This collection of studies examines the use of the written word in Celtic-speaking regions of Europe between c. 400 and c. 1500. Building on previous work as well as presenting the fruits of much new research, the book seeks to highlight the interest and impor-t of Celtic uses of literacy for the study both of medieval l generally and of the history and cultures of the Celtic c Please in the Middle Ages. Among the topics discussed are the significance of charter-writing, the interplay of oral and des in the composition and transmission of medieval Irish genealogies, prose narratives and poetry, the survival of re in Brittany and of Gaelic literacy in eastern Scotland lfth century, and pragmatic uses of literacy in later ales.

D1628366

Renewal
by interr
in persc
by phor

CAMBRIDGE STUDIES IN MEDIEVAL LITERATURE 33

Literacy in Medieval Celtic Societies

CAMBRIDGE STUDIES IN MEDIEVAL LITERATURE 33

General Editor: Professor Alastair Minnis, Professor of Medieval Literature,
University of York

Editorial Board
Professor Patrick Boyde, FBA (Serena Professor of Italian, Cambridge)
Professor John Burrow, FBA (Winterstoke Professor of English, Bristol)
Professor Rita Copeland (Professor of English, University of Minnesota)
Professor Alan Deyermond, FBA (Professor of Hispanic Studies, London)
Professor Peter Dronke, FBA (Professor of Medieval Latin Literature, Cambridge)
Dr Simon Gaunt (University of Cambridge)
Professor Nigel Palmer (Professor of German Medieval and Linguistic Studies,
Oxford)
Professor Winthrop Wetherbee (Professor of English, Cornell)

This series of critical books seeks to cover the whole area of literature written in the
major medieval languages – the main European vernaculars, and medieval Latin and
Greek – during the period *c.* 1100–1500. Its chief aim is to publish and stimulate fresh
scholarship and criticism on medieval literature, special emphasis being placed on
understanding major works of poetry, prose, and drama in relation to the contemporary culture and learning which fostered them.

Recent titles in the series

A complete list of titles in the series can be found at the back of the book

Literacy in Medieval Celtic Societies

EDITED BY

HUW PRYCE

Senior Lecturer in History
University of Wales, Bangor

CAMBRIDGE
UNIVERSITY PRESS

CAMBRIDGE UNIVERSITY PRESS
Cambridge, New York, Melbourne, Madrid, Cape Town, Singapore, São Paulo

Cambridge University Press
The Edinburgh Building, Cambridge CB2 2RU, UK

Published in the United States of America by Cambridge University Press, New York

www.cambridge.org
Information on this title: www.cambridge.org/9780521570398

First published 1998
This digitally printed first paperback version 2006

A catalogue record for this publication is available from the British Library

Library of Congress Cataloguing in Publication data
Pryce, Huw.
Literacy in medieval Celtic societies / by Huw Pryce.
p.   cm. – (Cambridge studies in medieval literature; 33)
Includes bibliographical references and index.
ISBN 0 521 57039 5 (hardback)
1. Celtic literature – History and criticism.
2. Written communication – Great Britain – History.
3. Civilization, Medieval, in literature.   4. Manuscripts, Medieval – Great Britain.
5. Civilization, Celtic, in literature.   6. Social history – Medieval, 500–1500.
7. Celtic language – Written Celtic.   8. Literacy – Scotland – History.
9. Literacy – Ireland – History.   10. Literacy – Wales – History.
I. Title.   II. Series.
PB1097.P78   1998
302.244′094109175916–dc21   97–9721   CIP

ISBN-13 978-0-521-57039-8 hardback
ISBN-10 0-521-57039-5 hardback

Contents

vii

Contents

Illustrations

Contributors

Dauvit Broun	Lecturer in Scottish History, University of Glasgow
A. D. Carr	Reader in Welsh History, University of Wales, Bangor
T. M. Charles-Edwards	Jesus Professor of Celtic, University of Oxford
Sioned Davies	Senior Lecturer in Welsh, University of Wales, Cardiff
Wendy Davies	Professor of History, University College London
Marie Therese Flanagan	Senior Lecturer in History, The Queen's University, Belfast
Katherine Forsyth	British Academy Institutional Research Fellow, Department of History, University College London
Ceridwen Lloyd-Morgan	Assistant Archivist, National Library of Wales, Aberystwyth
Huw Pryce	Senior Lecturer in History, University of Wales, Bangor
Katharine Simms	Senior Lecturer in Medieval History, Trinity College, Dublin
Patrick Sims-Williams	Professor of Celtic Studies, University of Wales, Aberystwyth
Llinos Beverley Smith	Senior Lecturer in Welsh History, University of Wales, Aberystwyth
David E. Thornton	Assistant Professor, Department of History, Bilkent University
Noël-Yves Tonnerre	Professor of Medieval History, Université d'Angers

Acknowledgements

This book contains, in revised form, thirteen of the fifteen papers delivered at a conference held in Neuadd John Morris-Jones at University of Wales, Bangor (UWB) in September 1994. The conference brought together a wide range of scholars with an interest in the uses of literacy in the medieval Celtic countries, and the resulting book has, I believe, benefited from the comments and discussions stimulated by its chapters' earlier incarnations as texts for oral delivery on that occasion. I am very grateful to the University of Wales Board of Celtic Studies for making a generous grant towards the costs of speakers attending the conference, and to the School of History and Welsh History at UWB for financial and other support. Thanks are also due to the following for their help in organizing and running the conference: K. Rees and June Hughes of the School of History and Welsh History; Meryl Wyn-Jones and her colleagues in the conference office; the hall staff of Neuadd John Morris-Jones; Trish Route and Karen Sherwood, the post-graduate helpers whose calm and capable assistance did so much to ensure the smooth running of the conference; and Tomos Roberts, Archivist at UWB, who organized an exhibition of medieval documents and manuscripts held in the University Library.

As editor of the present volume my greatest debt is, of course, to the contributors, not only for their readiness to contribute but also for their co-operation in responding to my queries and suggestions and for their patience: my warm thanks go to them all. In addition, I wish to thank Michael Gaches for translating Professor Tonnerre's chapter, David Thornton for checking some bibliographical references, and the institutions and individuals acknowledged elsewhere for supplying photographs. I am grateful to UWB for granting me a semester's sabbatical leave in 1996, some of which was used to finish editing the book. Last but not least, I am indebted to Nancy Edwards for much valuable advice and support at all stages of this project.

HP

Abbreviations

AC	*Annála Connacht: The Annals of Connacht (A.D. 1224–1544)*, ed. A. M. Freeman
A. Clonm.	*The Annals of Clonmacnoise*, ed. D. Murphy
AFM	*Annála Ríoghachta Éireann: Annals of the Kingdom of Ireland by the Four Masters*, ed. J. O'Donovan
AI	*The Annals of Inisfallen*, ed. S. Mac Airt
ALC	*The Annals of Loch Cé*, ed. W. M. Hennessy
'A. Tig.'	'The Annals of Tigernach', ed. W. Stokes
AU	*Annála Uladh: Annals of Ulster*, ed. W. M. Hennessy and B. MacCarthy
BBCS	*Bulletin of the Board of Celtic Studies*
BL	British Library
BN	*Bretha Nemed*
CCSL	Corpus Christianorum Series Latina
CGH	*Corpus Genealogiarum Hiberniae*, vol. 1, ed. M. A. O'Brien
CIH	*Corpus Iuris Hibernici*, ed. D. A. Binchy
CL	*Le Cartulaire de l'Abbaye de Landévennec*, ed. A. de la Borderie
CMCS	*Cambridge Medieval Celtic Studies (= Cambrian Medieval Celtic Studies* from no. 26, Winter 1993)
CR	*Le Cartulaire de Redon*, ed. A. de Courson
Chron. Scot.	*Chronicum Scotorum*, ed. W. M. Hennessy
ECMS	J. R. Allen and J. Anderson, *The Early Christian Monuments of Scotland*
ECMW	V. E. Nash-Williams, *The Early Christian Monuments of Wales*
EWGT	*Early Welsh Genealogical Tracts*, ed. P. C. Bartrum
HE	Bede, *Historia Ecclesiastica Gentis Anglorum*, ed. B. Colgrave and R. A. B. Mynors
Hib.	*Collectio Canonum Hibernensis: Die irische Kanonensammlung*, ed. H. Wasserschleben

Abbreviations

LL	*The Text of the Book of Llan Dâv*, ed. J. G. Evans with J. Rhys
MGH	Monumenta Germaniae Historica
NLW	National Library of Wales
NLWJ	*National Library of Wales Journal*
PCC	Prerogative Court of Canterbury
PRIA	*Proceedings of the Royal Irish Academy*
PRO	Public Record Office
RCAHMS	Royal Commission on the Ancient and Historical Monuments of Scotland
UWB	University of Wales, Bangor
UR	*Uraicecht na Ríar*, ed. L. Breatnach
WHR	*Welsh History Review*
ZCP	*Zeitschrift für celtische Philologie*

Note on references

All works, apart from those listed above and also unpublished manuscript sources, are referred to in the notes by the author and short title system; full bibliographical details are given in the list of Works Cited.

xiii

Introduction

HUW PRYCE

This book examines the uses of writing in Celtic-speaking societies between $c.$ 400 and $c.$ 1500. In common with much other recent work on medieval literacy, it is concerned not simply with who could read and write but also with the contexts in which written artefacts were used and with what this implies about the societies which produced them.[1] While its coverage is neither comprehensive nor exhaustive, the book is intended to be sufficiently wide-ranging to provide an introduction to the various approaches adopted in the study of literacy in the Celtic countries, as well as to indicate some questions and comparisons which could be pursued further in future work.

Literacy has been recognized as a topic of major significance for an understanding of medieval culture and society in recent years, attracting considerable scholarly attention reflected in a growing number of publications.[2] This interest in the uses of the written word has been shared by scholars working on the Celtic countries in the Middle Ages, as shown, for example, by studies of the beginnings of literacy in Ireland, distinctive forms of charter-writing, the interrelationship of oral and literate modes in the transmission and performance of Irish and Welsh vernacular literature, or pragmatic uses of literacy in later medieval Wales.[3] However, these studies have, quite properly, concentrated on specific genres of writing or particular Celtic countries, while discussions of literacy in medieval Europe more generally have tended to pay scant attention to evidence from the Celtic world. The present volume complements and builds on the work which has already been accomplished on literacy in medieval Celtic countries in two ways. First, it makes available the fruits of new research, and second, it provides an opportunity to identify similarities and differences between, and indeed within, the different Celtic societies covered as well as between different periods of the Middle Ages. It aims, therefore, to set the study of medieval Celtic

1

literacy in a broader geographical and chronological context than has hitherto been usual, while at the same time allowing a range and depth of discussion which would not be possible in a volume with a wider remit, embracing, say, the whole of medieval Europe or of Britain and Ireland. The result, it is hoped, will be to deepen understanding of how and why the written word was used in Celtic societies and hence to highlight the significance of the Celtic evidence for an assessment of medieval uses of literacy more generally.

A central assumption underlying the book is that Ireland, Scotland, Wales and Brittany – the countries on which these essays principally concentrate – shared sufficient connections and resemblances in the Middle Ages to make comparisons between them particularly fruitful. One point of connection, of course, was that speakers of the various Celtic languages were ultimately descended from the Celts of the first millennium BC. True, in the medieval period those speakers were not aware that the two main branches of the Celtic languages – Goedelic, comprising Irish, Scottish Gaelic and Manx, and Brittonic, including Welsh, Cornish and Breton – belonged to the same linguistic tree.[4] However, an awareness of the connections and linguistic similarities between Brittany, Cornwall and Wales is attested until at least the end of the twelfth century,[5] while Ireland and the Gaelic-speaking regions of Scotland formed a single cultural world sharing a common literary language until the seventeenth century.[6] In addition, common Celtic descent was a factor which helped to create some of the resemblances between the legends and literary motifs attested in the various Celtic countries, and hence the distinctive cultures of the latter.[7]

New links were forged between Celtic societies by the church, which, as elsewhere in early medieval Europe, played a fundamental role in introducing literacy and determining the uses to which it was put. Post-Roman Christianity in Celtic Britain made a crucial contribution to the making of Christianity not only in Ireland, and subsequently in Scotland via the Irish settlements in Dál Riada, but also in Brittany, thanks to the emigration of Britons, among them church leaders, to the Armorican peninsula in the fifth and sixth centuries. The Celtic churches, while emphatically not constituting a single 'Celtic church', maintained links with each other in the earlier Middle Ages which both reflected and helped to reinforce important institutional and cultural resemblances between them: the cultivation of an elaborate, rhetorical style of Latin indebted to late Roman education is one case in point, the exchange of Latin texts glossed in Celtic vernaculars another.[8]

The interaction between native, vernacular cultures and the Christian Latin written culture transmitted by the church is a theme of central importance in considering the uses made of literacy in medieval Celtic societies. In some Celtic areas this interaction was essentially one between two distinct, though overlapping, groups: clerics, and native men of learning. The latter included the *filid* and lawyers of early Christian Ireland and the poets and legal specialists of medieval Wales, whose social role it was to conserve and contribute to a multi-stranded body of learning and lore, combining both secular and Christian elements, known in Gaelic culture as *senchas* and in Wales as *cyfarwyddyd*.[9] Although their character, organization and influence varied, these native learned classes, who enjoyed high social prestige and whose expertise was usually transmitted within families, are well attested in Ireland, Scotland and Wales throughout the medieval period and may be regarded as a further distinguishing feature of those societies.[10]

Nevertheless, while all the societies studied in this volume shared connections and characteristics, particularly in the linguistic and cultural spheres, which justify labelling them as Celtic, they by no means formed a uniform whole. Indeed, by focusing on the specific contexts in which literacy was used the essays which follow highlight important differences between – and within – the Celtic countries. The most striking contrast is the differing amount and character of the written artefacts surviving from each of the societies under consideration. For example, a wealth of vernacular texts survives from Ireland from the seventh century onwards which is unparalleled in Europe, whereas texts in Welsh survive in any bulk only from the twelfth century, the earliest extant Breton texts (other than glosses) date from the middle of the fifteenth century, and few Gaelic manuscripts originally written in Scotland are earlier than the fifteenth century.[11] Or take the use of European-style Latin charters: only ten examples survive issued on behalf of twelfth-century Irish kings, by comparison with about sixty in the names of native Welsh rulers of the same period and 160 for Mael Coluim IV of Scotland (1153–65) alone.[12] Explaining such contrasts is obviously of central importance to any assessment of literacy: is the surviving evidence, even allowing for substantial losses, broadly representative of the uses made of writing in the different Celtic countries, or does it give a highly

3

distorted impression of those uses? And if the latter is the case, how far is it possible to draw comparisons across time and space?

These questions also arise, of course, in respect of other parts of medieval Europe: they lie, for instance, at the heart of disagreements about the importance of literacy in Anglo-Saxon England or the extent to which recourse to the written word increased from the twelfth century onwards in western Europe as a whole.[13] The issues which need to be addressed in attempting to resolve these questions in a Celtic context are brought into sharp relief by Patrick Sims-Williams in his discussion in this volume of pre-Norman Wales and, to a lesser extent, Scotland, two Celtic societies for which very little written evidence survives. He argues that minimalist estimates of the quantity and variety of written texts depend on a questionable combination of romantic assumptions about the predominance of oral culture and positivist interpretations of the extant written sources, and emphasizes that the surviving evidence can be used to support very different, yet equally valid, conclusions.

Patrick Sims-Williams thus highlights a concern which also engages the attention of a number of other contributors, especially with regard to the early Middle Ages, namely the difficulty of establishing how many and, more importantly, what kinds of written artefacts were produced in Celtic societies. A fundamental issue at stake here is that of textual transmission. What do the channels by which surviving texts were transmitted imply about the loss of other sources? The lack of enduring monastic libraries in early medieval Celtic countries may well have been one factor militating against the preservation of manuscripts within those countries themselves: it is striking that all surviving Welsh, and most Irish, manuscripts written before *c.* 1100 containing Latin texts were preserved in English and continental churches, whither they had been taken in the early Middle Ages.[14]

In addition, since many early medieval texts survive only in copies of the twelfth century and later, account needs to be taken of the ways in which later medieval attitudes to the written word determined whether and how early medieval texts survived. Thus the vernacular riches of early Christian Ireland are extant for the most part in manuscripts of the twelfth century and later, copied by scribes who sought to preserve those texts' original form; in Wales, on the other hand, scribes appear to have been readier to modernize texts.[15] Above all, though, survival depended on continued material support for native men of learning. In Ireland, this continuity was very strong,

4

although, as Katharine Simms shows, the institutional basis shifted from churches to hereditary secular families by the thirteenth century. In Wales, too, there is good evidence for continuity: ecclesiastical support for native written culture was maintained through the twelfth and thirteenth centuries, especially, it seems, amongst the Cistercians, with lay scribes and patrons playing a dominant role thereafter.[16] Scotland was less fortunate in this respect, and the written cultivation of Gaelic culture was restricted from the thirteenth century to the highlands and islands, while the enthusiasm with which Brittany's scholars embraced the learning of the northern French schools from the later eleventh century onwards was inimical to the preservation of earlier texts.[17]

True, as Patrick Sims-Williams warns us, some contrasts between Celtic societies may be more apparent than real, reflecting differing channels of transmission and hence differing survival rates for particular kinds of written artefacts. Yet differences in the transmission of texts themselves stem, at least in part, from differing historical experiences which need to be borne in mind in considering the forms literacy took in the societies under consideration here. Two closely connected variables which helped to shape those forms are, first, the impact of influences – both political and cultural – from non-Celtic societies and, second, patterns of state formation and political development. A brief consideration of these points will serve to provide some historical background and context for the essays which follow.

An obvious but fundamental factor, especially with regard to uses of literacy in the early Middle Ages (up to *c.* 1100), is that Ireland, and Scotland north of the walls, lay outside the Roman Empire whereas the regions which became Wales and Brittany fell within it. These contrasts help to explain differences in the reception of Latin literacy transmitted by the church and, allied to that, the higher prestige accorded to Irish than to British as a written vernacular in the fifth and sixth centuries.[18]

In terms of political development, a broad distinction can be drawn between the experiences of Ireland and Wales, on the one hand, and of Scotland and Brittany on the other.[19] Ireland and Wales were characterized by political fragmentation in this period, although from the tenth century some rulers achieved far more extensive hegemonies than had been established earlier. However, fragmentation was less marked in Wales, which also differed from Ireland in being the object of Anglo-Saxon rulers' ambitions, expressed in military campaigns

5

and conquests and the imposition of overlordship, notably by the West Saxon kings from Alfred (d. 899) to Edgar (d. 975).[20] Scotland and Brittany, by contrast, achieved a fair measure of political cohesion in the early Middle Ages. The kingdom of the Picts extended over most of Britain north of the Forth and Clyde and was a formidable power in the late seventh and eighth centuries. However, in the ninth century its kingship was seized by dynasts, most notably Cináed Mac Alpin (d. 858), from Dál Riada, a kingdom established in Argyll and the adjacent isles which was the most successful of the Irish conquests in post-Roman western Britain (there were also substantial Irish settlements in Wales and some in Cornwall). Thus from the middle of the ninth century a unitary kingdom of the Scots was forged which extended its authority southwards to embrace both Lothian, previously part of Northumbria, and the former British kingdom of Strathclyde in the early eleventh century, although most of the highlands and islands were under Norse control. By *c.* 900 this political change had resulted in the disappearance of Pictish identity, accompanied by the expansion of Gaelic and the fatal decline of the Pictish language.[21] Brittany was different again. It appears to have undergone substantial British settlement by the later sixth century but also lay on the periphery of Frankish power, and it was thanks to Carolingian intervention that a series of powerful Breton rulers, based in the south-east of the peninsula around Vannes and Nantes, succeeded in establishing themselves from the 830s. One consequence was the creation of 'two zones of distinct languages and cultural traditions', namely Breton in the west and Frankish in the east. True, Brittany suffered heavily from Viking attacks in the early tenth century, leading to a temporary diaspora of Breton churchmen, together with their manuscripts and relics; but after the return of Alan II in 936 from exile in England, ducal authority was restored and ecclesiastical communities returned.[22] By the later eleventh century, though, Brittany had fallen within the Anglo-Norman sphere of influence and its cultural integration into the northern French world grew apace.[23]

The varying impact on the Celtic countries of French and English influences is a major theme in the central and later Middle Ages.[24] As we have seen, exposure to external influences was not in itself something new. However, in Celtic Britain and Ireland, at least, the mediation of these influences by extensive conquest and/or settlement by speakers of French and English gave them an unprecedented intensity and durability. Wales and Ireland experienced both conquest

6

and settlement, but the chronology and impact of these differed between the two societies. The Normans began their conquests in Wales in the late eleventh century, but it was only with Edward I's conquest of 1282–3 that native Welsh political authority was finally extinguished, after which the country was divided between the king's lands or principality, comprising former domains of the native rulers of Gwynedd and Deheubarth, and forty or so marcher lordships; administrative unity was achieved only with Henry VIII's so-called Acts of Union of 1536 and 1543.[25] Anglo-Norman intervention began in Ireland a century later than in Wales (from 1167), and by c. 1240 English power extended over more than half of the island; thereafter, however, it was eroded by native Irish lords, and Ireland remained divided between these and the Anglo-Irish until it was conquered by the Tudors.[26]

Unlike Wales and Ireland, Scotland was not subjected to Anglo-Norman conquest in the twelfth century. However, the Scottish kings of that period, notably David I (1124–53), encouraged Norman and other French settlement as a means of strengthening their kingdom and were also highly receptive to Anglo-French cultural influences.[27] Having weathered the storm of Edward I's ultimately unsuccessful attempt at conquest and the civil wars precipitated by Robert Bruce's seizure of the throne, the kingdom successfully maintained its independence from the 1340s; Gaelic, however, receded to the highlands and western isles by the fourteenth century and Scots English was the vernacular in the rest of the kingdom.[28] Brittany, too, experienced domination by powerful neighbours – first the Angevins, then the Capetians – in the twelfth and thirteenth centuries. Nevertheless, from the late thirteenth century the duchy of Brittany became one of the most powerful principalities in France, and its rulers enjoyed a virtually autonomous, quasi-regal status vis-à-vis the kings of France.[29] Here, not surprisingly, French influence was predominant: ducal documents were normally written in French from the 1280s onwards, and there is no evidence that the later medieval dukes could speak Breton (in contrast to James IV of Scotland, who learnt Gaelic in the 1490s).[30]

The contributors to this volume respond in different ways to the challenge of recognizing the difficulties encountered in establishing the quantity and character of written artefacts produced in the medieval Celtic countries while making allowance for the differing historical experiences just outlined. But the different approaches taken in the essays which follow have a common objective: to assess how, why and in which contexts writing was used in those countries. Admittedly, in view of the hazards of arguing that certain forms of literacy were lacking or rare simply because they have left few if any traces in the surviving evidence, that assessment may well illuminate no more than part of a larger picture whose overall appearance can only be conjectured. Nevertheless the evidence that does survive offers valuable insights into at least *some* of the uses made of the written word in the societies considered in this book, and the following chapters allow some general conclusions to be drawn about literacy in medieval Celtic contexts.

With the exception of Llinos Beverley Smith's and A. D. Carr's studies of late medieval Wales, the essays in this volume provide little evidence of widespread pragmatic uses of literacy by lay men and women in administration and the transfer of property rights, including the ability to write documents themselves rather than relying on professional scribes. Admittedly this impression stems in part from the selection of topics covered and is thus to some extent misleading: the Scots kings turned increasingly to the written word as an administrative tool from the twelfth century, as did Breton dukes from the late thirteenth, and Anglo-Norman intervention in Ireland brought the bureaucratic administrative practices of the English kingdom in their wake.[31] Nevertheless, there is a good case for supposing that it was only in the later Middle Ages, and then only to a limited extent, that the Celtic countries witnessed the emergence of the kind of literate mentality argued by Michael Clanchy to have developed in twelfth- and thirteenth-century England as a consequence of the administrative demands of lords and rulers.[32] Moreover, in Celtic societies extensive recourse to documents in administration appears to have resulted from the imitation or imposition of literate modes originating outside them, primarily in England and France.

The adoption of forms of writing common to other parts of Europe from the twelfth century onwards is clearly an important aspect of wider changes in the societies discussed in this book.[33] This begs two questions, however: how was literacy used in those societies before they were exposed to such forms, and how far did the introduction of new uses of literacy lead to the displacement of traditional ones?

Up at least until the twelfth century, the acquisition and application of literate skills in Celtic societies were essentially restricted to the church and, particularly in Ireland, to native learned classes comprising both clerics and laymen. However, the uses of literacy adopted by these groups had a social impact well beyond those able to read (let alone write) texts for themselves. In part, this was because the time and resources required to acquire literate skills helped to reinforce privileged social status. In early Christian Ireland, moreover, literacy in the form of biblical scholarship became a qualification for high rank. This extended the social impact of the written word inasmuch as it was associated with aristocratic status and power.[34] On the other hand, there is nothing in the extant evidence to suggest that, in contrast to Merovingian and, especially, Carolingian Francia, early medieval Irish rulers sought to turn the written word – be it in Latin or Irish – into a privileged mode of communication for administrative purposes.[35] This is not to deny that writing was used by clerics and native *literati* in ways intended to sustain and proclaim royal power in early medieval Celtic societies. But the genres adopted tended to be primarily propagandistic and owed little to the bureaucratic model of government provided by imperial Rome. This is true even of the Latin inscriptions, cut in roman capitals, on memorial stones erected in fifth- and sixth-century western Britain: while these were almost certainly statements of *romanitas,* and therefore of political legitimacy,[36] they provide no grounds for assuming that their patrons were committed to adopting literate modes in administration. Inscribed monuments could express political and cultural self-confidence in other ways too. The ogam inscriptions in Irish proclaimed pride in the Irish language on the part of conquerors in a former province of the Roman Empire, while the only use of ogam for a vernacular other than Irish, namely in the Pictish inscriptions, may reflect a deliberate choice by the lay aristocracy in Pictland.[37] The genealogy of the kings of Powys on the Pillar of Elisse or the use of charter formulae on stones exemplify a similar monumental use of the written word. Though less public, literacy was also used for ideological purposes on vellum: genealogies and king lists sought to legitimize dynastic power, charters to protect ecclesiastical property rights.[38]

What of the impact of new forms of literacy from the twelfth century onwards? This is discussed with reference to Scotland by Dauvit Broun, who argues that a careful examination of orthography shows that Gaelic literacy survived, to an undefined extent, in the kingdom until the middle of the thirteenth century despite royal enthusiasm for Anglo-French culture from the reign of David I (1124–53).[39] In the later Middle Ages, however, patronage of Gaelic culture and its attendant literate products was restricted to the lordship of the Isles: English, not Gaelic, was the preferred vernacular in written records in the heartlands of the kingdom.[40] The contrast with Ireland and Wales is striking. In the former, the introduction of the Latin charter by native rulers and ecclesiastics before the Anglo-Norman intervention appears to have been primarily ideological in inspiration: the documents were signs of a desire to conform with European norms of ecclesiastical reform and styles of rulership, but the impact of such aspirations before the establishment of Anglo-Norman power was probably very limited.[41] Moreover, Gaelic literary culture survived the partial conquest of the island and continued to be fostered by a native learned class comprising, from the thirteenth century onwards, lay hereditary families patronized by native Irish lords.[42] In Wales, too, native literary culture survived the experience of conquest: indeed, production of manuscripts containing Welsh texts blossomed after 1282, in part as a cultural reaction to the end of native political rule.[43] It is notable that some of the native lords who administered the new literate administrative procedures introduced by the English crown and marcher lords were also the foremost patrons of vernacular literature: old and new uses of literacy co-existed. Nor did an increasing recourse to writing for pragmatic purposes by administrators and landowners mark an end to its symbolic and indeed quasi-magical uses in spells or charms, while land continued to be transferred without the use of documents in south-west Wales.[44]

Indeed, throughout the medieval period memory and the spoken – and sung – word were valued in all the societies examined here, and the relationship between oral and literate modes of communication is an important theme in many of the chapters which follow.[45] Widespread reliance on the spoken word was inevitable given most people's inability to read texts for themselves, and in certain circumstances distrust of documents may have led to their use being deliberately avoided.[46] However, several papers draw on other recent work on orality and literacy to warn against regarding these as two polar opposites, and to locate points of interaction between them. Thus genealogies could be composed and transmitted both orally and in writing, yet the written form with its 'propensity for augmentation' offered opportunities for manipulation lacking in purely oral compositions; this suggests in turn that extensive genealogies cannot be explained as written expressions of an oral genre but owed their detail and complexity to the use of the written word.[47] Likewise, Middle Welsh prose tales were carefully crafted written compositions whose oral stylistic features, while quite possibly derived from a tradition of oral composition, were aimed at the requirements of oral performance.[48] Of course, the extent to which the products of native oral culture were committed to writing varied according to circumstances and seems to have depended to a considerable degree on the existence of learned classes committed to the preservation of native lore and literature.[49] The lack of such a class may explain why in eleventh- and twelfth-century Brittany such material appears to have been transmitted orally on the whole.[50] Another determinant of the degree to which literature was composed and transmitted orally was gender: native learned classes were male preserves and in medieval Wales, as surely also in the other Celtic countries and elsewhere in Europe, women had less access to the means of textual production than men.[51]

That the written word co-existed and interacted with non-literate forms of communication serves to underline that the significance of literacy cannot be taken for granted but needs to be evaluated by examining the specific contexts in which it was used. In exploring some of those contexts in the medieval Celtic countries the following chapters not only throw light on the social and cultural histories of those countries but also have important implications for an understanding of medieval uses of literacy more generally. While this volume does not set out to make systematic comparisons between Celtic and other European uses of literacy, three points emerge which merit emphasis. The first is the unparalleled extent to which literacy was used in early medieval Ireland as a tool for fostering native culture in the vernacular; allied to that, secondly, is the crucial role played by learned classes in ensuring that the learning and lore they guarded was transmitted in writing. Thirdly, although they had used literacy for a variety of purposes since the late Roman or sub-Roman periods, the societies considered in this book seem to have shared only belatedly and to a limited degree in the huge proliferation and diversification of written texts which, it has been argued, characterized much of western Europe from the twelfth century onwards.[52] Just how distinctive those societies were in these and other respects will no doubt become clearer in the light of further work on the uses of writing in both Celtic and other European contexts. The essays in this volume will, it is hoped, help to stimulate such work by revealing some of the challenges and rewards offered by the study of literacy in medieval Celtic societies.[53]

NOTES

1 On the question of defining literacy, see, for example, Street, *Literacy*, p. 1; McKitterick (ed.), *Uses of Literacy*, pp. 2–5.

2 See, for example, Clanchy, *From Memory*; Stock, *Implications of Literacy*; McKitterick, *Carolingians*; McKitterick (ed.), *Uses of Literacy*; Keller *et al.* (eds.), *Pragmatische Schriftlichkeit*; D. H. Green, *Medieval Listening*.

3 On these topics see, for example, J. Stevenson, 'Beginnings of literacy'; A. Harvey, 'Early literacy'; *idem*, 'Latin'; W. Davies, 'Latin charter-tradition' (and cf. Broun, *Charters*, pp. 38–42); Tranter and Tristram (eds.), *Early Irish Literature*; S. Davies, *Crefft y Cyfarwydd*; Ll. B. Smith, 'Proofs of age'. Further relevant studies include Brett, 'Breton Latin literature', J. M. H. Smith, 'Oral and written', and Pryce, 'Origins'; others are referred to elsewhere in this volume.

4 Byrne, '*Senchas*', 144. The relationship between these languages is summarized in Russell, *Introduction*, pp. 14–18.

5 See Tonnerre, below, pp. 168–9.

6 Jackson, ' "Common Gaelic" ', 74–7, and cf. Russell, *Introduction*, pp. 61–2.

7 See, for example, Brett, 'Breton Latin literature', and Tonnerre, below, pp. 172–6.

8 W. Davies, 'Myth'; Charles-Edwards, below, pp. 65–7; J. M. H. Smith, *Province and Empire*, pp. 167–9, 173–4.

9 Byrne, '*Senchas*', esp. 138; Sims-Williams, 'Some functions', pp. 100–2; S. Davies, below, p. 135.

10 See, for example, Charles-Edwards, below, pp. 68–74 and Simms, below, pp. 238–46 (Ireland); D. S. Thomson, 'Gaelic learned orders' (Scotland); and Owen, 'Gwŷr dysg' (Wales). The existence of such a class in Brittany is doubtful: Brett, 'Breton Latin literature', 5–9.

11 Sims-Williams, below, pp. 19–33; Charles-Edwards, below, p. 62; Tonnerre, below, p. 169; Black, 'Gaelic manuscripts', pp. 154–60. On Man and Cornwall, see Russell, *Introduction*, pp. 28, 113–15.

12 Flanagan, below, p. 113; Maund, *Handlist*; *Regesta Regum Scottorum*, vol. 1, ed. Barrow.

13 Compare Wormald, 'Uses of literacy' with Campbell, *Essays*, pp. 157–8, 174–5, 178 and Keynes, 'Royal government', esp. pp. 228–9, 255–7; see also McKitterick (ed.), *Uses of Literacy*, p. 2.

14 Sims-Williams, below, pp. 20–1; Charles-Edwards, below, p. 62. It is worth noting that all surviving pre-eleventh-century Breton manuscripts, over 150 in number, are preserved outside Brittany in libraries to which they had been taken by monks and clergy fleeing from the Vikings, although the extent to which this reflects efforts to preserve the books of monasteries as opposed to other churches is unclear: J. M. H. Smith, *Province and Empire*, pp. 164–5.

15 Sims-Williams, below, p. 27; Simms, below, p. 242.

16 Below, p. 242; Huws, *Llyfrau Cymraeg*, pp. 12–14.

Introduction

17 Broun, below, pp. 196–7; Grant, *Independence*, pp. 200–2; Brett, 'Breton Latin literature', 22.

18 Forsyth, below, pp. 55, 58; Charles-Edwards, below, pp. 76–8; and compare Sims-Williams, below, pp. 31–2.

19 For a comparative view of some key developments, see W. Davies, 'Celtic kingships'.

20 W. Davies, *Wales*, esp. ch. 4.

21 Broun, 'Origin of Scottish identity'; Duncan, *Scotland*, chs. 3–5; Smyth, *Warlords*.

22 J. M. H. Smith, *Province and Empire*; quotation at p. 166.

23 M. Jones, *Creation of Brittany*, ch. 1; Tonnerre, below, pp. 166–8.

24 On Celtic Britain and Ireland, see R. R. Davies, *Domination and Conquest*; Frame, *Political Development*.

25 R. R. Davies, *Conquest*; G. Williams, *Renewal*, chs. 1–11.

26 Frame, *Colonial Ireland*; Cosgrove (ed.), *New History of Ireland*.

27 Broun, below, pp. 183–6.

28 Grant, *Independence*.

29 M. Jones, *Creation of Brittany*, ch. 1.

30 Ibid., pp. 122–3, M. Jones, 'L'aptitude à lire', 45 and n. 33; Grant, *Independence*, p. 202.

31 Ibid., pp. 148–9; M. Jones, *Creation of Brittany*, pp. 111–58; Frame, *Colonial Ireland*, pp. 93–110.

32 Smith, below; Grant, *Independence*, pp. 105–6.

33 Cf. R. Bartlett, *Making of Europe*, pp. 283–8, which sees the diffusion in the Celtic (and Slavic) lands of charters derived from Carolingian models as a symptom of those lands' 'Europeanization'.

34 Charles-Edwards, below, pp. 68–74.

35 Ibid., p. 62. Cf. Nelson, 'Literacy'.

36 Sims-Williams, below, p. 29.

37 Charles-Edwards, below, p. 78; Forsyth, below, p. 55.

38 Thornton, below, pp. 91–3; W. Davies, below, pp. 102–5.

39 Below, pp. 183–201.

40 Grant, *Independence*, pp. 103, 201–2.

41 Flanagan, below, pp. 113–32.

42 Simms, below, pp. 241–52.

43 Cf. Huws, *Llyfrau Cymraeg*, pp. 4–5, 12–13.

44 Smith, below, pp. 215–17.

45 Other recent discussions of this theme include Richter, *Formation*, esp. ch. 9, and J. Stevenson, 'Literacy and orality'.

46 Cf. Forsyth, below, pp. 42–3, and Smith, below, pp. 214–15. See also Grant, *Independence*, p. 212, for a rhetorical juxtaposition of the Campbells' use of charters with the Macdonalds' true Gaelic style of rulership, allegedly without reliance on documents, in the later medieval lordship of the Isles.

47 Thornton, below, pp. 86–91.

48 S. Davies, below, pp. 135–46.

49 This is not to argue that native men of learning always favoured the use of writing. For example, the reciters (*datgeiniaid*) who performed the compositions

13

of poets in later medieval Wales may have sought, with the poets' support, to ensure an exclusively oral transmission for those poems so as to preserve their monopoly of the bardic repertoire: Huws, 'Transmission', pp. 185–6.

50 Tonnerre, below, pp. 169–78; Brett, 'Breton Latin literature', 9; and cf. Constantine, *Breton Ballads*, p. 64.

51 Lloyd-Morgan, below, pp. 149–65.

52 See, for example, Keller, 'Entwicklung'.

53 I am grateful to Thomas Charles-Edwards for commenting on this Introduction. The responsibility for any errors or misinterpretations it contains is of course mine alone.

I

The uses of writing in early medieval Wales
PATRICK SIMS-WILLIAMS

Recently four foreign scholars were driving to a conference in Bangor. As their car crossed the Welsh border the driver noticed a solitary white cow in the field beside them. 'Ah,' he said, 'so the cattle are white in Wales.' 'No,' said the second scholar, 'some of them are white.' 'No,' said the third, 'at least one of them is white.' 'No,' said the fourth scholar, 'at least one of them is white on at least one side.'

Similar problems face scholars trying to assess the extent to which writing was used in the Celtic-speaking countries before the twelfth century. How far can they extrapolate from tiny amounts of evidence? How representative is what survives of what once existed? How far may their deductions be influenced by inherited preconceptions about what is likely, by national or institutional rivalries, or even by their own temperaments?

To some extent we can place estimates of the use of writing by early medieval Celtic-speakers on a scale ranging from the over-cautious positivism of some modern scholars back to the romantic view, held by some patriotic historians in the early modern period, that the Celtic countries were once as rich in historical records as England and the continent; the disappearance of these manuscripts was then explained by stories such as the conflagration of Welsh books in the Tower of London conducted by Ysgolan,[1] or the slightly less mythical removal of Scottish records by Edward I.[2] More familiar scapegoats in modern scholarship include the ubiquitous Vikings, who did indeed steal books, and the zealots of the Reformation, who did indeed destroy them. (The problem is that Vikings and Reformers were active outside the Celtic countries as well.) Conspiracy theories still crop up as well, for example the 'flight of fancy' according to which the monks of Lichfield appropriated the Lichfield Gospels from Llandeilo in belated revenge for the attack on them by Cynddylan of Powys.[3] By and large, however, the romantic-patriotic

15

vision of lost national manuscript cultures rivalling that of Anglo-Saxon England has long since been replaced by another Romantic vision – Romantic with a capital R this time: the exaltation of 'Celtic' culture as peculiarly oral and traditional, untrammelled and unsullied by the prosaic process of writing (despite the contrary epigraphical impression). The alliance of the minimizing positivists with the proponents of this newer Romantic vision of the orality of the Celtic-speaking peoples has been a powerful if unholy one, for it has subverted the simple early modern opposition between patriotic exaggerators and foreign belittlers. Once illiteracy was re-evaluated as orality it lost its stigma. The sacred Celtic cow, black on one side, was now an Indo-European rare breed.

So far as I know, the origin of the idea of Celtic orality has never been traced. I suspect that it should be seen as a Romantic re-evaluation of the perceived illiteracy of the Celts and should be added to the positive re-evaluations of earlier negative stereotypes listed by Malcolm Chapman.[4] In the eighteenth century, when outsiders looked at the culture of Celtic-speakers, particularly those in Catholic areas, they saw a mainly *oral* vernacular culture, with few manuscripts on view and printing in a rudimentary state. Ignoring the socio-economic and political reasons for this, and the possibility of what is now termed 'reoralization', it was easily assumed that stories, poems, and genealogies had never been written down, and had always been handed on by word of mouth. To outsiders this oral literature appeared quite different from the written works of medieval writers like Chaucer and Malory, which had long been available in printed books. In the Highlands of Scotland, according to William Collins *c.* 1749,

> Ev'n yet preserv'd, how often may'st thou hear,
>   Where to the pole the Boreal mountains run,
> Taught by the father to his list'ning son
>   Strange lays, whose power had charm'd a SPENCER's ear.[5]

According to Charles Topham Bowden in his *Tour through Ireland* in 1791, 'Amidst the unspeakable miseries of those half-fed wretches, they enjoy in a very exalted degree poetry and song. . . . I have sat under a hedge and listened to the rustic songs of those peasants, while at labour, with a pleasure which transcended any I had ever felt at Vauxhall.'[6] When the Revd Richard Warner visited Llangollen in 1797 the sexton repeated 'twice or thrice, with emphasis and delibera-

16

tion', the genealogy of the saint: 'St. Collen ap Gwynnawg ap Clydawg ap Cowrda ap Caradog Freichfras ap Lleyr Merim ap Einion Yrth ap Cunedda Wledig'; but Warner had to ask Thomas Pennant how to spell this.[7] In the Middle Ages, however, this sort of material *was* written down.[8] Gerald of Wales refers to the bards and others of his day having genealogies by heart *and* in writing in the Welsh language (*Descriptio Kambriae*, I.3 and 17),[9] though these books have perished, as has the manuscript of Merlin's prophecies that Gerald saw in Nefyn, presumably in the church there (*Itinerarium Kambriae*, II.6). By the eighteenth century, when copies of medieval Celtic poems first attracted the attention of outsiders, such medieval manuscripts as did survive were often unknown, unlocatable or inaccessible, and when arguments arose about authenticity – especially in connection with the *Poems of Ossian*, which *were* indeed forgeries – an obvious line of defence was to claim that the Celts had always relied on oral transmission and hadn't needed to write poetry down. This position was seemingly supported by the testimony of Caesar, who had stressed the way in which the druids of ancient Gaul preferred to pass on their *disciplina*, that is, their occult, largely(?) versified, knowledge, by word of mouth.[10] The influence of this testimony can no doubt be seen in the way in which the book-in-hand almost disappears from druidic iconography in the eighteenth century.[11]

Caesar's Gaul is surely too remote in time and space to be relevant to early medieval Britain and Ireland; but the Romantic idea of the 'Celts' was, and remains, through and through synthetic and anachronistic: if the ancient Celts preferred orality so must their descendants (an assumption no one would make in the case of the Anglo-Saxons vis-à-vis the ancient Germans). In actual fact, however, Caesar does not say that the Gaulish druids avoided writing altogether, specifically stating that they *did* use the Greek alphabet for many purposes other than their *disciplina*; and by now we have ample epigraphic evidence, in various alphabets, for the use of writing by the Gauls and other early Continental Celtic-speaking peoples,[12] and even, to judge by discoveries such as the Coligny Calendar and the Larzac and Chamalières tablets, for druidic or para-druidic purposes.[13] These discoveries, however, were made far too late to undermine the stereotype of the wilfully illiterate Celt.

In any case, scholars always seem to have tended to keep epigraphical and literary evidence in separate compartments, leaving the former to the antiquaries. We see this very clearly in the case of early Wales. So-called 'Class I' inscribed stones (approx. fifth to seventh centuries) survive in considerable numbers and have been well documented since Gibson's edition of Camden's *Britannia* appeared in 1695.[14] The influence on them from lost manuscript writing (whether on vellum or papyrus or wood or wax tablets)[15] is obvious. Nevertheless, they have rarely been cited in discussions of literacy and orality in 'Celtic' culture, apparently because of an unspoken assumption that they belong to a sub-Roman tradition as opposed to a native 'Celtic' and (almost by definition) oral culture. Such a view is contradicted by the distribution of the Class I stones, for instead of congregating in the 'Lowland Zone' of Romanized south-east Wales, they predominate in the 'Highland Zone' of western, central and northern Wales. An inadequate way of explaining this distribution would be to redefine them as 'Celtic' rather than 'sub-Roman', that is to say, as an indigenous response to the erection of ogam monuments by the Irish settlers in the same areas;[16] this would hardly explain the epigraphy and Latin formulae of the inscriptions, which point to Romano-British and Gallo-Roman influences. Instead, evidence such as the influence from sixth-century Lyon seen clearly at Penmachno in Gwynedd[17] should make us rethink and upgrade the role of writing, including manuscript writing, in the heart of 'native', 'Celtic' Wales. When we do so, we find that the resulting picture is wholly consonant with what Gildas tells us about the literary attainments of Maelgwn, king of Gwynedd, pupil of a *magister elegans* (probably a 'rhetor') as well as patron of *praecones* (probably 'beirdd', i.e. panegyric poets).[18] By the sixth century any division between the illiterate, native 'Highland Zone' and the literate, romanized 'Lowland Zone' must surely have been swept away by the upheavals of the Anglo-Saxon conquest and 'ruin' of lowland Britain.

The great stumbling block to redefining the role of literacy in the early medieval Insular Celtic societies is the lack of surviving manuscripts. To positivistically minded historians, attempts to explain – or explain away – the lack of manuscript evidence smack of special pleading. An example of such positivism is Kathleen Hughes's 1977 lecture 'Where are the writings of early Scotland?'[19] This is a particularly good example because her methodology is unusually explicit – more explicit than any comparable discussion of Wales – and thus reveals the inherent weakness in the positivists' position, their reliance on the *argumentum ex silentio*. This weakness is

The uses of writing in early medieval Wales

particularly apparent if one frees oneself from preconceptions about Celtic orality before reading her text.

The simple answer to Dr Hughes's question 'Where are the writings of early Scotland?' is, of course, that they hardly exist, at least in Scotland, although it is possible that some manuscripts emigrated to Ireland or the continent and survive there.[20] The question she really addresses, however, is the narrower one of why we have few works composed in early Scotland, in particular historical ones. Her main answer is that very little history (in our sense) was written down.[21] This gloomy conclusion depends on negative evidence. May it not be due merely to the ravages of time? Dr Hughes undertook to show the contrary, ingeniously but rather tendentiously. She argued that the depredations of sixteenth-century Protestants cannot alone explain the lack of extant pre-eleventh-century material because a large number of late medieval manuscripts and early printed books did escape the conflagrations. Yet might one not argue that if the number of *early* books extant in the sixteenth century was proportionally small, their total elimination then would not be statistically implausible, especially considering that very venerable-looking books might have been under a particular suspicion of popery? Dr Hughes also dismissed as a myth the story that ancient Scottish chronicles were appropriated by Edward I, on the grounds that the Scottish muniments held by the English in 1323 must have been 'administrative and legal texts, mainly of the thirteenth century'.[22] Yet, while this is doubtless true of the vast majority, can one be sure that there were no earlier records among them, especially as the 'inventory' of 1323 declines to give details 'because of the disorder of the writing and because of their trifling value' (which doesn't really suggest the thirteenth century)? Finally, Dr Hughes argued that already in the thirteenth century 'the historical sources for early Scottish history were as scanty as ours. The only chronicle they had was the known king-list' – because if more sources had been extant they would have been available to, and used by, historians of that time.[23] This is a dangerous approach. To adduce as an analogy what Dr Hughes herself says in another context, 'the argument put forward by the English when writing to Pope Boniface in 1301 is ultimately based on Geoffrey of Monmouth but this does not prove the disappearance of reliable English historical materials'.[24] One cannot argue that there never were early Scottish historical manuscripts because none are extant, for their absence may be merely a

19

facet of the loss of early Scottish manuscripts in general; there *must* have been numerous basic books for school and altar, as Dr Hughes says,[25] but they are not extant either. Indeed, many early charters may have perished with the Gospel Books in which they may have been written.[26]

Very few Insular Celtic manuscripts from before 1000 have survived in their countries of origin. The reason for this is unclear. One possibility is poor storage conditions coupled with damp and peat-smoke.[27] Another is the tendency for 'Celtic' monasteries to be laicized, or at least to change hands, and the absence of Benedictinism with its emphasis on the importance of the monastic library.[28] Whatever the reason, it is a fact that most extant early Irish and Welsh manuscripts have survived because they were taken to the continent or England at an early stage; it would therefore be worth considering whether this may have happened less to manuscripts from Scotland (the Schaffhausen *Vita Columbae* from Iona being a notable exception, if we count Iona as Scottish), perhaps because Scottish *peregrinatio* led more often to Ireland[29] than to the continent.

A further consideration is that, despite some evidence for antiquarian activity (such as the *Vitae* of St Kentigern), the twelfth-century Scottish church tended to be more Anglo-Norman and less backward-looking than the Irish church, as Hughes herself remarked[30] – or than the Welsh church, we may add. Now our knowledge of early Irish and Welsh charters and annals depends much less on the survival of such early manuscripts as the Book of Kells and Lichfield Gospels than on the activities of antiquarians and controversialists in the twelfth century and later, to whom Welsh historians, for example, owe the *Annales Cambriae* and the Book of Llandaf. This may point to an important part of the answer to the question 'Where are the writings of early Scotland?' Scottish writings may simply have ceased to be copied.

By comparison the problems presented by Ireland and Wales are slightly less acute, though still severe. In both countries we have to face the fact, mentioned above, that hardly any pre-eleventh-century manuscripts of any sort have survived continuously in the two countries themselves. Kenney estimated that 'only some ten manuscripts of older date than the year 1000 have survived on Irish soil. On the other hand, of the books which Irish emigrants carried with them to foreign lands well over fifty, complete or fragmentary, are still extant.'[31] (Contrast this with nearly a thousand manuscripts

The uses of writing in early medieval Wales

written or owned in England up to 1100 surviving, over three-quarters of them still in English libraries.)[32] Scaling down the Irish figures to take account of the relative smallness and poverty of Wales, it is hardly surprising that no pre-1000 books have survived within Wales itself and that only about ten or so early Welsh books or fragments have survived abroad, mostly in England. This is predictable when one considers that Welsh *peregrini* (insofar as there were any) seem mostly to have gone not to the continent but to Ireland, where their books will have suffered the general fate of early manuscripts in that island. Most of the few Welsh books which survive are ones like the Cambridge Juvencus, which was imported to England in the late Anglo-Saxon period, no doubt for the usefulness of its text of this popular Latin curriculum author – and certainly not for the sake of its precious incidental Welsh glosses and *englynion*.[33] This means that the picture which the surviving Welsh manuscripts give us may well be skewed by the selective way in which the Anglo-Saxons imported Welsh books. Those with ecclesiastical and school texts would have a greater interest than those with a purely Welsh historical or legal or vernacular interest; in fact, the fewer Welsh peculiarities in the way of script and glosses the better.[34] By contrast, manuscripts written on the continent by Irish scribes or taken to the continent by Irish *peregrini*, and preserved there by complacent librarians of large monastic libraries, are (not surprisingly) more catholic in content; one thinks above all of the remarkable ninth-century Irish scholar's notebook, the 'Reichenauer Schulhandschrift', or 'Codex Sancti Pauli', from Reichenau,[35] or *mutatis mutandis* of codices such as the Old English Vercelli Book. Even on the continent, of course, the great bulk of such manuscripts must have been lost. Bernhard Bischoff once suggested that less than a seventh survives of even the carefully conserved ninth-century Carolingian manuscript collections.[36]

The ten or so early manuscripts which survived in Ireland were ones like the Book of St Mulling and the Cathach of St Columba which were enshrined; presumably such books, while particularly vulnerable to theft, were also particularly jealously guarded and preserved by their successive keepers.[37] Though none now survives there, there were also such books in Wales, such as the eighth-century Gospels now at Lichfield but formerly at Llandeilo Fawr;[38] or the lost Gospel of St Gildas, still at Llancarfan c. 1100–30, allegedly written for St Cadog by Gildas himself;[39] or the lost St Asaph Gospels which the canons took on fund-raising tours in the thirteenth

21

century;[40] or the bejewelled Book of St Beuno or 'Tiboeth' at Clynnog Fawr, allegedly copied by St Twrog in the reign of the early-seventh-century king Cadfan. According to Sir Thomas Wiliems, who is the last person known to have seen this Book of St Beuno (in 1594), it took its name *Tiboeth* ('not hot'?) from having been unscathed when a fire struck Clynnog church,[41] and later folklore recounted that it survived three fires in the church, being encased in iron covers or an iron 'cistan'.[42] (Perhaps special measures were taken to preserve special books? For example, two Gospel Books are the only known survivors of the 1055 Welsh arson at Hereford.)[43] Despite this, the Book of St Beuno perished:

> Tybiwyd y cadwai '*Tiboeth*',
> Yn ei ffurf, oer na phoeth;
> Ond mwy nid oes dim un darn
> O'i gloer wiw, a'i glawr haiarn.[44]

> ('It was supposed that "Tiboeth" would keep in its shape, whether cold or hot; but now there is not one fragment of its splendid box and its iron cover'.)

Since the Book of St Beuno was lost so very late – after 1594 – Edward Lhuyd's comment seems reasonable rather than simply patriotic:

> Seeing therefore we find valuable Antiquities lost in an Age that was Curious, we can make no manner of Estimat at the number of MSS. lost the foregoing centuries, when such Ancient writings were called by the Incurious Monks *Vetusta & inutilia*; and when our Ancestors the Provincial *Britans* were perpetually either engag'd in War, among themselves or exposed to the Invasion of Forreigners; the *Picts, Scots, Saxons, Danes*, and *Normans*.[45]

Early Gospel Books like those mentioned above must have survived as long as they did because of their obvious value as relics, only to succumb to the eventual fate of nearly all such items of ecclesiastical wealth in Wales.[46] In the case of more utilitarian books, however, the obsolescence of Insular script in Wales from about the twelfth century onwards[47] must have militated against preservation – a factor which did not obtain in Ireland, where the use of Insular script continued. Unfortunately we have no early Welsh library catalogues or book lists by which to estimate survival rates. If we had, they might well have included disparaging notices of 'Vetusta &

inutilia', as Lhuyd surmises, or even dismissive references like those to books *in scottice scripti* in the St Gall catalogues.[48]

Even if we were so unwise as to take a hyper-positivistic line and restrict ourselves to the tiny sample of Welsh manuscripts that survive, we could still speak with certainty of quite a number of works certainly available in Wales before the middle of the twelfth century. We have a Gospel Book (the Lichfield Gospels, perhaps not written in Wales itself); various biblical and liturgical extracts; a Psalter and Martyrology; patristic works like Augustine's *De Trinitate*; Classical and Christian school texts such as Ovid's *Ars Amatoria* and Juvencus; Liberal Arts texts such as Martianus Capella, Boethius' translation of Porphyry's *Isagoge*, and Macrobius; Bede's *De Natura Rerum*, and computistical texts such as Bede's *De Temporum Ratione* (a fragment now in America), the vernacular Computus Fragment and the *De Mensuris et Ponderibus*; also original works such as the tract on the Alphabet of Nemniuus and the poetry by Sulien's family.[49] To these we must add works extant in copies from lost Welsh exemplars such as Pelagius on the Pauline Epistles (exemplar pre-800) and Boethius' *De Arithmetica* (exemplar pre-950),[50] and of course original works such as Gildas's *De Excidio Britanniae* (if written in Wales), the *Orationes Moucani*, the *Historia Brittonum*, Asser's *Life of Alfred*, the *Annales Cambriae* and Harleian Genealogies, and the saints' Lives by Rhygyfarch and Lifris;[51] all these are known only from non-Welsh copies and it is only internal evidence that allows us to assign them to Wales. For instance, the prayers of Moucan (Meugan) appear in an eighth-century Mercian manuscript from Worcester but can be included because of the author's Welsh name.[52] Most prayers in the manuscript are given anonymously, so others are perhaps Welsh but unidentifiable as such. (This applies *mutatis mutandis* to other anonymous early medieval Latin works; there is no easy diagnosis of specifically Welsh as opposed to Irish 'symptoms', and nearly all known anonymous Cambro-Latin works[53] have been identified as Welsh from their subject matter or manuscript context.) On top of all these texts, we have to add the Latin works quoted or alluded to by Welsh authors; for example, Ieuan and Rhygyfarch's library at (?)Llanbadarn seems to have included the works of Virgil, Ovid, Lucan, Prudentius, Caelius Sedulius, Aldhelm and others.[54] Listing all this evidence together it would be possible to draw up a quite substantial collection of *Fontes Cambrenses* to parallel the *Fontes Anglo-Saxonici* sponsored by the British Academy.

A hyper-positivist might object that some of these Latin texts may have been very rare birds in Welsh libraries and may have been little read even where they were available. The answer to this is threefold. Firstly, just as it would be absurd to suppose that the Gospels were rare in the Welsh church because only the Lichfield Gospels survive, so it would be unreasonable to deduce that Juvencus or Martianus Capella or Ovid's *Ars Amatoria* were rare because only single Welsh manuscripts of them survive (in Cambridge and Oxford). Indeed all three were also known to the Llanbadarn school. Obviously all our figures need to be scaled up by an unknown factor, all the more so because popular school books were often worn out of existence; only one complete Virgil survives from Anglo-Saxon England![55] Secondly, the books are clearly representative of widely divergent scriptoria and scribal traditions in Wales, not just one or two bastions of learning. Thirdly, the fact that the Latin texts *were* read is shown not only by quotations by Welsh authors but also by the physical appearance of the surviving manuscripts. Martin Irvine notes that 'the codices of grammatical *artes* and curriculum *auctores* usually bear the marks of utilitarian books', and he illustrates this with a page from the Cambridge Juvencus, densely glossed in Wales in Latin, Welsh and Old Irish (as well as in English Caroline after its importation into Anglo-Saxon England).[56] Preliminary studies of the glossators show that the Juvencus manuscript was studied industriously, in conjunction moreover with reference books such as Jerome's *Commentary on Matthew* and Isidore's *Etymologies* which must also be added to our *Fontes Cambrenses*, though no Welsh manuscripts of them are now extant.[57]

I turn now to the use of writing for non-theological and non-scholastic purposes. Here a cautious *communis opinio* is expressed by R. R. Davies. Citing M. T. Clanchy's formula 'a shift from sacred script to practical literacy' (a tendentious phrase for Anglo-Saxonists), he says:

> The art of writing in Wales was on the whole reserved for other purposes [than record documentation] until the twelfth century, and in most respects until the thirteenth. Charters written in Latin and employing distinctively 'Celtic' formulae were certainly composed at various ecclesiastical centres in Wales both before and after the coming of the Normans; and the marginal entry in the eighth-century Lichfield Gospels shows that an attempt could be made to record a legal dispute in a mixture of Latin and Welsh. But writing was mainly reserved for theological and hagiographical works in

24

Latin. The vernacular literary and legal traditions in Wales were carefully nurtured in professional 'schools'; but they were taught and transmitted orally. No literary manuscript, as opposed to an occasional fragment, in Welsh pre-dates the mid-thirteenth century. The regulation of native Welsh society's affairs was likewise dependent on the spoken word and the collective memory. In these circumstances the documents and records which are the essential grist for the social historian's mill are largely lacking; they were never composed.[58]

How far do these cautious conclusions depend on a combination of negative evidence and assumptions about Celtic orality?

Our only concrete contemporary evidence of record keeping consists of the charters, the manumission, and the *Surexit* legal-dispute memorandum inserted at Llandeilo Fawr in the margins of the Lichfield Gospels, the only Gospel Book from early Wales to survive.[59] That is to say, our direct knowledge of these three classes of record is due to late Anglo-Saxon importation and preservation of a single book, one valued of course for its sacred text not for its marginalia. Any such records written on single sheets or 'dedicated' codices (i.e. cartularies) would hardly have found their way to England, or have been preserved there if they had. While the minimalist can indeed say that we have only one example of a Welsh Gospel Book containing records, the maximalist can equally well reply that we have no Welsh Gospel Book that does *not* contain them! We are back with the single white cow. How many Gospel Books were there in Welsh churches and how many similar records perished with them? And if only one example survives of something so basic and universal as a Gospel Book, how many cartularies and single-sheet charters may have perished altogether?

That the Llandeilo charters in the Lichfield Gospels do not stand alone is happily borne out, as Wendy Davies has shown,[60] by copies or adaptations of similar and indeed earlier charters in the twelfth-century cartularies of Llandaf and Llancarfan, the former in 'St Teilo's Book' (*Liber Landavensis*), a codex got up to look like a Gospel Book,[61] and the latter drawing on a Book of St Cadog at Llancarfan,[62] conceivably identical with the Gospel of Gildas mentioned above. The south-eastern orientation of this copying activity may be due not to some hypothetical original restriction of 'Celtic' charter composition to the Romanized south-east, but rather to the fact that the 'cartularization' was precipitated by the early Norman encroachments

25

in that part of Wales. By the time the Normans had penetrated further, Welsh churchman had learnt the lesson that the sword is mightier than the pen. But even in the north-west, at Clynnog Fawr, there were putative seventh- to twelfth-century 'Celtic' charters in the Book of St Beuno, lost in the seventeenth century. We only know this because of the one-off chance that the man who became provost of Clynnog about 1470, Geoffrey Trefnant, happened to be related to Piers Beaupie of Welshpool, one of Edward IV's loyal servants, and through Beaupie was able to obtain a royal confirmation of the Clynnog donations.[63]

While such later evidence shows that the Lichfield Gospel's charters are not isolated freaks, it does not do the same for the Gospel's manumission and legal memorandum. But this is to be expected. No later religious house would have preserved such *inutilia*; we shall never know whether the Books of St Cadog and St Beuno contained manumissions and dispute records, for no one would have been interested in copying them into a cartulary or confirmation charter. There is therefore no reason to assume that manumissions and dispute records were not committed to writing as often in Wales as they were in Anglo-Saxon England or Cornwall. The stark contrast between *one* example of lawsuit *notitia* from Wales and *ninety-five* from Anglo-Saxon England[64] may be illusory.

Much the same applies to other genres: for example, the complete lack of surviving letters, despite the fact that letters must surely have been exchanged. In the early Middle Ages original letters stood little chance of preservation; it is symptomatic that a twelfth-century Canterbury archivist wrote *Epistola inutilis* on the oldest extant letter on vellum or parchment in western Europe (*c.* 704).[65] The Insular letters with the best chance of survival were those sent to distinguished recipients on the continent, such as Lull and Alcuin, whose collected correspondence was copied and preserved. Here the relative isolation of the Welsh church told against it. Significantly, the early-ninth-century letter about the so-called Bamberg cryptogram, the only surviving text of a letter sent from Wales (or more likely shortly after leaving Wales), was written by four Irishmen to another Irish scholar and was preserved on the continent.[66] The text of the cryptogram which it contains, however – *Mermin rex Conchen salutem* – suggests that the king of Gwynedd (Merfyn Frych) did send letters.[67]

No one has been able to prove the writing of legal texts in pre-

26

Norman Wales, despite tantalizing eleventh-century hints.[68] Yet it should be admitted that purely oral law-schools may be as much a figment of the imagination as the lawbook of Hywel Dda, if not more so. *Prima facie*, there seems no reason why Welsh law should not have been written down as early as that of Ireland. The absence of pre-Norman manuscripts is neither here nor there, for the same is equally true of the undoubtedly early Irish laws. Legal codices were not likely to be exported and survive elsewhere. Whereas the antiquity of the Irish laws is clear because their copyists were concerned to transmit the *ipsissima verba* of the 'canonical text', that, as Thomas Charles-Edwards has pointed out, was not a concern of the medieval Welsh jurists, who updated both the content and the language of the texts they inherited in a way typical of Middle Welsh prose in general.[69] A further philological obstacle may be transmission in and out of Latin.[70] The result is that exact scholars have been able plausibly to come to different conclusions about when laws were first written in Wales.

The history of written Old Welsh prose is possibly not only obscured by linguistic modernizing out of recognition, but also skewed by the fact that all our visible Old Welsh evidence is from books preserved outside Wales for the sake of their Latin contents.[71] If this evidence is taken at face value, as it is by positivists such as D. Simon Evans in his lecture *Llafar a Llyfr yn yr Hen Gyfnod*,[72] we get a picture of a painful progress from brief ninth-century glosses to the glories of *Culhwch and Olwen*. This may be right, or it may be dictated by the nature of the surviving evidence; it may be rather as if one were to try and chart the history of Irish prose by comparing the Würzburg glosses with the Leabhar Breac.[73] To make a fair comparison between prose in Wales and Ireland we have to leave out on the Irish side domestically preserved early manuscripts such as the Book of Armagh and Stowe Missal, and also forgo the evidence afforded by later scribes preserving Old Irish linguistic features. A further example of positivism is Proinsias Mac Cana on the *Surexit* memorandum:

> Given that in many early societies law is the first, or one of the first, branches of native tradition to be consigned to writing, one might perhaps infer that the memorandum is one of the first rudimentary attempts at a functional written prose in Welsh. The corollary is that a developed 'literary' or narrative prose still lay some distance in the future.[74]

Jenkins and Owen rightly object that 'This argument seems to misunderstand the genre of "Surexit". The memorandum is very different from the kind of legal material which breaks the ice of writing for a national language.'[75] Mac Cana's argument also forgets that no Welsh manuscript, in *any* language, survives from before the time of the Lichfield Gospels marginalia, and that the mixture of Latin and the vernacular in *Surexit* is also to be found in the roughly contemporary Book of Armagh, which few would place at the beginning of continuous narrative written prose in Irish. The mixing of Latin and the vernacular in these manuscripts admits of various explanations,[76] of which inexperience in writing the vernacular is the least likely. Indeed, both in Anglo-Saxon England and in Ireland one has the impression that it was writing Latin rather than the vernacular that presented problems in the ninth and tenth centuries.[77] In Wales, Latin may have been rather stronger (the *Historia Brittonum* and Asser come to mind), but there is simply not enough evidence to pose the question as to whether or not vernacular prose was relatively weak. Certainly it would be perilous to argue that if there had been a flourishing vernacular Welsh prose literature in the Alfredian period, then the scribes of the surviving fourteenth-century vernacular codices such as the Book of the Anchorite of Llanddewibrefi would have known and preserved it. Hence we simply do not know whether or not homilies were written and delivered in the vernacular in Wales, as in Ireland and Anglo-Saxon England,[78] or solely in Latin; we have evidence for neither language.

The unfortunate fact is that we are not in a position to say quite where the boundaries between Latin and the vernacular were set in early Wales, owing to the massive loss of manuscript evidence, and analogies with the rest of Europe are merely suggestive.[79] One very visible area where Latin was definitely preferred to Welsh, however, was in inscriptions. The Welsh were evidently determined to use Latin even if the Latin merely calqued a Welsh construction: *Moridic surexit hunc lapidem* ('Moriddig raised this stone').[80] No Welsh-language inscriptions are extant before the unusual one at Tywyn of *c.* 800.[81] This does not indicate that the non-inscriptional writing of the vernacular only began *c.* 800, for the fact is that Latin continued to be almost exclusively the chosen language for inscriptions for centuries *after* 800, when we know for certain from manuscripts that the vernacular was being used for other purposes. We see therefore a genre-related preference. The script and language of publicly dis-

The uses of writing in early medieval Wales

played writings were probably important semiotically; the medium was part of the message, even with an illiterate audience in mind, as St Boniface recognized when he asked Eadburg of (?)Wimborne for a codex copied in gold to impress the pagan Germans.[82] In Wales, the use of roman capitals and (later) half-uncials may have constituted an assertion of Romano-British and Christian legitimacy, in contra-distinction to the Irish use of ogam and Germanic use of runes.[83] Probably for the same reason, the Welsh studiously avoided the addition of symbols to the roman alphabet, useful though they might have been in the writing of Welsh names,[84] and preserved an archaic orthography in inscriptions (e.g. *CATAMANVS*, where *Catman* or *Catuan* would be permitted in a charter).[85] And since the epigraphic tradition of Roman Britain was exclusively Latin (the only known exceptions being one or two curse-tablets deposited at Bath, not public inscriptions),[86] Latin was naturally the language of Welsh memorial stones: while an Irish settler in Anglesey might be commemorated with a vernacular formula such as *CAMVLORIS HOI*, even when roman rather than ogam letters were used,[87] a Welshman would always prefer *HIC IACET N.* and the like. This Welsh preference for Latin inscriptions is interesting and culturally signifi cant, especially in comparison with Ireland, but cannot necessarily be used in arguments about the use of the vernacular in non-monumental situations.

Linguistically early vernacular poetry is extant in a range of genres,[88] largely thanks to the survival of some major thirteenth- and fourteenth-century codices (the Black Book of Carmarthen, Book of Aneirin, Book of Taliesin, White Book of Rhydderch, Red Book of Hergest). The possible oral background of these texts is debatable. It seems likely enough (if strictly unprovable on internal evidence)[89] that early medieval Welsh poets, like many modern poets, composed without pen in hand and that they committed their own and others' poems to memory. Faulty memorization, but not necessarily oral transmission from reciter to reciter, almost certainly explains some of the variations between the A and B texts of the *Gododdin* or between the two versions of the Gereint fab Erbin *englynion*, in particular the dislocation of stanzas within sequences joined by incremental repeti-tion or *cymeriadau*.[90] All this is far from conceding that the poets necessarily operated in an illiterate environment. For all we can prove to the contrary, the ninth- or tenth-century(?) poet of *Etmic Dinbych* may not have been untypical in his consultation of writings in a cell.[91]

29

His poem (in the fourteenth-century Book of Taliesin) may even have come down to us from a copy written there. Asser's picture of King Alfred learning Old English poems both from performance and from readings from a book[92] may not have been untypical of his own Welsh experience.

This sort of speculation runs up against modern assumptions about the orality of Celtic bardic art. For example, Rachel Bromwich, referring to stories of spontaneous verse rejoinders by Celtic poets, to the *beirdd gwlad* and *ymryson y beirdd* of modern Wales, and to the hypothetical importance of 'extemporary verse-repartee' in medieval bardic contests and early modern *eisteddfodau* and Courts of Poetry, sums up:

> My point is that the practice of writing is non-essential and even alien to such a tradition, and that where poetry is concerned – as distinct from prose-composition, whose history differs in important respects – the power of the written word has never succeeded in gaining final domination over it.[93]

If we could assume that the progess of literacy in the Celtic countries has been slow but inexorable, we could project modern evidence for orality back into the early Middle Ages. This would be a dangerous assumption, however, as we have seen. Quite possibly the role of writing increased and decreased from period to period and genre to genre; for example, if it is legitimate to judge by the surviving textual evidence, the transmission of the poems of Cynddelw from the twelfth century onwards may have been less oral than those of the Cywyddwyr in the fourteenth century.[94] It is worth comparing pre-twelfth-century Ireland, where there is legal evidence for a distinction between the learned *fili* and the humbler *bard*, between 'the practitioners of bardic competition and verses' (the *baird*) and 'the champions of knowledge and poetic art' (the *filid*): 'although knowledge of letters and metrics is not required of the bards, it is required of them to perceive and recognise their proper measure by ear and nature. It is thus that the free bards make their bardic poetry'.[95] It stands to reason that the early Irish poetry which actually survives is more likely to be the work of the learned poets than the orally orientated (if not actually illiterate) *baird*, and the same could be true of extant early Welsh poetry.

The idea of an exclusively oral milieu for poetry in early Wales stems partly from the fact that we have no codex of Welsh poetry earlier than the mid-thirteenth-century Black Book of Carmarthen. Here again we must remember manuscript survival. The fact is that there are no all-vernacular codices *of any sort* before this period, so it is not a matter of poetry being a specially oral case which reached book form relatively late. Moreover, the orthography and palaeographical errors of manuscripts like the Book of Aneirin show that there must have been comparable codices in the Old Welsh period.[96] And in the marginal *englynion* in the Juvencus manuscript in Cambridge we have tangible evidence[97] that religious and secular poetry was being written down by the early tenth century. Admittedly, these verses were incidental marginalia, but it is not to be expected that purely vernacular poetic manuscripts of this early period would have been conserved abroad. The position is much the same for early Irish literature; with the exception of the poems in the unique ninth-century Codex Sancti Pauli miscellany mentioned above (which includes, for instance, the only Irish panegyric poem extant in an early manuscript),[98] *all* the tiny corpus of vernacular Irish verse extant in early manuscripts is incidental or marginal to the Latin works for which the manuscripts were preserved on the continent.[99]

It is difficult to know how far back beyond the tenth century the written transmission of Welsh poetry can be pushed, but John T. Koch's ongoing search for traces of exemplars in Archaic Old Welsh orthography is eminently reasonable in principle.[100] It conflicts, of course, with the late David Greene's theory that the Welsh *literati* despised their vernacular until the ninth century, when the Irish example inspired them to start writing glosses and stray stanzas in their margins.[101] Professor Greene's ideas on this point, however, were based on negative evidence (such as the 'weak scriptorial tradition of the Welsh monastic system') and misconceptions. The writing of marginal verses cannot be shown to be of Irish inspiration.[102] Nor was the orthography of Old Welsh due to ninth-century imitation of Old Irish, since it can be seen to emerge naturally from the Archaic Old Welsh orthography used for personal names in the Llandaf and Llancarfan charters in the seventh and eighth centuries.[103] Nor does Gildas object to vernacular Welsh language and literature in themselves, but rather to bardic praise of earthly rulers,[104] a view in any case probably not generally shared: it is noteworthy that the early-ninth-century author of the *Historia Brittonum* says that Aneirin, Taliesin, and other poets *claruerunt* in sixth-century British poetry, an annalistic formula which implicitly puts them on a par with

31

Latin poets such as Virgil.[105] To judge by this formula, the Welsh admiration for *Latinitas*, upon which Greene builds so much, by no means excluded admiration for the vernacular, at least in its proper place.

There was an element of deliberate provocation in Greene's positivism – Jackson-baiting and Welsh-baiting rolled into one – and also something more significant. Proinsias Mac Cana recalls that

> in this instance as in others he enjoyed trailing his coat a little, for he evinced a huge delight at some of the indignant reactions to his magisterial pronouncements. But there was more to it than cocking a snook at convention: the fact is that he disliked ambiguity, indecision or suspension of judgement, even when the matter in hand might seem to leave little choice.[106]

I am not trying to claim decisively that Welsh churchmen were writing down vernacular poetry as early as the late sixth century, as Colmán mac Léléni is believed to have been doing in Ireland;[107] merely that a similar horizon in both countries is not inherently unlikely. Pending completion of Koch's investigations, 'not proven' is the safest verdict. Faced only with negative evidence, we are in the position which Emily Lyle calls 'parity of ignorance'. Her example is the Scottish ballad 'Sir Colin', whose written transmission Child thought to have begun in the seventeenth century. This was disproved in 1972 by the discovery of a dilapidated sixteenth-century manuscript. Lyle's point is

> that it is not sufficient to admit, when an early Scottish form of 'Sir Colin' comes to light, that a mistake was made in this single instance. It is necessary to see that the mistake belongs to a class of mistakes resulting from an underlying, insidious error in methodology that needs to be strenuously rebutted. As events turned out, we know that it would have been wiser of Child to conclude that it was 'not proven' whether or not there had been an early Scottish form of 'Sir Colin'.[108]

Should we not take the same line with regard to an early written *Gododdin* (Scottish or otherwise)? If you don't like suspension of judgement, the Dark Age kitchen is not for you!

It cannot, of course, be supposed that vernacular manuscript production in the various Celtic-speaking countries was always comparable; that seems not to have been the case in 1250–1350, for example, when Welsh production was much more buoyant than Irish and Scottish Gaelic was – or at least seems to have been.[109] But comparison is not inherently unreasonable. Why should early Wales have been radically different from Ireland or England?

I have been sitting on the fence contemplating the Welsh cow for long enough. I am not going to disturb the reader by getting off the fence and declaring that half a white cow is the tip of an iceberg! All I am claiming is that if there was much more and wider and more varied literacy in early Wales that we have hitherto suspected, the evidence might well look exactly like what actually survives. A man once doubted that the earth went round the sun 'because it doesn't look like that'. The scientist replied: 'And how would you expect it to look if it was as it is?'

NOTES

1 Jarman, 'Cerdd Ysgolan', 57–62.
2 See below, p. 19.
3 Richards, '"Lichfield" Gospels', 144.
4 Chapman, *Celts*, pp. 210–14.
5 William Collins, *Ode on the Popular Superstitions of the Highlands of Scotland, considered as the Subject of Poetry* (not published till 1788), in *Poetical Works of Gray*, ed. Poole, p. 301 (vv. 36–9). ('Spencer' refers to Edmund Spenser on the Irish bards.)
6 Bowden, *Tour* (Dublin, 1791), pp. 165–6, quoted by Leerssen, *Mere Irish*, p. 81. For further quotations of this sort see my 'Invention of Celtic nature poetry', pp. 108–10, also a telling quotation from E. Souvestre, *Les derniers Bretons* (1834), in Constantine, *Breton Ballads*, p. 179.
7 Warner, *Walk through Wales*, p. 185.
8 See Thornton, below, pp. 83–4.
9 Cf. Sims-Williams, 'Historical need', 28–9.
10 *De Bello Gallico*, VI.14. For some recent comments on this passage by Insular Celtic scholars see: J. E. C. Williams, 'Celtic literature', p. 124; Tristram, 'Early modes', pp. 431–4; A. Harvey, 'Latin', pp. 18 and 20–1; Russell, *Introduction*, pp. 198–9. Compare the dismissive remarks of Kendrick, *Druids*, pp. 117–20.
11 Piggott, *Druids*, p. 162. But note that the 'Chief Druid' facing p. 65 of Henry Rowlands's *Mona Antiqua Restaurata* (Dublin, 1723), regains his book (but loses his sandals) in the second edition (London, 1766).
12 Usefully surveyed by Russell, *Introduction*, pp. 2–7 and 198–207, and by Lambert, *La langue gauloise*.
13 Meid, *Gaulish Inscriptions*, p. 56, n. 101, would accommodate this evidence to the traditional view, noting that 'the bronze plate on which this calendar was engraved was deliberately destroyed before it was hidden in the earth'. Compare also Guyonvarc'h and Le Roux, *Les druides*, p. 264, n. 4: 'Un emploi de l'écriture

33

lié à des pratiques magiques est, dans notre documentation actuelle, presque toujours, en Gaule, un signe de décadence et de survivance tardive'

14 A useful modern survey is Redknap, *Christian Celts*; see also Charles-Edwards, below, pp. 63–5, and the comparative statistics for half-uncial inscriptions in Wales, Scotland and England given by Forsyth, below, pp. 44, 53–4. The epigraphical dating of Class I stones is now controversial (e.g. Dark, 'Class I inscribed stones'). A middle way is suggested by Higgitt in his review of Okasha, *Corpus*. Close philological dating is impossible, but valid linguistic trends are visible; cf. Sims-Williams, 'Dating the transition', pp. 236–7.

15 On the last three media cf. J. Stevenson, 'Literacy in Ireland', pp. 20–1, and S. Kelly, 'Anglo-Saxon lay society', pp. 41–2. For early Welsh references to writing on wax see Haycock, 'Tree-list', pp. 307 and 319 n. 87.

16 Cf. C. Thomas, *Mute Stones*, p. 70.

17 Knight, 'Penmachno'.

18 See Charles-Edwards, below, pp. 64–5.

19 In Hughes, *Celtic Britain*, pp. 1–21 (cf. my review). On Scotland see also Forsyth, below, pp. 39–44.

20 Very hypothetically, Hughes mentions the Book of Kells, and 'Garland of Howth' in this connection (*Celtic Britain*, pp. 11, and 15 n. 96, and cf. p. 41). Dr Dauvit Broun pointed out in discussion that some Irish manuscripts, such as the Drummond Missal, have certainly moved *to* Scotland.

21 Ibid., p. 20.

22 Ibid., p. 4.

23 Ibid., pp. 5–6 and 17.

24 Ibid., p. 7. In fact elsewhere (p. 98, cf. p. 10) she admitted the existence of an early Pictish Chronicle.

25 Ibid., p. 11. Compare early Anglo-Saxon England where in theory (Ecgberht's *Penitential*) every priest was supposed to be equipped with a psalter, lectionary, antiphonary, missal, baptismal order and martyrology, although only miserable fragments survive: Sims-Williams, *Religion and Literature*, p. 273.

26 Cf. Broun, *Charters*, and more generally below, pp. 25–6.

27 Adverse climatic conditions are not a sufficient explanation alone, as would emerge if manuscript survival were mapped against rainfall across a wider area of Europe. For the effects of damp and peat-smoke see Black, 'Gaelic manuscripts', pp. 164–5.

28 Various members of the audience in Bangor suggested this, noting that Benedictine libraries survive better than those of other orders, and that there are relatively few Anglo-Saxon manuscripts from before the tenth-century Benedictine Revival.

29 A Pictish example is given by Hughes, *Celtic Britain*, p. 41.

30 Ibid., p. 15.

31 Kenney, *Sources*, p. 9. The significance of these statistics (which need updating) is taken up by Sims-Williams, 'Evidence for vernacular influence', p. 240, and by A. Harvey, 'Latin', p. 19. For more recent statistics, positivistically interpreted, see Mostert, 'Celtic, Anglo-Saxon or Insular?'

32 Gneuss, 'Preliminary list'. The great bulk of these belong to the period of the tenth-century monastic revival and later. On the massive loss of the earliest manuscripts see Dumville, 'Importation of Mediterranean manuscripts'.

The uses of writing in early medieval Wales

33 Cf. Sims-Williams, 'Evidence for vernacular influence', p. 240. Professor Dumville has in hand a study of Anglo-Saxon importation of Welsh and Breton books.

34 This may mean that some Welsh books surviving in Anglo-Saxon England cannot easily be identified as such, a possible example being the eighth-century Hereford Gospel Book. Cf. Sims-Williams, *Religion and Literature*, p. 181.

35 Benediktinerstift St Paul, St Paul in Lavanttal, Austria, MS 86b/1. On this see bibliography in Berschin, *Greek Letters*, pp. 153 and 321, n. 120, to which add Oskamp, 'Irish material'.

36 McKitterick, *Carolingians*, p. 163.

37 Cf. ibid., pp. 135–6. An example, perhaps the Book of Kells itself, is the 'Great Gospel of Colum Cille' stolen from Kells and recovered in 1007; see Herbert, 'Charter material', p. 60. See also the next note.

38 The Lichfield Gospels include an early-ninth-century memorandum that Gelhi son of Arihtiud acquired this Gospel Book from Cingal in exchange for a horse and placed it on the altar of St Teilo: *LL*, p. xliii; Jenkins and Owen, 'Lichfield Gospels, Part I', 50 and 56.

39 *Vitae Sanctorum Britanniae*, ed. Wade-Evans, pp. 94–7; Pryce, 'Ecclesiastical wealth', p. 26, also noting a possible Insular Gospel Book at Valle Crucis.

40 G. Williams, *Welsh Church*, pp. 43 and 89. The supposed and actual dates of this book are uncertain.

41 *Gwaith Iolo Goch*, ed. Johnston, p. 323. Butler, 'Fire at Clynnog', 100, suggests that the fire in question was the early-sixteenth-century one (rather than the destruction in 978, as previously supposed), but this is ruled out by Iolo Goch's reference to *y Tiboeth* in the fourteenth century (unless *tiboeth = di-buelh* is a secondary folk etymology).

42 E. T[homas], 'Clynnog Fawr', 43.

43 Cf. Sims-Williams, 'William of Malmesbury', 13, n. 24.

44 Eben Fardd, *Cyff Beuno*, p. 64.

45 *Archaeologia Britannica*, p. 225.

46 See Pryce, 'Ecclesiastical wealth'.

47 See Huws, *Llyfrau Cymraeg*, pp. 2–3.

48 McKitterick, *Carolingians*, p. 183; cf. Mostert, 'Celtic, Anglo-Saxon or Insular?', pp. 95–6. Contrast the survival of book lists from England: Lapidge, 'Surviving booklists'.

49 Lindsay, *Early Welsh Script*; Peden, 'Science and philosophy'; Huws, 'Welsh manuscript'; Lambert, ' "Thirty" and "sixty" ', 37–9 on *De Mensuris*; I. Williams, 'Notes on Nennius'; Lapidge, 'Welsh-Latin poetry'. The above list is intended to give a general impression, not to be complete. I owe my knowledge of the ninth-century *De Temporum Ratione* to Prof. Malcolm Parkes.

50 Dumville, 'Late-seventh- or eighth-century evidence'; Bishop, 'Corpus Martianus Capella', 259–62.

51 See Lapidge and Sharpe, *Bibliography*, passim.

52 British Library, Royal 2 A.xx. See Sims-Williams, *Religion and Literature*, pp. 15, 169, 280, 320–2, and 327; Howlett, 'Orationes Moucani'. On the Welshness of the name see my review of *The Welsh Life of Saint David*, ed. D. S. Evans. In addition to the etymology mentioned there, note the possibility of a hypocoristic *M'Eucan < M'Oucan : Avicantus* (R. J. Thomas, 'Enwau afonydd', 32).

35

53 Lapidge and Sharpe, *Bibliography*, §§81ff. On Welsh 'symptoms' cf. Lapidge, 'Latin learning', pp. 93–7 and 102.
54 Lapidge, 'Welsh-Latin Poetry', 69.
55 Orchard, *Poetic Art of Aldhelm*, pp. 131–2. On whether the fifth-century 'Vergilius Romanus' comes from sub-Roman Britain see Dumville, 'Importation of Mediterranean manuscripts', pp. 113–14.
56 Irvine, *Making of Textual Culture*, pp. 372–3.
57 A. Harvey, 'Cambridge Juvencus Glosses'; Lapidge, 'Latin learning', pp. 97–102.
58 R. R. Davies, *Conquest*, pp. 111–12. Cf. Keynes, 'Royal government'.
59 Unless the Hereford Gospel Book comes from Wales (see above, n. 34), and this in fact contains comparable marginalia referring to Scandinavian, English and Welsh disputants, entered in Hereford; see Jenkins and Owen, 'Lichfield Gospels, Part I', 61–2, also 'Lichfield Gospels, Part II', 113–14. The Lichfield marginalia are in *LL*, pp. xliii–xlviii. In general see D. Jenkins, 'From Wales to Weltenburg?'
60 W. Davies, 'Latin charter-tradition'; cf. Broun, *Charters*, pp. 38–42. For an assessment of the south-eastern material see my review of W. Davies, *Llandaff Charters* and *Early Welsh Microcosm*. Charter-formulae also seem to occur in south-eastern inscriptions from Ogmore and Merthyr Mawr; see ibid., 128, and W. Davies, 'Latin charter-tradition', pp. 259 and 270, n. 40, and below, p. 104.
61 G. Williams, *Welsh Church*, p. 444; Huws, 'Making of *Liber Landavensis*'.
62 *Vitae Sanctorum Britanniae*, ed. Wade-Evans, p. 126 (§56).
63 Sims-Williams, 'Edward IV's confirmation charter'. The earliest copy is in a manuscript (BL Harley 696) mostly copied in 1503 at Caernarfon by Richard Foxwist, on whom see Smith, below, p. 208.
64 Wormald, 'Handlist', 259–65. For manumissions see S. Kelly, 'Anglo-Saxon lay society', p. 50.
65 Chaplais, 'Letter from Bishop Wealdhere'; Sims-Williams, *Religion and Literature*, p. 211.
66 Berschin, *Greek Letters*, pp. 144–5.
67 This is assumed by Chadwick, 'Early culture', p. 95. 'Conchen' is usually identified with Cyngen, king of Powys; cf. Sims-Williams, 'Historical need', 26 and n. 88.
68 T. M. Charles-Edwards, *Welsh Laws*, pp. 81–2; Pryce, *Native Law*, p. 26.
69 *Welsh Laws*, pp. 21–2. The two texts of *Culhwch and Olwen* are a good parallel, although linguistic modernization is not the only factor there; the later text sometimes makes explicit features essential for oral delivery which are abbreviated in the earlier text (S. Davies, 'Llafar v. ysgrifenedig').
70 See, for example, Pryce, 'Early Irish canons', 115.
71 I assume this is true of the book from which the Old Welsh Computus Fragment came (Lindsay, *Early Welsh Script*, pp. 18–19 and plate VIII).
72 D. S. Evans, *Llafar a Llyfr*.
73 A. Harvey, 'Latin', p. 22, rightly objects to the idea that vernacular prose-writing was the 'result of separate glosses' being, as it were, joined up'. Cf. Tristram, ' "Cattle-Raid" ', p. 72.
74 Mac Cana, *Mabinogi*, p. 12. See also *idem*, 'Rhyddiaith Gymraeg', 82.
75 Jenkins and Owen, 'Lichfield Gospels, Part II', 112.
76 Ibid., pp. 112–13 and n. 10; McCone, 'Zur Frage der Register'; *idem*, *Pagan Past*,

pp. 35–6. Nor would one date the emergence of English prose on the basis of the material discussed by Wenzel, *Macaronic Sermons*.

77 For Ireland see Sharpe, *Medieval Irish Saints' Lives*, pp. 19–26 (with review by J. Carey), also Flanagan, below, p. 114. For England see S. Kelly, 'Anglo-Saxon lay society'.

78 Compared by Tristram, *Early Insular Preaching*.

79 Cf. Richter, 'Writing the vernacular'. For example, no one would venture to suppose that Irish and Welsh were used liturgically, though Slavonic was for a time (ibid., p. 223).

80 *ECMW*, no. 61 (tenth- or eleventh-century). Welsh *cyfodi* meant 'raise' as well as 'arise'.

81 I would now tentatively prefer this date: see Sims-Williams, 'Emergence', 23.

82 Sims-Williams, *Religion and Literature*, p. 209. On the symbolic power of writing see ibid., pp. 180–1, 210, 270, 287, 293–5; J. Stevenson, 'Literacy in Ireland', pp. 16–17 and 20–2 (on Patrick's *apgitoria*, cf. Sims-Williams, 'Byrhtferth's ogam signature'). See also Flanagan on the symbolic function of script in charters, below, pp. 115–17.

83 Cf. Charles-Edwards and Forsyth, below, pp. 63–4 and 54–5; also A. Harvey, 'Early literacy', 14, and 'Latin', p. 21.

84 This is the point behind the story of the Alphabet of Nemniuus (I. Williams, 'Notes on Nennius', 380–1). Contrast other nations' willingness to add letters: Sims-Williams, 'Additional letters'.

85 See Sims-Williams, 'Emergence'.

86 See Tomlin, *Tabellae Sulis*, pp. 128–9 and 133; *idem*, 'Ancient British Celtic'.

87 'Here [lies] Camulorix': see Sims-Williams, 'Additional letters', 48–9.

88 Rowland, 'Genres'. With what follows cf. my 'Early Welsh Arthurian poems', esp. pp. 33–7.

89 Orchard, *Poetic Art of Aldhelm*, pp. 112–25, has shown that even a highly literate poet can 'pass' the 'five tests for orality' devised by B. Peabody. In any case, the techniques of 'oral-formulaic improvisation' do not appear in early Welsh poetry; see Jackson, *Gododdin*, p. 60, n. 1; Haycock, 'Early Welsh poetry', pp. 112 and 123. For an 'exception which proves the rule' see my ' "Is it fog or smoke?" ', 512, and Conran, 'Ballad', 23, n. 13. For the compositional techniques of the Welsh poets see Haycock, 'Medd a mêl farddoni'.

90 For the *Gododdin* see charts in Owen, ' "Hwn yw e Gododin" ', pp. 125–6, and Dumville, 'Early Welsh poetry', p. 9. (G. R. Isaac's assumption of non-oral transmission, 'Canu Aneirin', seems more convenient than logical; cf. Roberts, 'Oral tradition', 65.) For the Gereint *englynion* see Rowland, *Early Welsh Saga Poetry*, pp. 457–61.

91 Sims-Williams, 'Gildas and vernacular poetry', p. 172. Cf. J. T. Koch, 'When was Welsh literature?', 65, n. 1.

92 S. Kelly, 'Anglo-Saxon lay society', p. 60.

93 Bromwich, 'Celtic literatures', pp. 47–8.

94 Huws, *Five Ancient Books*, p. 23. For a Cynddelw poem preserved in two early manuscripts see, for example, *Gwaith Cynddelw Brydydd Mawr I*, ed. Jones and Parry Owen, no. 7 (but cf. oral[?] variation in no. 9). On the use of books by bards see E. I. Rowlands, 'Bardic lore'.

95 Quoted and discussed by McCone, *Pagan Past*, pp. 27, 166–7 and 225–7; cf. my review, 188.

96 Cf. Huws, *Llyfrau Cymraeg*, p. 2.

97 All too tangible in the case of Edward Lhuyd, who cut three off; the same fate has now met the only other similar evidence of written poetry in the Old Welsh period, the *englyn* on Padarn's staff; see Haycock, *Blodeugerdd Barddas*, pp. 3 and 241.

98 The poem to Áed mentioned by Simms, below, p. 240. On the Codex Sancti Pauli see above, n. 35.

99 See Sims-Williams, 'Evidence for vernacular influence', pp. 240–1.

100 See J. T. Koch, 'When was Welsh literature?'; 'Cynfeirdd poetry'; 'Gleanings'; 'Thoughts'. Cf. Sims-Williams, 'Emergence', 78–9; Rowland, 'Horses in the *Gododdin*', 39.

101 Greene, 'Linguistic considerations', 2–3.

102 Sims-Williams, 'Evidence for vernacular influence', pp. 239–41.

103 Sims-Williams, 'Emergence'.

104 Sims-Williams, 'Gildas and vernacular poetry', pp. 174–9.

105 Dumville, 'Historical value', 17.

106 Mac Cana, 'David Greene', 5.

107 Thurneysen, 'Colmán mac Lénéni'; cf. Carney, 'Three Old Irish poems', 63–5. Carney suggested much earlier dates for the composition, if not the writing down, of the so-called 'Leinster' poems; see, however, Liam Breatnach's review of Tranter and Tristram (eds.), *Early Irish Literature*, 120, also Sims-Williams, 'Gildas and vernacular poetry', p. 173, n. 29, and J. T. Koch, 'Conversion', 41. In general see Corthals, 'Irland'.

108 Lyle, 'Parity of ignorance', p. 113.

109 Huws, *Llyfrau Cymraeg*, p. 4; Carney, 'Literature in Irish', p. 689; Black, 'Gaelic manuscripts', p. 160.

2

Literacy in Pictland

KATHERINE FORSYTH

Discussions of early medieval literacy on the continent are framed, necessarily, in terms of a contraction from the Roman period. But what of the regions beyond the territory of the former Empire, areas without the legacy of imperial bureaucratic and personal literacy? Work by Harvey[1] and Stevenson[2] has demonstrated that through contact with the Roman world the Irish developed a literacy using a script of their own devising – ogam.[3] The introduction of Christianity promoted a different kind of literacy, in the roman alphabet, but orthographical studies have shown a degree of continuity with the earlier form. The nature of this roman-alphabet literacy in Ireland has been ably discussed by Jane Stevenson[4] and Thomas Charles-Edwards.[5] This chapter is an attempt to extend the enquiry to that other Celtic-speaking region beyond the *limes* – Scotland. In many respects, Gaelic-speaking Dál Riada (Argyll and adjacent islands) is part of the Irish sphere; discussion will focus instead on the Brittonic-speaking east, that is, Pictland (the rest of Scotland north of the Forth–Clyde line, including the Outer Hebrides and the Northern Isles). Since the Picts were politically, linguistically and culturally eclipsed by their Gaelic-speaking neighbours in the second half of the ninth century, AD 900 provides a convenient terminus.

The first obstacle to a study of literacy in Pictland is the complete lack of any surviving Pictish manuscripts. Of course, few enough pre-900 manuscripts survive from anywhere in the British Isles.[6] More difficult to explain away is the lack of any texts from Pictland preserved in later manuscript copies. Kathleen Hughes addressed the question in detail and came up with a number of reasons particular to Scotland why putative Pictish manuscripts would have failed to be preserved, from the predations of Edward I to seventeenth- and eighteenth-century Presbyterian lack of interest in the history of the early church.[7] Notwithstanding these potential losses, she concluded

39

that the reason why Pictish material demonstrably had not been available to Scottish historians of the thirteenth century was that it had never existed in the first place. Although she provided a plausible explanation for why texts have not survived, equally one might add the four hundred years of Pictish political, administrative, cultural and linguistic obsolescence before 1300. Taking into consideration the abandonment or even suppression of Pictish identity, identified by Broun and Wormald as attendant on the ninth- and tenth-century Gaelic ascendancy,[8] there seems ample reason why such manuscripts would not be preserved.

Since what we know of Scottish history in the post-Pictish period suggests that any earlier documents would be extremely unlikely to survive, we are at a methodological impasse. The evidential outcome would be the same whether the texts were never written in the first place, or whether they had all been lost in the intervening period; thus the absence of manuscripts can tell us nothing. As the archaeologists remind us, absence of evidence is not evidence of absence; but neither is it licence to posit Pictish scriptoria churning out documents, only for them all to perish subsequently.[9] Have we any reason to think the inhabitants of eastern Scotland were any more literate in the seventh and eighth centuries than they were in the third and fourth?

Without digressing into the contested ground of the earliest Pictish Christianity, one can assert the growing consensus that possibly by the early, and certainly by the late, seventh century the church was well established in Pictland.[10] No biblical or liturgical texts have survived from the Pictish church,[11] yet it is inconceivable that they did not exist: the church simply could not have functioned without them. Equally one might ask, where are the contents of the great library at York? The material remains of the Pictish church, including *de luxe* ecclesiastical metalwork such as the Monymusk reliquary,[12] and, above all, the impressive body of monumental sculpture,[13] indicate a vibrant ecclesiastical culture open to influences from Ireland, England and beyond. The argument is not, as Hughes complained, that 'outstanding stone-work necessarily presupposes outstanding scriptoria',[14] but simply that, artistically and intellectually, the monuments could have been produced only in a milieu familiar with manuscripts. There are numerous depictions on Pictish sculpture of figures holding or reading from books – as at Nigg, St Vigeans 11 and 17, Aberlemno 3 and Invergowrie[15] – or in the case of Papil, carrying book satchels (Fig. 1).[16] The point has been closely

Fig. 1 Detail of cross-slab from Papil, Shetland, showing figures with
book-satchels.

argued by art historians at a number of levels, from the general
observation that the layout of cross-slab panels reflects a manuscript-
derived aesthetic to the more specific contention that the Picts
developed skills in setting out interlace, key and spiral patterns on
other media before they first applied them to relief sculpture in the
early eighth century.[17] In one very specific instance, distinctive
imagery and multi-layered symbolism prompted R. B. K. Stevenson
to argue for the late eighth-century presence near Meigle, Perthshire,
of an illuminated medical manuscript 'and a library through which
ideas came, as they did to Jarrow, Iona and the rest, from afar and
were redistributed'.[18] The artists may not have been learned in Latin,
but the sometimes ambitious iconographic programmes of the great
cross-slabs reflect the calibre of Pictish theology and biblical exegesis.

The extant physical evidence is supported by the few scattered
documentary references to the state of the Pictish church. The early
eighth-century snap-shot provided by Bede presents the Pictish

church as literate in Latin.[19] There is nothing in either the physical or documentary evidence to suggest that the Pictish church was intellectually or culturally deviant. In enquiring about Paschal doctrine King Nechtan is described as having 'no small measure of knowledge on these matters' after 'assiduous study of ecclesiastical writings'.[20] In the light of this it may not be exceeding the evidence to see Nechtan, who later retired to a monastery,[21] as a philosopher-king in the Aldfrith mould.[22] The response to Nechtan's enquiries, reproduced in full by Bede, is a long letter presupposing mature ecclesiastical literacy.[23] Bede presents Pictish monasteries as possessing existing computistical texts and able to copy and adopt new ones. A natural extension of computistics is the annal-keeping at the monastery of Applecross, in north-west Pictland, posited by Henderson for the seventh century;[24] and the rudimentary historical writing, similarly discerned by Mrs Anderson, in mid-eighth-century Fortrenn.[25] To assert the use in Pictland of biblical, liturgical, computistical and exegetical texts in Latin should be uncontroversial. Is there anything to indicate the use of literacy beyond the confines of the church?

Underlying much scholarship on the subject of literacy is an implicit belief in humankind's 'will to write': the assumption that once the technology of writing is available to a given society, its, to us, manifest advantages will necessarily lead to its being adopted, and that through time its use will be maximized wherever possible.[26] Thus a society's lack of literacy will be interpreted as a lack of exposure or access to literacy rather than as cultural indifference or outright hostility.[27] Not only is this to substitute possibly inappropriate cultural priorities,[28] but such technological determinism also denies an active role to knowledgeable social actors.[29] Does the elevation of administrative literacy to the normative standard, or even universal goal, stem from an overly restrictive conception of political organization and administration? The role of literacy in enabling the development of embryonic state structures has been acknowledged, but does an emphasis on writing as a technology of social control blind us to the possibilities of orally conducted government in a society which attaches greater importance to interpersonal relations?

As so often, a telling counter-example is provided by early medieval Ireland, where there is ample evidence for 'literary' literacy in Latin and the vernacular, but apparently no evidence for what could be termed 'administrative' literacy.[30] The very limited role accorded written evidence in Irish vernacular law is in keeping with attitudes prevalent elsewhere.[31] More striking, however, is the failure of the church's apparent attempts to introduce the charter to Ireland in the seventh century.[32] Elsewhere in Europe churches and monasteries employed their literacy to record and formalize donations and to secure them against the claims of later generations. Irish churches appear not to have done this. Rather, in Ireland, it seems, complex transactions of wealth and resources in the church, in secular society and between the two were effectively administered without written texts. Clearly, a high level of literacy in one sphere cannot be taken to imply literacy in another. To see Nechtan as versed in theology and computistics is one thing; to argue on this basis that he would have used literacy to govern his kingdom is unwarranted. There is no reason for assuming that his *exactatores* ('tax-gatherers'?), killed at the battle of *Monith-Carno* in 729,[33] need have been competent in using written documents.

Margaret Nieke has written of the use of writing by 'the secular authorities' in Dál Riada as 'just one of a series of measures these early rulers were taking to strengthen their control over the kingdom.'[34] I find myself unable to endorse her view. The annals to which she refers are primarily ecclesiastical documents whose interest in secular affairs is a natural reflection of the church's position in the world; the genealogies are manifestations of existing oral genres of propaganda put into writing by the clergy. There seems no evidence for 'practical' secular literacy in Dál Riada, no bureaucratic record-keeping, administrative or legal writing. Whatever its original purposes, the usefulness of the *Senchas Fer nAlban*[35] as a practical document has surely been overstated. It is better seen not as a 'Domesday' survey, but rather as a propagandistic statement of ethno-political ideology framed in genealogical terms. Certainly, this was the reason for its preservation. The document is indeed 'unique within the Celtic lands',[36] and even if it did have its origin in an actual administrative survey, it was an unprecedented early experiment in a genre which appears not to have been pursued in either Scotland or Ireland.

Dalriadic attitudes to literacy appear to have been drawn, not surprisingly, from Ireland. But what of Pictland? The Picts were in a position to draw on the cultural heritage of both Ireland and Anglo-Saxon England. From which did they derive their ideas about writing? Or did their unique historical position lead them to attitudes of their own? As in Ireland, there is no evidence for Pictish administrative literacy, but unlike Ireland, there is no evidence for written vernacular literature in Pictland, despite the claim that extant texts of Brittonic poetry 'had their genesis in a Strathclyde scriptorium sometime in the latter half of the seventh century'.[37] The roots in the Pictish period of the precocious political development of the kingdom of Scotland have been remarked upon,[38] but was this achieved through Anglo-Saxon-style administrative literacy (the traces of which have not survived), or, perhaps more remarkably, without recourse to the technology of writing? These important questions are not easily answered on present evidence.

In assessing Pictish attitudes to the uses of literacy, the scatter of indirect documentary references, mentioned above, and the nebulous testimony of the sculpture permit nothing more than the vaguest of statements. The only other material is a heterogeneous corpus of inscriptions. As the only written documentation to survive from Pictland this epigraphic material assumes an importance far greater than its volume suggests. As concrete realizations of literate skill and the physical manifestation of attitudes to literacy, inscriptions have the potential to make a major contribution to the debate. The extant Pictish inscriptions come from a greater range of social contexts than the other material discussed so far: from public statements on grand monuments to informal graffiti scratched on slabs, from domestic as well as ecclesiastical and landscape sites, and from areas of the country, such as Shetland and the Outer Isles, for which there is no documentary evidence at all. Their potential is, however, tempered by the fact that they are few in number, often fragmentary and frequently difficult to interpret.

Two alphabets were in use in Pictland, roman and ogam, and thirty-seven inscriptions survive in one or other of them (Map 1). Two monuments (Dupplin and Newton) are inscribed with both. There are eight roman-alphabet inscriptions extant in Pictland, thinly scattered from the Tay to Shetland.[39] All, bar one, are on formal public stone monuments. As an item of *de luxe* metalwork, the exception, the inscribed silver chape from St Ninian's Isle, also has a display aspect. No informal roman-alphabet inscriptions survive in Pictland. The cross-slab from Papa Stronsay, inscribed DNEDI (for *domine dei*?), is now lost and cannot be dated. The Newton stone remains undeciphered and presents many problems. Though the text offers no clues as to date, as a monument it sits most happily with the individual inscribed memorials of Celtic Britain, most of which date

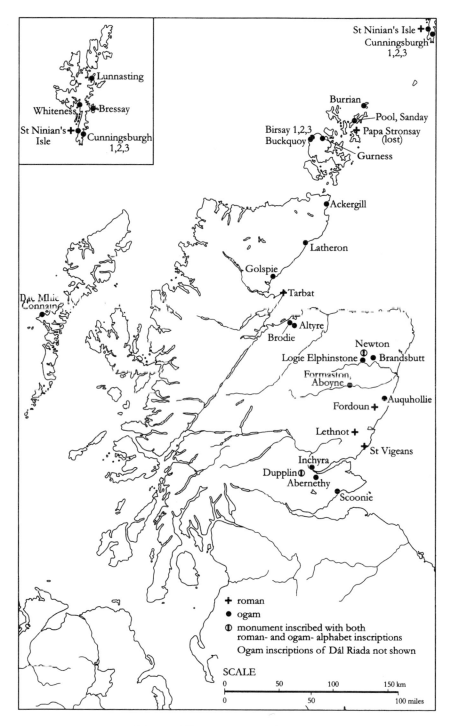

Map 1   The inscriptions of Pictland

45

Fig. 2   Fragment of cross-slab from Tarbat, Ross-shire (0.48m tall). Carved in relief:
In nomine IHU XPI crux XPI in commemoratione Reo[. . .]

Fig. 3   Fragment of cross-shaft from Lethnot, Angus (0.24m tall), inscribed [. . .]
filii Medicii.

from the sixth and seventh centuries.[40] Palaeographic and art-historical criteria can be used to date the remaining inscriptions, and though none is datable with precision, they appear to range from the mid-eighth to the mid-ninth centuries. Following Okasha's dating, they are: Fordoun (eighth century, text incomplete: personal name, perhaps text in vernacular); St Ninian's Isle (late eighth century: Latin with personal names);[41] Tarbat (late eighth or early ninth century, text incomplete: Latin with fragmentary personal names) (Fig. 2);[42] Lethnot (ninth century, or late eighth, text incomplete: Latin with personal name) (Fig. 3); St Vigeans (early ninth century, personal names only, or perhaps with minimal connecting text in the vernacular); and Dupplin (early ninth century, text only partially legible: Latin with personal names, accompanying ogam inscription illegible).[43]

The ogam inscriptions of Pictland are both more numerous and more heterogeneous.[44] Twenty-nine are extant, scattered throughout Pictland, including the Western and Northern Isles (a further six from Dál Riada are excluded from the following discussion). These include two pillars and one slab with text only, four 'Class I' Pictish symbol stones, five 'Class II' cross-slabs with Pictish symbols, four cross-slabs, one free-standing cross, five small fragments of carved stone, four building slabs inscribed with graffiti, two knife handles and one spindle whorl. A minority have been dated using archaeological or art-historical methods, and range from the sixth century (Pool) to the tenth century (Whiteness). The majority fall somewhere in the seventh, eighth and ninth centuries, though in individual cases the date is sometimes little more than a guess. Six are too fragmentary to be of linguistic significance, containing no more than three or four letters in sequence (Abernethy, Birsay 2, Birsay 3, Cunningsburgh 2, Cunningsburgh 3, Whiteness). A seventh is too weathered to be read at all (Dupplin). Two others are highly weathered and are legible only in snatches (Auquhollie, Brodie). This leaves only twenty, about two-thirds of the total, which are completely or substantially legible.

By its very nature, the ogam script is prone to damage and confusion and presents many problems of interpretation. In our case, the problems are compounded by the sparseness with which the Pictish language is otherwise attested. Thus the usual difficulties of handling epigraphic material are sorely exacerbated.[45] None the less, some Pictish ogams can be fully interpreted without difficulty, many can be substantially interpreted. Only a minority resist all explanation. In the case of this last group, much of the blame must rest with our ignorance rather than any deliberate obscurity on the part of the carvers of the texts.

The inscriptions are all fairly short and consist entirely or predominantly of personal names. The substantial inscriptions comprise two inconclusive pieces of graffiti (Pool and Birsay 1); three texts consisting of a single Celtic personal name (Ackergill, Bac Mhic Connain, Scoonie) (Fig. 4); two slightly longer texts containing single Celtic personal names and additional material either incomplete or not wholly legible (Cunningsburgh 1, Newton); four texts of the form X

MAQQ Y, 'X son of Y', with the X and Y being personal names, mostly identifiably Celtic (Altyre, Golspie, Latheron, St Ninian's Isle); one text has been recently reinterpreted as a Christian blessing in Old Irish (Buckquoy);[46] and one text, consisting of five letters carved in a circle, appears to have cryptic or magical rather than straightforwardly linguistic meaning (Logie Elphinstone). The remaining seven present varying degrees of difficulty. One is legible but unintelligible (Brandsbutt); one is largely unintelligible but may contain attested personal names (Inchyra); a third is inconclusive (Gurness). Although one word remains obscure, the Pictish text of the Burrian cross-slab can be tentatively read as 'X made this cross'. The Bressay inscription appears to identify the slab as the cross of a woman with a Norse name; a man with a Celtic name is also mentioned, though it is not known whether he is the person commemorated or the craftsman. Two of the words in the Lunnasting text are obscure, but the other two are probably Celtic male personal names. The Formaston stone also contains known Celtic male personal names.

How are we to interrogate this evidence? Similar methodological problems of an archaeological nature affect inscriptions in both scripts and these must always be borne in mind. An unquantifiable amount of material will have failed to survive, but not at a uniform rate across all categories of evidence. For instance, small inscribed chattels in bone and wood will be under-represented in comparison with large stone monuments. While it can never be proven, it is at least possible that blank panels on some stone monuments once bore painted texts. Two likely contenders are the cross-slabs Meigle 5[47] and St Andrews 14,[48] the latter having a panel in the usual position for texts on Irish crosses.[49] Patterns of survival and recovery are rendered uneven by local variations in such diverse factors as geology, modern agricultural improvement, antiquarian and archaeological interest. It is thus impossible to quantify how representative the sample is and distribution maps can be used only with extreme caution. The small size of the sample, the many centuries it spans and the great range of sites from which it comes make it difficult to generalize about Pictland.

Beyond the presumption, at a crude level, that a highly literate society would leave more written material than one with little emphasis on writing, to what extent is it possible to use inscriptions for evidence of literacy? A number of attempts have been made to

Fig. 4   Detail of cross-slab with hunting scene from Scoonie, Fife (1.07m tall). It is inscribed with a Pictish symbol and, vertically up the right edge, in ogam with the male personal name *Eddarrnonn* (Ethernan).

evaluate the literate skills of the carvers of individual texts,[50] and examples of undoubtable solecisms have been identified in botched and muddled inscriptions,[51] though these are very rare. Not every irregularity is an error, however, nor each deviation from Classical norms a mistake. The recurrence of certain inverted or reversed letterforms on post-Roman inscriptions in western Britain, for instance, suggests a regional fashion rather than straightforward palaeographic incompetence.[52] A further consideration is that concerns of design and display on elaborate public monuments may override those of straightforward legibility.[53]

Even if we can be sure our variant is a 'mistake', whose skill are we measuring? That of the *scriptor* who drafted the text, that of the *lapidarius* who carved it on stone or that of the patron, with whom rested ultimate 'quality control'? Only at the informal end of the scale, where graffiti and other texts are composed and executed by the one individual, can levels of literacy be more simply discerned. But such texts are often in poorly attested vernaculars and it is difficult to distinguish casual sloppiness from illiteracy. The only Pictish inscriptions in this category are in ogam, and we are sorely ignorant about the norms of ogam palaeography. We are not in a position to evaluate the orthographical accuracy of most of the roman-alphabet inscriptions of Pictland, but they are skilfully carved in accomplished and sometimes ambitious scripts,[54] the carving of display capitals in relief at Tarbat being particularly impressive.[55] Higgitt has emphasized the two-way connections between the epigraphic and manuscript traditions at Insular monasteries,[56] but to what extent can individual monuments be taken as representative of more general levels of literacy either within or beyond centres of excellence? Public inscriptions need not necessarily reflect the highest of literate standards in a society and, in fact, poorer inscriptions may reflect a 'democratization' of literacy, as do the non-standard spellings on some eighteenth- and early nineteenth-century Scottish grave-slabs.[57]

A disturbing example of the lack of correspondence between epigraphic and manuscript accomplishment is provided by the Dál Riadic monastery of Iona. There is ample evidence for liturgical, historical, literary and scientific writing there,[58] and a strong case exists for the Iona origin of one of the greatest early medieval illuminated manuscripts – the Book of Kells.[59] Thus the island provides an almost unique opportunity to evaluate how the highest standards of learning and manuscript production might be reflected in the epigraphic tradition. The comparison is instructive. What strikes one most forcibly is the remarkable *lack* of inscriptions on Iona. The high degree of ecclesiastical and secular patronage is clear in the extensive corpus of ambitious stone sculpture, yet only a tiny percentage of the extant monuments is inscribed.[60] Only one of the great high crosses bears a text, a short and extremely weathered inscription which is perhaps to be interpreted as a request in Irish for a prayer on behalf of the patron or craftsman of the cross.[61] Apart from one early Latin grave-marker,[62] the only other inscribed monuments are seven rather unprepossessing recumbent grave-slabs dating from the eighth and ninth centuries.[63] These are incised with a simple cross and a request in Irish for a prayer on behalf of the deceased, who is identified by his name only. The letters are uneven and the layout casual, but the quality of the script cannot be attributed, as we have seen, either to an absence of fine models or to a lack of skilled carvers. The small percentage of inscribed slabs on this hyper-literate little island reflects a positive choice to leave most grave-slabs anonymous. The well-documented case of Iona alerts us to the fact that neither quality nor quantity of inscriptions is necessarily an indication of level of interest or skill in literacy.

It is understandably hard to distance oneself from a deeply engrained textual aesthetic concerning uniform letter-height, even letter and line spacing, and balanced layout of text within panels, and thus to avoid inappropriate value judgements about seemingly eccentric inscriptions (this is particularly true of unfamiliar ogam). There is a contrast between the generally neat and orderly Anglo-Saxon inscriptions and their Irish counterparts, which are relaxed almost to the point of dishevelment. The distinction does not result from greater literacy, more advanced technical ability or higher aesthetic standards on the part of the English, but, as Higgitt has explained, reflects differing manuscript practice in the two cultures, with the Anglo-Saxon taste for *de luxe* manuscripts contrasting with more utilitarian attitudes to the written word on the part of the Irish.[64] Significantly, the influence of both strains can be detected in the corpus of Pictish roman-alphabet inscriptions.

Much more difficult to assess is the readership of inscriptions.[65] Taking into account Wormald's warnings about the 'fallacy of the intended audience',[66] Higgitt has argued that 'most early medieval inscriptions in Britain and Ireland had a practical function and some sort of readership in mind'.[67] He concludes that, while a few inscrip-

Literacy in Pictland

tions address a restricted, learned, clerical audience, 'many more seem to concern a much wider public – in some cases literally an audience – that could be reached through the medieval habit of sharing texts by reading them aloud'.[68] This potential for participation in literacy by those unable to read is, of course, as true of manuscripts as of inscriptions.

For all the suggestiveness of the epigraphic evidence, its testimony regarding literacy remains unsatisfactorily inconclusive. While it is possible to evaluate the standard of individual inscriptions, and to speculate on authorship and audience, the fundamental and insurmountable problem is that it is simply impossible to quantify what is essentially qualitative evidence. The extant inscriptions constitute random snap-shots of information which it is impossible to systematize into a general picture. They embody high levels of writing skill and an interest in communicating through literacy, at certain kinds of site in certain parts of Pictland at certain periods, but they simply will not tell us how many people could read or write. That is not, however, the only, nor even the most interesting, question, that the historian can ask.

Ramsay MacMullen has asserted that 'knowing how to communicate in writing is one thing; doing so is another'.[69] The distribution of inscribed monuments in the pre-Norman British Isles indicates that there is no simple correlation between the extent of non-epigraphic literacy and the incidence of inscriptions. For instance, according to Okasha 72% of surviving Anglo-Saxon sculpture comes from the north, yet the same area contains 80% of the roman-alphabet inscriptions.[70] If the sample is limited solely to (non-runic) lapidary inscriptions from the ninth century or earlier, i.e. the period of the historical Picts, the figure rises to 100%.[71] Yet no satisfactory reason has been provided as to why Southumbria should be completely lacking in such monuments. The geographical spread of roman-alphabet inscriptions in Ireland is more even, but still there is remarkable clumping at some sites, all of them monastic. Macalister lists about 430 early medieval lapidary inscriptions in the roman alphabet, of which over 250 come from a single site, the monastery and pilgrimage focus of Clonmacnoise.[72] Subsequent discoveries at Clonmacnoise mean that the figures need to be revised upwards.[73] Why should this one site have more extant roman inscriptions than the rest of the post-seventh-century British Isles put together?

MacMullen has discussed how, in the Classical world, inscribing

53

activity was not a direct reflection of literacy as such, but rather an indication of the 'epigraphic habit'. He rejected political and economic factors as primarily responsible for fluctuations in the number of inscriptions, and prioritized instead 'very broad psychological shift[s]', such as a declining faith in posterity.[74] Similarly, work on inscribed memorials in Pictland, south-west Britain and Scandinavia has emphasized cultural motivations, characterizing the emergence of this type of monument as an expression of new social statuses and linking its decline to the rise of alternative sources of authority.[75] Thus an examination of the inscriptions of Pictland holds out the exciting possibility of recovering aspects of Pictish social structures and *mentalités*. The extant epigraphic corpus has already been discussed. To compare it with contemporary inscriptions elsewhere in the British Isles reveals a number of ways in which the Pictish material differs markedly.

In contrast to the other Celtic-speaking regions, Pictland lacks individual inscribed memorials of the kind dated to the seventh century and earlier, the distribution of which stops suddenly at the Forth.[76] In fact, the appearance in Pictland of book-hand roman-alphabet inscriptions in the middle of the eighth century is at least a generation later than in neighbouring Dál Riada, southern Scotland and Northumbria. One of the most striking things about Pictland is the marked preference there for non-roman script. Elsewhere, after the seventh century, lapidary inscriptions in non-roman scripts are only a small minority of the extant total: ogams represent less than 1% of the later Irish epigraphic corpus and in England runes account for roughly 15%,[77] while in post-seventh-century Wales there are no non-roman inscriptions at all.[78] Yet in Pictland they are in a distinct majority; there are three-and-a-half times as many ogam as roman inscriptions. The carving of ogam begins at least two centuries before roman, and continues to the end of the period. Not only is it used more, but ogam is used in different ways. While ogam was the only script in monumental use in Ireland before the seventh century, thereafter it assumed a very marginal position, and is never found in formal contexts.[79] In marked contrast, ogam in Pictland enjoyed an elevated status as a formal epigraphic script and is to be found prominently displayed on grand public monuments, such as Brodie, Scoonie, Brandsbutt, Altyre and Bressay. There are also cursive examples of the script, for instance Burrian, Birsay and Buckquoy. Scraps of ogam graffiti and the handful of ogam-inscribed personal belongings from domestic sites give a tantalizing glimpse of lay literacy in the script.

The largely complementary distribution of roman- and ogam-alphabet inscriptions in Pictland, and the fact that only the latter appear in non-ecclesiastical and informal contexts, are our two main leads in investigating the use of the two scripts. One could speculate at length, but a key consideration must be the apparent difference in patterns of sculptural patronage in Pictland. Like Wales, Pictland lacks collections of the 'mass-produced' monastic grave-slabs typical of both Ireland and England.[80] Instead we find large and sometimes elaborate monuments with presumably dedicatory texts.

There is no doubt that the great cross-slabs of Pictland are Christian monuments – their most prominent feature is the Christian cross, and they display well-known scriptural scenes – but this notwithstanding, Pictish sculpture has a remarkably secular tinge. The most common imagery is that of the horseman and the hunt which, even if it can bear a Christian message, is still a celebration of the activities of the warrior aristocracy. Military might, kingship and violent animals are the common images, and scriptural iconography, though present, is less prominent than on either Irish or Anglo-Saxon monuments. If the cross-slabs are the fruit of a partnership between the secular nobility and the church, then in the ogam inscriptions we may be hearing the voice of the secular magnates, proclaiming their name and lineage. Their motivation for choosing the ogam script remains opaque. It may have stemmed from the choice of the vernacular, or perhaps even had an artistic objective. It is clear from the symbol stones that the Picts had a developed spatial aesthetic and this would have been disrupted by panels of horizontal text. Vertical ogam was much more discreet and could be tucked away at the side, or better still up the edge, without disrupting the design. If there was indeed lay literacy in ogam then use of that script may have given access to a wider audience.

Like the Anglo-Saxons and the Irish, the Picts had two scripts at their disposal for different purposes. Uniquely, however, they had a third writing system, which they used more widely than either. I have argued elsewhere that the famous Pictish symbols have claim to be regarded as a script,[81] but it is not necessary to accept this contention to see that the Picts *used* the symbols as they did alphabetic scripts. Thomas has shown how, in archaeological terms, the Class I Pictish symbol stones are the exact equivalent of the individual inscribed

55

Fig. 5   Two re-used prehistoric standing-stones moved to Newton House, Aberdeenshire, in the early nineteenth century (2.05m tall). One is inscribed with a pair of Pictish symbols, the other with an ogam containing the same name as at Scoonie and with an undeciphered inscription in what is presumably some form of the roman alphabet.

memorials found throughout the rest of the Celtic-speaking British Isles (Fig. 5),[82] and a close examination of the Class II symbol-inscribed cross-slabs suggests that the symbol statements, in my opinion almost certainly personal names, refer to the patron in the manner of alphabetic inscriptions elsewhere. In a few instances the patron appears to be depicted armed on horseback, or peacefully at her loom, with a symbol statement label at his or her shoulder (Kirriemuir 2 and 1, respectively) (Fig. 6).[83] A parallel may be drawn between the two-, three- or four-symbol statements appearing on certain cross-slabs and the listing of secular patron, ecclesiastical supervisor and master-craftsman on Irish high crosses (and possibly at St Vigeans?), or of patron, honorand and saint on certain Welsh ones.

Fig. 6   Reverse of cross-slab from Dunfallandy, Perthshire (1.58m tall), showing figures 'labelled' with Pictish symbols.

Precise comparisons are difficult because of the complexities of dating, but *if monastic grave-slabs are left out of the equation,*[84] Pictland has a sizeable proportion of the inscribed Insular monuments from the seventh, eighth and ninth centuries. Leaving aside the 160-odd Class I symbol stones, many or most of which are probably earlier, if one adds to the total of Pictish ogam and roman-alphabet inscriptions the fifty-seven or so symbol-inscribed cross-slabs[85] then Pictland becomes the region by far the most richly endowed with inscribed crosses/cross-slabs. Peter Harbison has identified the middle of the ninth century as the point at which Irish kings began to exploit the power of the written word by recording their patronage on inscribed crosses.[86] If the Dupplin cross is correctly dated to the beginning of that century, then Picts had beaten them to it by a generation.[87]

What then can be said in conclusion about literacy in Pictland? The direct evidence is limited, but none the less we can perceive that the Pictish churches were probably as literate as their peers, no more, no less. The surviving evidence is not enough to make positive statements about the extent, nature and quality of Pictish ecclesiastical literary culture, but to deny the existence of literary culture is to fly in the face of that evidence. While the introduction of the roman alphabet was attendant on the arrival of Christianity, writing in ogam may pre-date Christianization. The lack of ecclesiastical association may in part account for the remarkable prominence of ogam in post-seventh-century Pictland. The adoption of the script by the Picts reflects an active desire to use literacy in their own vernacular. Why they should contemplate a vernacular literacy, rather than a Latin one, is a question that remains to be answered, but the difficulty of generating an orthography for a previously unwritten language should not be underestimated and testifies to a certain linguistic sophistication on the part of those who attempted it.[88] The factor which above all others distinguishes Pictish attitudes to literacy is, of course, the creation of the unique symbols, a complex and independent-minded response to Latin-letter literacy on the part of a culture well able to produce alphabetic writing when it so desired.[89]

NOTES

1 A. Harvey, 'Early literacy'; 'Latin'.
2 J. Stevenson, 'Beginnings of literacy'.
3 For a general discussion of ogam, see McManus, *Guide*.
4 J. Stevenson, 'Literacy in Ireland'.
5 Below, pp. 62–82.
6 For pre-800 manuscripts, see Lowe, *Codices Latini Antiquiores*, esp. vol. 2.
7 Hughes, 'Where are the writings?'
8 Broun, 'Origin of Scottish identity'; Wormald, 'Emergence of the *regnum Scottorum*'.
9 Sims-Williams, above, pp. 18–20.
10 Hughes's argument that the Pictish church expanded only in the early eighth century, set out in her 'Early Christianity', has been searchingly criticized by Henderson, 'Early Christian monuments', esp. p. 48.

11 The only ninth-century manuscript surviving from eastern Scotland is the Book of Deer (Cambridge UL MS Ii.6.32): see Hughes, 'Book of Deer'.

12 Youngs (ed.), *'Work of Angels'*, pp. 134–5.

13 *ECMS.*

14 Hughes, 'Where are the writings?', p. 11.

15 *ECMS*, pp. 75–83, fig. 72; 271–2, fig. 282; 275, fig. 288; 214–15, fig. 228; 255–6, fig. 277 respectively.

16 *ECMS*, pp. 10–15, fig. 6.

17 Henderson, 'Shape and decoration', p. 212.

18 R. B. K. Stevenson, 'Further thoughts', p. 24.

19 In *HE* I. 1, pp. 16–17 Bede emphasizes that *all* the four peoples of Britain are united in their use of Latin.

20 *HE* V. 21, pp. 532–3.

21 'A. Tig.', s.a. 724.

22 I owe this suggestion to Dr Thomas Owen Clancy, University of Glasgow.

23 *HE* V. 21, pp. 534–51. For a discussion of the context of this letter, see Duncan, 'Bede'.

24 Henderson, *Picts*, pp. 167–8. See also Hughes 'Early Christianity', p. 45.

25 Anderson, *Kings and Kingship*, 2nd edn, p. 101.

26 A view justly criticized by Houston, 'Literacy', p. 33.

27 A notable exception is Greg Woolf's study of varying native responses to Classical literacy in Mediterranean Gaul: 'Power'.

28 See Woolf, 'Power', p. 85, for 'the shift in the moral valency of writing'. For the possibilities of an early medieval 'barbarian counter-culture' indifferent to literacy see Wormald, 'Uses of literacy'.

29 Such 'need' need not be bureaucratic. See Woolf, 'Power', p. 88, for the use of literacy for ethnic or cultural self-definition.

30 Cf. Charles-Edwards, below, p. 62.

31 F. Kelly, *Guide*, p. 204. For changing attitudes to the value of written documents in England, see Clanchy, *From Memory*.

32 J. Stevenson, 'Literacy in Ireland', pp. 27–32.

33 *AU*, s.a.

34 Nieke, 'Literacy', p. 248.

35 Bannerman, *Studies.*

36 Nieke, 'Literacy', p. 246.

37 Gruffydd, *'Rhaeadr Derwennydd'*. See also J. T. Koch, 'Thoughts'.

38 Duncan, *Scotland*, p. 110.

39 For full references, see Okasha, 'Non-ogam inscriptions'; for Dupplin, see Forsyth, 'Dupplin'.

40 C. Thomas, *Mute Stones*, chs. 2–3.

41 See also Brown, 'St Ninian's Isle'.

42 See also Higgitt, 'Pictish Latin inscription'.

43 The cross-slab from Brechin, inscribed *S MARIA M[ATE]R XHI*, is dated on art-historical grounds to the late ninth or early tenth century, and is therefore outside the Pictish period proper.

44 Padel, 'Inscriptions of Pictland'; Forsyth, 'Ogham inscriptions'.

45 For the difficulties of interpreting damaged and fragmentary inscriptions in Anglo-Saxon England, see Okasha, *Hand-list*, and Page, *Introduction*.
46 Forsyth, 'Spindle-whorl'.
47 *ECMS*, pp. 300–1, fig. 314b.
48 *ECMS*, p. 359, fig. 373b.
49 On the positioning of text on Insular crosses, see Higgitt, 'Words and crosses'.
50 For example, Okasha, 'Literacy'.
51 For example, C. Thomas, *Mute Stones*, p. 263.
52 Okasha, *Corpus*, pp. 18–28; C. Thomas, *Mute Stones*, figs. 7.2, 7.3.
53 As, for example, at Ruthwell: Okasha, *Hand-list*, pp. 108–12.
54 In T. Julian Brown's opinion, 'by the end of the eighth century, at the latest, Pictish scribes had little to learn about Insular handwriting, whether from Iona in the West or from Northumbria in the South': 'St Ninian's Isle', p. 251.
55 Higgitt, 'Pictish Latin inscription', 314–15; 'Stone-cutter', pp. 155–7; 'Display script'.
56 Higgitt, 'Stone-cutter'.
57 For their 'touching disregard for spelling' see Wilsher and Hunter, *Stones*, p. 7.
58 For discussion of the contents of the library at Iona see Clancy and Markús, *Iona*, pp. 211–22.
59 Henderson, 'Pictish art'.
60 RCAHMS, *Iona*.
61 St Martin's Cross, no. 83. R. A. S. Macalister interpreted it as *oroit do Gillacrist do ringe in chrossa* (*Corpus*, vol. 2, no. 1070); the RCAHMS could see only 'traces of lettering' (*Iona*, p. 206).
62 RCAHMS, *Iona*, pp. 182–3, no. 22 (probably seventh century).
63 Ibid., nos. 22, 31, 37, 45, 46, 47, 68. The other inscription, no. 69, is a tenth-century runic one.
64 'Stone-cutter', p. 160, drawing on comments by Malcolm Parkes.
65 Cf. Page, *Introduction*, p. 15.
66 'Uses of literacy', 96.
67 Higgitt, '*Legentes quoque uel audientes*'.
68 Ibid.
69 MacMullen, 'Epigraphic habit', 233.
70 Okasha, *Hand-list*, p. 5.
71 Calculation based on Okasha, *Hand-list* and 'Supplement'.
72 Macalister, *Corpus*, nos. 1, 19, 170, 186, 521–967 (minus late examples and metalwork).
73 Edwards, *Archaeology*, pp. 170–1.
74 MacMullen, 'Epigraphic habit', 246. But see Meyer, 'Explaining the epigraphic habit', for an alternative socio-cultural explanation.
75 Driscoll, 'Power'; C. Thomas, *Mute Stones*; Randsborg, *Viking Age*, p. 25. For an alternative view of runic monuments as a response to social and religious change, see Sawyer, 'Viking-Age rune-stones'.
76 The solitary Auquollie ogam pillar and the anomalous Newton stone excepted. For southern Scotland, see C. Thomas, 'Early Christian inscriptions'.
77 Calculation based on Macalister, *Corpus*, and Okasha, 'Vernacular or Latin?'
78 *ECMW*.

60

Literacy in Pictland

79 The sole exception is the eleventh-century runic-ogam slab from Killaloe (Macalister, *Corpus*, no. 54) which reflects later Norse attitudes to ogam seen elsewhere in Man and in the Northern Isles.

80 As at Clonmacnoise, Kilbrecan (Aran), Toureen Peakaun, Iona, Hartlepool, Lindisfarne and Whitby.

81 Forsyth, 'Symbols'.

82 C. Thomas, *Mute Stones*, p. 20. Though neither is in its original location, the current juxtaposition of the Newton symbol stone and the Newton ogam/Roman inscribed stone provides a striking comparison which demonstrates that these are indeed cognate monument-types.

83 *ECMS*, pp. 226–8, figs. 239–40.

84 See n. 80.

85 Ritchie and Fraser, *Pictish Symbol Stones*.

86 Harbison, 'Royal patronage'.

87 Forsyth, 'Dupplin'.

88 For contrasting attitudes to the prestige of Celtic vernaculars, especially as reflected in the epigraphic record, see T. M. Charles-Edwards, 'Language and society'.

89 I am indebted to John Higgitt, Richard Sharpe and Patrick Wormald, not only for their incisive comments on a draft of this chapter, but also for numerous stimulating discussions of, and disagreements over, the uses of literacy in early Scotland. All errors of fact and judgement remain, of course, my own responsibility.

Since this chapter was written two further ogam inscriptions have come to light in Pictland: a small fragment of worked bone from Borinish, South Uist, and a large cross-marked stone from Mains of Afforsk, Aberdeenshire. Neither has yet been published.

61

3

The context and uses of literacy in early Christian Ireland

T. M. CHARLES-EDWARDS

A scholar turning from early medieval continental Europe to Ireland in the same period must be struck by three things: how much written material survives; how much of it is in the vernacular; and how little of it is designed to do the jobs usually performed by the more utilitarian written documents in ancient, medieval or later literate societies.[1] Admittedly there are major problems of transmission: almost always early Irish Latin texts survived only if they were taken to Carolingian Europe, while vernacular texts survived if they continued to be copied into the central and later Middle Ages. What survives is probably not representative.[2] The difficulties of transmission, therefore, show that of the three things which strike our continental scholar, the one that is undoubtedly remarkable is the quantity of what survives both in Latin and in the vernacular rather than the paucity of utilitarian documents. On the latter, there may be grounds for suspecting that the tradition of charter-writing demonstrated by Wendy Davies[3] was not as productive as was Irish scholarship and literature, but charters may well have been relatively unsuccessful in passing through the filters which would have prevented their preservation. What stands out as confirmed fact is the quantity of texts of high culture, rather than the paucity of documents. This, then, is the problem I shall address: how to explain the richness of early Irish literature, both the literature of scholarship and of the imagination, whether in Latin or in Irish. It is an old question, but I shall examine it in a slightly different form, namely, why did literacy take the form particularly of scholarship?

Recent discussions of ogam have shown that, in part at least, the problem goes back to the late Roman or post-Roman period. Opinions still differ about the date and context of the invention of the ogam alphabet, but no one denies that it already existed in the fifth century.[4] It is generally agreed that it was invented by one or more

62

persons who were bilingual in Latin and Irish, in response to, but not as a cipher for, a Latin alphabet.[5] I shall confine my discussion to western Britain (here usually meaning Wales and Cornwall) and, in particular, to those points which are crucial to my argument. I shall not attempt anything remotely resembling a comprehensive account of ogam.

What is crucial about the ogam alphabet is that it was used for Irish rather than for Latin; that the values given to the letters may be distinguished from those found in the later standard Old Irish; and that in the Irish colonies in western Britain it was used in areas in which inscriptions were also cut in Latin and in varieties of roman capitals; sometimes inscriptions were bilingual. Post-Roman Britain used a variety of scripts for different purposes.[6] In particular, there was a clear distinction between the letter-forms employed for inscriptions and those used for books. In inscriptions, however, half-uncial was apparently not used until the seventh century. In other words, in the fifth and sixth centuries books and inscriptions each had their own distinctive letter-forms, while in the seventh century the grander book-script, half-uncial, came to be used in inscriptions and not only, as before, in books. The view implied by Kenneth Jackson, by which the letter-forms found in seventh-century inscriptions were a linear development from those used on stones a hundred years earlier, is based on a confusion.[7] An Insular **g** may ultimately be a descendant of a square capital **g**, but that evolution occurred centuries before, in the Roman Empire. What happened *c.* 600 was a switch among those inscribing stones from one old set of letter-forms to another. Half-uncial is itself, of course, an ancient Roman script; it was probably invented, as an Irish scholar's note declares, in Africa.[8] There is thus no epigraphical difficulty whatsoever in dating the Catamanus stone to *c.* 625: although it uses half-uncial letter-forms, this does not signify that there must be a considerable gap between this inscription and those which used roman capitals.

The change of fashion by which roman capitals came to be abandoned *c.* 600 coincides with the approximate date given by Kenneth Jackson for the extinction of the British spoken form of Latin. The early inscriptions of western and south-western Britain demonstrate that Latin was spoken even in the west in the fifth and sixth centuries.[9] They also show that, while British spoken Latin may have been, as Jackson argued, phonologically conservative,[10] John Koch is entirely correct in arguing that the decay of nominal inflexion had progressed even further in Britain than it had in northern Gaul.[11] It is also very likely that the influence of British on British Latin is often the reason why it is sometimes conservative and sometimes prone to more rapid change. The bilingual inscriptions of western Britain thus enable us to achieve some limited understanding of a very interesting period of language contact in the British Isles. They are especially helpful because, at the same period, British missionaries were active in Ireland itself and were thus agents of a similar pattern of language contact on the western side of the Irish Sea.

What we have, then, at this period, is the contact of three languages, Latin, Irish and British. I shall return to Irish later, but first we must follow the fortunes of Insular Latin from its British origins to its flowering in Ireland. Latin, we know, had grander and less grand forms, was written in books, inscribed on stones and spoken at home. It had immense cultural prestige, even though, as a spoken language, it was steadily declining. The most powerful of Gildas's sixth-century British kings, Maelgwn, king of Gwynedd, was taught an elegant form of Latin in a school which was evidently a descendant of the schools of the rhetors under the Empire.[12] The practice had been to have three levels of schooling: elementary, in which children were taught to read and write; the school of the grammarian, in which they learned to read some of the classics of Latin literature, especially Virgil; and finally the school of the rhetor, where they learned to argue a case in refined Latin according to ancient rules of forensic eloquence.[13] Only a very small minority went through all three levels.[14] Yet Maelgwn had reached a point that corresponds to the third level. It was thus still possible even as late as the sixth century for high rank to be associated with high Latin culture and the prolonged education necessary to attain it.

Gildas has a famous reference to people whom scholars have interpreted as British bards. He denounces Maelgwn for allowing himself to be praised by panegyrists foaming at the mouth with mendacious flattery. Admittedly, Gildas was primarily concerned with the outrageous untruthfulness of the praises rather than with the language in which they were delivered.[15] Yet there remains a contrast between the refinement of Maelgwn's Latin education and his present situation, surrounded by bards whose lies were broadcast as undiscriminatingly as their spittle. Moreover, this contrast within the career of Maelgwn needs to be brought into relation with another contrast found in the inscriptions. While Irish was admitted in Britain to the dignity of being used on memorial inscriptions, British was not. Further back in time, some evidence for British may be emerging in the curse tablets found at Bath, but such texts were very far from having the public status of memorial inscriptions in stone, as their cursive script and the context in which they were found demonstrate;[16] and, moreover, no such texts have been found from the post-Roman period. They only reinforce the general epigraphic evidence for the lower social prestige of British.

Gildas's own Latin, as Michael Lapidge has argued, also attests the existence of what we would call tertiary-level teaching, namely the instruction of a rhetor.[17] This was no longer part of that urban culture which the Empire sought to impose on its northern provinces, but it was still available, presumably in the form of private teaching, such as that formerly found in late Roman aristocratic households.[18] Another significant conclusion we may draw from Gildas's style is the contrast it offers with such sixth-century figures as Caesarius of Arles Caesarius' monastic background and pastoral purpose entailed a style that eschewed any overt links to the Classical rhetoric of the past. The language was simpler and references to pagan authors were avoided.[19] Given Gildas's conscious adoption of the role of Old Testament prophet, one might have expected a corresponding austerity of style. Yet, whereas Caesarius avoids all Virgilian echoes and quotations, Gildas parades them.[20] From this we may deduce that in Britain there was not the same association between plain prose and austere virtue as on the Continent. The contrary association, between a fundamentally traditional eloquence and the persuasiveness required of a religious prophet is not merely implied by Gildas's practice but is also set out in what he says about the 'refined teacher' under whom Maelgwn studied, for he insists with great care that because Maelgwn had that particular teacher, he cannot have escaped being warned by a wise man. The teacher may have been *elegans*, 'refined', but he also had *sapientia*, the wisdom portrayed in the Old Testament and sought by the student of Scripture.[21]

Such assumptions were not confined to Gildas. The *Amra Choluim Chille*, an elegy on Columba very probably composed at his death in 597, celebrates his learning, using for the purpose several loans from Latin: Columba is both *docht* (from *doctus*) and a *sui*, the vernacular word sometimes used for Latin *sapiens*.[22] There is no contrast here between a secular learning which entitled someone to be called *doctus* and a religious learning conferring the title *sapiens*. The *Amra* is poles

65

apart from Gregory the Great's judgement on Benedict, 'scienter nescius et sapienter indoctus', roughly 'showing discernment in his very lack of knowledge and wisely unlearned'.[23] Michael Winterbottom has demonstrated that the links between Columbanus and Gildas are stylistic and are not confined to the Irishman's interest in the Briton's writings.[24] They are most obvious in his Fifth Letter, addressed to Pope Boniface, in which, by implication, he treats the Italian Christians of 615 – divided into Arians, Trecapitoline Catholics and those Catholics in communion with Rome – as in a spiritual situation comparable with Gildas's Britain. Yet Columbanus' monastic vocation would, in the Gaul or Italy of a century earlier, have suggested a much less pronounced readiness to use heightened language. Columbanus' hagiographer, Jonas of Susa, gives a most important account of the saint's education.[25] Its pattern would have been clearly recognizable two centuries earlier. It was organized according to the traditional ages of man. Columbanus' education must have begun with the instruction in reading and writing characteristic of the first stage of Roman education, but this seems to be beneath Jonas's notice. He then progressed in his *pueritia* to *liberalium litterarum doctrinae* and *grammaticorum studia*, the second stage which lasted into adolescence. All of this took place in his native Leinster. Subsequently he left Leinster and went to a teacher called Sinilis (Sinell). With him he studied scripture, *scripturarum sacrarum scientia*, to such effect that before his adolescence was over he had written a commentary on the psalms *elevato sermone*, 'in a distinguished style'.[26] The different periods of education may be compared as follows:[27]

	Roman education	Columbanus' education
primary	7–11/12	[end of *infantia* or beginning of *pueritia*]
grammaticus	11/12–15/16	*pueritia* + *adolescentia*
rhetor	15/16–20+	exegesis: *adolescentia*

If we leave aside, then, the first stage, learning to read and write, we are left with an apparent identity in the second stage – grammar – and a clear difference in the third: the study of the Bible has taken the place of learning the arts of the orator. Moreover, the second and third stages, those to which Jonas pays attention, are particularly clearly distinct in Columbanus' case, since he studied grammar and liberal letters in Leinster, but exegesis outside his native province.

Yet there remain problems. Columbanus' own writings show that his education included a training in the art of persuasive writing in

Latin. What may, therefore, have happened is that grammar and rhetoric were combined in a single stage, in order to make room for exegesis as the culmination of education. Rhetoric may be included under the umbrella term 'liberal letters', as is suggested by the list given later in the same chapter: 'grammar, rhetoric, geometry'. In this latter list, however, is included 'the series of the divine scriptures', as if Columbanus had also studied Scripture in his first period of education in Leinster, and not just at the school of Sinilis. Some study of the Bible must probably be allowed for at the earlier stages of Irish education, as elsewhere in Christian Europe: the psalms in particular were learnt by heart at an early stage, and were thus useful when teaching children to read and write.[28] Such a context may explain the Springmount Bog tablets, which contain a part of one of the psalms.[29] Similarly, Insular grammars, the earliest of them probably Irish, normally used Scriptural examples in place of Classical ones and even ecclesiastical words in their paradigms. no longer did one decline *musa, musa, musam* but *ecclesia, ecclesia, ecclesiam*.[30]

Confirmation of this broad division of early Irish education into two stages comes from the subject matter of the *Hisperica Famina*, which suggests an origin in a school devoted to imparting linguistic skills, *eloquentia*,[31] as well as from the scholastic colloquies, which appear to have the same home.[32] The combination of the two, linguistic skill and Scriptural learning, emerges from the character of Cummian's Letter to Ségéne and Béccán on the paschal question, which is both rhetorical and argues as one exegete to another.[33] Evidence for the central importance of exegesis is widespread: much of the *Amra Choluim Chille* celebrates Columba's learning as an exegete;[34] Bede's account of Englishmen resorting to Irish schools in the period 651–64 envisages them as going to study exegesis. When he praises Aldfrith, king of Northumbria, for the learning he obtained in Ireland before he became king, he describes him as 'most learned in the Scriptures'.[35] Some of the intellectual procedures of Irish exegesis, on the other hand, demonstrate that the authors had had a grounding in Latin grammar, such as the formula used for explaining texts: a proper discussion of a text should include the time and place of composition, the author and the reason why the text was written (*tempus, locus, persona, et causa scribendi*).[36]

Although there appear to have been two distinct stages in education, and perhaps some teachers would only cover one stage, the pre-eminent goal was knowledge of the Bible. For this reason the laws envisage a single hierarchy of Latin learning, that of the *ecnae* or *suí litre*.[37] They do not make it clear which of these grades may have taught grammar. The *Collectio Canonum Hibernensis* shows that the scriptural scholar was responsible for much of Irish canon law and was also charged with exercising the function of an ecclesiastical judge.[38] Partly as a consequence, leading scholars had the right to participate in ecclesiastical synods. We find several, for example, among the participants in the all-Irish assembly convened by Adomnán at Birr in 697.[39] Scriptural scholarship thus had an even more central position in the early Irish church than in other churches at the time. Not merely was knowledge of the Bible the accepted goal of the higher levels of education, but the expertise of a *sapiens* entitled him to sit in authority alongside bishops and the abbots of the greater monasteries. The Irish church was ruled by synods, so that the right to participate was crucial. It was, no doubt, for this reason that several bishops and abbots were also *sapientes*.[40] A knowledge of letters was necessary for admission to the ecclesiastical grades; high scholarship, however, gave a man authority in the church.

Given the central position in the church of the ecclesiastical scholar, the *ecnae* or *suí litre*, it is a little surprising to turn to the vernacular law tracts on status and to find that he does not have quite so central a position in their conception of Irish social structure. As Liam Breatnach's work on the law tract dealing with the status of poets, *Uraicecht na Ríar*, has shown, the central issue for Irish lawyers was to relate the hierarchies of the *filid* and the church.[41] The hierarchy of the church in question, however, was not that of the scholars, but the standard one descending from bishop to doorkeeper. As Breatnach observes, it is only the *filid* and the church which are divided into seven main grades and four subordinate grades (*fográda*).[42] As for the ecclesiastical scholars, the *ecnai* or *sapientes*, they are usually, but not always, divided into seven grades; moreover, the names of the grades vary from text to text, whereas the names of the grades of the church and of the *filid* are relatively fixed.[43]

This preoccupation with the relationship between the ordinary grades of the church and those of the *filid* may be termed ideological by contrast with another, more immediately practical concern, which was to relate the grades of the *filid* to those of lay society. When the laws talk in terms of such-and-such a grade of *filid* being of equivalent rank to another, the other is frequently a grade of secular society. Just as the church and lay society were paired together in the law tract

Córus Béscnai as if they were partners to a contract, so also were the poets and lay society.[44] The reason is clear enough: the flow of patronage was from lay society to the *filid* or the church as the case might be. Similarly, the laity had the duty to protect both the *filid* and the church, especially since it was characteristic of both poet and churchman that they often worked outside the borders of their native territories. In terms of such crucial marks of rank as honour-price or the size of one's company, it was vital to drive home the claim on behalf of either poet or churchman that he was entitled to as much as a given grade of lay society. In terms of both the flow of wealth and of the power to give protection, the lay hierarchy from king down to *ócaire* was the central pillar of society, on which were dependent the parallel hierarchies of church and *filid*.

Neither in the ideological preoccupation with the relationship between church and *filid* nor in the more practical concern with their relationship with lay society were the *ecnai* central. This is odd, on a number of counts. First, the *Collectio Canonum Hibernensis* was a compilation by two *ecnai*, put together early in the eighth century.[45] It is careful to set out, in its first books, the scheme of the seven grades of the church and its three subordinate grades — the very scheme which was precisely echoed in the hierarchy of the *filid*.[46] Elsewhere, in the Irish Synods edited by Bieler, we have an assertion of the equivalent high rank of three churchmen, an ecclesiastical scholar, a so-called 'distinguished *princeps*' and a bishop;[47] yet even here there is no full statement of the grades of scholars. Yet the *Hibernensis* is quite clear that there are specifically ecclesiastical scholars, to be distinguished from the 'wise man of the world', the *mundialis sapiens*, who is encouraged to steer clear of church cases;[48] it is also clear that these ecclesiastical scholars perform a judicial role in the church, just as, by implication, the *mundialis sapiens* performs a judicial role among the laity.[49] Ecclesiastical scholars, therefore, both compiled the *Hibernensis* and were prominent among the persons who were expected to know and enforce its rules. Furthermore, it is generally accepted that the reason why in Ireland the scheme of the seven grades became the norm was that it was adopted within the church and imitated by others, as *Críth Gablach* says of the lay grades.[50] In Christendom as a whole, there was no such virtual unanimity as is found in early Christian Ireland: the seven grades elsewhere competed with other schemes for the ranking of the clergy.[51] Within the Irish church one would have expected the scholars to be responsible for the sevenfold scheme; and yet they did not apply it to themselves with anything like the rigour that was shown with respect to the ordinary grades of the church.

However much uncertainty there may have been about the names and number of ranks among Irish ecclesiastical scholars, they apparently had no doubt that they comprised a distinct order in society. That this was indeed the case is amply borne out by the annals, which are full of the obits of ecclesiastical scholars, among them the compilers of the *Hibernensis*.[52] Moreover, in the vernacular laws the *ecnai* remained a distinct order, distinguished not only from the standard grades of the church, but also from *filid* and *brithemain*.[53] What, then, is one to make of the evidence of the law of status, most fully elaborated in the vernacular laws, but enough elements of which are referred to in canon law texts to show that the essential pattern was generally accepted? In particular what are we to make of the lawyers' consistent preference for distinguishing different orders, each with its own hierarchy?

It has become fashionable recently to speak of the Irish learned orders in the early Christian period as forming a single mandarin class.[54] It has thus been claimed that the same people, in essence, composed vernacular laws as wrote canon law and exegesis. It is also asserted that the *filid* formed part of this single mandarin class; that what marked them out from the inferior bards was their learning; and that this learning was nothing other than the learning of the ecclesiastical schools. Interpreted in one way, this view has much to be said for it, but understood as it sometimes has been, it seems to me to fly in the face of the evidence I have been discussing and much other evidence besides. The distinction I propose to make is based upon a text from the *Bretha Nemed*.[55] Its significance can best be assessed if we first consider what *Uraicecht na Ríar*, a law tract which Breatnach has assigned to the second half of the eighth century and to Munster, has to say on the subject of hereditary status among the *filid*.

Uraicecht na Ríar combines together two principles which are not naturally yoked together. First, it assumes that the basis of a *fili*'s rank is his knowledge and professional art:[56] 'That is a poet whose qualifications are complete and genuine, who is not found to be perplexed in the mass of his craft.' On the other hand, it also wishes to assert that the norm is the hereditary transmission of the craft from father to son.[57] Personal skill is the proper basis of poetic rank, yet the family dominates poetry. The solution to this difficulty is the rule that if one's father and grandfather were not poets, one is only entitled to half the honour-price that would otherwise be due to one by virtue of professional knowledge and art.[58] Precisely the same rule also separated the thriving commoner from recognized nobility.[59] There is thus a single attitude to all the hierarchies of Irish society: recent wealth and recent poetic art do not confer as high a rank as old wealth and inherited poetic art.

When presented in this fashion, the principle appears to be solely directed at restraining upward social mobility from the ranks of mere commoners into the ranks of those privileged, whether by being lords of clients or by being possessed of special knowledge or skill. What remains unclear is whether the same bar also operates in a horizontal as well as a vertical direction. For example, the third poetic grade, that of the *clí*, has an honour-price equivalent to the *aire désa*, the ordinary noble lord of clients.[60] Let us suppose that a son of an *aire désa* learns the craft of poetry to the level required of a *clí*. Is he debarred from enjoying the rank of a *clí* because his father was not a poet? Or does the equivalence between the two ranks mean that he is free from any such restraint in his progress up the ladder of the *filid*?

Our choice of which interpretation to follow will make a considerable difference to our view of the shape of early Irish society. If the bar operates both vertically and horizontally, the various hierarchies of status are each separate hereditary groups. There are then three aristocracies, quite distinct one from another: the church from the lay aristocracy, the *filid* from the church. If the bar operates only vertically, there are still distinct professions, but there is easy movement from one to another and from the lay aristocracy into the professions. In that case, it will be possible to talk of a single, largely hereditary aristocracy, whose members enjoy high rank, now from their wealth in cattle and clients, now from their position in the church, now from their attainments as poets. *Uraicecht na Ríar* does not, unfortunately, provide any answer to this question. Admittedly, in § 4 it states the bar for *suíd* as a whole, a term which ought to include ecclesiastical scholars as well as poets. In § 11 it reiterates the bar for both *filid* and secular lords. It seems to be thinking of the privileged as a group, whether they enjoy high rank because of the number of their clients or because of the depth of their learning; and to think of the privileged as a group would be entirely natural if

71

someone could move easily from one hierarchy of status to an equivalent rank in another. These are, however, only clues; to get anything more we need to turn to the passage from the *Bretha Nemed* to which I have already referred: 'for he who is not the child of a noble, or a poet, or an ecclesiastical scholar, sues for only half honour-price until he serve learning doubly.'[61] One might suppose initially that this passage, too, can be interpreted in such a way as to allow a bar on easy horizontal movement between the different privileged orders. Yet when the text says 'until he serve learning doubly', it is clearly thinking of an order the basis of whose status is knowledge or skill. In the context, in fact, it must be thinking of entry into the order of the *filid* in particular. The implication must now be, therefore, that if an aspirant poet is the child of a lay noble or an ecclesiastical scholar, there will be no bar on his ascent up the ranks of the *filid*.

It is only this interpretation which is consistent with non-legal evidence. We may take as an example the situation at Trim in the eighth century, as it has been revealed to us by Professor Byrne.[62]

Trim (Áth Truimm):

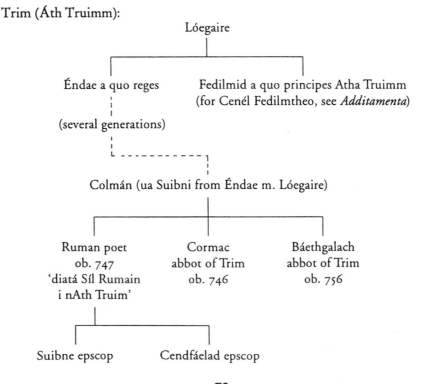

The context and uses of literacy in early Christian Ireland

The descendants of Fedelmid had controlled the church of Trim in the kingdom of Cenél Lóegairi up to the early eighth century, but were then displaced by a cadet branch of the royal lineage, Cenél nÉndai. The range of offices held by this branch in the eighth century demonstrates that it was entirely possible to have horizontal movement between the secular aristocracy, the poets and the church. Eighth-century Trim is also a well-known example of the pattern by which royal lineages shed branches who then turn to the church.[63] This pattern shows again how, although the church and the *filid* might be central to an ideological conception of hierarchy in early Irish society, the lay aristocracy, headed by royalty, was central in practice.

Usually, therefore, movement was from royal families into the church or into the ranks of the *filid*, and not vice versa. Yet this is not an absolute rule. There are several early Irish rulers, especially in Munster, who appear to have been churchmen.[64] The *Bretha Nemed* cite examples of kings who were also poets;[65] although they are described as being bards rather than as being learned poets (*filid*), that may only reflect the circumstance that, being kings, they would not need to claim rank by virtue of their poetic craft. A further example, no less relevant because it concerns a Northumbrian whose mother was Irish, is that of Aldfrith, who ruled from 686 to 705. We know that he was not expected to succeed to the Northumbrian throne, and that before he did so he had lived among the Irish and achieved the rank of *sapiens* or *ecnae*.[66] This case may serve to remind us that succession was often uncertain in spite of such devices as the heir-apparent, the *tánaise ríg*. Since members of a ruling family uncertain of their prospects of succession might well be wise to hedge their bets and acquire qualifications for high status other than royal office, learning within royal dynasties is likely to have been commoner than we suppose.

The legal material, allied to such specimen cases as the church of Trim or King Aldfrith, makes it possible to re-assess the notion of a mandarin class in pre-Viking Ireland. What is crucial is the pattern by which movement up the various hierarchies was restrained by a hereditary principle, whereas movement from one hierarchy to another was not. It implies that Ireland was ruled by an aristocracy in which hereditary status was crucial but might be sustained in several different ways: by secular power, by such standard ecclesiastical offices as bishop, or by learning. This was a single aristocracy, in which learning was recognized as a possible source of high rank, and in that sense it is fair enough to call it a mandarin class. On the other hand, it included the lay nobility as much as it did ecclesiastical office-holders or scholars. Learning was not a requirement for high rank. Moreover, movement from the lay nobility into the ranks of the learned orders was not merely as fully recognized as was movement within the learned orders, it may even have been more common. The early Irish aristocracy had a crucial problem, how to avoid social descent; and it therefore sought to multiply ways in which it could avoid degradation. Since the grounds of status were kept as varied as possible, rather than depending upon a single mandarin qualification, it seems better to characterize it as a complex aristocracy rather than as a mandarin class.

High-ranking families were, therefore, anxious to place their members in positions of prestige; competition for such positions made the whole business uncertain, and hence learning was of direct social and political concern to the aristocracy, including ruling lineages. This cannot have failed to have its implications for the extent of literacy. To see what may have been the pattern, we may return for a moment to Columbanus' education. What was notable about it was its two-part structure. Admittedly, Jonas tells us nothing about the stage of learning to read and write, but after that we seem to get two kinds of school: that of the grammarian, who may also have taught elements of rhetoric; and that of the *ecnae* or *sapiens* proper, who taught the exegesis of the Bible. In Columbanus' case, the school of the grammarian was situated in Leinster; that of the *sapiens*, Sinilis, outside Leinster. Finally, it is worth noting that Columbanus became a monk only after he had attended the school run by Sinilis. Someone could perfectly well have followed the same education as Columbanus and have ended up as a bishop or a *fili* or even, like Aldfrith or Cormac mac Cuilennáin, as a king. Aldfrith was *doctissimus in scripturis*, but it may have been commoner for those who might enter the ranks of the learned, but were not definitely destined for such a career, to complete only the first stage.

The evidence for this is only indirect, a matter of the style of such texts as *Auraicept na nÉces*, the Primer of the Poets, of many law tracts, and of the first of the metrical tracts edited in Thurneysen's *Mittelirische Verslehren*. All of them exhibit what I have called Standard Old Irish Textbook Style, derived from manuals of Latin grammar.[67] The influence of Latin grammar appears to have been

The context and uses of literacy in early Christian Ireland

pervasive in didactic texts associated with all the learned orders from
c. 700 onwards. On the other hand, there is a distinction between the
form of argument found in Irish canon law and in the vernacular
laws. Alongside the contrast of language and other contrasts to which
we shall come in a moment, there is the crucial one that it was the
norm for rules of canon law to be justified by exegesis, while this is
only occasionally true for the vernacular texts. The compilers and the
intended users of the *Collectio Canonum Hibernensis* had been to
both types of school, to the school of the grammarian and to that of
the exegete. Moreover, although the influence of the Textbook Style –
derived, it will be remembered, from Latin grammar – is to be found
in both exegesis and canon law, it is not nearly so widespread in the
latter as it is in the vernacular laws;[68] and, while recent work on the
relationship between canon and vernacular law has shown borrowings
in both directions, it has perhaps tended to neglect the more widespread influence of Latin grammar on Irish vernacular law.

It is of course the school of the exegete that gets most attention, for
in early Christian Ireland exegesis is the pinnacle of the culture. Bede,
for example, has his English converts going to Ireland partly to visit
the schools of exegesis. Moreover, he explicitly says that they did so
on what amounted to Irish scholarships.[69] I do not know of any
evidence to confirm what Bede says, but it is still worth pondering its
implications. Annalistic obits suggest that schools run by *ecnai* were
situated in most of the principal churches.[70] The implication would
seem to be that it was Irish churches that were providing free board
and lodging and free books and teaching for these English students.
Such provision goes well beyond what even well-heeled municipal
schools achieved in the Late Empire.[71] Municipal schools had, of
course, perished with the decline of the late Roman city; but I wonder
whether the British church had not taken over some of the responsibilities for education that the city was increasingly unable to fulfil.
There is one compelling reason why it should have had a greater
concern with Latin education than was shown by its counterparts in
Gaul or Italy: some Britons spoke Latin from childhood, some did
not. In order to recruit from those who did not, the British church
needed to ensure the survival of an organized education which took
linguistic instruction as a central aim. This would explain the greater
continuity with the old rhetorical tradition to be found in a Gildas or
in a Columbanus than in Caesarius of Arles or Benedict of Nursia.
No doubt the provision for Bede's English students was due to a very

75

particular situation, a widespread concern for missionary work in England. There is good reason to suppose that, even if Bede's remarks are literally true, native Irish students did not receive a free education.[72] In particular, even if it was an accepted duty of the principal Irish churches to provide a school of exegesis, that says nothing about teaching in grammar. This will help to explain why learning might often be associated with high rank: the young noble will have had the resources to gain an education out of the reach of many of his contemporaries.

The text which, more than any other, gives us some idea of the relationship between Latin and vernacular culture in pre-Viking Ireland is *Auraicept na nÉces*, the Primer of the Poets, dated by its most recent editor, Anders Ahlqvist, to the early Old Irish period (before *c.* 750).[73] Its concern is with the vernacular counterpart to Latin grammar, and in its opening section it provides a fascinating argument about the origin and status of the Irish language. Moreover, since it conceives of ogam as the native alphabet of the Irish, it provides a link with that early period of language contact in the fifth and sixth centuries when Latin, British and Irish were in contact and sometimes in competition. The story of the invention of Irish is attached, as one might expect, to the account in Genesis of the Tower of Babel. Yet, although Irish was invented at the Tower, its origins were ten years after the dispersal of peoples which took place when God divided the human race into many languages. Irish, then, did not originate in the sin of pride which led to the building of the Tower. It was not part of God's plan to confound the presumption of the human race. Irish was invented by Fénius Farsaid in a school;[74] and the method of its invention was this: Fénius extracted what was best from the existing languages of the world. Moreover, not only was Irish, therefore, the best of languages but it was invented in a school and for a school: when Fénius was living by Nimrod's Tower, identified with the Tower of Babel and placed in Egypt, he was asked by his school 'to extract a language out of the many languages'.[75] The *Auraicept* is a notable enemy of racialism: when the dispersal took place from the Tower of Babel, 'it was everyone who spoke the same language that went from there to his own territory, and not everyone of the same descent'.[76] The origin of Irish national identity is thus declared to be the language of a school. Given that Fénius was evidently a student of many languages, and given also the grammatical material to follow in the rest of the *Auraicept*, the school in question was that of the grammarian. Irish identity was a matter of the letters of the ogam alphabet, of genders and declensions.

There are perhaps two kinds of reason for this pride in the Irish language, apart from the professional propaganda of the schoolmaster. They are implicit in the two names used for Irish. First, it is the language of the Féni, and its inventor was Fénius Farsaid. At the time when the *Auraicept* was composed, it was still possible to think of Ireland as inhabited by different *cenéla*, of which the Féni, the people to which the Uí Néill, the Connachta and the Éoganachta belonged, were only one, alongside the Ulaid and the Laigin.[77] Moreover, just as the origin story of the Irish language was evidently part of that tradition of speculation about national origins which issued in the *Lebor Gabála*, so it is possible that an early stage of the *Lebor Gabála* was primarily concerned to relate the northern Féni – the Connachta and the Uí Néill – to the southern Féni, the Éoganachta: hence the ancestor figures, two sons of Míl Espáine, Éber and Eremóin, identified one with the north and one with the south. The standpoint of the *Auraicept*, however, was different: with its insistence on the primacy of a shared language over any question of descent, it was well-placed to argue for the unity of the Irish people as a whole. At that stage, the Ulaid and the Laigin may not yet have been regarded in the schools as descendants of Míl Espáine; but, nevertheless, they all spoke Irish. Subsequently, this linguistic perception of Irish identity, conjoined with an origin legend of the Féni, encouraged the Irish *literati* to invent further sons of Míl and so establish a genealogical unity of the Irish. In the end, therefore, the Irish came to be a *cenél*, a people that perceived its identity in terms of common descent, a view anticipated and rejected by the *Auraicept*.

The other name used by the *Auraicept* for Irish was *Goídelc*. The name is traced from a certain Goídel who was a Greek, yet in origin it appears to be the British word for the Irish and their language, Welsh *Gwyddel* and *Gwyddeleg*. One area in which such a sense of linguistic identity, fostered by contact with other languages, is traceable is in the Irish settlements in western Britain. The bilingual inscriptions show not only two languages side by side, Irish and Latin, but also two alphabets, Latin and ogam. Even in the eighth-century *Auraicept*, the ogam alphabet is associated with the Irish language and thus with Irish national identity.[78] Admittedly, ogam appears to be the junior partner in the inscriptions: it sometimes contains less information than the Latin, and never contains more.[79]

77

There are, too, a few inscriptions in which the layout betrays the primacy of the Latin text.[80] Underlying the anxiety of the *Auraicept* to proclaim itself the best of all languages, one may perhaps detect the same cultural primacy of Latin: the author of the *Auraicept* is well aware of the doctrine whereby there were three principal languages in the world, Hebrew, Greek and Latin.[81] While it claims that a legal disciple of Fénius, Caí Caínbrethach was a Hebrew and that Goídel was a Greek, it has no such figure to relate Latin to Irish. Instead it is busy comparing the teaching of the Laitneóir, the Latin grammarian, with what the *Auraicept* has to offer for Irish. Just as, in terms of subject matter, the Bible is at the apex of early Christian Irish culture, so, in terms of language, Latin has a clear pre-eminence. Irish is like that poet envisaged by the lawyers, who, because he lacked a poetic lineage, had to run twice as fast to keep up with his more highly born rival; hence the ingenious and ambitious claims of the *Auraicept*.

Yet the comparison with British remains stark: Irish was fit to be used alongside Latin in inscriptions commemorating great men; British was not.[82] The fundamental explanation must be that Irish was the language of rulers who had established themselves within the Empire and could talk with the likes of Ambrosius Aurelianus, 'last of the Romans', on more or less equal terms. By contrast with other invaders of the Empire, it had a stronger and more professionalized culture: if we may import the attitudes of the *Auraicept* back into the fifth century, the Goídel knew that Irish was his language and the vehicle of his culture. The use he made of ogam and of his own language shows that he was ready to sustain an identity separate from that of the Romans. The first 'nativists', perhaps, were the Irish settlers in Britain.

My task was to explain the scholarly propensities of the Irish in the early Christian period. The explanation is necessarily complex. One line runs from the schools of grammar and rhetoric in the cities of Late Antiquity through Gildas and Columbanus, to the concerns with language and grammar shown by Irish scholars. Another starts from the crucial fact that Irishmen learned Latin in schools and needed the Latin they learned from grammars in order to gain access to Christian Latin culture, above all to the Bible. They could not afford the contrast made by Caesarius of Arles or Gregory of Tours between the rhetorical Latin of the schools and the rustic Latin which would be intelligible to a preacher's audience.[83] Nor could they afford the notion that rusticity might be a mark of monastic sanctity. It is also, however, necessary to remember the Irish sense of the worth of their language and culture as compared with Latin, a sense fed by the experience of conquest in a Roman province. One of the fundamental principles used by Columbanus in his Fifth Letter was that although all the Irish were the disciples of St Peter and St Paul, they were not and never had been subjects of the Roman State.[84] He could therefore argue the cause of St Peter's Rome to Arian Lombard and Trecapitoline Catholic, each, for his own reasons, highly suspicious of the emperor and of a papacy still upholding the orthodoxy of Justinian and Vigilius. Columbanus had no allegiance to the emperor but looked only to Peter. By his time, Irish churchmen had managed the delicate feat of plundering the Egyptians, taking what seemed to them best in their former enemy Rome, but retaining a sense of their separate identity. The social context of this feat was the existence of a complex aristocracy, lords of clients, churchmen, ecclesiastical scholars whose medium was Latin, and *filid* and *brithemain* whose medium was Irish. Both Irish and Latin had made their home within this complex aristocracy. What was remarkable about the Irish contribution to the Carolingian Renaissance at the end of our period was the simple number of scholars who left Ireland for Francia.[85] The explanation of this phenomenon stretches back into sub-Roman Britain, to the jockeying of three languages, Latin, British and Irish, but it must rely also on the character of the Irish aristocracy: single in terms of family recruitment, but complex in terms of the grounds for privileged rank.

NOTES

1 I have deliberately avoided covering the same ground as two important papers by Jane Stevenson, 'Beginnings of literacy', and 'Literacy in Ireland'.
2 See Sims-Williams, above, pp. 15–38.
3 W. Davies, 'Latin charter-tradition'.
4 McManus, *Guide*, p. 41; Sims-Williams, 'Some problems', 135.
5 A. Harvey, 'Early literacy'.
6 Brown, 'Oldest Irish manuscripts'.
7 Compare *ECMW*, pp. 12–13, where Nash-Williams is quite clear on the nature of the change (from one pre-existing form of lettering to another) with Appendix II which could be taken to imply gradual development from one to the other; Jackson, *Language and History*, pp. 160–1, is aware that the change involves a switch from a traditional inscriptional form of lettering to using the contemporary

book-script on stone as well as on parchment, but he then argues that the process must have taken a long time; this, however, implies the latter view.

8 Bischoff, 'Die alten Namen'.

9 T. M. Charles-Edwards, 'Language and society', pp. 715–18.

10 Jackson, *Language and History*, pp. 74–94, criticized by Gratwick, '*Latinitas Britannica*'; Gratwick was, in turn, criticized by McManus, '*Linguarum diversitas*', and by Russell, 'Recent work'.

11 J. T. Koch, 'Loss of final syllables'.

12 This is implied by the phrase *magister elegans* in *De Excidio Britanniae*, ch. 36: see Lapidge, 'Gildas's education', p. 50.

13 Marrou, *History of Education*, pp. 265–98.

14 Cf. Augustine, *Confessiones*, II. 3, ed. Verheijen, pp. 19–20.

15 Sims-Williams, 'Gildas and vernacular poetry', p. 177.

16 Tomlin, *Tabellae Sulis*.

17 Lapidge, 'Gildas's education', pp. 40–8.

18 Ibid., p. 49.

19 Cf. Norberg, *Manuel pratique*, pp. 93–104.

20 N. Wright, 'Gildas's prose style', p. 114.

21 On the notion of *elegantia* see, for example, Augustine, *De Ciuitate Dei*, IX. 4, ed. Dombart and Kalb, p. 252: 'A. Gellius, uir elegantissimi eloquii et multae undecumque scientiae'.

22 Columba is a *suí* or has *suíthe* (*Amra Choluim Chille*, §§ 12, 26, 72, 91), is a support of the *ecnaid* or *ecnae* (§ 81) and is *docht* (§§ 27, 65): ed. W. Stokes, 'Bodleian Amra Choluim Chille', 162, 168, 260, 262, 266, 270.

23 Gregory the Great, *Dialogues*, Bk. II, Prologue, ed. de Vogüé, p. 126.

24 Winterbottom, 'Columbanus', 310–17.

25 Jonas, *Vita S. Columbani*, I. 3, ed. Krusch, p. 155.

26 Krusch's text (p. 158, 12) has *elimato sermone* where *elimato = elevato*.

27 Marrou, *History of Education*, p. 265.

28 *HE* III. 5, pp. 226–7.

29 Lowe, *Codices Latini Antiquiores*, Suppl., p. 1684; Armstrong and Macalister, 'Wooden book'; D. Wright, 'Tablets from Springmount'.

30 Law, *Insular Latin Grammarians*, pp. 30–41.

31 *Hisperica Famina*, ed. Herren, pp. 39–44; Herren, 'Hisperic Latin'.

32 Winterbottom, 'On *Hisperica Famina*'.

33 Cummian's rhetorical skills are already clear in the *uerba excusationis* with which he opens (*Cummian's Letter*, ed. Walsh and Ó Cróinín, pp. 56–8).

34 *Amra Choluim Chille*, §§ 54–60, ed. Stokes, 'Bodleian Amra Choluim Chille', 252–6.

35 *HE* IV. 26/24, pp. 430–1.

36 Bischoff, 'Wendepunkte', 206–9 (repr., pp. 217–18).

37 For example, *CIH* 585.34–586.29; 2279.16–31; for further details see *UR*, pp. 84–5.

38 *Hib*. XXI. 1–2, pp. 62–3.

39 Ní Dhonnchadha, 'Guarantor list', 180: most of those numbered 26–40 in the list may be in this category.

40 I have discussed the participation of scholars in synods and the combination of different offices in one churchman in a chapter of my *Early Christian Ireland*.

The context and uses of literacy in early Christian Ireland

41 *UR*, p. 86 and *passim*.
42 Ibid., p. 87.
43 Ibid., pp. 83–5.
44 *BN* I in *UR*, pp. 20–8.
45 Kenney, *Sources*, no. 82.
46 *Hib.*, Bks. I–IX, pp. 3–27.
47 *Canones Hibernenses*, IV. 1, 9; V. 11, in *Irish Penitentials*, ed. Bieler, pp. 170–5.
48 *Hib.* XXI. 26. *b*, p. 72.
49 The *scriba* of *Hib.* XXI. 1–2, pp. 62–3, judges ecclesiastical cases.
50 *Críth Gablach*, ed. Binchy, lines 6–9.
51 Reynolds, ' "At sixes and sevens" '.
52 *AU*, s.aa. 725, 747.
53 *UR*, pp. 84–5.
54 Ó Corráin, 'Nationality and kingship', p. 19.
55 *BN* IX, in *UR*, p. 46.
56 *UR*, § 3.
57 Ibid., §§ 4, 7, 11.
58 Ibid., §§ 4, 11.
59 *Críth Gablach*, ed. Binchy, lines 256–9.
60 *BN* II; line 6, *BN* X, line 4, in *UR*, pp. 28–30, 47.
61 *BN* IX in *UR*, pp. 45–6.
62 Byrne, 'Trim and Sletty', commenting on the *Additamenta* in the Book of
   Armagh, §§ 1–4, in *Patrician Texts*, ed. Bieler, pp. 166–70; *Book of Leinster*, ed.
   Best *et al.*, vol. 6, lines 48744–7 = *Corpus Genealogiarum Sanctorum*, ed. Ó Riain,
   p. 690. 4; *Martyrology of Tallaght*, ed. Best and Lawlor, 17 February, 11 October.
63 Ó Corráin, 'Nationality and kingship', pp. 18–20.
64 Byrne, *Irish Kings*, pp. 211–15. Some of the most prominent of the Uí Néill kings
   had periods as clerics from which they returned to rule as king, such as Fínsnechtae
   mac Dúnchada and Domnall mac Murchada (*AU*, s.aa. 688.3; 689.2; 744.2).
65 *CIH* 1131. 25–7.
66 Anonymous *Vita S. Cuthberti*, III. 6, in *Two Lives*, ed. Colgrave, p. 106; Bede,
   Vita S. Cuthberti Prosaica, c. 24, ibid., p. 236; *HE* IV. 26/24, p. 430: 'uir in
   scripturis doctissimus, qui frater eius et filius Osuiu regis esse dicebatur'; *AU*, s.a.
   704: 'Aldfrith m. Ossu sapiens'.
67 T. M. Charles-Edwards, 'Review article', 146–52.
68 One of the few examples in *Hib.* is XXV. 9, pp. 78–9, a quotation from Jerome's
   Commentary on Matthew, illustrating the origin of the style in Late Antique
   schoolroom techniques.
69 *HE* III. 27, pp. 312–13.
70 These are discussed in my *Early Christian Ireland*.
71 Marrou, *History of Education*, pp. 303–5.
72 Cf. the 'ounce [of silver] for godly instruction' (*uinge forcetail déodae*) mentioned
   in a fragment of *Córus Béscnai*, *CIH* 1819.35; the commentary, however, suggests
   that this was payable if the person's own church had refused to educate him.
73 *Auraicept*, ed. Ahlqvist, pp. 36–7.
74 For Fénius Farsaid, see Carey, 'Fénius Farsaid'.
75 *Auraicept*, ed. Ahlqvist, § 1.

81

T. M. Charles-Edwards

76 Ibid.
77 'Saga of Fergus mac Léti', ed. Binchy, § 1, p. 37, trans. p. 39.
78 *Auraicept*, ed. Ahlqvist, §§ 1–2.
79 The patronymic is only in the Latin in *ECMW*, nos. 70, 84, 127, 298, 308, 390.
80 Ibid., no. 142.
81 *Auraicept*, ed. Ahlqvist, § 7, 1.
82 T. M. Charles-Edwards, 'Language and society', pp. 715–18, 735.
83 Caesarius of Arles, *Sermones*, no. 86, ed. Morin, p. 353; and the trenchant words of Gregory of Tours's mother in Gregory of Tours, *Libri de Virtutibus*, I. Praef., ed. Krusch, pp. 585–6.
84 Columbanus, *Ep.* 5, § 11 in *Sancti Columbani Opera*, ed. Walker, p. 48.
85 Contreni, 'Irish contribution', pp. 79–80.

4

Orality, literacy and genealogy in early medieval Ireland and Wales

DAVID E. THORNTON

For historians of early medieval Ireland and Wales the genealogical sources, along with the chronicles, constitute the primary means of reconstructing dynasties, and thereby of understanding the transmission of power and analysing power structures.[1] Given this evident importance, it is regrettable that for many scholars genealogies have, in the words of John Kelleher, 'all the charm of an obsolete telephone directory from some small, remote capital'.[2] One of the most striking features of early medieval Celtic genealogies – especially those from Ireland – is the very quantity involved.[3] It has been suggested, for instance, that this large volume of genealogy is a reflection of earlier 'barbarian', that is pagan and pre-literate, practices.[4] Such an interpretation could be supported by references to the isolated examples of oral rendition of genealogies in the historical period along with a sideways glance at the Gaulish druids. Indeed, James Carney argued that some of the so-called 'archaic' Leinster genealogical poems were composed in the middle of the fifth century or even earlier, and urged that references to pagan gods should be considered 'with utmost seriousness'.[5] However, such an approach is no longer in vogue in Celtic studies, and scholars have increasingly argued that the early medieval Celts were in tune with developments in contemporary Europe rather than simply regurgitating elements of a pre-Christian, Indo-European past.[6] Thus, the extant genealogies betray a significant biblical and Classical – and therefore literary – influence and were the product of what has been termed (for Ireland) 'a mandarin caste' of literate, aristocratically minded and hereditary clergy, working for the most part in monasteries but concerned directly with (and often related closely to) their secular cousins.[7] Furthermore, it has been demonstrated that the archaic poems were not only revised, but also composed, in the early Christian context of the seventh century.[8] The situation for Wales is comparable: the earliest surviving genealogical

83

sources reflect clear biblical and Classical influences, and the earliest extant collection was probably drawn up at St David's, under the watchful eye of Owain ap Hywel, king of Dyfed (d. 988).[9] Furthermore, attempts to identify pagan gods in the early medieval Welsh pedigrees have not always fared well.[10] Consequently, we must surely take the literate and Christian context of the Irish and Welsh genealogies as understood.

Of course, we are only able to discuss these early medieval Celtic genealogies precisely because they have been preserved in successive manuscript copies. The earliest extant Irish genealogical collections (the Book of Leinster and Rawlinson MS B.502) date from the twelfth century, but some material therein may have been composed four or five centuries earlier; while for Wales, the earliest collection, composed in the middle of the tenth century, is preserved in London, British Library, MS Harley 3859, a (probably) continental manuscript of *c*.1100. All other genealogical sources survive in manuscripts from the late medieval or early modern periods. Therefore, it is not always possible to be absolutely certain of the layout and structure of the underlying genealogical material, though some general comments can be ventured. For example, both the Welsh and Irish tracts are linguistic, not diagrammatic, in their representation of genealogical relationships.[11] Layout on the page often depended upon the type of genealogical information being conveyed. On the one hand, in the Irish codices, linear retrograde patrilines of the form *Donnchad m. Aeda m. Congaile m. Néill* are often set out as series of columns with one (sometimes two) names per line. On the other hand, sections outlining segmentary genealogical relationships (entitled *míniugud senchasa* or *craeb coibnessa*) employed the standard two-columnar format of the manuscripts.[12] The scribes sought to follow this layout whenever the texts were suitable, though it was not always possible to do so. However, the fact that these genealogies were written down does not exclude the possibility of oral transmission as well. For example, Gerald of Wales (writing in the late twelfth century) stated that while the Welsh bards 'kept accurate copies of the genealogies of these princes in their old manuscripts . . . they would also recite them from memory'.[13] Similarly, elements of oral transmission have been detected among the Irish genealogies.[14] These points should be borne in mind when analysing the effects of the oral and literary media on genealogical sources.

In this chapter, I shall briefly review the orality–literacy debate as it has come to bear upon the cultivation of genealogy in general and upon the early medieval Celtic material in particular, before proceeding to consider both the structural and functional effects of the literary medium upon these genealogies. The functional effects will be divided into two themes in which students of literacy have taken a particular interest and for which genealogy has some importance: namely, literacy and power, and literacy and history.[15] It should be stressed that the patterns and themes discussed are not regarded as simply the result of literacy alone (the so-called 'autonomous' model); rather, the use of that medium may have facilitated the development of those patterns within the specific context of early medieval Irish and Welsh political structures, kinship and genealogy.[16]

ORALITY–LITERACY

The relationship of genealogies to the orality–literacy debate is important for Celtic studies, not only because Celticists have benefited from comparative work on oral genealogies when analysing those generated in early medieval Ireland and Wales, but also because genealogies and origin-legends were often central to the development of the debate among anthropologists in the 1950s and 1960s. The thrust of this debate may be summarized as follows: oral genealogies tend to be more 'fluid' than their written counterparts, and thereby can be manipulated more effectively in order to represent changes in political or social structures. In the two most oft-cited African case-studies, of the Tiv and the Gonja, anthropologists demonstrated that the native genealogies which had been related orally were significantly different from those recorded earlier in the century by British colonial administrators and preserved in official documents, and these differences were seen to relate directly to the changes in tribal structures during the intervening years.[17] The oral genealogies functioned as 'charters' for prevailing political and social structures by means of a process termed *structural amnesia* or 'the homeostatic process of forgetting': elements of the genealogy no longer relevant or necessary would be collectively forgotten and new elements could be silently incorporated. This, it was argued, was possible only because no formally recorded version of the genealogy had been kept by the tribe which could contradict the revised account. Thus, literacy is anathema to this process: 'To prefer one genealogy throughout time is to make rigid a charter which, if it is to work, must remain fluid – and to a certain extent is also to make rigid a fluid social structure.'[18]

However, a number of qualifications and criticisms have been raised against this 'oralist' interpretation of genealogical manipulation, regarding both the general principles involved and genealogies in particular. For example, we are no longer encouraged to regard orality and literacy as two mutually exclusive and opposing positions, but rather as points of a continuum or spectrum.[19] Societies are not necessarily exclusively oral or literate in their modes of communication, nor need societies exist in total isolation from one another. Thus, scholars have come to realize that the 'traditions' of pre-literate societies can be affected significantly by contact with literate ones: elements of the written tradition are seen to 'feed back' into the oral milieu.[20] Jack Goody has gone so far as to suggest that the practice of drawing up lists (of which genealogies constitute a specific type) should be linked *causally* to the advent of literacy, even if individual lists are drawn up orally: 'While I do not see the making of tables, lists and formulae as originating entirely with the coming of writing, I would maintain that the shift from utterance to text led to significant developments of a sort that might be loosely referred to as a change in consciousness and which in part arose from the great extension of formal operations to a graphic kind.'[21] Now clearly this is not to suggest that genealogical lists should be found *only* in literate societies, since we have direct evidence to the contrary; but it has been argued that when genealogies are kept in oral societies (especially longer genealogies) it is likely that some form of feedback is to be suspected.[22]

We need therefore to re-define the distinction between oral and written genealogies. Of course, whatever the original inspiration for the development and continued transmission of genealogies in a pre-literate society, the point still remains that as long as these genealogies are not written down – at least by members of the relevant society – then their relative fluidity is guaranteed. However, it can be demonstrated that this oral–literate distinction regarding the function of genealogies as social and political charters is not wholly accurate: written genealogies (by the very fact of being written down) are *not* necessarily doomed to be less fluid as means of representing political and social structures. For example, the fact that Celticists, as well as historians in other literate contexts such as ancient Greece and biblical Israel, have compared written genealogies with those studied by anthropologists, identified similar patterns, and thereby achieved a greater understanding of the written text, demonstrates that the distinction is not absolute.[23] Evidence for comparable genealogical manipulation has also been presented by anthropologists for contemporary literate and quasi-literate contexts.[24] Furthermore, scholars have stressed that oral transmission is not as automatically fluid as the extreme 'oralist' position would have us believe.[25]

Some examples from early medieval Wales and Ireland should suffice to illustrate these contentions. Here, one must distinguish between what appears to have been the genealogy at the time of composition and what is extant in our manuscript sources: it is often possible to be certain that a genealogy has undergone change only if more than one version has been preserved, or if later genealogists/scribes have drawn attention to alternative lines of descent. This is the phenomenon which I term *genealogical schizophrenia*: that is, where a dynasty appears to claim more than one origin or, in effect, more than one genealogical 'personality'. This schizophrenia may be more apparent than real: apparent to the medieval scribe and modern historian, but not necessarily to the earlier dynast whose pedigree is under scrutiny. Manipulation of written genealogies can take a number of forms. On the one hand, it is possible to find instances of complete alteration of a genealogy to accommodate significant political changes: this, in effect, would differ very little from the 'amnesia' of oral genealogies. On the other hand, it is possible to identify a process of *augmentation* – characteristic, I shall argue, of written genealogies in particular – whereby political change is expressed by means of additions to an existing genealogical scheme rather than its complete re-composition.

A good example of genealogical manipulation is represented by the different versions of the royal genealogy of early medieval Dyfed.[26] According to the Old Irish text 'The Expulsion of the Déisi', the kings of eighth-century Dyfed were the descendants of Irish immigrants.[27] The Harleian and later genealogies, however, derive the dynasty from Macsen Wledig (Magnus Maximus).[28] Here we have two entirely different lines of descent requiring resolution. I would argue that the Irish version is the earlier (though not necessarily wholly accurate) account, because the use of Magnus Maximus (regarded, in medieval Welsh pseudo-history, as the last representative of Roman power in Britain) would suit the political aspirations of Owain ap Hywel (d. 988), whose father's rule had extended over a large part of Wales and whose mother was of the Dimetian royal line. The overall scheme of the Harleian genealogies was to prove that the Second Dynasty, and especially Owain, was the legitimate successor of pre-Roman, Roman and post-Roman rule over the Britons. It is worth stressing that, in this example of complete genealogical change in a written context, part of the evidence stands outside the main corpus of Welsh genealogical manuscripts. In the later manuscripts, the scribes appear to have sought to reconcile the different accounts by creating hybrid pedigrees. The implication seems to be that the literate context for the composition and initial transmission of these genealogies posed no obstacle to the manipulation of them for political ends, but that the resulting variant accounts could pose problems for later genealogists divorced from these immediate circumstances.

The Irish example of genealogical schizophrenia is the genealogy of the ruling line of Conaille Muirtheimne (in modern Co. Louth).[29] In this case the extant manuscripts (the early modern Book of Lecan and Book of Ballymote) cite these variant lines of descent, all of which sought to connect the dynasty of the Conaille to the neighbouring kingdoms of the Ulaid. There are three main stems which diverge at the person of Conall Anglonnach (eponymous ancestor of the Conaille): one associates them with the Uí Echach Coba and Dál nAraide; the second with the Dál Fiatach; and the third with 'pre-historic' figures mentioned in the Ulster-Cycle tales. The schizophrenia may be explained synchronically or diachronically. The overkingship of the Ulaid had alternated between the Dál nAraide and the Dál Fiatach until late in the tenth century; thereafter it was monopolized by the latter. The variants in the genealogy may therefore represent attempts to account for this periodic change in overlord. Alternatively, the Conaille may have earlier claimed affiliation with the neighbouring Uí Echach Coba (and thence the Dál nAraide), only to find it necessary to shift allegiance to the more powerful Dál Fiatach from the 970s onwards. Either way, literacy was no impediment to genealogical change.

These two examples demonstrate that the written genealogies of early medieval Ireland and Wales could exhibit a significant degree of fluidity, comparable to that characteristic of their oral counterparts. The examples chosen involve not mere adaptation or extension, but wholesale alteration of the relevant part of the genealogy in order to reflect changes in political aspirations or circumstances. One *could* argue that the survival of the different versions is proof of the relative rigidity of these written genealogies; but, at least in the Welsh cases, the variants are only preserved (in the first instance) outside the *extant* manuscript tradition. Anyway, the existence of these variants does *not* appear to have prevented the manipulation in the first place.

SIZE AND AUGMENTATION

The redaction of genealogies also has implications for their overall structure and in particular their size: this is one of the factors underlying what might be termed the 'propensity for augmentation', a characteristic of written genealogies which facilitates their manipulation.[30] The most obvious structural implication of literacy for genealogy is that (vellum permitting) it enables theoretically unlimited extension of an individual pedigree or of the corpus as a whole. By contrast, as we have seen, oral genealogies are self-regulating and (with certain notable exceptions, such as those from Polynesia) relatively short. This is partly because there is no need for the retention of unnecessary elements (such as extinct segments or distant generations) and partly no doubt because human memory has its limitations. In oral societies, royal genealogies will often tend to be longer than those of the subject lineages (though these latter may be more segmentary).[31] Non-royal genealogies may, as a whole, be relatively complex, but individual knowledge will often be restricted to no more than four, five or six generations above *ego*.[32] These levels may correspond to the extent of the minimal kindred-group (like the early Irish *derbfine* or *gelfine*) through which the individual's interaction with other members of society is defined. Also, it is worth stressing that in some cases where oral genealogies longer than those discussed here are encountered, anthropologists suspect either feedback from literate contact or generation by a semi-literate society.

Obviously, such limitations are not presented by the written medium. Here the Irish material in particular comes into its own. For example, estimates of the total number of different entries given in the index to O'Brien's *Corpus Genealogiarum Hiberniae*, vol. 1, stand at about 12,000, and this by no means represents the whole corpus.[33] Individual pedigrees can be very long: for example, the pedigree of the mid-eleventh-century kings of Osraige covers over 100 generations to Noah, and the segmentary genealogies of even quite minor kingdoms can contain the names of as many as three or four hundred different individuals. The degree of segmentation can be very large, again surely beyond the scope of an oral genealogist, however competent. Indeed, even the literate Irish genealogists found it necessary to draw up short tracts summarizing the segmentation by naming the main apical ancestors and the major groups descended from them.[34]

As we have seen earlier, the written medium need not be (and was not) an impediment to the manipulation of genealogies along the lines usually associated more with their oral counterparts. However, this (theoretically) unlimited size of written genealogies facilitated another type of manipulation which I term the 'propensity for augmentation', whereby genealogies would be added to or 'augmented' (rather than silently altered) in order to reflect concomitant political change. This process accounts for the supposed rigidity of written genealogies (as identified by the oralist interpretation) by employing the structural advantage (in terms of size) of the written medium. Augmentation can take a number of forms: horizontal (that is segmentary), vertical (the grafting of one pedigree onto another), or often a combination of the two. The end product is a 'layered' genealogy which has in effect evolved over more than one stage: old lineages have not been discarded but newly emerged ones have been incorporated. The genealogical position of the new political circumstances is represented not as a wholly new phenomenon, which in political reality it may well be, but as a continuation or extension of the earlier genealogy.

Horizontal augmentation, at its crudest, entails the very common tendency for the offspring of (say) an important ancestor-figure to grow, as, for example, new lineages or kingdoms are brought into closer political association with that ancestor's descendants. Such a pattern *can* be found among oral genealogies, except that extinct lineages will, in that case, be eventually forgotten. Take, for example, the sons of Cunedda Wledig (ancestor of the main dynasties of Gwynedd): these sons can be shown to be eponymous ancestors of various north Welsh kingdoms in the early Middle Ages.[35] In the *Historia Brittonum* they are said to number eight (no names are given). In the Harleian genealogies the figure has nudged up to nine (and names and pedigrees are given); this is followed in the Jesus College collection, which adds two daughters for good measure; while in the later medieval and early modern codices the number of sons named is up to twelve or thirteen and the daughters (through a scribal error) to three. The possible total progeny of sixteen is thus double that of the earliest account. Another notable Welsh example of filial augmentation is that of Brychan Brycheiniog, whose offspring numbered about thirty in our oldest surviving accounts and increased to about fifty in the later manuscripts (here the number of daughters remains relatively stable and the sons double).[36] Similar Irish cases can be found of maximal-lineage founders with large progenies which tended to grow in size over time: Niall Noígiallach of the Uí Néill, Cathaír Mór of the Laigin, Ailill Ólom of the Eoganachta and other Munster groups, and so on. And of course, perhaps the best-known example from Munster is that of the Dál Cais. Originally derived from one of the subject Déisi groups in Munster, the Dál Cais came to challenge and replace the Eoganachta in the overkingship of the province during the course of the tenth and eleventh centuries. Their genealogy was altered accordingly: they rendered their eponymous ancestor Cormac Cass as son of Ailill Ólom and thereby placed themselves on a parallel or equal genealogical footing to the Eoganachta. The Dál Cais validated their changed political fortunes by augmenting (not replacing) the existing genealogical scheme.

Such a propensity for augmentation is, I would argue, characteristic in particular of written genealogies: admittedly some of the elements can be found in oral examples, but it is the combination of factors associated with the written form (namely, a theoretically unlimited size and a pre-existing written model) which makes augmentation so common among literate genealogical traditions.

I have so far been concerned more with the structural implications of orality and literacy for genealogies, and (to an extent) with providing a defence of written genealogy. I would like to proceed now to a consideration of the functional implications of literacy for genealogy (naturally taking on board the main themes discussed already). In particular, I shall concentrate on genealogy in terms, first, of literacy and power, and second, of literacy and history.

LITERACY AND POWER

It has become fashionable in recent decades to discuss literacy in terms of the exercise of power and government, that is, of the extent to which the development of the written medium of communication has been employed to achieve, maintain and regulate the position of particular social, political or religious élites.[37] This is inevitably important for genealogies which have a special role in the wielding of power, whether in the validation of an individual ruler's or dynasty's position, or, more subtly, of the regulation of relationships between rulers and the ruled.

At the most fundamental level, the use of an appropriate genealogy to validate an individual king's position as king would differ little between the oral and written media. But literacy does offer some new possibilities in this regard. Take, for example, the earliest 'literate' genealogies that survive: epigraphic genealogies from the ancient Near and Middle East. Analysis of these pedigrees has suggested that those over three generations in length were inscribed during periods of political instability or imperialistic expansion.[38] The famous trilingual inscription of Darius I at Behistun concludes his pedigree with the statement: 'From long ago our family have been kings . . . eight of my family previously exercised kingship. I am the ninth.'[39] It is no doubt significant that this inscription was erected after a power struggle with an alleged pretender and that it served to reinforce Darius' (probably) tenuous position in the immediate aftermath. In such cases the genealogy is used monumentally: the ruler has a point to make, and does so in a visible manner (requiring much economic and human effort) as a testimony to his own power.[40] Literacy has facilitated the process.

Compare this with the pedigree of Cyngen ap Cadell of Powys (d. 854/5) on the so-called Pillar of Elisse.[41] Cyngen claimed to have erected the inscription in memory of his great-grandfather Elisse ap Gwylog, who, we are told, had recovered the 'inheritance' of Powys from the English. This stress on the English is significant here, since it appears that during Cyngen's reign (808–54) they, and especially the Mercians, made important incursions into Wales at the expense of Powys. In 816 the English are said to have invaded as far as Snowdonia and Rhufoniog. In 821, Cenwulf of Mercia was (according to Geoffrey Gaimar) at Basingwerk when he died, and in the following year the English destroyed Degannwy and took Powys into their power. Finally, the Welsh are said to have submitted to Ecgbert of Wessex in 828/830. Under such circumstances it is perhaps not surprising that Cyngen would wish to emphasize earlier Powysian successes against the English and, by means of his epigraphic pedigree, to connect himself directly to their perpetrator. The kingdom may also have faced pressure from the west, from the emerging Second Dynasty of Gwynedd. The inscribing of the pillar must, given its contents, be understood in the light of these contemporary events. The written genealogy was used monumentally in order to support the position of the dynasty and of Cyngen in particular.

This example illustrates one of the uses of written genealogies in terms of power in the abstract. Literacy also has implications for the practical exercise of power expressed through genealogical relationships, especially for the relative status and reciprocal relationships between dynasties. The Irish genealogies are especially significant in this regard; and here genealogy must not be taken in isolation, but used in conjunction with other texts such as those outlining the reciprocal dues of overking and sub-kings (the *frithfolaid* tracts and *Lebor na Cert*) and the long lists of categories of peoples/kingdoms: *aithechthuatha* ('vassal peoples'), *saerclanna* ('free kindreds'), *daerclanna* ('unfree kindreds'), *fortuatha* ('outside peoples') and so on. The basic principle involved may be summarized as follows: the greater the genealogical distance between the dynasty of a given sub-kingdom and the macro-dynasty which exercised the overkingship, the lower the relative status of that minor dynasty. This could have significant implications for the client-king in terms of the services, dues and tribute he owed to his provincial overking.[42] For example, in the twelfth-century *Lebor na Cert* (Book of Rights) there is a clear distinction between those groups which paid tribute to the overking and those which did not: analysis of these groups genealogically reveals that the non-tribute payers were those whose ruling dynasties were regarded as genealogically part of or closely related to the appropriate provincial macro-dynasty (the Eoganachta, the Uí Néill, the Ulaid, the Connachta).[43] Those whose genealogy placed them beyond the relevant point (whether this entailed extra-provincial origin or not) were liable to pay tribute. Of course, the scheme was not always applied rigidly: for instance, there were certain Eoganachta who were considered among the 'unfree' *clanna* of Cashel,[44] but the general pattern does usually hold. There is something of 'the chicken and the egg' about this: groups could strive for a less onerous situation and would *perforce* have their genealogy altered accordingly. This may explain some of the cases where the number of sons of the main dynastic founder was augmented over time.

LITERACY AND HISTORY

Anthropologists have argued that literacy facilitates the development of what has been termed 'true' or 'objective' history in that, first, the existence of a written account of the past, independent of the writer and reader, is thought to distance the past from the present (unlike in oral accounts); and second, the existence of written accounts permits the comparison of different versions.[45] Of course, this is not to suggest that the committing to writing of an account of the past *ipso facto* guarantees its accuracy and objectivity, but (to quote Ruth Finnegan) this would allow at least for 'the possibility of a detached and self-conscious check on the truth of historical accounts'.[46] Genealogy is important in this regard, since it is in itself concerned with the past as directly connected to and affecting the present, and because many early examples of historical and pseudo-historical writing have a genealogical flavour. However, it should be reiterated that the redaction of genealogies does not ensure their accuracy, nor does it necessarily impose a single standard version.

These points are reflected in the following passage, which possibly once introduced a version of the Irish genealogies:

> The foolish Irish nation, forgetful of its history, boasts of incredible or completely fabulous deeds, since it has been careless about *committing to writing* any of its achievements. Therefore, I propose to *write down* the genealogies of the Irish race: firstly, the race of Éber, secondly the race of Éremón, thirdly the race of Ír, and fourthly the race of Lugaid mac Ítha.[47]

Similar ideas can be found in other medieval genealogical sources, such as the Icelandic *Landnámabók*.[48] In the Irish example quoted, genealogy is an integral aspect of 'national' history. Furthermore, in both the Irish and Icelandic cases, the act of committing the genealogies to writing is regarded as a means of demonstrating the 'truth' of that history, whether to counter the excessive claims of natives or the denigrating criticisms of foreigners. This is not merely a medieval *topos*, but reflects the important function of literacy for the development of genealogy and history.

For both the early medieval Irish and Welsh, the tracing of national origins and genealogical history was inevitably linked to Latin literacy, since the very channel for the introduction of the literary medium – namely, Christianity – brought with it a whole series of biblical, Classical and patristic teachings concerning the origins of peoples. Any self-respecting Christian people would naturally seek to find their particular niche within the overall scheme, and the early medieval Celts were not alone in tracing their origins to one of the

Orality, literacy, genealogy in early medieval Ireland and Wales

sons of Noah as given in the Table of Nations.[49] Furthermore, this was not simply a matter of crudely grafting some pagan or pre-literate genealogical scheme on to that of Book 10 of Genesis. In the case of the Irish, the development of the famous tripartite Milesian scheme – which, as the passage quoted above illustrates, pervades all the genealogies – can be derived in part from Latin Christian learning (probably in the seventh century) and has been described by Donnchadh Ó Corráin as 'one of the most transparent literary inventions'.[50] The early medieval Welsh fare no better: the earliest extant account is to be found in the *Historia Brittonum* and derives the Britons from the Trojan Brutus – an equally literate invention. The scheme up to biblical levels draws on various sources, including the so-called 'Frankish Table of Nations' (in fact, probably composed in Ostrogothic Italy or Byzantium in the early sixth century) and Isidore's *Etymologiae*, as well as some Irish material. This scheme no doubt inspired Geoffrey of Monmouth's twelfth-century account of British origins which in turn 'fed back' into the native genealogies.[51] Even the earlier Welsh genealogies betray the Christian and Latin literate context of their composition: the kings of Powys sought to associate themselves with St Germanus and Magnus Maximus (on the Pillar of Elisse); and in the Harleian genealogies the important ancestor Beli Magnus (Beli Mawr) is probably to be derived not from a pagan Celtic god as some have suggested, but, through the *Historia Brittonum*, from a Briton mentioned by Orosius and (ultimately) Suetonius.[52] Thus it can be seen that use of the written word not only enabled the early medieval Irish and Welsh to speculate as to their history and genealogical origins within a wider framework (however inaccurate and unhistorical this may seem to us today), but also provided the very means by which they did so.

Literate historical enquiry also had structural implications for the genealogies of early medieval Ireland and Wales. It is necessary to distinguish between the genealogies as they have been preserved (as part of often vast genealogical collections copied into later manuscripts) and as they may have existed at the time of composition (for instance, as shorter tracts on individual dynastic groups drawn up at the local monastery). The extant manuscripts often contain more than one version of a genealogy. Indeed, Ó Corráin has termed the manuscripts 'work-books (or rather copies of them) . . . from which the learned classes met the needs of their patrons'.[53] These Irish genealogists in particular were careful to keep record of variant lines of

95

descent in the genealogies, employing such formulae as *ut alii dicunt* ('as others say'). I have already mentioned the three, very different, ancestries of the Conaille Muirtheimne given in the same tract. Such practices could sometimes be on a larger scale. For example, an eighth-century tract on the Déisi Muman concludes with what appears to be an appendix covering much the same ground as the main tract but with significant differences (additional names, alternative lines of descent and so on).[54] On occasion, the genealogists were not so careful. The section on the Déisi in the fourteenth-century Book of Lecan sought to synthesize this tract with later (and in places very different) genealogies of the Déisi: the result is an often very confusing hybrid which can only be understood if the separate strands are distinguished. I have suggested that a similar process occurred for the Welsh example of Dyfed, where the later genealogists sought to harmonize the divergent ancestries by incorporating names from one into the other. In such cases, the original (if divergent) versions can possibly be understood when analysed in terms of ninth- and tenth-century politics; but these later hybrids often serve only to confuse modern historians just as they confused their medieval predecessors! However, in both cases – either variant citation or hybrid – the underlying motive would seem to be a desire to identify the truer genealogy.

I have attempted to illustrate some of the ways in which literacy determined the character of the genealogical sources from early medieval Ireland and Wales. While we must revise the now-dated distinction between orality and literacy as mutually exclusive modes of communication, and thereby re-define our understanding of oral versus written genealogies, it is evident that the use of writing did have significant consequences for genealogy, both structurally and functionally. For example, the literary form, by facilitating the growth in quantity of genealogy, produced a means of manipulation (here termed 'augmentation') less suited to the oral medium. Thus, we return to the alleged 'barbarian' pre-literate origin of the Celtic practice of maintaining a large number of long genealogies noted in the first paragraph. If my arguments regarding the correspondence of literacy and volume are accepted, then these long genealogies did not have a pre-literate origin and the explanation for their length must be sought elsewhere – for instance, in the segmentary nature of dynastic succession. Functionally, the written form affected the two aspects of genealogy in which Celtic historians are most interested: its connection to the exercise of power; and the manner in which it described the past. Any attempt to understand the early medieval Irish and Welsh genealogies must therefore take the implications of literacy into account.

NOTES

1 This chapter will concentrate on Ireland and Wales before *c.* 1100, but it should be borne in mind that other medieval Celtic-speaking areas produced genealogical material, though in smaller amounts. See the chapters in this volume by Broun and Tonnerre.
2 Kelleher was referring specifically to the *Irish* genealogies: 'Irish genealogies', 138.
3 Dumville, 'Kingship', pp. 76–7.
4 Genicot, *Généalogies*, pp. 14, 16–17. For similar arguments for Old English genealogies, see Moisl, 'Anglo-Saxon royal genealogies'.
5 Carney, 'Archaic Irish verse', pp. 39, 50.
6 McCone, *Pagan Past*.
7 Ó Corráin, 'Early Irish churches', pp. 330–1; *idem*, 'Historical need', pp. 142–3; *idem*, 'Legend', pp. 26–7. For further thoughts on this concept of the 'mandarin caste', see Charles-Edwards, above, pp. 70–4.
8 Ó Corráin, 'Irish origin legends', pp. 56–68.
9 *EWGT*, pp. 9–13; Phillimore, '*Annales Cambriae*'.
10 See, for example, the case of Beli Mawr given on p. 95.
11 On non-Celtic diagrammatic genealogies, see Klapisch-Zuber, 'Genesis'.
12 Modern editions of Irish genealogies maintain this distinction by giving the pedigrees as two columns of names but the segmentary genealogies as ordinary narrative across the whole page: see *CGH*.
13 *Giraldi Cambrensis Opera*, ed. Brewer *et al.*, vol. 6, p. 168.
14 For example, Nicholls, 'Mac Coghlans', 445.
15 Much of what follows is a reduced version of Thornton, 'Power', ch. 1.
16 See, for example, Street, *Literacy*.
17 Bohannen, 'Genealogical charter'; Goody and Watt, 'Consequences'.
18 Bohannen, 'Genealogical charter', 314.
19 The literature here is vast. See, for example, Finnegan, *Literacy*, p. 175; Goody, *Domestication*, pp. 80–2; Havelock, 'Oral–literate equation', p. 11.
20 Henige, *Oral Historiography*, pp. 81–7; Finnegan, *Literacy*, pp. 117–20.
21 Goody, *Domestication*, p. 75; note also Ong, *Orality*, pp. 99–101.
22 Vansina, *Oral Tradition as History*, p. 178; Henige, 'Disease of writing', pp. 240–61; Henige, 'Truths yet unborn?'
23 Dumville, 'Kingship'; Ó Corráin, 'Irish origin legends'; R. Thomas, *Oral Tradition*; Wilson, *Genealogy*.
24 For example, I. M. Lewis, 'Literacy'; Gough, 'Literacy'; Freedman, *Chinese Lineage*.

25 Vansina, *Oral Tradition as History*, pp. 120–3.
26 Thornton, 'Power', pp. 79–93; also Thornton, *Kings*, ch. 3.
27 For the texts, see Meyer, 'Expulsion of the Dessi'; *idem*, 'Expulsion of the Déssi'; Pender, 'Two unpublished versions'.
28 *EWGT*, pp. 9–10, 45–6, 106.
29 On the Conaille, see Thornton, *Kings*, ch. 4. For their genealogies, see *Book of Ballymote*, ed. Atkinson, p. 152d19; *Book of Lecan*, ed. Mulchrone, fo. 115rc18; also note *CGH*, p. 327.
30 See Thornton, 'Power', pp. 11–12.
31 Vansina, *Oral Tradition: A Study*, p. 153.
32 Thornton, 'Power', pp. 6–8; Henige, *Chronology*, p. 27.
33 Ó Cuív, Review of *CGH*, 330; Byrne, 'Senchas', 139; Ó Corráin, 'Irish origin legends', pp. 55–6.
34 *CGH*, pp. 137–8, 153, 358.
35 Miller, 'Foundation-legend'.
36 Compare the lists given in *EWGT*, pp. 14–19, 42–4, 81–4.
37 This was no doubt inspired in no small part by Clanchy, *From Memory*. See also Bowman and Woolf (eds.), *Literacy*; Lerer, *Literacy*; Goody, *Logic*; Pattison, *On Literacy*.
38 Wilson, *Genealogy*, pp. 58–72.
39 Benedict and von Voigtlander, 'Bisitun inscription'.
40 Bowman and Woolf (eds.), *Literacy*, pp. 8–9.
41 *EWGT*, pp. 1–3. For recent discussions of Powysian politics in this period, see Sims-Williams, 'Historical need', and Thornton, 'Power', pp. 66–78.
42 T. M. Charles-Edwards, 'Early medieval kingships', pp. 38–9.
43 *Lebor na Cert*, ed. Dillon.
44 See the list in Royal Irish Academy, MS 1234 (Stowe C.i.2), fo. 40r.
45 Goody and Watt, 'Consequences', p. 67; Finnegan, *Literacy*, p. 19; Clanchy, 'Remembering', 176. For some general considerations, see Ong, 'Writing', pp. 36–45.
46 Finnegan, *Literacy*, p. 21.
47 This passage is based on *CGH*, p. 192 with emendations and translation by Byrne, 'Senchas', 137. (My italics.)
48 See the passage quoted in *Book of Settlements*, trans. Pálsson and Edwards, p. 6; the text occurs in the *Þórðarbók*-recension. Byrne, 'Senchas' compared the Irish passage with the 'Nennian' preface to the *Historia Brittonum* and Gregory of Tours's introduction to his Books of Histories.
49 For discussion of some examples, see Thornton, 'Power', pp. 34–49.
50 Ó Corráin, 'Irish origin legends', pp. 64–5.
51 On this, see Thornton, 'Neglected genealogy'.
52 Zimmer, *Nennius*, pp. 272–3; Rhys, *Lectures*, pp. 37, 89–91; *Trioedd Ynys Prydein*, ed. Bromwich, pp. 75, 282. For fuller discussion, see Thornton, 'Power', pp. 110–11.
53 Ó Corráin, 'Historical need', p. 142.
54 Thornton, *Kings*, ch. 3.

5

Charter-writing and its uses in early medieval Celtic societies

WENDY DAVIES

Just as looking at one occurrence of a word gives you only a snapshot from its full semantic range, so reading the text of a single charter transmits but one moment from a network of relationships:[1] one charter is never going to reveal everything (or even the most important things) about the people and places it mentions in that moment. But it can tell you something about the moment, and the greater the number of texts, the greater our chances of insight into distant worlds.

To use charters like this is to use them – quite justifiably – as records. Indeed, at one level charters are no more than records of the transfer of property rights. But charters were more than mere records: they were also signs, like other types of medieval written text, and in the early Middle Ages they had several uses. If we take some care (and remember the limitations) we can begin to 'read the signs' and proceed from sign to function; thus, multiplying our insights, we can approach the 'diverse uses' of writing in early medieval societies.

In considering charter-writing and its uses, I am going to range across some of the texts I have studied in the past twenty years, and do so in a discursive way. I am not therefore going to focus much on detail, nor am I going to say much about charter form. I *am*, however, going to do my best to concentrate on 'uses'.

EASTERN BRITTANY

Let me start with charter-writing in eastern Brittany in the late eighth and ninth centuries. Communities in this area at this period must be viewed as Celtic societies, since their vernacular language, and a very high proportion of personal and place nomenclature, are linguistically Celtic. There are, however, differences between these eastern communities and those of regions farther west; hence, I will begin in the east and then move west and north.

Village communities of eastern Brittany were record-using societies in the late eighth and ninth centuries (at least there is about 100 years of very good documentation surviving from that period, but the record-using habit may of course have been older). These were peasant communities, village-based, agricultural. I do not suppose a high degree of lay literacy in them (although in fact we have no evidence on this point), but it is perfectly clear that transactions in landed property and in persons were recorded, and that records were kept by lay owners, vendors, purchasers and others with a full or limited interest. These records were kept safe, brought out when there were problems, and passed on to the new owners if property changed hands. The records were made according to charter form; they were made locally (that is, local to the village) by local scribes, who are frequently identified by name in the record (very often one of the village priests); and they were occasionally made at the machtiern's residence (*lis*), perhaps functioning as some sort of local registry.[2]

The form of the record varied with the nature of the transaction and with its precise location, but essentially there were two approaches to charter-writing: (i) consistent practices with regard to form and to formulas, of – apparently – purely local origin, sometimes, although only very rarely in this area, of 'Celtic' type;[3] (ii) use of material that we find in the seventh-century west Frankish formularies, much of which is ultimately of late Roman origin.[4] The latter practice does not have to mean that the scribes were using precisely the same formularies that survive today, but it does indicate that they were using some kind of closely related formulary. This material must have been extremely antiquated by the early ninth century: people were writing within a very old tradition, a throwback to a totally different world, and in many ways a relic. The fact that scribes used such an old tradition is of considerable interest and itself tells us something about the nature of writing in these rural communities.

There were three principal uses for these records in eastern Brittany: the records were, in a formal way, part of the process of transfer of property; they were a useful source of evidence in cases of dispute; and, where there were ecclesiastical interests in the property transferred, they were part of the church's armoury of protective mechanisms. The latter use is common to charter-writing and charter-keeping in all Celtic areas; the former uses are much less so. I shall discuss each of them in turn, beginning with the east Breton material and moving from that to other Celtic parts in order to note similarities and differences.

CHARTERS AND THE TRANSFER PROCESS

I do not want to suggest, for any Celtic area, that charters had a formal dispositive function, of the type supposed in the classic German literature; in other words, that the production of a charter was a necessary part of the transfer of property rights, without which you could not acquire property.[5] It may therefore have been unusual for a charter to be handed over as part of the ceremony of transfer, although this certainly did sometimes happen in eastern Brittany: 'I have *publiciter* handed over the charter of sale' was written of a transaction in 830 near Lusanger.[6] I would, however, suggest that new lay owners in east Breton villages felt more comfortable if they had a written record of the change: it was part of the mechanics of transfer to get hold of a record, especially in cases of sale. (This must be *in part* because the ninth century was a period of some mobility of property; many things changed; people felt a need to have some evidence of changes.)[7] It is certainly the case that transfer of property rights was a matter of public performance: there were gathered together, at least, the two contracting parties, with witnesses; the transaction took place on the land, in church, or in a public open space in the village; and things happened: a rod or a stick or a sod was handed over;[8] a cloak was placed on the altar; documents changed hands. If, for some reason, the transaction was performed away from the village, for example at the monastery of Redon, then the locals were still formally notified, in public.

The fact that we sometimes have two, slightly different, written versions of the same transaction suggests that the new owners were not the only people who were anxious to have a record; whether occasionally or commonly, two parties in a transaction sometimes did so.[9]

The function of the record in these cases was to provide some element of proof of ownership after transfer. This was especially important for sales. The record was also to provide a means of identifying witnesses to the transaction in case of future problems. Participants seem to have thought about future problems in a fairly short-term way; finding witnesses in later years, and talking to them, was a real option, and could have a significant bearing on problems that arose.[10] So, when the machtiern Ratfred produced 'neither witnesses nor proof', soon after 857, he failed to demonstrate before the *princeps* Salomon his right to lands in Bains and Sixt and thereby was found guilty of harassing the owner.[11]

These procedures are clear enough for eastern Brittany. In other Celtic areas – western Brittany, Cornwall, Wales, Ireland, Scotland – keeping records of transactions was a much more ecclesiastical process (or, at least, the evidence that survives suggests this). There is not much evidence to indicate that having a document was considered desirable by the mass of lay owners. From Cornwall there are records of the lay manumission of slaves, but even this was done at the altar and there was a strong ecclesiastical hand in the making of the records.[12] From south Wales the *marginalia* of the Lichfield Gospels preserve a similar record of manumission and a record of the resolution of a lay dispute – but these too seem to have been made at or near a monastery, in this case Llandeilo Fawr.[13] Both types of case are not so much evidence of the lay desire for a record of a major transaction as of their desire for religious backing, a special protection; this is a different mental framework.

CHARTERS AS A SOURCE OF EVIDENCE

Whatever the primary reason for making the record, a subsequent use of the record in eastern Brittany was as evidence in disputes. Here the written record had a use as proof of ownership. It was not the only sort of proof, even in eastern Brittany, for witnesses could be recalled, or evidence taken by a panel of enquiry, or compurgatory oaths sworn.[14] However, in cases of contested ownership or rights, the written proof could be produced. If the case went to court the text would be read out in public: in 860 (or 866) Wobrian accused Wetenoc of working more of his land in Ruffiac than Wetenoc had bought from him a generation previously; the accused produced the original documents; 'then Wobrian, vanquished as much by the charter as by the witnesses and guarantors, confessed'.[15] Note, however, that written charters were not necessarily the decisive proof: in 841 Wrbudic accused the abbot of Redon of holding a weir by right of a false charter. The accusation was disputed and the case was finally settled by the verbal testimony of locals.[16]

Outside eastern Brittany there can be no doubt that some people considered a written record as valid proof of ownership. There is an Irish heptad of *c.* 700, in which 'old writing' (in fact, *godly* old writing) is listed with valid witnesses, immovable stones, *ráth*-sureties and a bequest as viable proofs of ownership.[17] From Saint-Pol-de-Léon in north-western Brittany come references, in the later ninth century, to the belief that people should be notified of transactions in writing.[18] In Welsh material of the ninth, tenth and eleventh centuries (especially but not exclusively), there occurs a stock phrase that seems to invoke the same respect for the written record: *in sempiterno graphio* (this transaction is recorded . . . 'in an eternal writing'). By implication, writing the record made the action recorded eternal: writing was a way of making things *last*. There are examples from the monastery of Llancarfan and the bishopric of St David's, as also in charters from Dorset and Somerset in south-west England.[19] Although the mode of expression is different, there is something of the same spirit in the use of the word *monumentum* for the so-called 'foundation charter' of St Andrews, a document which claims to have been drawn up in the ninth century: 'Thana son of Dudabrach wrote this monument for the king . . .'.[20]

In implicit ways, then, the idea that the written record could be proof of ownership can be found in several Celtic areas. (I would not want to make a point of the lack of Scottish examples, given the paucity of early medieval Scottish material in general – an issue raised by Patrick Sims-Williams above.)[21] All of the examples are ecclesiastical; I know of no example of the *use* of written records in lay disputes (that is, use intended to affect the outcome of the dispute). Such records were, however, used in a way in ecclesiastical disputes, in many Celtic areas.

It is of considerable interest that a special word for writing about property, in effect for 'charter-writing', seems to have been used in Brittonic areas in the early Middle Ages. On the list that follows I give the word *chirograph* (meaning 'subscription', 'deed', 'charter' and widely used throughout Europe) at the top, and Brittonic variants beneath. These variants are a distinctive Brittonic usage (the English examples are western); the only other comparable examples cited by Niermeyer, of which there are three, are Italian, where the word *graphia* appears as a feminine noun.[22]

cyrographum

graphium	England/Wales IX-XIIth cent.
grafium	Brittany XIth cent.
grafum	Wales pre-XVIth cent.
grefium	Wales XIth cent.
grefiat	Wales IXth cent.
graffiare	Brittany X–XIth cent.

It is especially interesting that the word chirograph was borrowed into the Welsh language by the tenth (or even ninth) century in the word *grefiat*, which occurs in the Lichfield Gospel *marginale* recording the settlement of a property dispute;[23] and that it occurs in Latin on a stone monument from Merthyr Mawr (*in grefium in proprium*) ('[this was done] in a writing into ownership', perhaps meaning something like 'ownership was registered').[24] In central Brittany, in early tenth-century charters from the bishopric of Vannes, well beyond the recording practices of Redon, the word became the verb *graffiare*, 'to register a change of ownership'.[25] We have here a distinctive usage in Brittonic areas in the ninth to eleventh centuries which underlines the importance of the idea of writing as *permanent* 'proof': it was a type of guarantee, to add to the personal sureties who were those societies' main enforcing mechanisms.

It is interesting to look beyond charter-writing to consider the writing on the Merthyr Mawr stone. Writing as proof of ownership did not have to occur in charters: it could occur in other media, especially on stones (perhaps extending a much older habit, related to the use of boundary stones).[26] The Irish heptad mentioned above refers to immovable stones, symbols of permanence.[27] At Blair Athol in Perthshire there is a low stone called Clach na h-Iobairt ('the stone of the offering', where *iobairt* is the Gaelic equivalent of Latin *immolavit*, a distinctive dispositive word used for making grants in 'Celtic' charters).[28] The eighth-century Kilnasaggart stone in County Armagh also records a grant of the place (*in loc*) it marks to the Apostle Peter, as seventh-/ninth- and eleventh-century Welsh stones found at Llanllŷr (Cardigan) and Ogmore (Glamorgan) record grants too (the latter of a field – *ager* – to God and local saints).[29] People perceived writing as a mechanism for achieving or ensuring permanence of possession or use (absolute ownership was not so important), although they were clearly mistaken in this belief. The same perception led to the writing of charters into Gospel Books and hagiographic texts.[30] These are again techniques for emphasizing permanence, although such writing had other functions too.

ECCLESIASTICAL CHARTER-WRITING AND PROTECTIVE MECHANISMS

In eastern Brittany charters were not only produced in and for village communities. They were also produced by and for the interests of major monasteries and bishoprics. At one level the reason for making the record was much the same as the reason in the villages: it was to demonstrate ownership, especially when there had been a change. To this extent ecclesiastical owners were no different from (lay) peasants. However, the reasons for, and the uses of, charter-writing for large-scale ecclesiastical owners went further. And these further uses were by no means restricted to eastern Brittany.

Let me deal with this in two parts: management and making claims.

By the ninth century ecclesiastical charter-writing was also an aspect of property management; it helped the owner know what rights he had in landed property (an interest also demonstrated by the concern with defining space and with precise boundaries of land, recorded either by short limits or by describing perambulations at length); what income he might expect from it; and from whom and whence he might expect that income. In the case of the east Breton cartulary material, there is a marked difference in the way the monastery of Redon made its records in 850 and thereafter from the way it made them in the two previous decades, 832 to 850: in 832–50 the records were long, elaborate and written in the first person; from 850 they were much shorter, third-person records (although the long form was kept for special people, as in *CR* 35 or *CR* 52).[31] This is significant. The change arises from the increasing volume of business and of data that had to be handled. The years 850–5 mark a phase when the monks' attitude towards management started to change. Under Abbot Ritcant, 867–71, there was some basic organization and re-organization of the Redon archive, and at the same time the abbot was very active in acquiring confirmations of previous grants, making tenants renew tenancies, and persuading dependants to make personal commitments to himself. By 871 the monks must have been very conscious of management.

This development of the management approach is particularly well evidenced at Redon in the ninth century; it is hinted at in Saint-Pol in

105

the late ninth century; and in essence, without the detail, the same is true of Landévennec and its archive, in western Brittany, in the middle of the tenth century.[32] At Landévennec the records were organized geographically; and charters, such as *CL* 22 of its cartulary, were created *ab initio* in the mid-tenth century to provide evidence for renders which must have been regularly received for some time previously. The bishopric of Llandaf, in south Wales, had the same approach to its archive: there was major reorganization in the second quarter of the eleventh century.[33] The monastery of Llancarfan, not far from Llandaf, seems to have been similarly engaged no later than the late eleventh century.[34] It was possibly also true of St Serfs, Loch Leven, in the eleventh century (there are nine St Serfs records, largely eleventh-century but the first dated *c.* 950, in the later 'St Andrews Cartulary', and the record implies that there had been more – originally in Gaelic).[35] This process was certainly happening in Wales and Brittany; and probably in southern Scotland too. I exclude the Book of Armagh collection from northern Ireland, of basically seventh-century documents, copied in the early ninth century.[36] This collection might perfectly reasonably be described as a late eighth-century attempt to establish an ecclesiastical archive, but there is little to suggest that this activity was related to ambitions to manage the lands and the income more efficiently.[37]

Secondly, ecclesiastical charter-writing and record keeping could also be for making claims, and/or establishing or maintaining a proprietary position. Records could be massaged a little in order to support an existing position: at Redon endorsements were added to the Redon copy of a text, or at a time when Redon received a pack of existing documentation with a new property. This meant altering or elaborating or adding to the original text, not necessarily by claiming untrue things or by misrepresenting the situation (although this could happen). Hence, the record of a lay grant of the 850s to a local village priest was emended to read 'grant to a local *monk*' (as the priest subsequently became), so that the priest's property could go with him to the monastery.[38] There were also interpolations to emphasize the totality of ownership of the pledgor if a pledge transaction (a type of mortgage) should never be redeemed, as happened of property in Bains in 835; or to emphasize the totality of ownership of vendor or purchaser, as in Brain in 849.[39] These are reinforcements of the original contents, added to records of transactions which preceded the grants which passed the property to the monastery. They were made

106

in order to make clear that the donor to the monastery really had full powers of alienation. The changes were made to protect the monastery, or add to its protection, by providing some documentary 'proof', from subsequent claims by the donor's family.

Massaging existing texts, by endorsements on the original or expansion in recopying, was certainly not confined to Redon and to eastern Brittany. It is nevertheless very fortunate that such changes can be demonstrated in the Redon collection, because this collection is not regarded as forged, it is early, and the changes are very small-scale. But the same processes happened elsewhere (and not only in Celtic areas, of course). On a larger scale: the first twenty or so charters of the Landévennec Cartulary were put together in the mid-to late tenth century to demonstrate the absorption of small monasteries and churches by the larger community of Landévennec. This was done using a standard format: 'St N [e.g. St Rioc] came and commended himself, and all he owned, to St Winwaloe.' Thereafter Landévennec owned St Rioc's monastery.[40]

It could also take place on a much grander scale: there are cases in the Llandaf collection of charters which seem to have been invented from nothing, from no pre-existing texts (for example *LL* 125a, recording a supposed grant from King Maredudd to St Teilo), although the business was much more usually one of changing and expanding than inventing from scratch. The Llandaf enterprise (episcopal in this case) was altogether large-scale. Reduced to its essentials, it was a process of (i) taking existing text to create an episcopal archive for Llandaf, having inherited the episcopal traditions of other places, rightly or wrongly (Llandeilo Fawr, Welsh Bicknor and so on) – basically a process of the second quarter of the eleventh century; (ii) then in the early twelfth century taking, expanding and elaborating that archive in order to claim a territorial diocese, particularly as against the claims of the neighbouring bishoprics.[41] This twelfth-century activity was extremely elaborate, and involved visits to Rome, presentation of documents to the pope and receipt of papal letters and privileges. The business, partly successful, partly not, was conducted in terms of documents: words and signs were manipulated, for local political and material ends. At this level, charter-writing was about making large claims about local power, property rights and position; and securing public recognition of those claims, whether true or false.

This is an extreme example of the way writing became part of the ecclesiastical armoury, but the methods were not confined to south

Wales, nor to the twelfth century. Churches needed mechanisms to protect themselves against predators, the more property they accumulated, the greater the need. 'Predators' were the people who intruded upon or limited their property rights, from the tenants guilty of very small-scale non-payment of renders to the petty nobles who seized the *convivium* prepared for the bishop and made counter-claims to ownership; they also included the (foreign) rulers who made long-ranging raids. The need for mechanisms was not confined to Celtic areas; however, we certainly become conscious of their development in Celtic areas across the ninth, tenth and eleventh centuries.

The mechanisms were various, and involved developing techniques of persuading people to keep off (that is, respect) church property, or keep *on* it and do what was required of them – dig, pay, harvest and so on. The techniques included the use of ritual – walking bounds and moving about in solemn processions; the use of anathema and cursing, whether practical, liturgical or written (the frequent occurrence of religious sanctions in Celtic charters is distinctive, and stories like that of *CL* 9, in which bad men attack the monastery and come to grief, abound); the development of cult, for property was the possession of the saint and hence protected by him, and gifts could be encouraged from those who benefited from the saint's powers;[42] the development of the specially protected area, within which especial penalties were applied for incursion, such as *noddfeydd* in Wales, 'chartered' and 'privileged' sanctuaries in Cornwall and north Britain;[43] and use of charters, writing, written signs and symbols. It was not just the content of the words that was important but the fact of the writing. Hence, charters were written or copied into Gospel Books, like those of Lichfield (when it was at Llandeilo Fawr), Bodmin, Deer and Kells, as well as the Books of Armagh and Durrow, and the Leofric Missal.[44] Writing in the Gospel Book had several functions: putting the writing in that place gave the transaction especial protection by God and the saints and emphasized the permanence of the gift;[45] recording God as witness, *deus testis* in the Lichfield *marginalia*, also made the point.[46] But it was also a visible symbol to those who looked at the book. It is worth remembering in this context the significance of the topos of blinding: blinding was, hagiographically, what happened if someone ignored the warnings and intruded upon or invaded church property; those who wanted to warn chose this particular topos of blinding for those who could not read the signs.

Charter-writing and its uses in early medieval Celtic societies

Charter-writing is but one of the array of non-military techniques developed by churches to protect themselves; 'peace' oaths were another such technique developed on the Continent.[47] This type of charter-writing is a characteristically ecclesiastical thing. It was particularly notable in the ninth, tenth and eleventh centuries. It was notable in eastern, central and western Brittany in the late ninth century: there is material from Vannes, from Saint-Malo, from Saint-Pol and from Landévennec. In Wales the process is evident from the middle of the ninth century, in the Lichfield *marginalia* initially, and in the earliest of the long Llandaf original narrations. It is evident in Scotland at least in the eleventh and twelfth centuries, in material from Deer and from St Serfs.[48]

In Ireland, by contrast, charter-writing does not seem to have been a major protective technique used in the ninth to eleventh centuries. The notion that the written record had value as proof of ownership was current in Ireland by the late seventh century and was obviously influential in the Armagh sphere in the late seventh and eighth centuries; it is perhaps evident in material collected at eighth-century Lorrha, and it also surfaced later in the copies in the Books of Kells and Durrow which were made in the twelfth century.[49] The influence of charter-writing can also be seen in other traditions, especially those of central southern Ireland, in Latin hagiographic material from Kinnitty, Lismore and Clonfertmulloe;[50] and in texts such as the seventh-/eighth-century *Cáin Éimíne* from Monasterevin, Co. Offaly, whose 'legal core', as Erich Poppe puts it (at clauses 9, 10), is in essence a vernacular derivation from a Latin charter model.[51] It is therefore likely that some charter-writing took place at some centres in Ireland through the ninth to eleventh centuries, and that the charter tradition influenced the formulation of written property claims both in Latin and the vernacular, but it was clearly not taken up in Ireland in the way that it was in other Celtic parts. And when it *was* taken up, it was used in subtly different ways from those of the Brittonic mainstream: the Irish habit of citing the names of guarantors rather than of witnesses indicates a different approach to the transfer of property rights.[52]

Charter-writing had different uses, from visual sign to political argument and evidential dossier. All uses were not equally significant in all Celtic areas. There is, of course, an exceptionally strong ecclesiastical interest in charter-writing, throughout, and an excep-

109

tionally strong ecclesiastical motivation. However, there were circumstances in which it had significance for the laity too. The amount and quality of lay interest and its importance for the laity is arguable but is worth pursuing further. It is, for example, of particular interest that the Kells and Durrow charters are recorded in the vernacular, that the St Serfs charters seem to have been translated from the vernacular (both Irish), and that sections of the Lichfield *marginalia* are in the vernacular (Welsh).[53] This material may well have been more accessible to the laity than Latin texts and may be a hint of wider lay participation than that for which evidence survives. The relationship between writing and permanence, between writing and eternity, is a major social issue and is potentially of as much significance for the property-owning laity as for the clergy. Though change is likely to have been slow, in time the introduction of the new instrument of writing must have brought changes in practice. Our evidence is too patchy for us to trace the rate and course of change, but of the fact of change we should have no doubts.

NOTES

1 See Reuter, 'Property transactions', pp. 169–73.
2 For all this see W. Davies, 'People and places', pp. 65–70.
3 For 'Celtic' charter-writing, see W. Davies, 'Latin charter-tradition'. Additional examples have been identified since the original publication of this paper: see, for example, La Borderie, 'Chartes inédites', 98–9 – located by Julia Smith; Poppe on *Cáin Éimíne*, below nn. 51–2; Brett, 'John Leland', 179–80; and Pryce, 'Church of Trefeglwys'.
4 W. Davies, 'Redon cartulary', 79–80.
5 See Fichtenau, *Urkundenwesen*, pp. 73–87; cf. *traditio per cartam* in Visigothic Spain, Levy, *Vulgar Law*, pp. 146–8, 165–6.
6 *CR*, no. 229; cf. *CR*, no. 228, from nearby, a decade earlier.
7 See further below, p. 102.
8 W. Davies, *Small Worlds*, p. 134.
9 See W. Davies, 'Redon cartulary', 79.
10 Compare the attention paid to recording the witnesses present at transactions in late Roman contexts; the Constantinian legislation on the subject; and the influence of both on early Frankish and Visigothic records: W. Davies, 'Latin charter-tradition', pp. 275–6. Both Breton/Frankish and Irish texts of the seventh/eighth centuries provide for the confirmation of sale (and bequest) by witnesses: 'Excerpta de libris Romanorum et Francorum' in *Irish Penitentials*, ed. Bieler, pp. 140, 144; *Hib.* XXXIV.7, pp. 123–4. See also Tim Reuter's comments, 'Property transactions', p. 188.

11 *CR*, no. 105; cf. W. Davies, 'People and places', pp. 72–3.
12 Bodmin manumissions: Förster, 'Die Freilassungsurkunden'. For some revised dating, see Olson, *Early Monasteries*, pp. 71–2. See also Pelteret, *Slavery*, pp. 131–63.
13 *LL*, pp. xliii, xlvi, for the texts; for full discussion, see Jenkins and Owen, 'Lichfield Gospels Part I'; 'Lichfield Gospels Part II'.
14 See W. Davies, *Small Worlds*, pp. 149–50.
15 *CR*, no. 139.
16 *CR*, no. 195.
17 It is included in the text *Berrad Airechta*, ed. Thurneysen, p. 21, and trans. Stacey, p. 221.
18 W. Davies, 'Latin charter-tradition', p. 268.
19 Ibid.
20 *Chronicles of the Picts*, ed. Skene, p. 188. The text, apparently of mid-twelfth-century origin, is from the lost 'Register of St Andrews', a fourteenth-century collection, of which parts were copied and summarized 1708–29: see Anderson, *Kings and Kingship*, 1st edn, pp. 54–9; see also Miller, 'Disputed historical horizon', 3, 16, 33, for aspects of the textual history.
21 Sims-Williams, above, pp. 18–20.
22 Niermeyer, *Lexicon*, s.v. *graphia*.
23 Jenkins and Owen, 'Lichfield Gospels Part I', 56–61. Their translation emphasizes the permanence associated with the document: 'A document (*grefiat*) [was made] afterwards: Tudfwlch and his kin will not want it for ever and ever [i.e. Tudfwlch will not be without it for ever]' (Jenkins and Owen, 'Lichfield Gospels Part II', 91–2).
24 *ECMW*, no. 240. Cf. the *cirografum* on the Devon stone noted below, n. 29.
25 *CR*, nos. 275, 276, 278.
26 See T. M. Charles-Edwards on the use of stones as property markers in Ireland: 'Boundaries in Irish law', pp. 84–5.
27 See Thornton, above, pp. 92–3, on the permanence of the Pillar of Elisse as a platform for a dynastic claim in its record of the (manipulated) pedigree of Cyngen ap Cadell.
28 Watson, *Celtic Place-Names*, pp. 254, 310.
29 W. Davies, 'Latin charter-tradition', pp. 259, 261; *ECMW*, nos. 124, 255; C. Thomas, *Mute Stones*, pp. 100, 110, n. 31. The (?) late twelfth-century reference to a stone blocking the *cirografum* on a slab in the floor of the church at Stoke near Hartland in north Devon may well be a reference to an inscribed stone with intelligible writing about property – given the specific *cirografum* – pace Charles Thomas's ingenious alternative explanation, *Mute Stones*, pp. 177, 181, n. 24. Cf. the lengthy charter on stone from late ninth-century Milan, *Codex Diplomaticus Langobardiae*, ed. Porro-Lambertenghi, no. 308.
30 See below, p. 108; W. Davies, 'Latin charter-tradition', pp. 271–4; see also below, n. 45.
31 W. Davies, 'Redon cartulary', 77–8.
32 W. Davies, 'Cartulaire de Landévennec', pp. 86–95.
33 W. Davies, *Llandaff Charters*, pp. 23–8.
34 The Llancarfan charters were added to the manuscript containing Lifris's

eleventh-century Life of St Cadog *c.* 1200; nothing suggests that they were created *c.* 1200 and many things in Lifris's Life point to attention to property rights in eleventh-century Llancarfan: see W. Davies, 'Property rights', pp. 525–8.

35 Lawrie, *Early Scottish Charters*, nos. 3, 5, 6, 7, 8, 11, 13, 14, 23; see Anderson, *Kings and Kingship*, 1st edn, pp. 57–8. Cf. Broun, below, p. 188, on translating the Loch Leven records from Gaelic.

36 *Patrician Texts*, ed. Bieler, pp. 166–78.

37 See Sharpe, 'Palaeographical considerations', which includes consideration of the function of the collection; cf. Swift, 'Tírechán's motives'.

38 *CR*, no. 143.

39 *CR*, nos. 199, 58; for more detail, see W. Davies, 'Forgery', pp. 271–2.

40 W. Davies, 'Cartulaire de Landévennec', pp. 93–5. Cf., for the same purposes, *CL*, no. 13, which has reference to a donor who was a *transmarinus*, in other words an alien, a person without kin liable to make counter-claims.

41 W. Davies, *Llandaff Charters*, pp. 23–5.

42 Cf. *CL*, no. 45, where healing by the saint in the early eleventh century resulted in a gift from Count Budic – an entirely credible record with no apparent element of fabrication.

43 Pryce, *Native Law*, pp. 165–74; see also W. Davies, 'Protected space', pp. 7–8.

44 See Jenkins and Owen, 'Lichfield Gospels Part I', 61–6; also W. Davies, 'Latin charter-tradition', p. 259.

45 See further D. Jenkins, 'From Wales to Weltenburg?', pp. 79–86.

46 *LL*, p. xlv; see Jenkins and Owen, 'Lichfield Gospels Part I', 60.

47 For the 'peace of God' movement, see Head and Landes (eds.), *Peace of God*.

48 Jackson, *Gaelic Notes*; Lawrie, *Early Scottish Charters*, nos. 3, 5, 6, 7, 8, 11, 13, 14, 23.

49 For Lorrha, see P. Ó Riain's note on *Leabhar Sochair Lothra*, which he describes as 'an eighth-century charter or revenue book' used by the compilers of the Múscraighe section of the Psalter of Cashel recension of the corpus of secular pedigrees: 'Psalter of Cashel', 117, n. 50.

50 *Vitae Sanctorum Hiberniae*, ed. Plummer: 'Vita Sancti Finani', vol. 2, pp. 89, 92; 'Vita Sancti Carthagi (sive Mochutu)', vol. 1, pp. 195, 196; 'Vita Sancti Moluae', vol. 2, p. 222; cf. 'Vita Sancti Endei', vol. 2, p. 66.

51 See Poppe, 'New edition', 42–4, and Poppe, 'List of sureties', 592.

52 See Poppe, 'List of sureties'. The evidence of *Cáin Éimíne*, as also the much more elaborate list of guarantors of *Cáin Adomnáin*, from a comparable period, demonstrates that the distinctive Irish response to this charter form was already developing in about AD 700: see Ní Dhonnchadha, 'Guarantor list'.

53 See further Flanagan, below, pp. 123–4, 128, on the Irish charters.

6

The context and uses of the Latin charter in twelfth-century Ireland

MARIE THERESE FLANAGAN

The twelfth century saw the introduction of a new form of written record into Ireland, namely the Latin charter in the European tradition, a document which, in its external appearance – its handwriting and method of authentication by a seal – as well as its internal characteristics – its language and formulae – was used increasingly widely in medieval Europe from the late eleventh century onwards and was readily recognizable as a charter.

The earliest extant Latin charter-text in the European tradition attested from Ireland is that of Muirchertach Mac Lochlainn, king of Cenél nEógain, and high king of Ireland, in favour of the Cistercian abbey of Newry, 1156–7.[1] Only two charters issued by Irish kings which pre-date 1200 survive as originals: a charter of Diarmait Mac Murchada, king of Leinster, issued between 1162 and 1165, and a charter of Domnall Ua Briain, king of Thomond, with a date-range of 1168–85.[2] Diarmait Mac Murchada's charter provides secure evidence that the adoption of the Latin charter in the European tradition in Ireland occurred independently of, and before, the Anglo-Norman intervention which began in 1167. In addition to these two originals, eight charter-texts issued by Irish kings (including the above-mentioned charter of Muirchertach Mac Lochlainn) survive in transcripts of later date. The sum total of ten twelfth-century Irish royal charter-texts from six different Irish kings compares adversely with surviving English royal charters: 1,500 in the name of Henry I have been traced, while almost 3,000 charters of Henry II survive, approximately 400 of which are extant as originals;[3] or to take a French analogy, the approximately 360 charter-texts of Louis VI, king of France (1098–1137).[4] In addition to the two surviving original Irish royal charters which predate 1200, six original charters issued by Irish ecclesiastics survive which pre-date 1200, four of which still have seals,[5] as well as approximately forty-five transcripts of charter-texts. Again, this is a very small number by comparison with episcopal charter-texts extant from twelfth-century England. The number of twelfth-century Latin charters of Irish provenance therefore is very small, although it is difficult to gauge just how much, or how little, of the entire corpus may have survived. Following Anglo-Norman intervention, Latin charters were issued by both Anglo-Norman lay lords and ecclesiastics in or relating to Ireland, but my concern here is solely with Latin charters of indigenous provenance which pre-date 1200.

The context for the introduction of the Latin charter in the European tradition into twelfth-century Ireland undoubtedly was the reform movement which dominated the western church from about 1050 onwards and which began to have a discernible impact on the Irish church from no later than 1100. One of the by-products of the church reform movement was the promotion of an international culture, which increasingly bound together the diverse peoples of Europe. The twelfth-century reform movement in Ireland sought to bring about the Europeanization of the Irish church. It is in this context that the adoption in Ireland of the Latin charter in the European tradition most plausibly is placed. All the extant charters from twelfth-century Ireland were issued in favour of ecclesiastical beneficiaries, or by ecclesiastics. The Irish royal charters were issued in favour of monastic houses of reform observances, such as Cistercians and Augustinians, or in one instance in favour of a cathedral church; and the charters issued by Irish ecclesiastics relate overwhelmingly to the disposition of parochial tithes and may be set in the context of a reform strategy for the establishment of diocesan and parochial institutions.

The Irish charters reflect contemporary European usage with regard to language and script. The language of the charters is Latin. The seventh and eighth centuries had been the heyday of the production of Latin texts in Ireland.[6] From the ninth century onwards there was a shift towards the vernacular, illustrated in the increased proportion of entries made in Irish in the annals, and in the production of vernacular saints' lives, liturgical texts and monastic rules; additionally, texts originally written in Latin, including such undemanding and repetitive texts as penitentials, began to be translated into Irish. By the tenth century the Irish literary milieu was dominated by the vernacular, and it is only from about the middle of the eleventh century that there was a slow return to the active use of Latin, which quickened throughout the twelfth century. Reversion to the use of

Latin was a reflection of the fact that some sections of the Irish clergy again began to see themselves as part of a wider clerical and scholarly community and to return to the use of the universal language of western Christendom. The adoption of the Latin charter in the European tradition in twelfth-century Ireland reflects a renewed commitment to the Latin language. From the very accurate spellings of vernacular personal and place-names which the Latin charter-texts contain, including the use of length marks, the Greek *spiritus asper* to indicate lenition and the declension of genitive forms, there can be no doubt that the drafters of the Latin charters were literate in the Irish language and could write it accurately: their choice of Latin was therefore a deliberate one. The Latin charter in the European tradition, however, demanded an ability not just to write Latin, but to write it technically: it required drafters who had a command of the technical format and formulae which distinguished the document as a charter and constituted one of the criteria of its authenticity.

Handwriting also marked a new departure: of the eight extant twelfth-century originals, two royal and six ecclesiastical, none was written in Irish script (or Insular minuscule). All are written either in a Romanesque bookhand, or in a cursive curial or charter hand, which bears analogy with hands developed on the Continent and in England specifically for the writing of documents. The earliest extant original, that of Diarmait Mac Murchada, king of Leinster, datable to between 1162 and 1165, is written in a Romanesque bookhand; it constitutes the earliest surviving example of a non-Insular hand in Ireland (Fig. 7). Its use is noteworthy given that there survive twelfth-century manuscripts written in Ireland containing texts in Latin for which Irish script was employed: for example, a number of Gospel Books and psalters, and also Latin texts, such as pope Gregory the Great's *Moralia in Job*, Clemens Scottus' *Ars grammatica* and Calcidius' commentary on Plato's *Timaeus*.[7] Noteworthy also is the missal now in Corpus Christi College, Oxford, of twelfth-century date in an Irish hand, notwithstanding the fact that it reflects contemporary liturgical usages of the Latin church, rather than the Celtic rite; if Aubrey Gwynn is correct, it was commissioned by Tomaltach Ua Conchobuir, bishop of Elphin, on the occasion of his translation to the see of Armagh, which would date it as late as 1180.[8] The use of Romanesque minuscule for Diarmait Mac Murchada's charter therefore affords evidence of a deliberate choice to conform to the contemporary writing practices of medieval Christendom. It may also

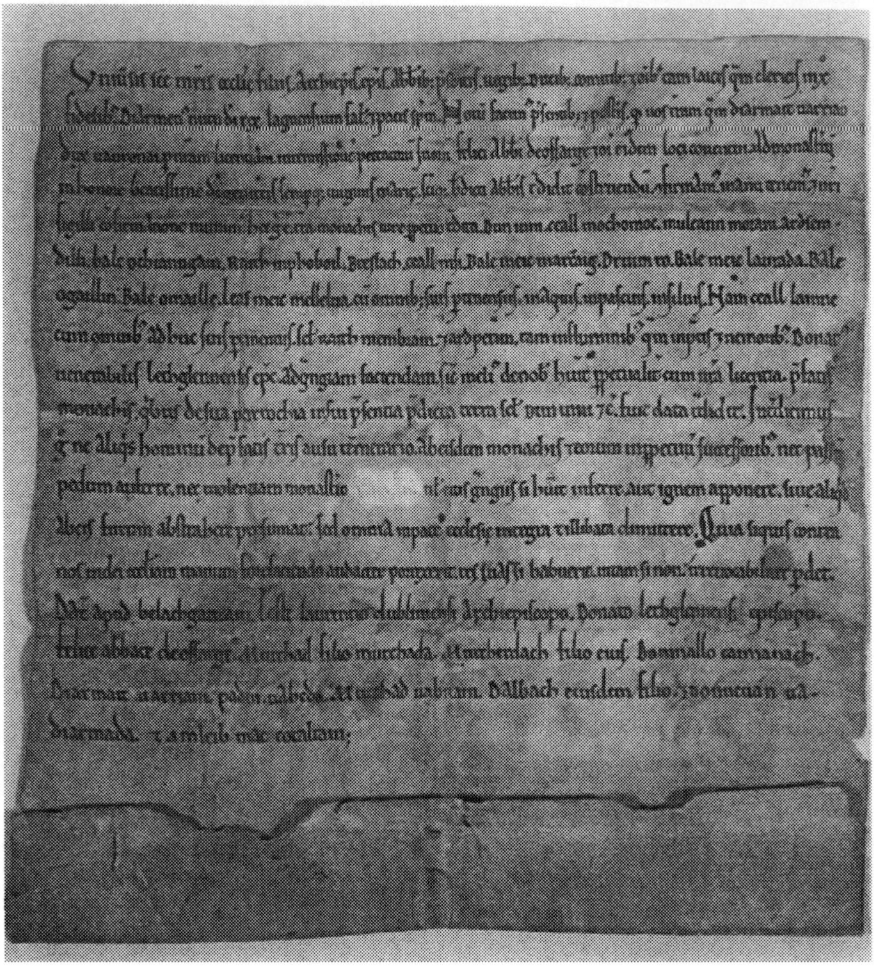

Fig. 7 The only surviving original charter of Diarmait Mac Murchada, issued in favour of Felix, abbot of Osraige, between 1162 and 1165. Dublin, National Library of Ireland, Deed 1.

be said to reveal an awareness of the appropriateness of one kind of script as against another for particular texts. This is borne out by the other extant original twelfth-century charter of an Irish king, that of Domnall Ua Briain, king of Thomond, datable to between 1168 and 1185, which is written in an elaborately elongated curial hand that bears analogy with contemporary scripts of the papal chancery and of the German imperial chancery. The six extant original charters of

116

Irish ecclesiastics, likewise, are all written in non-Irish script, either in bookhands or cursive charter hands.

While Professor Wendy Davies has demonstrated that there was a distinctive Celtic charter-tradition, which is manifest also in Ireland,[9] that tradition had little discernible influence on the Latin charters issued in twelfth-century Ireland. This is perhaps not surprising given the context in which the European Latin charter was introduced, namely a reform movement which had as its aim the Europeanization of the Irish church. Marked regional variations in the Latin charter produced in Ireland would have negated its function as a form of document which had credence throughout western Christendom. Hence, too, the avoidance of Irish script.

While reform-minded Irish ecclesiastics might be expected to deploy the European Latin charter as a badge of the international culture of western Christendom, its adoption by Irish kings also requires explanation. Twelfth century Irish royal charters are clearly a product of collaboration between Irish kings and ecclesiastics. The extant evidence, such as it is, suggests that the charters issued in the name of Irish kings were drafted by the ecclesiastical beneficiaries and presented to the individual kings for authentication by the appending of their seal. Variations in the four extant charter-texts of Diarmait Mac Murchada indicate that it was the beneficiaries and not a royal writing office who drafted the charter-texts. There is no evidence to suggest that Irish kings routinely retained writing offices of their own, or that members of their household were responsible for the actual drafting of the charter-text. This is not unusual in a twelfth-century European context: although by the twelfth century the German emperors, the kings of England and the kings of France had writing offices which were becoming ever more professional, nevertheless it was still not uncommon for an ecclesiastical beneficiary to present a charter to one of these rulers for authentication by his seal.

What is impressive is the extent to which Irish kings were not simply passive agents, but were able actively to exploit the charter-form as a literary vehicle for furthering their own agendas. The charters of Diarmait Mac Murchada, king of Leinster, are appropriate for illustrative purposes, since there survive one original charter issued in his name, the full texts of two other charters, the partial text of a fourth, a paraphrase of a fifth in a later confirmation and mention of a now lost sixth charter, all issued by Mac Murchada prior to Anglo-Norman intervention in Ireland.[10] Additionally, four charter-texts issued in the name of his daughters, Aífe and Derbforgaill, survive; and although they post-date the advent of the Anglo-Normans, nevertheless they serve to emphasize the commitment of the Mac Murchada family to this new form of written document.[11]

Diarmait Mac Murchada's sole surviving original charter was issued in favour of Felix, abbot of Osraige, a Benedictine community which was later to adopt the Cistercian rule and came to be known as the abbey of Killenny.[12] An incomplete text of another charter from Diarmait to Abbot Felix also survives.[13] Both were drafted in the form of confirmations, in which it is stated that Diarmait confirmed lands which had been granted to Felix's monastic community by Diarmait Ua Riain, *dux* of Uí Dróna, the more traditional title of king being denied to Ua Riain. The lands confirmed by Mac Murchada to Killenny are stated to have been granted by Ua Riain with the consent (*per licentiam*) of Diarmait Mac Murchada. The charter also confirms a grant of land and jurisdiction bestowed on Abbot Felix by Dungal Ua Cáellaide, bishop of Leighlin, in whose diocese the monastic community was situated, which similarly is stated to have been made *cum nostra licentia* ('with our consent').

Diarmait Mac Murchada's charter asserted that both Diarmait Ua Riain and Dungal Ua Cáellaide had to seek his consent before they could transfer land or ecclesiastical jurisdiction. The format of a confirmation charter, the use of the royal plural and the denial of a royal title not only to Diarmait Ua Riain in the main body of the text, but also to others of royal status in the witness list, all served to emphasize Mac Murchada's claims as overking of Leinster and were very deliberate choices on the part of the drafter. The charter-text was being deployed as a vehicle of propaganda to articulate the political aspirations of Diarmait Mac Murchada. His superior power is further emphasized by a protection clause forbidding attacks on the monastic community and the threat that any miscreant will forfeit his property, or if he has none, his life, if he breaches the protection now afforded by Diarmait Mac Murchada. It would be unwise to assume that the adoption of a new form of written document necessarily reflected profound changes in political or social realities, but Mac Murchada's charters afford a valuable insight into how he, or his agents, conceived his authority.

The deployment of the European Latin charter as a vehicle of self-proclamation and self-aggrandizement is evident also in Diarmait Mac Murchada's charter in favour of Áed Ua Cáellaide, bishop of Louth, granting land within the Hiberno-Norse kingdom of Dublin to a newly established Augustinian community in the city of Dublin.[14] Mac Murchada is styled not only 'king of the men of Leinster' but also 'king of the men of Dublin'. The charter includes a clause warranting the protection of the community and forbidding the exaction of hospitality or billeting of troops. The church-reform aspiration of freedom from secular exactions is harnessed to advance Mac Murchada's status as overking at the expense of local aristocratic families, who were deprived of the opportunity of exploiting to their advantage church lands in their immediate locality.

When the religious community was situated within the heartland of Mac Murchada's sphere of influence, his relationship, as expressed in his charter, took a somewhat different form: a charter-text in favour of the abbey of Ferns attests to a strategy for retaining influence in a monastic community which was located in the *caput* of his patrimonial kingdom of Uí Chennselaig.[15] Mac Murchada is described as founder of a monastery for Augustinian canons at Ferns; in reality, an Augustinian community was introduced at the pre-existing early Irish ecclesiastical site of Ferns, which had long-standing connections with Mac Murchada's family and had been exploited by it as a centre of influence.[16] A clause guarantees free abbatial election to the Augustinian community, which was to constitute the electoral body in accordance with the rule of St Augustine, and explicitly states that none of Diarmait's heirs shall forcibly intrude themselves into the abbacy, an appropriate stipulation in view of past practices of Mac Murchada's lineage in installing its own nominees in the ecclesiastical offices of the monastery. However, the canonically chosen electee shall be presented *causa dominii* to Diarmait, to his successor or his *senescallus*, in order to secure the lord's assent. In effect, Diarmait was retaining a veto on the election, albeit expressed in terms which conformed with contemporary requirements of canon law. The charter-texts issued in Diarmait Mac Murchada's name indicate a close understanding between Diarmait and his ecclesiastical associates, and an effective exploitation to his advantage both of the charter-form and of reform ideology.

How far was the adoption by Irish kings of the Latin charter in the European tradition pragmatic or functional, how far ideologically inspired? How were these charters intended to be deployed, and how did they relate to contemporary Irish legal procedures regarding transfers of property and rights of jurisdiction? There is a near-total dearth of evidence for legal procedures in twelfth-century Ireland. Some inferences, however, may be drawn by considering the purpose of the Latin charter in the European tradition as deployed on the Continent and in England in the twelfth century. The purpose of a charter was to supply a written record for the future of a legal transaction which had already taken place. That transaction generally took the form of a public ceremony at which the grantor transferred possession to the beneficiary by a symbolic act. Since a charter was intended to provide a written record of an event which had already occurred, its function was evidentiary, not dispositive: that is, the writing of the charter and its transfer to the grantee did not constitute a juridical act of bestowal. This distinction explains why charters were cast in the form of an openly sealed letter and couched in the past tense, informing a general public of an event which had already taken place; and since the charter recorded a past event, a time-date was not normally considered necessary. Since it was the public declaration and transfer in the presence of witnesses that constituted the valid legal act, not every grant was necessarily accompanied by a charter. The written record was optional and additional, not essential.

The function of the Latin charter in the European tradition adopted in twelfth-century Ireland can also be assumed to have been probative or evidentiary, not dispositive, given that the charters conform to standard practice in being cast in the past tense, with a general address and no time-date, and not least because there is so little evidence for the routine use of documentary records in property transactions in pre-Norman Ireland. The charters may be presumed to have served as an optional written record of a past event. As such, they could be of practical use to their ecclesiastical beneficiaries as one of a number of strategies which might be deployed to protect and preserve church property.[17] But from the viewpoint of the Irish kings who issued them, charters, given their optional and probative nature, may have been as much symbolic as functional, and their symbolic attributes, in turn, afforded Irish kings the possibility of exploiting them as vehicles of propaganda.

Placing the adoption by Irish kings of the European Latin charter in the context of the twelfth-century church reform movement must necessarily accord to ecclesiastics a major role in its introduction and production. None the less, although the charter-texts undoubtedly were drafted for the most part by ecclesiastics, the degree to which Irish royal charters contain echoes of other contemporary royal *acta* is noteworthy and affords clear evidence of their deployment as vehicles of royal propaganda. A charter of Diarmait Mac Carthaig, king of Desmond, of about 1173–7,[18] reflects stylistic influence from the German imperial chancery. The royal style, 'Diarmitius divina favente clementia rex Momiensium', may be compared with contemporary charters of, for example, Emperor Frederick I, where the form is 'Fridericus divina favente clementia imperator Romanorum'.[19] Although Diarmait Mac Carthaig was no more than king of Desmond, or the southern half of Munster, he is grandiloquently and exaggeratedly described as king of the men of Munster. Like Diarmait Mac Murchada, Diarmait Mac Carthaig deployed the charter as a means of self-proclamation and self-aggrandizement. Another echo of contemporary German imperial charters is the phrase 'in nostram tuitionem suscepimus'.[20] German influence in a charter of Diarmait Mac Carthaig need not occasion surprise, given the known involvement of Diarmait's family in the *Schottenklöster* of southern Germany and Austria. In the late eleventh century a number of monastic communities of Irish origin were established in southern Germany, foremost among them the monastery of St James at Regensburg which was to become the mother-house of a congregation of houses following the Benedictine rule, and which actively sought Irish recruits.[21] These communities, which enjoyed imperial patronage, and incidentally were in receipt of imperial charters, maintained contact with their homeland and forged particularly close links with Munster. A direct link with the Mac Carthaig family was occasioned by the fact that Christianus, third abbot of Regensburg, was a kinsman of Cormac Mac Carthaig, father of Diarmait whose charter-text survives; Abbot Christianus is known to have undertaken at least two fund-raising and recruiting missions to Munster, on the second of which he died and was buried in the church of Cashel.[22]

The monastery of Regensburg had a very active scriptorium in the twelfth century which was prepared to divert some of its resources to producing texts which actively promoted the kings of Munster, both the Meic Carthaig and the Uí Briain. In the *Visio Tnugdali*, or Otherworld Vision of Tnugdal, which was written by an Irish monk at Regensburg in 1148–9, during the abbacy of Christianus Mac Carthaig, pride of place among the denizens of heaven went to Cormac Mac Carthaig, king of Munster, whom Tnugdal in his vision saw in a beautiful palace decorated with gold, silver and precious stones, sitting on a golden throne and being served by all the pilgrims and poor whom he had helped during his lifetime.[23] The Vision of Tnugdal, with prominence afforded to Cormac Mac Carthaig, serves to highlight both the direct channels between Regensburg and the Meic Carthaig in the twelfth century, and the preparedness of *Schottenklöster* to further the political cause of their Irish patrons by disseminating pro-Mac Carthaig propaganda. At about the same time the Ua Briain kings of Thomond, or north Munster, were able to avail themselves of the services of a hagiographer who had been trained in southern Germany and also exhibited strong imperialist tendencies, and who wrote a Life of St Flannan of Killaloe depicting him as the patronal saint of the Ua Briain family.[24] It is in this context of demonstrable continental contacts that the elaborate elongated script of Domnall Ua Briain's charter in favour of Holycross Abbey should be placed, a script which bears close analogy with the contemporary usage of the papal chancery. It may also be borne in mind that Domnall Ua Briain's great-grandfather Toirrdelbach (d. 1089) had been in receipt of a letter from Pope Gregory VII, which is known only because it survives in a twelfth-century manuscript of Worcester provenance.[25] It is impossible to gauge how many other papal letters, or what other continental correspondence, the Uí Briain, or other Irish kings, may have received.

While Diarmait Mac Carthaig's charter affords the clearest evidence of direct channels of transmission from the Continent to Ireland during the twelfth century, there are some suggestive indications of continental influence in other Irish royal charters. Diarmait Mac Murchada's charter in favour of Áed Ua Cáellaide, bishop of Louth, is headed by the invocation 'in nomine sancte et individue trinitatis' ('in the name of the holy and undivided Trinity'). This is a feature of continental royal charters, both French and German; it does not occur in English royal charters, or very rarely so, although it occurs in England in ecclesiastical contexts.[26] Diarmait's charters in favour of Felix, abbot of Osraige, use the royal style 'nutu dei rex' ('king by the will of God'), which also suggests continental rather than English influence.[27] Other continental reflexes include a preference for the verb *tradere* ('to hand over') over *dare* ('to give') and the use of the phrase *sigillo signare* ('to mark with a seal'). Evidence for continental transmission of the Latin charter to Ireland is strong, and arguably stronger than for borrowings into Ireland via Britain. Diarmait Mac Murchada was in receipt of a letter of confraternity from Bernard of Clairvaux, which survives only in a continental letter collection.[28]

The context and uses of the Latin charter in twelfth-century Ireland

About 1162 Pope Alexander III addressed a letter to an Irish king in which the pope referred to a letter that he had received from the Irish king.[29] The king's name was not transcribed in the letter collection in which the papal letter has been preserved, but the pope mentions his association with the abbot of Mellifont (Co. Louth) and he may possibly have been Muirchertach Mac Lochlainn, king of Cenél nEógain, and claimant to the high kingship of Ireland, whose charter to Newry Abbey constitutes the earliest surviving charter-text of an Irish king.

By comparison with discernible continental influence, evidence for a pre-existing Celtic charter tradition influencing the European Latin charter as used in twelfth-century Ireland is much slighter. Possible evidence is afforded by Muirchertach Mac Lochlainn's charter-text to Newry Abbey, which may be dated to 1156–7.[30] In the witness list of this charter Gilla Mac Liag, archbishop of Armagh, is described as holding the staff of Jesus in his hand ('tenens baculum Iesu in manu sua'). The *Bachall Isú* ('staff of Jesus') was one of the most important insignia of the head of the church of Armagh. The phrase bears analogy with a vernacular charter of Celtic type relating to a transaction of about 1033–49 which was transcribed into the Book of Kells in the third quarter of the twelfth century, in which the list of sureties is headed by Amalgaid, 'comarba Pátraic co mbachaill Isu' ('successor of Patrick with the staff of Jesus').[31] There is also a vernacular Celtic-type charter in the name of Muirchertach Mac Lochlainn in the Book of Kells, which may be dated to about 1161 and in which Gilla Mac Liag is named, but there he is referred to simply as *comarba Pátraic*.[32] A direct correspondence between Muirchertach's Latin charter and the vernacular charter in his name in the Book of Kells is not therefore apparent.

Another possible instance of influence of a pre-existing Celtic charter tradition on the European Latin charter in twelfth-century Ireland is the occurrence of the phrase *testes et fideiussores* ('witnesses and sureties') in Muirchertach Mac Lochlainn's charter to Newry Abbey. The use of the nominative form in the witness list and the inclusion of the term *fideiussores* is distinctive; more usual was the ablative *testibus* or *hiis testibus*. It could be argued that the *testes et fideiussores* of Muirchertach Mac Lochlainn's charter to Newry affords evidence for a borrowing from the Celtic charter tradition, and represents a Latin rendering of the vernacular pairs *slána ocus dílse, slána ocus ráta* or *slána ocus soire, commairche ocus slána,*

123

attested in the vernacular charters in the Book of Kells. The Latin term *fideiussor* occurs in the *Collectio Canonum Hibernensis* compiled *c.* AD 700, where it is used as a general term for surety, while *stipulator* was used more specifically for the enforcing surety and an artificial Latin term *rata* was coined to correspond to the Irish *ráth* or paying surety.[33] However, *fideiussor* can occur also in non-Celtic contexts, such as German imperial charters of the twelfth century,[34] so that even if its inclusion in Muirchertach Mac Lochlainn's Newry charter was influenced by a pre-existing indigenous charter tradition (and the evidence is inconclusive) it might occur also in the context of the European Latin charter.

Another possible reflex of an indigenous charter tradition is the fact that a significant number of the Latin charters issued by Irish kings are in favour of named individuals who are given more prominence than the corporate institutions which they represented. Diarmait Mac Murchada's charter, which is described often as the foundation charter of Killenny Abbey, was issued in favour of Abbot Felix of Osraige; and what is usually termed Mac Murchada's foundation charter for All Hallows, Dublin was issued in favour of Áed Ua Cáellaide, bishop of Louth, in his capacity as head of the Augustinian communities in Ireland which were affiliated to Arrouaise.[35] Similarly, Domnall Ua Briain issued a charter in favour of Bishop Brictius of Limerick rather than the cathedral church of St Mary, Limerick, while Domnall's charter to Holycross Abbey named Abbot Gregory.[36] The naming of specific individuals as beneficiaries instead of, or alongside, the corporate institution which they represented may also be said to be a feature of the vernacular charters in the Celtic tradition entered into the Book of Kells, where the founder saint, or his contemporary successor, is named. Possibly this reflects a specifically Irish concept of ecclesiastical property as a benefit enjoyed by an individual during his lifetime, rather than the property of a corporate institution. But apart from these few possible instances, evidence for the impact of an indigenous charter tradition on the Latin charters issued in twelfth-century Ireland is slight.

By comparison with the extant Latin charters issued in the name of Irish kings, those issued by Irish ecclesiastics exhibit fewer individual features; they have the appearance of more routine documents and afford less forensic evidence, which makes it more difficult to pinpoint possible channels of transmission and influence. With only one possible exception,[37] no *acta* from Irish ecclesiastics survive which pre-date Anglo-Norman intervention, although they must have existed: the context of the twelfth-century church reform movement, which saw a major redistribution of landed resources and ecclesiastical jurisdiction to bishops of newly established territorial dioceses, would have provided ample opportunity for the use of charters as probative documents. Dungal Ua Cáellaide, bishop of Leighlin, for example, may have issued a charter in favour of Felix, abbot of Osraige, although his involvement with the Osraige community is known only via Diarmait Mac Murchada's confirmation charter.

A substantial number of the twelfth-century ecclesiastical charter-texts which do survive owe their preservation to the circumstances of Anglo-Norman intervention: almost all are contained in cartularies of fourteenth- and fifteenth-century date from religious houses which enjoyed Anglo-Norman patronage. The greatest number of twelfth-century Irish episcopal charter-texts survives in the cartulary of St Thomas's Abbey, Dublin, an abbey founded by Henry II in 1177 in reparation for the murder of Thomas Becket, and which was patronized almost exclusively by Anglo-Normans.[38] This necessarily means that the twelfth-century Irish episcopal charters which it contains relate only to areas which experienced Anglo-Norman settlement and post-date 1167, and this, in turn, may distort the evidence regarding their use by Irish ecclesiastics as well as their survival.

Given the chronological and geographical limitations of surviving twelfth-century Irish episcopal *acta* it is difficult to gauge how far and for what purposes the Irish episcopate used written *acta* before the Anglo-Norman incursion. Pope Alexander III in his letter addressed to the Irish bishops in 1172 stated that they had given letters under their seals to Henry II.[39] The use of seals pre-supposes the routine issue of documents. The decrees of the reforming synods of Cashel, Ráith Bressail and Kells must have circulated as written texts, possibly under the seals of the bishops. The chance nature of the survival of evidence relating to the twelfth-century church reform movement in Ireland cannot be overemphasized. It is highlighted by the fact that the only extant reform tract, Bishop Gilbert of Limerick's *De Statu Ecclesiae* of c. 1111, survives in manuscripts of English provenance.[40] And a very different assessment of the church reform movement might be made were it not for St Bernard of Clairvaux's Life of St Malachy of Armagh and the continental Life of St Laurence O'Toole.

Almost all the Irish episcopal charters which pre-date 1200 relate to grants or confirmations of tithes or ecclesiastical benefices to monastic houses patronized by Anglo-Normans. By 1152, the year in which the synod of Kells met under the auspices of the papal legate, Cardinal John Paparo, who gave formal papal ratification to the Irish diocesan structure, the reform party in the Irish church had succeeded in the formidable task of establishing a hierarchical episcopate of primate, archbishops and bishops, and a territorial framework of dioceses and provinces analogous to the jurisdictional structures of western Christendom. However, it is generally agreed that within the individual dioceses the task of organizing a pastoral ministry around local churches with territorially delimited parishes, in which a resident priest was to be supported by the collection of tithes from his flock, was less well advanced, and that Anglo-Norman intervention in Ireland contributed materially to the spread, if not to the initiation, of the parish network. The ecclesiastical canons, which Gratian had revived, vested the stewardship of tithes and of landed revenues in the bishop of the diocese and not in individual local churches.[41] The Anglo-Norman settlers generally chose to allocate the ecclesiastical revenues of their newly acquired Irish lands to monastic houses of Anglo-Norman foundation. This meant that Irish bishops necessarily had to be involved in the process of Anglo-Norman settlement, since in accordance with canon law they had to assent to the appropriation of tithes to monastic houses.

On the evidence of the extant twelfth-century charter-texts of Irish bishops, Anglo-Norman settlers did secure the consent of Irish bishops to allocate parochial tithes and ecclesiastical benefices to monastic houses of their choice. While the charters of the Irish bishops recording these appropriations were, like those of the twelfth-century Irish kings, probative documents providing a written record of dispositive acts which had taken place, they nevertheless might be said to have had a more immediately practical use. Ecclesiastical benefices and lands came within the remit of ecclesiastical courts. The charters issued by Irish bishops might be produced as evidence in ecclesiastical courts, which were, in effect, the bishops' own courts. Confirmations of charters of their immediate predecessors, issued by Irish bishops, suggest that the circumstances arising from Anglo-Norman intervention may have stimulated recourse to charters: the upheaval in landholding caused by Anglo-Norman incursions, which gave rise to speculative and sometimes conflicting grants, may have increased recourse to the written testimony of charters, and this circumstance may be reflected in the surviving episcopal *acta* and may have had a distorting effect on the evidence.

Twelfth-century Irish episcopal *acta* convey the impression of ready co-operation on the part of Irish bishops with Anglo-Norman settlers in the disposition of ecclesiastical benefices. Irish bishops may have exploited Anglo-Norman intervention as an opportunity for transforming local proprietary churches, churches which were in lay ownership or lay control, into parish churches; they may have consented to their appropriation in the expectation that suitable reform-trained clergy for those parish churches would then be provided by the monastic orders. While the twelfth-century *acta* of Irish bishops implicitly conceded a right to the secular Anglo-Norman lord to allocate the ecclesiastical benefices of newly acquired lands to monastic communities, from the bishop's standpoint this may have had the positive benefit of recovering churches and church lands from entrenched local lay control, and of staffing those churches with appropriately trained clergy at a time when there may have been a shortage in Ireland. The reiteration by twelfth-century Irish synods of the need for payment of tithes by the laity reflects the economic pressures on the new diocesan structure. The difficulties which bishops may have had in ensuring a secure source of income and maintenance for themselves and their secular clergy must be borne in mind. The ability of twelfth-century Irish reforming bishops to issue Latin charters in the European tradition, which accorded also with the contemporary documentary practices of the incoming Anglo-Normans, could be strategically deployed by them as one of a variety of mechanisms at the expense of secularized or unreformed clergy, who had not acquired the technical expertise to draft such charters. In furthering the development of parochial structures, parchment may have been as useful as the sword. Just as Irish kings may have exploited the European Latin charter to further their own self-aggrandizing agendas, so Irish bishops also may have been able to exploit it as an agent of reform.

The adoption of the European Latin charter in twelfth-century Ireland should be set in the context of forces both without and within Ireland which were working to shape a new international culture and to make the Irish church a part of it. However, those very forces promoting uniformity might also have a fragmenting impact, for in the process of trying to achieve uniformity, new divisions in society might be created, divisions which could develop into reaction and protest. Certainly, there is evidence for a reactive, if not reactionary, response from some Irish churchmen in the twelfth century. The impact of the reform movement in traditional ecclesiastical circles is indicated by the restructuring of the Columban filiation of churches which took place under Abbot Flaithbertach Ua Brolcháin of Derry, who, by espousing the cause of reform, secured a shift in the headship of the Columban federation from Kells to Derry in the middle of the twelfth century.[42]

The insertion of vernacular charters and memoranda into the Gospel Book of Kells in the third quarter of the twelfth century may represent a defensive response on the part of unreconstructed local clergy of the church at Kells. The latest entry inserted into the Book of Kells recorded a confirmation by Muirchertach Mac Lochlainn, in his capacity as high king of Ireland, of freedom from secular exactions to the church of Ardbraccan, Co. Meath, which may be dated on internal evidence to about 1161.[43] This written record inserted into the Book of Kells was contemporaneous with the actual grant of immunity. Assuming that an original document may have lain behind the entry, and there is no evidence to suggest what the physical appearance of a Celtic-type charter might have been, it is difficult to explain the impetus for transcribing it into the Book of Kells at a date so nearly contemporaneous with the transaction, unless there was a perceived need to invest it with the authority afforded by a venerable Gospel Book. On the evidence of Muirchertach Mac Lochlainn's Latin charter to Newry Abbey, about 1156–7, Muirchertach possessed a seal and was in a position by that date to authenticate Latin charters in the European tradition. That the Kells clergy did not obtain such a Latin charter from Muirchertach may have been determined by the fact that they were incapable of drafting it themselves, that they did not have access to the technical expertise. The next best which they could manage was a vernacular record in the style of a Celtic-type charter inserted into the Book of Kells, as a means of investing it with authenticity at a time when the Latin charter and the seal pendant were not only in use in twelfth-century Ireland but had been used by Muirchertach Mac Lochlainn.

A problem which remains unconsidered is the possible tensions and divisions between vernacular Irish culture and international Latin culture which may have manifested themselves as the church-reform movement gathered momentum in Ireland in the second half of the twelfth century. A return to the use of Latin was a reflection of the fact that Irish clergy once again began to see themselves as part of Latin Christendom. That readjustment, however, cannot have been effected without tensions within the ranks of the learned élite; it may have created a rift between those who remained committed to the vernacular Irish literary tradition and those who were opting for international Latin culture. We may speculate on how far the Latin charter in the European tradition may have been used by the advocates of church reform in Ireland as an ideological medium, as a badge of the reform party. Its potential for restrictiveness could have been exploited, in that it could exclude those elements of the Irish clergy, or learned élite, who had not embraced the revived use of Latin and acquired the technical expertise to draft charters and use the appropriate form of handwriting. The Latin charter could have been exploited by the reform party as a defining attribute of group identification and group exclusiveness. The literary form and style made the charters part of the discourse of Latin Christendom, and afforded reforming churchmen the opportunity of exploiting a new written medium at the expense of those who remained committed to vernacular Irish culture and the unreconstructed Irish church.

All the extant Latin charter-texts from twelfth-century Ireland were written by or for ecclesiastics. From the viewpoint of churchmen, charters served the practical function of providing written evidence which might be deployed as one of a series of strategies by churches for the protection of their property. While allowing for this practical function, an ideological dimension was relevant to the twelfth-century Irish context in which the Latin charter in the European tradition was adopted, for both the ecclesiastics who drafted and issued charters and the kings in whose name they were produced. The European Latin charter was exploited effectively as a vehicle of self-promotion by, or on behalf of, those Irish kings who had access to it via their support for the church-reform movement. It was deployed as a form of propaganda to proclaim and elevate their royal status at the expense of political rivals, and to signify their membership of a wider community of European rulers. From the standpoint of Irish ecclesiastics, alongside its utilitarian function as a protective device for church property the Latin charter additionally may have conveyed an ideological message, signifying a commitment to and conformity with the norms of contemporary western Christendom; and Anglo-Norman intervention may have afforded other opportunities to Irish ecclesiastics to exploit the international currency of this literary medium, which was common also to Anglo-Norman society, at the expense of more conservative Irish groups.

The Latin charter in the European tradition adopted in twelfth-century Ireland may be presumed to have had both ideological and pragmatic dimensions. There was always a close linkage between the practical use of writing and its symbolic function in medieval society, and the two cannot realistically be separated. None the less, it may be suggested that the symbolic functions of the European Latin charter were more immediately significant in twelfth-century Ireland than any practical uses. The Latin charter could function as a privileged mode of communication – initially, at any rate, even a somewhat artificial mode of communication, in that it was based on a documentary form which ultimately derived from an external source outside the established Irish written tradition. Anglo-Norman intervention in Ireland from 1167 onwards was to provide Irish ecclesiastics, if not Irish kings, with further opportunities to expand the practical functions of this particular written medium.

NOTES

1 Dugdale, *Monasticon*, vol. 6, part 2, pp. 1133–4; O'Donovan, 'Charter of Newry'; this and other charters discussed here will be included in my forthcoming edition of Irish royal charters.

2 Butler and Bernard, 'Charters of Duiske', 5–6; for Domnall Ua Briain's charter see *Facsimiles*, ed. Gilbert, vol. 2, no. lxii; Dugdale, *Monasticon*, vol. 6, part 2, p. 1137. The seals are missing from both charters.

3 Mortimer, 'Charters of Henry II', 119.

4 Fawtier, *Capetian Kings*, p. 8.

5 For an original charter of Malachy, bishop of Down (1176–1202), see Richardson, 'Some Norman monastic foundations'; for a charter of the canons of Holy Trinity *c.* 1176–8, and of Laurence, archbishop of Dublin, *c.* 1176–8, see Sheehy, 'Diplomatica', 126–8; for charters of Cristin, bishop of Louth, *c.* 1190, of Donatus, prior of Louth, *c.* 1188–97, of Matthew, archbishop of Cashel, *c.* 1198–1206 and of Thomas, abbot of Glendalough, *c.* 1200–7, see *Calendar of Ormond Deeds*, vol. 1, nos. 9, 12, 16, 20.

6 Evidenced in the listings in Lapidge and Sharpe, *Bibliography*.

7 Ibid., nos. 529, 530, 531; Byrne, *One Thousand Years*, nos. 5, 6, 7, 8; Bischoff and Bieler, 'Fragmente'.

8 Gwynn, 'Irish missal', and *idem*, 'Tomaltach Ua Conchobair', 260–273.

9 W. Davies, 'Latin charter-tradition'.

10 For an additional charter to Felix, abbot of Osraige, see Butler and Bernard, 'Charters of Duiske', 7; charter to All Hallows, Dublin, in *Registrum Prioratus Omnium Sanctorum*, ed. Butler, pp. 50–1; charter to Ferns in Dugdale, *Monasticon*, vol. 6, part 2, pp. 1141–2; a confirmation by John, lord of Ireland, to the Cistercian abbey of Baltinglass refers to a charter of Diarmait Mac Murchada 'sicut carta memorati regis Darmatii quam ipsi habent testatur': Nicholls, 'Charter of John', 191; a charter issued by Richard fitz Gilbert, alias Strongbow, to Thomas, abbot of Glendalough, confirmed him in the abbacy and its possessions 'sicut mihi in verbo veritatis Diarmicius rex testatus est': *Chartae, Privilegia et Immunitates*, p. 1; *Crede Mihi*, ed. Gilbert, pp. 46–7. It is possible that Thomas had also received a charter, or charters, from Diarmait Mac Murchada.

11 *Chartularies of St Mary's*, ed. Gilbert, vol. 1, pp. 31–2; *Crede Mihi*, ed. Gilbert, p. 50; Flanagan, *Irish Society*, p. 125.

12 The complex background is discussed in Ó Conbhuidhe, 'Origins of Jerpoint'.

13 Above, n. 10.

14 Ibid.

15 Ibid.

16 Doherty, 'Irish hagiographer'.

17 Cf. W. Davies, above, pp. 106–9.

18 Blake, 'Dermot Mac Carthy's charter'; Webster, *History of the Diocese of Cork*, pp. 375–6.

19 'Frederick with the favour of divine clemency emperor of the Romans'; *Urkunden Friedrichs I.*, ed. Appelt, vols. 2 and 3, *passim*.

20 'We have received into our protection'; *Urkunden Konrads III.*, ed. Hausmann, pp. 11, 35, 74, 129, 248, 273, 283, 309, 338, 367, 420, 434, 459–60, 463 and *passim*; *Urkunden Friedrichs I.*, ed. Appelt, vol. 2, pp. 756, 761–2, vol. 3, pp. 570, 574–5.

21 P. A. Breatnach, 'Origins of the Irish monastic tradition' and the references there cited, and also his edition of *Die Regensburger Schottenlegende*.

22 Ibid., pp. 62–3, 253–60.

23 *Visio Tnugdali*, ed. Wagner; Picard and de Pontfarcy, *Vision of Tnugdal*, pp. 144–5. A notice of Diarmait Mac Carthaig's death in 1185 was incorporated into the annals kept at the *Schottenkloster* of Vienna: Ó Riain-Raedel, 'Twelfth- and thirteenth-century Irish annals', 132; *obits* for both Cormac and Diarmait Mac Carthaig were incorporated into the necrology of the *Schottenklosterkongregation: eadem*, 'Irish kings and bishops', 401–3. For the Munster bias of the hagiographical pursuits of the *Schottenklöster*, see also *eadem*, 'Aspects of the promotion'.

24 Ó Corráin, 'Foreign connections'.

25 Sheehy, *Pontificia Hibernica*, vol. 1, no. 2. Toirrdelbach Ua Briain also received a letter from Lanfranc, archbishop of Canterbury: *Letters of Lanfranc*, ed. Clover and Gibson, no. 10.

26 Cf. *Urkunden und erzählende Quellen*, ed. Helbig and Weinrich, where, of 150 charters comprising imperial, episcopal and comital charters, 65 contain the invocation *in nomine sancte et individue trinitatis* and a further 23 contain variations such as *in nomine domini Amen*.

27 Dabbs, *Dei Gratia*, pp. 89–91.

28 Flanagan, *Irish Society*, p. 103, n. 80.

29 Falkenstein, 'Ein vergessener Brief'.
30 See above, n. 1.
31 *Notitiae*, ed. MacNiocaill, p. 10, and *idem*, 'Irish charters', p. 157. For other instances of the identity and status of clerics being described in terms of the insignia which accompanied them, see *Notitiae*, ed. MacNiocaill, pp. 18–19, and *idem*, 'Irish charters', pp. 156–7.
32 *Notitiae*, ed. MacNiocaill, pp. 34–7, and *idem*, 'Irish charters', p. 159.
33 *Hib.*, Bk XXXIV, pp. 122–4; Sheehy, 'Influences'.
34 Cf. *Urkunden Friedrichs I.*, ed. Appelt, vol. 3, pp. 58, line 34, 474, line 19.
35 Flanagan, 'St Mary's Abbey'.
36 *Black Book of Limerick*, ed. MacCaffrey, p. 34, and see also above n. 2.
37 *Crede Mihi*, ed. Gilbert, pp. 55–6; *Calendar of Archbishop Alen's Register*, ed. MacNeill, p. 8.
38 *Register of the Abbey of St Thomas*, ed. Gilbert, pp. 209–11, 219–23, 252–60, 285, 291–4, 311–13.
39 Sheehy, *Pontificia Hibernica*, vol. 1, no. 5.
40 Lapidge and Sharpe, *Bibliography*, no. 312.
41 Morris, *Papal Monarchy*, pp. 221, 389–92, 531, 536.
42 Herbert, *Iona, Kells, and Derry*, pp. 109–23.
43 See above, n. 32.

7

Written text as performance: the implications for Middle Welsh prose narratives

SIONED DAVIES

Over the past thirty years the study of orality and literacy, and the interaction between them, has developed into an extremely fruitful multi-disciplinary field of research. Much scholarship has concentrated on the *effects* of literacy, the main thesis being that literacy leads to a number of social, literary and cognitive changes.[1] The contention is that the development of writing (and communication media in general, including print and telecommunication) leads to general developments or social patterns, which are seen as beneficial to society – the results of literacy are discussed in such terms as 'progress', 'development', 'modernization'.[2] This 'autonomous' model, informed by technological determinism, has been challenged in particular by Street's 'ideological' model and Finnegan's 'weak' theory of literacy.[3] They argue that the picture is far more complex, and that the effects of literacy may be diverse rather than single. To them, the 'Great Divide Theory', a term coined by Finnegan, claims too much; literacy and orality have co-existed and interacted along the centuries, and continue to do so. As Street emphasizes, 'the social reality is always a mix'.[4] This is certainly true of medieval Wales.

This essay will focus on the collection of eleven medieval Welsh prose tales known as the *Mabinogion*, a collective title which was first used in Lady Charlotte Guest's English translation of the tales.[5] It must be stressed that the term is almost certainly a scribal error found in a single manuscript. Nevertheless, it has become a convenient label to describe this corpus of medieval tales, although they should not be perceived as a unified collection of any kind – they all vary in date, authorship, sources, background and content. The eleven tales survive in the Red Book of Hergest (*c.* 1400), while ten (some incomplete) are to be found in the White Book of Rhydderch (*c.* 1350).[6] Fragments also occur in manuscripts earlier by a hundred years or so. It is unclear whether the texts represent the earliest attempts at recording narrative prose in the Welsh language, or whether they are merely the earliest surviving examples.[7] The chronology and dating of the tales are also problematic, which complicates issues concerning the relationship between individual texts. However, it is probably safe to assume that they were written down some time between the end of the eleventh and the beginning of the fourteenth centuries, against a background of vast change in the history of Wales.[8] During this period the Welsh struggled to retain their independence in the face of the Anglo-Norman conquest which ultimately transformed the society, economy and church of Wales. On a cultural level there were changes too: for example, foreign influences on native prose and poetry, although it must be remembered that literary influences were not all one-way, as reflected clearly in the transmission of Welsh Arthurian material to the Continent. As regards content, the tales vary greatly. Resonances of Celtic mythology are found in the *Four Branches of the Mabinogi*, as the author uses traditional material to reinforce his own views regarding proper social conduct. *Culhwch and Olwen*'s dove-tailing of two well-known international themes, the Giant's Daughter and the Jealous Stepmother, serves as a framework for a series of independent Arthurian tales, in which Arthur, together with warriors such as Cai and Bedwyr, helps Culhwch win his bride. The relationship between *Owein, Peredur* and *Gereint* (known collectively as the three 'romances') and the corresponding metrical romances of Chrétien de Troyes has been a source of much controversy. The Welsh romances certainly betray foreign influences, yet remain structurally and stylistically within the Welsh narrative tradition. *The Encounter of Lludd and Llefelys* first appears, in an abbreviated form, in a thirteenth-century translation of Geoffrey of Monmouth's *Historia Regum Britanniae*. The story relates how Lludd overcomes three oppressions that came to Britain, and draws on the same pseudo-historical background as *The Dream of Maxen*. In his dream, the Roman emperor Magnus Maximus meets a maiden whom he eventually marries, and this is followed by a collection of onomastic tales and an account of the founding of Brittany. A second dream, *The Dream of Rhonabwy*, presents a satirical view of the Arthurian past, and is an extremely sophisticated piece of writing, probably the latest tale of the corpus.[9]

These eleven tales are not written versions of oral stories, but rather the result of composition-in-writing. However, it is certain that the authors were drawing on oral material to varying degrees: these are what can be termed as 'oral-derived texts' rather than 'unambiguously oral texts'.[10] The author of the *Four Branches of the Mabinogi*, for example, states clearly on three separate occasions that he is drawing on *cyfarwyddyd* (traditional tales), implying that he is using more than one tale and combining them to form a composite work.[11] If the authors of the written texts are to a large extent dependent on traditional material as regards *what* they say, then is the same true of *how* they say it? Or are the stylistic features of the written texts totally divorced from the oral performance of the *cyfarwyddiaid* (story-tellers)? Roberts argues, rightly, that the oral narrator's relationship to his text is different from that of the author. He continues:

> In the one case we see a performer, a variable text, a knowledgeable audience; stylistically we have a composition based on formulae, or at least conventional phrases, and familiar situations; structurally the text will be linear, chronological, and sequential. The written text, however, is fixed and it will be read rather than performed; its narration may be less direct but will lend itself to experimentation and its style will be less bound by convention, but it will be open to audience participation of a different kind, as listeners ponder the meaning of the narrative or enjoy literary skills more subtle than the purely aural.[12]

However, the majority of medieval written texts were composed for *oral* delivery, and as such it could be argued that they, too, were *performances* in their own right: their actual enactment was necessarily a vital part of their impact. As stressed by Finnegan, the audience would see as well as hear the reader, so that kinesic elements such as gestures and facial expressions would continue to play an important part, as well as any other communication media (musical features, acoustic and visual elements).[13] As with an oral performance, aural audiences still had only the spoken moment in which to grasp meaning: 'the mediaeval listeners could not glance back a few pages if they lost track of the story for a moment'.[14] It should be emphasized, therefore, that although the composer now has the time to create at leisure, although he is free from the pressures of extempore composition, nevertheless he still has to bear in mind the *reception* and *dissemination* of his work. Coleman argues convincingly that medieval audiences actually *chose* to listen to readings, even if they were themselves literate, because of 'the excitement of live performance, the intensification of aesthetic experience, the social bonding, the intellectual stimulation, and the cultural affirmation available in the high-context environment of public reading', so that there would be a continuous interaction between text, reader and hearers, rendering the parchment 'interactive'.[15]

Unfortunately, direct evidence for the reading aloud of narrative texts in medieval Wales is scanty. It is probably safe to assume that many of the patrons of medieval Welsh manuscripts could themselves read. However, comparative evidence would suggest that oral and aural (and visual) culture was the only choice for the majority. Turning to the *Mabinogion* corpus, we find few references to books and to reading. The colophon at the end of *The Dream of Rhonabwy* claims that neither poet nor story-teller knew the tale 'heb lyuyr' ('without a book'), suggesting that the tale was commonly read, not recited. In the second branch of the *Mabinogi*, Branwen's letter is read out to her brother, the king – compare the role of the priest at the king's court, who must, according to the evidence of the law-books, be 'ready and unintoxicated at the king's need, to write letters and to read them'.[16] Gerald of Wales refers more than once to reading aloud, as, for instance, in the following passage, which provides an example of voluntary aurality: 'While we were in Brecon, I, Gerald, the Archdeacon of the place, presented to the Archbishop a copy of my own far from negligible work called *The Topography of Ireland*. The Archbishop received it graciously and read a portion of it with close attention each day during the journey, or else had it read to him.'[17] A few references to reading are found in the works of the medieval Welsh poets, although the research has been far from exhaustive. In the fourteenth century Iolo Goch describes Ithel Ddu as 'orau . . . darlleawdr ar dir Llëyn' ('the best reader in the land of Llŷn'),[18] while Lewys Glyn Cothi in the fifteenth century draws a comparison between reading and reciting from memory, and mentions reading aloud to his patron.[19] Therefore, although the Welsh evidence is scanty, one must accept the possibility of a twofold reception of literature in a society largely but not completely illiterate: public as well as private reading. References to an acoustic reception may be missing because it was regarded as so self-evident as not to warrant mention. Indeed, this is supported by an examination of some of the structural and stylistic features of the *Mabinogion* tales.[20]

The main thesis, therefore, is that the stylistic and structural features of Welsh narrative prose tales have been greatly influenced by (1) the art of the oral story-teller and (2) the aural reception of the written texts: in other words by the demands of *performance*, so that those traits that are usually described as 'oral' should not be regarded merely as a residue of the oral past, but as functional within a literate context. For the purposes of this essay, a few illustrations will have to suffice, and comments will be confined to reflections on the structure of the tales, and the use of formulae.[21]

In the field of narrative structure, the discussion will focus on three features that are generally recognized as important in the context of an oral performance because of their significance in the *reception processes* of oral narrative. First, the length of and unit of performance will be considered. Clover argues that the medieval Icelandic prose sagas reflect a literary development – a phenomenon linked perhaps to memory, for the performer cannot compose or the audience remember tales that are beyond a certain length.[22] Long prose forms, she argues, came into existence only with the emergence of a reading class. She looks towards non-European traditions to support her thesis, and quotes Biebuyck's remarks on the contemporary Mwindo material, and Finnegan's on the *Lianja*: 'It is not at all certain that the traditional pattern was not in fact a very loosely related bundle of separate episodes, told on separate occasions and not necessarily thought of as one single work of art . . . By now, of course, its circulation as a composite written narrative among sophisticated audiences has, in a sense, established 'The Tale of Lianja' as a kind of (prose) epic in its own right'.[23] However, although it could be argued that the episode was the all-important narrative unit, Biebuyck, Okpewho and others have argued convincingly that the 'whole' did exist as an immanent or potential entity. Kellogg outlines the theory:

> Every performance of traditional narrative takes place in a vast context of story, and must be understood so by the critic . . . I am left, therefore, with skepticism that a long narrative can exist in oral tradition as a single 'work' separate from the tradition as a whole . . . The usual instruction to the performer would be 'sing us the episode of such and such', with its fit into the unperformed whole being a task for members of the audience, accomplished more or less satisfactorily depending on their knowledge of tradition.[24]

Secondly, repetition (of narrative events and of verbal phrases or formulae) is generally regarded as one of the main characteristics of oral literature. This makes sense in practice, due to the ephemeral nature of oral prose or poetry.[25] Olrik, in his seminal article 'Epic laws of folk narrative', draws particular attention to tripartite repetition – *das Gesetz der Dreizahl* – which, he argues, creates suspense,

137

focuses attention, and is an integral part of the structure of western European oral narrative.[26] Finally, comparative evidence suggests that the structure of oral prose narrative *tends* to be linear, chronological and sequential, with a tendency towards conjunctive cohesion. One reason for this is surely the influence of memory on any orally performed narrative. Compare, for example, Rosenberg's remarks on the structure of sermons:

> Memory . . . exerts pressure on the sequence of clauses within a sentence. Clauses tend to be generated chronologically, matching their sequence to the sequence of the sentences describing them. Memory performs better with temporally arranged sentences . . . Clearly the events have an effect on the way sentences are organized. The simplest sort of plot structure characterizes the stories in the sermons: a straightforward single-strand narrative, each episode of which is introduced by such formulas as 'after a while' and 'by and by'.[27]

Such structural features also ease the process of listening, understanding and transmitting, as reflected in the pioneering work of Bartlett and other cognitive psychologists who have examined how story patterns are stored in the mind.[28]

These three features are reflected in varying degrees in the synchronic or horizontal structure of the *Mabinogion* tales. First, an attempt was made to discover how the authors (or scribes) viewed their own texts, and whether the presentation of the written material betrayed contemporary ideas regarding the arrangement of narrative. As noted by Doyle and Parkes, 'layout and decoration function like punctuation: they are part of the presentation of a text which facilitates its use by a reader'.[29] Huws emphasizes that the Welsh scribes were not as sophisticated as their continental counterparts in their use of capitals to divide their texts, yet examples of the technique can be found.[30] One further consideration in this context is to what extent we can attribute to the scribe himself a dynamic and determinative role. A. N. Doane, in his discussion of Anglo-Saxon poetry, argues that the scribe is a special kind of speaking performer, in the ethnographic sense: as he copies from one manuscript to another, he recreates the transmitted message through his own performance within the tradition, reflecting his communicative competence within that tradition. This is reflected beyond verbal variation, in features such as spacing and word division which, Doane suggests, 'seem to stand for the very features of phonic speech that modern textuality does not formally mark, such as rhetorical pauses, rhetorical word-stress, and variation of pitch and loudness'.[31] This seems to be an avenue well worth exploring in the medieval Welsh manuscripts. Instances can be found in the Red Book of Hergest, for example, where rubrication is used, in the absence of speech markers, to highlight character switching in dialogue passages. For the purpose of this essay, however, since the focus is on the macro-structure of the texts, remarks will be confined to the use of large initials. There are no divisions within the *Four Branches*, apart from large initials at the beginning of each branch, nor within the short *Encounter of Lludd and Llefelys* and the two dream visions. *Owein* is divided into five sections in the Red Book version (three sections are of a similar length). There are three sections to *Gereint* in the White Book, and only two in the Red Book version, but it should be noted that the divisions occur towards the beginning of the narrative, and draw attention to scene and character switching ('his story so far', 'Gereint's story so far', 'their story so far'), which is surely a mark of written narrative. Yet this tells us nothing of the reception: compare the use of *uchod* ('above') in the third branch.[32] The Red and White Book versions of *Peredur* are divided into three sections of 35, $13\frac{3}{4}$ and 13 columns. However, it must be stressed that *Peredur* has a complex manuscript tradition, for fragments of the tale also occur in Peniarth MSS 7 and 14, raising questions regarding the 'fixed' version of *Peredur*.[33] The text of *Culhwch and Olwen* is divided sixteen times by large initials, with slight variation between the Red and White Book versions. Nine examples appear in the final section of the tale, which relates the accomplishing of the tasks set by the giant, and some of these episodes are extremely short, a few lines in some instances. The pattern in *Culhwch* is, therefore, rather different, implying that several independent tales were brought together for the final part of the quest and that the scribe saw them as such since the divisions are visually marked in the manuscript. It is difficult to decide what is represented by this final section; some scholars have drawn comparisons with the 'summary style' of Old Irish tales, and have argued that the story-teller would expand his material during the performance.[34] Perhaps the summarized sections of *Culhwch and Olwen* are merely an outline of what could be accomplished during an oral performance. This tale certainly makes demands on a reader, as reflected in the summarized formulae which would surely be expanded during a public reading.

Since the manuscript layout on the whole did not prove to be very revealing, the next step was to examine whether any other evidence of narrative division was apparent in the written material. Phrases relating to time, such as 'once upon a time', 'one afternoon', 'one day', often function as a boundary between one event and the next in oral narrative, fulfilling what Bauman calls a 'scene-setting function'.[35] Such phrases were found to be extremely common in many of the *Mabinogion* tales, and were often found to coincide with the few examples of large initials in the manuscripts. It was also found that episodes were 'framed' by verbal repetition or phrases, common to single tales rather than to the corpus as a whole. The implication is that such repetition would function as a signal to a listening audience, clearly emphasizing the beginning of a new episode. The basic structure of the *Four Branches*, for example, is chronological and highly episodic. 'Once', 'one day', 'one afternoon' are often employed to mark new episodes, together with verbal repetition. For example, the beginning of the second major episode of the first branch echoes the opening of the tale: 'And once he was at Arberth, a chief court of his.' The journey also seems to function as a boundary between one episode and the next, linked with a return to Arberth in the first and third branches, and to travel to and from Ireland in the second branch. Indeed, it could be argued that the *episodes* were the narrative units that were taken by the author from oral tradition, and that on the model proposed by Clover, he was the first to combine them into a long composite text, arranged into four 'branches', although audiences may have been aware of an immanent whole.[36] This is borne out by the author's references to his sources, for he refers to several sources rather than one *cyfarwyddyd*, and also by the fact that medieval triads and poetry refer to individual characters and events rather than to the 'branches' as organic units.[37] As well as large initials, verbal repetition has a narrative function in *Culhwch and Olwen* too. Arthur's words 'Which of the marvels is it best to seek first?' open three episodes, while use is also made of scene-setting phrases such as 'one day'. It should also be noted that verbal repetition is an important feature in the giant's listing of the tasks. The dialogue between Culhwch and the giant – 'Hawd yw genhyf gaffel hynny kyd tybyckych na bo hawd. Kyt keffych hynny yssyd ny cheffych.' ('It is easy for me to get that, although you think it will not be easy.' 'Although you may get that, there is something you will not get.') – is written out in full several times, then summarized in

140

various permutations until it eventually becomes two words – 'Hawd. Kyt' ('Easy. Although'). This section is therefore held together by the verbal repetition which functions as a chorus of sorts, as suggested by Matchak – 'the formulas act as structural conjunctions which ease the process of listing the anoetheu' – and, I would add, the process of listening to them.[38] Turning to the 'romances', a variation on the phrase 'The emperor Arthur was at Caer Llion on Usk' opens *Owein* and *Gereint,* while the phrase occurs once again in *Gereint* and twice in *Peredur* to signal a new major episode. The romance, of course, is episodic by nature as the hero undergoes a series of adventures. Verbal repetition links the episodes in *Gereint* and *Peredur* ('And he went on his way', or a variation on the formula), while in *Owein* the phrase 'he travelled the bounds of the world and its wilderness' occurs three times to mark sub-episodes in the penultimate section of the tale. In the romances, the episodes are not usually causally linked, but rather they form a series of juxtaposed events, and cohesion is maintained by means of this 'chorus effect'.[39] The three shorter tales of the *Mabinogion* corpus can be regarded as complete entities. Although based on the theme of the *three* oppressors, the *Encounter of Lludd and Llefelys* draws little on the art of the story-teller. The *Dream of Maxen* is basically composed of two moves, each move ending with an onomastic tag which, as noted by Hunter, would have been an important aide-mémoire to the oral story-teller.[40] The structure of *The Dream of Rhonabwy* is rather different in that the first section is chronological, but then the tale proceeds in disjointed narrative fragments, rather like a real dream. Indeed, the narrative runs backwards, parodying the *ordo naturalis* of the other tales, and surely making more demands on the audience.[41] Yet the author makes use of verbal repetition as Rhonabwy asks his guide nine times for an explanation of events, thus employing a traditional technique not to link episodes, but rather to give information to the audience.

Once an attempt had been made to recognize the major divisions in the longer narrative texts, their length was then analysed, together with the lengths of the complete shorter tales. Chaytor, among others, has argued that many medieval romances were intended to be recited in episodes, and so the unity of action is not always apparent: 'how much recitation at a time was either demanded by the audience or supported by the reciter is a matter of sheer conjecture; but the "lay-out" of the matter indicates that convenient halting-places were clearly marked'.[42] Some scholars have undertaken mathematical analyses of medieval texts,[43] and have argued for mathematical symmetry in the metrical narratives of Chrétien de Troyes. Ryding is sceptical, and argues that most such speculation is circular: 'the usual thing is to divide the story first into logically coherent units, then to estimate their average length, and then to assume that to have been the length of the performance'.[44] Some tentative suggestions can be made regarding narrative divisions in the *Mabinogion*, based on the methodology outlined above. The major episodes within the *Four Branches* average between 8 and 12 columns of the White Book text.[45] *The Dream of Maxen* is $12\frac{3}{4}$ columns in total, and *The Encounter of Lludd and Llefelys* is $8\frac{1}{2}$ columns in total; the three main sections of *Owein* occupy between 10 and 11 columns, while two of the three major sections of *Peredur* are of similar length ($13\frac{3}{4}$ and 13 columns). *Culhwch and Olwen* is composed of very short episodes, yet it has been argued that the tale has an overall tripartite structure (separated by the listing of Arthur's men and the listing of the tasks) of 20, 14 and 21 columns.[46] *The Dream of Rhonabwy* is $22\frac{1}{4}$ columns in total, *Branwen* $23\frac{1}{4}$ columns, and *Manawydan* 20 columns. These figures may well suggest some sort of numerical clustering. However, it is acknowledged that the methodology needs much refining, and that further research needs to be undertaken in the reading aloud and timing of narrative sections.

Examples of repetition (and especially tripartite repetition) are abundant within the corpus. In the *Four Branches*, for example, Pwyll sees Rhiannon on three consecutive days; Gwydion and Gilfaethwy are transformed three times into animals; Aranrhod places three curses on her son. However, the technique can be used to a literary effect as in the first section of *The Dream of Maxen* and in *Owein*, where the narrative focuses on three journeys.[47] The author of *The Dream of Rhonabwy*, in particular, plays with the technique in the overtly mechanical description of the chess game. Repetition arising from the giving of advice and instructions also features prominently in the tales, such as Arawn's instructions to Pwyll that he should give but one blow to Hafgan, and Bendigeidfran's instructions to the seven survivors regarding the talismanic burial of his head. Nicolaisen's comment on Irish folktales is relevant, namely that characters are given anticipatory advice which 'often takes the form of lengthy, sequential and, in their compulsory detail, bizarre instructions which demand absolute adherence if the dangerous task is to be successfully accomplished'.[48] Not only is an element of suspense introduced into the narrative, but such repetition ensures that the listener is continuously reminded of the course of events.

As regards the micro-structure of the written texts, conjunctive cohesion is certainly a feature that has been explored by many wishing to draw up a list of benchmarks of oral composition.[49] A survey of contemporary oral narrative in the Welsh Folk Museum Archive further proves the point: short clauses, linked by *a* ('and'), *yna* ('then') are the norm. This feature, it has been argued, is a reflection of the fragmented nature of spoken language, as opposed to the integrated nature of written language, and of the theory that spoken language is produced in spurts, or idea units.[50] Each of the *Mabinogion* tales depends heavily on conjunctive cohesion. However, it should be noted that this is a common feature of medieval Welsh prose in general. There has been, as yet, no detailed comparative research in this field, although one is left with the impression that *a* ('and') occurs far more frequently in the native tales.[51]

Reference has already been made to the function of verbal repetition within individual texts. However, a close analysis of the *Mabinogion* tales shows that certain phrases are common to more than one tale, that is, the authors seem to be drawing on a common pool of formulae or traditional patterns. Much has been written on the significance of the formula in oral poetry, ever since the work of Milman Parry and Albert Lord on Homeric diction and South Slavic heroic songs.[52] However, there is little agreement on whether formulaic style must imply oral composition, whether literacy and oral composition are always mutually exclusive. Evidence of formulaic diction is plentiful in medieval poetry, although composition was in writing. As Bäuml argues, 'In general, medieval vernacular literacy exhibits characteristics of orality in the processes of composition as well as reception. These characteristics doubtless included some of the functions of formulae and themes: though they no longer served as necessary tools for composition and reception, they yet facilitated the retention, and therefore the reception, of the read or heard written text.'[53] Metre is an integral part of the Parry–Lord formula. However, many scholars have shown that formulae are also a distinct feature of orally transmitted prose, and have been critical of the disproportionate emphasis which has been placed on verse narration in formula research.[54] Admittedly, these are not formulae in the Parry–Lord sense, yet they are an integral part of oral prose narrative. Their presence in medieval written literature certainly does not point to oral

143

composition, but rather implies that the authors were aware of the technique and realized its usefulness as far as composition and reception were concerned.

The authors of the *Mabinogion* tales draw on a stock of stereotyped forms of expression or formulae.[55] *Verbatim formulae* are restricted to greetings and oaths, while *variable formulae*, where identity is established by similar structural patterns and repetition of key words, are far more common. The latter may be divided into two categories. First, formulaic units are combined to give a longer formula, when describing physical appearance, combat, approach to a building or location, feasting, transition from one day to the next. In the second category there is but a single formulaic unit, employed to open and close a tale, to take counsel, and to describe horses. Opening formulae, for example, are important in any oral performance: it is a common practice to open with a phrase setting the tale in the remote past, such as 'one day', 'one afternoon'.[56] In the *Mabinogion* tales this is often preceded with a reference to the hero, his status and location: for example, 'Pwyll pendeuic dyuet a oed yn arglwyd ar seith cantref dyuet' ('Pwyll prince of Dyfed was lord over the seven cantrefs of Dyfed'). Often in oral performances, there will be a direct address to the audience before the tale begins, as reflected in English and French romances,[57] although this may have become conventionalized diction in written texts. There are no examples in the native Welsh corpus, in contrast to the opening of the Middle Welsh translation of *Otinel* where the author asks for silence.[58] The closing formulae, on the other hand, close the frame and bring the performance to an end. In the *Mabinogion* tales it is either stated categorically that the tale is at an end – 'velly y tervyna . . .' ('and so ends . . .') – or the title of the tale is given, 'a'r chwedyl hwn a elwir . . .' ('and this tale is called . . .') – or both features are combined. Such formulae give us an insight into contemporary views regarding the idea of a 'text'. The closing formula of the White and Red Book versions of *Peredur*, for example, refers only to the last episode – 'Ac velly y treythir o Gaer yr Ynryfedodeu' ('And so is it told of the Castle of Wonders') – while a common formula closes the Peniarth 7 version which ends in Peredur's marriage to the empress – 'Ac y velly y t[er]vyna kynnyd paredur ap Efrawc' ('And so ends the progress of Peredur son of Efrog'). This raises questions regarding not only the performance of *Peredur* but also, as noted earlier, the very nature of the 'fixed' text.

The *Mabinogion* corpus displays many more features that are an integral part of oral narrative performance and that create *involvement* between the story-teller and his audience, for example the use of direct speech, and (perhaps) tense switching. The suggestion is, therefore, that the *Mabinogion* tales, in their written form, were tales to be performed – some, I would argue, more successfully than others. Needless to say, this has been a general overview, a procedure which, I admit, is in itself open to criticism. A closer analysis would show that each tale has its own particular structural and stylistic features, yet this can only be fully appreciated in the general context of the medieval Welsh prose narrative tradition. The written texts are a window on medieval oral story-telling; they provide us with an insight into the narrative techniques and performance of the *cyfarwydd* and encode vestiges of oral traditional performances. But, as has been suggested, they are also performances in their own right. The authors *chose* to include traditional formulae in their written narratives: they made use of tripartism, of chronological, episodic structure, of verbal repetition, of conjunctive cohesion, of formulaic diction, not only because they had inherited these techniques from oral tradition, but also because they viewed their written texts as performances for a hearing public – such techniques were functional within a literate context. It could also be argued that these texts are 'performances' in the folkloristic sense, based upon an understanding of performance as a 'mode of speaking':

> performance represents a transformation of the basic referential . . . uses of language. In other words, in artistic performance of this kind, there is something going on in the communicative interchange which says to the auditor, 'interpret what I say in some special sense; do not take it to mean what the words alone, taken literally, would convey.' This may lead to the further suggestion that performance sets up, or represents, an interpretive frame within which the messages being communicated are to be understood, and that this frame contrasts with at least one other frame, the literal.[59]

As emphasized by Foley, the situated 'words' encode a set of different, highly focused meanings within this performance frame or arena, and convey a message indexed by other than textual strategies (for example, the use of onomastics, place-names, nicknames, triads), so that the listener must 'fill out' spoken images.[60] Such 'word power' stems from the empowering event of performance. Features that are employed to 'key performance', that is to mark the discourse as a communication to be received by co-participants in a particular way, can be seen to exist in the *Mabinogion* texts: for example, special formulae, parallelism, appeal to tradition. However, we today must be aware of such signals, and must attempt to decode them if we are to reinvest the *Mabinogion* texts with their power of performance.

NOTES

1 See, for example, Havelock, *Preface to Plato*, and *Muse Learns to Write*; Goody, *Domestication*, and *Interface*; Goody (ed.), *Literacy*; Ong, *Orality*.

2 For an excellent overview, see Finnegan, *Literacy*, pp. 1–15.

3 Street, *Literacy*; Finnegan, *Literacy*.

4 Street, *Literacy*, p. 61.

5 *Mabinogion*, trans. Guest. For a more recent translation, see *Mabinogion*, trans. Jones and Jones.

6 For a discussion of the manuscripts, see Huws, 'Llyfr Gwyn Rhydderch', and G. Charles-Edwards, 'Scribes'.

7 Cf. Sims-Williams, above, pp. 27–8.

8 For the historical background, see, for example, R. R. Davies, *Conquest* and Walker, *Medieval Wales*.

9 For a general introduction to the tales and their background, see Mac Cana, *Mabinogi*, and Roberts, *Studies on Middle Welsh Literature*.

10 These terms are defined by Foley, *Traditional Oral Epic*, pp. 5–8.

11 It should be noted that *cyfarwyddyd*, meaning 'tale' or 'narrative', reflects the later semantic development of a noun which originally meant 'traditional lore' or 'traditional learning' (see Roberts, *Studies on Middle Welsh Literature*, p. 2). The term itself is connected etymologically with 'knowledge', 'guidance', 'perception'. The *cyfarwydd* was therefore the 'guide', 'well-informed person', 'expert', and later the 'story-teller': Mac Cana, *Learned Tales*, pp. 132–41.

12 Roberts, *Studies on Middle Welsh Literature*, p. 82.

13 Finnegan, *Literacy*, p. 78. For an introduction to current theories on 'performance', see Finnegan, *Oral Traditions*, pp. 91–111.

14 Crosby, 'Oral delivery', 107.

15 Coleman, 'Interactive parchment', 79. See also *eadem*, 'Solace of hearing' and *Public Reading*.

16 *Cyfreithiau Hywel Dda*, ed. Williams and Powell, p. 13. My translation.

17 Gerald of Wales, *Journey*, trans. Thorpe, pp. 80–1.

18 *Gwaith Iolo Goch*, ed. Johnston, p. 99.

19 Roberts, 'Ystoria', 14.

20 D. H. Green, *Medieval Listening* examines the whole spectrum of genres, and considers the criteria for assessing what works were destined for listeners, what examples anticipated readers and how far both modes of reception could apply to one work. It would be extremely useful to adapt his methodology, as far as possible, to the Welsh data.

21 For a detailed analysis of the stylistic and structural features of all eleven tales, see S. Davies, *Crefft y Cyfarwydd*.

22 Clover, 'Long prose form'.
23 Finnegan, *Oral Literature*, pp. 109–10. See also Biebuyck, 'Epic', and Okpewho, 'Does the epic exist?'.
24 Kellogg, 'Varieties of tradition', pp. 124–5.
25 See, for example, Finnegan, *Oral Poetry*, pp. 126–9. Cf. Ong's comment: 'redundancy, repetition of the just-said, keeps both speaker and hearer surely on the track': *Orality*, p. 40. However, it must be emphasized that repetition should not be used as a touchstone for differentiating between oral and written styles, for repetition has great aesthetic value in a literary work.
26 Olrik, 'Epic laws'. M. Lüthi, on the other hand, prefers to discuss tripartite repetition in terms of imitation and anticipation – repetition is a static phenomenon, while anticipation is dynamic and leads to realization: see 'Imitation'. Cf. also R. M. Jones's remarks on tripartism in Welsh literature: 'Tri mewn llenyddiaeth'.
27 Rosenberg, 'Message', p. 154.
28 F. C. Bartlett, *Remembering*. For a detailed discussion of medieval memory, see Carruthers, *Book of Memory*.
29 Doyle and Parkes, 'Production of copies', p. 186.
30 Huws, 'Llyfrau Cymraeg', 10. See McCann's analysis of the three Welsh romances: 'Adeiledd y Tair Rhamant'. The layout of all eleven tales is discussed in detail in my *Crefft y Cyfarwydd*.
31 Doane, 'Ethnography', 425.
32 The third branch is a continuation of the second, and opens thus: 'When the seven men we spoke of above had buried the head of Bendigeidfran in the White Mount in London . . .' (*Mabinogion*, trans. Jones and Jones, p. 41).
33 Lloyd-Morgan discusses the structure of the tale in detail in 'Narrative structure'.
34 For details, see Ó Coileáin, 'Oral or Literary?' Delargy, too, argues that the literary sagas of the twelfth to the fifteenth centuries are tale summaries, 'containing all the essential framework and detail which the *sgélaige* [story-teller] expanded when reciting the tales to an audience': 'Gaelic story-teller', 206. Murphy, 'Saga and myth', pp. 98–9 on the other hand, argues that the style of the early Irish tales is a reflection of the problems that arise in the process of transcribing oral performances, and adds: 'several of the best manuscript texts begin well, but tail off badly as the story proceeds. This strange procedure can be easily explained on the hypothesis of recording from oral recitation'. Note that the most important of the tasks, the hunting of the *twrch trwyth* (the wild boar), is mentioned in the *Historia Brittonum*: Nennius, ed. Morris, pp. 42, 83 (c. 73).
35 Bauman, *Verbal Art*, p. 21. See also Nicolaisen, 'Time in folk-narrative'.
36 In Turkic tradition, the Köroglu epic is told as several independent plots, each called a *kol* (arm); the term for a comparable unit in medieval Icelandic sagas was *þáttr* (strand, of a rope). One cannot help noticing the semantic similarity between the terms *cainc*, *kol* and *þáttr*.
37 R. M. M. Davies, 'Moral structure', pp. 65–114.
38 Matchak, 'Aspects of structure', p. 113.
39 Fentress and Wickham, *Social Memory*, p. 55, suggest that the syntactic simplicity of such a paratactic structure 'made it an appropriate vehicle for oral poetry. The poet could concentrate on generating a succession of images, which he endea-

voured to render brilliant and striking, without having to embed these images in a syntax which articulated logical and causal relations.'

40 Hunter, 'Onomastic lore'.
41 See Edgar M. Slotkin's excellent analysis, 'Fabula, story, and text'. Radner, 'Interpreting irony', argues that the author of *Culhwch and Olwen*, too, is playing with traditional forms, and that his treatment of oral tradition may well be a consequence of the act of writing itself.
42 Chaytor, *From Script*, p. 58.
43 See, for example, Eggers, *Symmetrie*, and Zumthor, *Histoire littéraire*.
44 Ryding, *Structure*, p. 32.
45 J. Gwenogvryn Evans's facsimile edition (*White Book Mabinogion*) is used here when calculating the length of each tale and its divisions.
46 Roberts, *Studies on Middle Welsh Literature*, p. 92. However, as was suggested above, the reader may well have expanded parts of the text during an oral delivery.
47 For a discussion of tripartism in *Owein*, and of the similarities between the tale and the European *volksmärchen*, see Hunt, 'Art of *Iarlles y Ffynnawn*'.
48 Nicolaisen, 'Concepts of time', p. 154.
49 See, for example, Mac Cana, 'Mongán Mac Fiachna'.
50 See, for example, Chafe, 'Integration'.
51 Chaytor, *From Script*, p. 142 also draws attention to this feature: 'Medieval literature, written to be recited . . . naturally preserved certain syntactical mannerisms which were eliminated in the course of progress towards literary style. . . . Early language is inclined to avoid subordinate clauses; the elaboration of the Ciceronian period is but little attempted, for the reason that auditors with acoustic, but with no visualising capacity, are likely to lose the thread of a lengthy sentence, unless it is presented to them in co-ordinate clauses.'
52 Parry, *Homeric Verse*; Lord, *Singer of Tales*. See also Foley (ed.), *Oral-Formulaic Theory*.
53 Bäuml, 'Medieval texts', 39.
54 See, for example, Basgöz, 'Formula'; Finnegan, *Oral Literature*; Okpewho, 'Does the epic exist?'; Ross, 'Formulaic composition'; Bruford, *Gaelic Folk-Tales*, and 'Recitation or re-creation?'; and Delargy, 'Gaelic story-teller'.
55 For a detailed discussion of formulae in the *Mabinogion*, see S. Davies, *Four Branches*, and *Crefft y Cyfarwydd*.
56 Compare the phrases relating to time that function as a boundary marker between episodes within a narrative.
57 See Crosby, 'Oral delivery', 100–1.
58 *Ystorya de Carolo Magno*, ed. Williams, p. 43.
59 Bauman, *Verbal Art*, p. 9.
60 See Foley, 'Word-power', and also *idem, Singer of Tales*.

8

More written about than writing? Welsh women and the written word

CERIDWEN LLOYD-MORGAN

Most papers in this volume are, explicitly or otherwise, concerned with men and their contact with the written word. To establish the degree to which women had access to books or to a written culture is far more problematic. Little if any detailed research has yet been undertaken on this subject with reference to Welsh women, and the present chapter is intended only as a preliminary overview, which will, I hope, be superseded by further work by other scholars. Nevertheless, it should be borne in mind that even in those western European countries such as England, France or Germany, on which much research has already been done, women's access to literacy, even at its most basic level, appears to have been rare, and restricted mainly to a minority within the most privileged social groups. Small wonder that Lesley Smith and Jane Taylor suggested recently, referring to studies of English and continental European women, that 'solid archival research offers convincing and depressing evidence of a female oral world and a male textual world, where women listened rather than read, heard rather than preached'.[1]

Welsh women are highly visible in Middle Welsh poetry and prose, but almost invariably as characters or subjects. In the prose tales, from those of native provenance such as the *Four Branches of the Mabinogi* to the later romantic tales which have encountered French influence in the course of their evolution, strong female characters stand out by reason of their great individuality and often resourcefulness, but of course they are essentially fictional beings. None the less, the poetry of both the *Gogynfeirdd*, the poets of the princes, and the later *cywyddwyr* includes songs for and about real women. There, however, women are often portrayed by these male poets as lovers, such as Dafydd ap Gwilym's Dyddgu and Morfydd, or potential lovers, whilst women from noble families are commemorated in elegies, when their importance may often be identified as their lineage,

149

their suitability as someone's wife, or their capacity to bear sons, only very rarely for their learning. That the fourteenth-century poet Rhisierdyn should state that Myfanwy, wife of Goronwy ap Tudur of Penmynydd in Anglesey, had learned to read ('Llythyr a ddysgodd') appears to be quite exceptional, even for women of such high rank.[2] Thus their presence in the men's poetry is defined largely in terms of their gender and their relationship to the masculine world. This need not mean, however, that women's role within medieval Welsh literature was a somewhat passive and/or marginal one. In this chapter I hope to show that there is evidence that women did have a more active and creative role in the production and transmission of literature, but I shall consider first of all the question of literacy amongst Welsh women and the related questions of book ownership and patronage.

At this point it must be stressed that I shall be limiting my remarks to indigenous, Welsh-speaking women, rather than women of English or Norman families. There was, of course, contact and intermarriage between these groups, but it seems unlikely that any other than women from Welsh-speaking families would have owned, read or written books in Welsh, or been involved in the production and transmission of literature. Inevitably it is mostly women from Norman or Angevin families whose names appear in written documents such as charters or correspondence. An early exception is *Thaderech* daughter of *Katherech*, party to three charters from Glamorgan which G. T. Clark dated *c.* 1197.[3] By the fourteenth century it is not uncommon to find women as parties to deeds.[4] Similarly, cases are recorded of women with Welsh names attaching their own seal to a document, for example the *Thaderech* mentioned above and also Gwenhwyfar, widow of Hywel ap Gruffydd, who issued a receipt for ten marks in respect of war damages in November 1284.[5] None the less, although being party to a deed or attaching one's seal to a document may indicate a person's status, wealth or power, or reflect the importance attached to a written record by an individual or their community, it certainly does not prove that that individual – or indeed anyone but the scribe – could either read or write.[6]

One area which has provided generous materials in other cultures is, of course, iconography. But in Wales iconographic evidence of any kind from the medieval period is scarcer than in England or some continental countries, and visual representations of medieval women with books are hard to find. Wendy Armstead, for example, in her research on misericords in Welsh churches has not found a single instance of a woman being depicted with a book.[7] There are, however, two well-documented examples of stained-glass windows with such images, both of them in Gresford parish church near Wrexham, and both from the very end of the fifteenth century. In both cases St Apollonia, the patroness of the toothache sufferer, appears holding her dentist's pincers in one hand and a book in the other. However, Gresford is not far from the English border, and there is a strong possibility that the artist and craftsmen were not all local, but English, or English-influenced. In his study of stained glass in north Wales, Mostyn Lewis draws attention to the similarity in style between much of the work from the second half of the fifteenth century surviving in the north-east and glass in York Minster, suggesting that artists and artisans from England may have been responsible;[8] this would be analogous to the production of inlaid tiles by itinerant specialists in Cistercian abbeys.[9] A further problem with the St Apollonia windows, of course, is that the woman with the book is a saint, and a foreign saint at that. Similarly, another window in Gresford church, dated 1498, shows St Anne praying in her garden with an open book before her, and at Llandyrnog, again in east Denbighshire, the east window (*c.* 1500) depicts the Annunciation, with an open book on Mary's lap. These are all conventional treatments of common religious scenes, and it cannot, therefore, be assumed that such visual representations have any genuine link with the realities of contemporary Welsh cultural life, at least as far as women's relationship with books is concerned. By the same token, the *vitae* of Welsh female saints must be approached with caution. Although the Life of Gwenfrewi (St Winifred) states that her father decided to 'devote' her to the liberal arts, we are not told how or where this occurred or whether she was first taught to read and write.[10] The *vita* also states that St Beuno gave her daily Scripture lessons, but again this statement need not imply that Gwenfrewi was literate, for cases are attested in England of illiterate women who had an extensive and exact Bible knowledge acquired aurally.[11] Moreover, in the realm of hagiography biographical statements often owe more to convention or eulogy than to fact, and this consideration, as well as the lengthy time gap between the supposed lifetime of the saint and the surviving texts, means that they may not be reliable. In short, the *vita* of a saint – especially one who apparently survived beheading –

can not be taken as evidence for normal, secular female experience at a given period.

Another area where visual evidence might be found and is available in profusion in other cultures is manuscript illustrations. In France and Germany women, some of them named, are known to have worked as illuminators: one of them, Claricia, included a portrait of a young girl swinging on a letter Q in a twelfth-century psalter from Augsburg.[12] Unfortunately, however, the Welsh manuscript tradition is largely one without pictures. We cannot boast substantial illuminated manuscripts filled with detailed miniatures which provide a window – or even a distorting mirror – on contemporary life. Manuscripts can be found containing scribal doodles, sketches, caricatures, diagrams or even the occasional illustration, but the number which contain a planned series of more than two or three pictures is tiny. Three of these will serve to show the comparatively low level of development of a visual tradition in indigenous manuscripts.

The first is Peniarth MS 23 in the National Library of Wales, copied in the late fifteenth century. It is the latest of the three, written in Welsh, and contains a version of *Brut y Brenhinedd*, a Welsh translation of Geoffrey of Monmouth's *Historia Regum Britanniae*. It contains a large number of pictures of kings and queens, mostly very crudely executed. A number of the queens are depicted holding various objects, generally symbols of royal power, and there is not a book amongst them. Two further illustrations are included, *hors série*, one showing the Crucifixion and the other the Nativity. The latter is extremely unusual in so far as it shows a completely barebreasted Virgin Mary, but again, understandably, books are absent.

My second example is Peniarth MS 28, containing a thirteenth-century Latin redaction of native Welsh law, and remarkable for its series of more than twenty illustrations.[13] These are closely related to the text and so include, for example, officials of the king's court, animals, trees and so on. There are only two depictions of women: one (fo. 5^r) shows a woman and a man kissing, probably representing two servants, whilst the other (fo. 17^v), stands at the beginning of the section devoted to the law concerning women, and shows a woman carrying a dish. Like the laws themselves, these illustrations reflect only certain aspects of female experience, those relating to their role in relation to men. It is not surprising, therefore, that there is no linking of women with books. The only person shown with a book is the court judge, pictured with what is presumably his law-book.

Welsh women and the written word

More promising at first sight is NLW MS 17520A, now known as the Llanbeblig Hours from its provenance, the parish in which the castle and town of Caernarfon are situated. This manuscript contains six miniatures, one of them depicting the Annunciation, the Virgin Mary having an open book on her lap, as in the Llandyrnog Annunciation window. Again this is a commonplace feature of a standard religious image, and in that sense it is purely conventional, but it is worth noting since visual representations of any female in close proximity to a book in medieval Wales are not plentiful. Moreover, the first owner of this manuscript was a woman, which suggests that the book was commissioned for her if not by her. Her death, in 1413, was noted in the manuscript by a hand not that of the main scribe, but her name, Isabella Godynogh, is an English one. Although it is not impossible that Isabella was of mixed parentage or had married into an English family, it cannot be established that she was Welsh by birth and language. The town of Caernarfon, of course, was a borough, established as part of the Edwardian settlement, and remained largely dominated by English incomers until the Acts of Union.[14] It seems likely that this was the social context to which Isabella Godynogh belonged, so the Llanbeblig Hours cannot be taken as evidence about book ownership or literacy among Welsh-women.

However, this link between a woman and a religious book raises the wider connection between literacy and religion in medieval Wales. In general, this connection was a very close one, since so many of the surviving manuscripts containing Welsh literature, including secular literature, have links with religious houses, notably the Cistercian houses, including Strata Florida in Cardiganshire, Neath and Margam in Glamorgan and Basingwerk in Flintshire. The Cistercian abbeys also – in contrast to the Benedictines – recruited locally and tended to ally themselves with native rulers rather than with the English, even though they might suffer as a result.[15] We must consider, therefore, whether the Cistercians' involvement in the physical production of Welsh books, and with literacy in general, ever extended to women, and, more specifically, whether Cistercian nunneries for Welsh women provided access to books as well as teaching women to read and even to write. Outside Wales, in Germany and Flanders especially, there is evidence of much scribal activity amongst nuns, even into the fifteenth century.[16] Amongst English nuns, however, the level of education was not always very high, especially in the four-

153

teenth and fifteenth centuries, so we cannot necessarily assume that the existence of a nunnery will presuppose literacy amongst all its inmates. In Wales, moreover, there is little evidence for proper monastic schools in the male establishments, far less so for the nunneries.[17] A Benedictine nunnery at Usk, founded before 1236, claimed to admit girls of gentle birth, which has led some scholars in the past to suggest that it was a kind of finishing school, but there seems to be no firm evidence to support this contention. Like other Welsh nunneries, this was a small establishment, having only about five nuns at its foundation, later increased to thirteen. But in any case, it is uncertain to what extent this house catered for Welsh-speaking women, since not only was it Benedictine but it lay in an area which had undergone very heavy and early Norman settlement: Usk was not part of *pura Wallia*.

There were, however, a few Cistercian nunneries where we can be confident that the inmates were indigenous. One of them, Llansan-ffraid-yn-Elfael, was probably short-lived, for Gerald of Wales states that Enoch, the abbot of Strata Marcella, who was also the founder of the nunnery, eloped with one of the nuns.[18] Enoch, we are told, later repented and was restored to the bosom of the church, but, in a classic case of the double standard, the scandal had more serious repercussions for women, for the nunnery is said to have been closed down as a result. Gerald is known to have become prejudiced against the Cistercians, so his story should perhaps be taken with a pinch of salt, especially since there is little or no independent evidence for the very existence of the nunnery. However, since he does repeat the same story in at least three contexts, it is possible that there is some truth at its core, and that a nunnery did exist which came under a cloud because of charges of immorality. It would not have been unique in Europe in that respect.

We are on firmer ground with the other two Cistercian nunneries, Llanllŷr in Cardiganshire and Llanllugan in Montgomeryshire. Both were founded and endowed by indigenous noblemen in the late twelfth century, but they had few members. In 1377 there were only four nuns and the abbess living at Llanllugan, though they do seem to have been Welshwomen, and were served by a chaplain whose name, Griffin, indicates that he too was Welsh; at the Dissolution there were only three nuns. Not only were their numbers so few that they could hardly have had much impact on the statistics of female literacy amongst the Welsh, but also the sparse surviving documentary evidence gives little indication of reading or writing skills. Two receipts for compensation for war damage to the convent of Llanllŷr are extant, both issued in November 1284, but one of these was given on the nuns' behalf by their procurator, a monk of Strata Florida.[19] The other was issued and sealed by the abbess herself, but, as we have already noted, this cannot in itself be taken as proof of literacy.

Other surviving references to the Welsh convents focus not on literacy or book ownership but on the nuns' other activities. Although Dafydd ap Gwilym in the middle of the fourteenth century refers to Llanllugan in a *cywydd, Cyrchu Lleian* ('Fetch me a nun'), the context, as one would expect with Dafydd, sheds no light on the nuns' literacy, for its theme is their desirability as sexual partners.[20] The poem has clear affinities with Gerald's story about Llansanffraid, hence David Williams's suggestion that it was with a nun from Llanllugan that Abbot Enoch eloped.

The abbess of Llanllŷr in 1299 was perhaps more interested in forestry, for a fine was imposed on her for having an oak tree felled in royal woodland. (She was later pardoned.) Agriculture was important over the years, for by the Dissolution Llanllŷr had become known for its herd of pedigree dairy cattle. Dame Annes, who was abbess in the late 1460s, is also revealed in an unscholarly light in a poem by the Montgomeryshire poet Huw Cae Llwyd. In a satirical *cywydd gofyn* he asks Sir William Herbert, earl of Pembroke, for the gift of an ape for her to keep as a pet.[21] Although the absence of evidence does not prove that little reading or writing went on at these nunneries, it is none the less striking that what does survive relates exclusively to other activities: agriculture, forestry, keeping pets, and possibly sex. Perhaps it is only fair to add that by 1530 Llanllugan seems to have been known for its frugal and strict regime. But certainly the nuns cannot have been renowned for their literacy, and although one could argue that the evidence for that may have been suppressed or disappeared through natural causes, its absence is consistent with the fact that there is no evidence concerning manuscripts held at these nunneries, far less written within their walls. It is true that only limited evidence is available with regard to the male religious houses, compared with that found in other European countries, and that even in England or France documentary evidence for the literacy of nuns or their ownership of books is patchy, but it is striking that in the case of Welsh nunneries the absence is total. There is no evidence that Welsh nuns had any books, let alone libraries.

In terms of lay ownership of books, the evidence is also absent or hidden. We have no large body of surviving wills for men or women such as are available in many parts of England and provide valuable information about female ownership of books: men's wills may include bequests of books to female relatives, and women's wills bequests of books to relatives of either sex.[22] Probate evidence is not necessarily representative, however, for only a very small percentage of the population would leave written wills, survival rates will vary from place to place and at different periods, and most potential female testators would be unmarried or widows. Within the archives of the ecclesiastical probate registries in Wales, now held at the National Library, no wills survive from before the 1500s, and they are mostly available only from the 1560s at the earliest. Despite considerable variation from one archdeaconry to another, it can be said that surviving wills are rare until the end of the sixteenth century; the same is true, for example, of the Welsh wills that were preserved at the Chester District Probate Registry. Further wills of Welsh testators were proved at the Prerogative Court of Canterbury, and here the survival rate is better, but even in this group, wills are scarce before the second half of the sixteenth century. Wills were proved at Canterbury rather than in Wales if the testator held property in more than one county or had a complex or extensive estate; hence they reflect the most privileged stratum of society. Yet even here women's surviving wills are few and far between. From Glamorgan, for example, one of the counties where gentry might boast a comparatively high standard of living compared with those in, say, the northwest, and where there was a strong tradition of literary and manuscript production, only eleven wills survive from before 1500. In just one of these cases the testator was female: Agnes Rodney held lands in Herefordshire and in Glamorgan, but her will, dated 1420, mentions no books. Furthermore, in view of her name and Hereford connections her cultural and linguistic identity is at the very least open to doubt. Between 1500 and 1536 a further eighteen Glamorgan wills proved at Canterbury survive, but none of them was made by a woman.[23] A very small number of stray wills of women with Welsh names has been preserved amongst other archives at the National Library of Wales and county record offices, but the numbers are still too small to be statistically significant, and even these appear to contain no references to books.[24]

None the less, other documentary evidence about female ownership

156

of books does exist,[25] and we do have one possible, albeit isolated, case of a woman patron commissioning a text from a male cleric. This is the Welsh translation of the Athanasian Creed or *Quicumque vult*, which opens with the following statement by the translator: 'Thus, since I understood that you, honoured Efa daughter of Maredudd, wished to have the Creed of St Athanasius in Welsh, I took upon myself a little labour to turn this Creed into a language that you can read and understand.' There then follows a discussion of translation as an art. Finally the text ends with this colophon: 'This is called the Creed of St Athanasius and Brother Gruffudd Bola translated it from Latin into Welsh for the love and honour of Efa daughter of Maredudd ab Owain.'[26]

Efa's brother, Gruffudd ap Maredudd, was active around 1265–82 so presumably she too lived in the third quarter of the thirteenth century. The family was a noble one, with a long tradition of patronage. It is significant that in Efa's day her brother Gruffudd undoubtedly commissioned two translations from Latin into Welsh: another religious text, the *Transitus Mariae*, and a secular narrative, the *Chronicle of Turpin*. The words of Gruffudd Bola addressed to Efa, 'ieith y gellych ti y darllein' ('a language which you can read'), prove that he knew that she was literate in Welsh; it was not the skill of reading but the Latin language that was the obstacle between her and the text. The translator must also have assumed that she was an intelligent, even an intellectual woman, otherwise he would scarcely have wasted time expounding translation theory. However, the exact wording casts a doubt on whether she actually commissioned the text herself. Gruffudd Bola says that he 'understood that she wished to have' a Welsh version of this text, and that he has undertaken the task for the love and honour he bears her ('yr caryat Eua ... a'e henryded'), and also for the good of her soul and her comfort ('Hynn weithon a gymereis i arnaf y wneuthur yr lles ysprydaul a didanuch yti ac yn enryded y'r Trindaut o'r nef'). This sounds less like a commission than a man of the cloth giving a woman a text he thinks is good for her. (I take *didanuch* in this context to mean 'solace', 'comfort').[27] A further difficulty is that the formulae used by Gruffudd Bola differ from those used when men commission work for themselves. Another translator, Madog ap Selyf, states that he undertook work 'o adolwyn a deissyf' ('at the request and desire') of Efa's brother, Gruffudd, whilst in the late fourteenth century the scribe Hywel Fychan and the translator Syr Dafydd Bychein, working for

Hopcyn ap Thomas and Rhys ap Thomas respectively, use 'o arch a gorchymun' ('at the request and command') or 'o arch a dymunet' ('at the request and wish'), both of which imply a deliberate request or a command by the patron directly.[28] Reluctantly I suggest, therefore, that it is safest to leave open the possibility that Efa may not have commissioned the translation herself, at least directly: it could well have been her brother, for example, who actually commissioned it. Whatever the truth of the matter, however, at least we have in Efa ferch Maredudd an unambiguous case, in the thirteenth century, of a woman who could read Welsh, but not Latin, and who owned at least one text.

It is possible that other women had texts copied for them in an indirect fashion. My colleague Graham Thomas recently suggested to me, only partly in jest, that Llyfr Gwyn Rhydderch (the White Book of Rhydderch, now Peniarth MSS 4–5 in the National Library of Wales), one of the most important Middle Welsh manuscript compendia, could perhaps have been intended not for Rhydderch ab Ieuan Llwyd of Llangeitho, with whose name it has become associated, but for his wife. The gender of the audience of both the native and French-influenced tales included in this manuscript is uncertain, but it is significant that a group of *vitae* of female saints, namely Catrin, Marged and Mary of Egypt, were included, and copied as a series.[29] It is worth noting that lives of these particular saints are often found in books owned by women in England.[30] The White Book also contains, in close proximity to these *vitae*, copies of other Christian texts relating to females: an account of Elen's finding of the True Cross, the miracles of the Virgin Mary and the *Transitus Mariae*.[31] Whilst great caution is necessary in linking particular texts with a particular kind of audience at a period where the social context of literature is not richly documented, further research might reveal more about the composition in terms of gender of the audience for whom these medieval Welsh texts were intended.

There are a few scattered references within literary texts to contact between women and the written word, including at least one case in the White Book itself. This is the reference in the second branch of the *Mabinogi* to Branwen secretly sending a letter to her brother Bran to tell him of her plight, attaching the letter to the wing of a pet starling. The bird flies to Bran in Wales and the letter is discovered and read. However, this episode poses a number of problems. First, it is possible that the detail of the letter was not present in the original version, for the preceding sentence describes how Branwen 'reared a starling . . . and taught it words and instructed the bird what manner of man her brother was'. If the bird could convey the message orally, there would be no need for the letter, which may well be a later accretion. It is significant that when Bran receives the letter the text does not state that he himself read it, and the use of the impersonal form of the verb, in contrast to the personal form used for his reaction, strongly suggests that the letter was read aloud to him: 'And when the letter was read he grieved to hear of the affliction that was upon Branwen.'[32] It must be stressed also that these are fictional, even mythical characters, and so cannot be taken to reflect any contemporary reality, at the time of the copying of the White Book or earlier; but it would still be unexpected, to say the least, to find that an aristocratic male was unable to read whilst his sister could write.

References in medieval poetry can be equally inconclusive. A poem by Hywel Dafi of Gwent, who was active between 1450 and 1480, opens with the poet looking through a keyhole at a girl reciting psalms before an image of the Virgin Mary: 'a'i llafar oll mewn llyfr aur, / adrodd gair bron Mair o'i min / salmau ar dalau'i deulin' ('with all her speech in a golden book, / reciting psalms from her mouth / on her knees before Mary').[33] The context and the description of the book as 'golden' suggest an illuminated book of hours or psalter, and since the girl in this classic male sexual fantasy is later referred to by name as Gwenonwy, the poet clearly indicates that she is Welsh. Unless the fantasy extends far beyond the sexual element, the poem does provide a rare example of a woman in possession of a book. The description of her dress, even allowing for hyperbole, defines her as a lay woman of some wealth, which in other European contexts would be entirely consistent with ownership of such a book. It is perhaps significant that the poem is attributed to a poet from south-east Wales, where one might expect ownership of books to be more common, especially since there are comparatively few surviving books of hours or other volumes for personal devotion produced in Wales or owned by Welsh families. It should not necessarily be assumed, however, that the object of Hywel Dafi's fantasy could read. Outside Wales, learning the psalms was often regarded as sufficient education for girls, and in England the psalter was accordingly one of the commonest books in female ownership recorded in wills, so that if a woman was to own any book at all, this would very likely be a psalter.[34] But ownership of a book cannot be taken as proof of

159

literacy, and an illuminated manuscript could be seen by its owner primarily as a religious icon or a status symbol rather than as a text to be read. It should also be remembered that even in communities which placed great value on the written word within their religious devotions, such as the English Lollards and the Cathars of Languedoc, women's literacy, even of the most basic kind, lagged far behind that of men, with the women learning their texts aurally.[35] The poet does not describe the woman as reading, he states only that she was reciting the psalms and that the text was available to her in the book. The use of the term *adrodd* ('to recite'), seems in fact to preclude actual reading. It may well be that Gwenonwy had learned her psalter by heart, but used her illuminated book as an aid to devotion, and, perhaps, a symbol of her wealth and status. The inclusion of an image of the Virgin Mary in the scene glimpsed through the keyhole may imply that she was in a private chapel, a further indication of her social position.

If the evidence for women owning books or reading them is limited, so far I have found no instance of a woman scribe in medieval Wales. Many scribes are anonymous and it is possible that women were involved in literary book production, but it is striking that there appear to be no known cases of named women copying extant literary manuscripts in Welsh before the early eighteenth century. By the sixteenth century, however, there is far more evidence of simple literacy: for example, Richard Owen's reference in 1552, in his translation from the Latin of *Dysgeidiaeth Cristionoges o Ferch* ('The Instruction of a Christian Woman') to women reading his text or hearing it read.[36] From the sixteenth century too there survive letters from female members of the noble families associated with Clenennau and Gwydir, although it is worth noting that those ladies wrote in English not Welsh.[37] As far as the medieval period is concerned, however, extant letters of Welsh provenance and sent by women seem to be restricted to non-natives, whether Norman or English.[38]

But the lack of evidence of women's involvement in the physical production of manuscripts does not mean that they were not involved in the production of literature. Early examples of active female participation in the indigenous oral culture are found in the account by Gerald of Wales of the woman who accosted Henry II of England at St David's and quoted one of the prophecies of Merlin, and the reference in *Historia Gruffud vab Kenan* to the *gureic brud* ('woman of prophecy') Tangwystl, although these women were probably transmitters and at best adapters rather than original composers of their pronouncements.[39] But women were authors too. The survival of a substantial and varied corpus of work by Gwerful Mechain, a Montgomeryshire poet of the late fifteenth century, shows that Welsh poetry was not a purely male preserve as some would like to think.[40]

In the case of Gwerful Mechain's male contemporaries and even predecessors, it is sometimes possible to find manuscript copies of their poems made during the poet's lifetime. The fourteenth-century poet Dafydd ap Gwilym, at least one of whose poems was attributed to Gwerful and vice versa, can boast a contemporary manuscript, whilst a hundred years later Lewys Glyn Cothi, for example, is known as a scribe as well as a poet. But in Gwerful's case not one manuscript seems to have survived from her lifetime, and much of her output is found only in late, even very late, manuscripts. The great disparity between the versions of her poems found in copies of the sixteenth, seventeenth and even eighteenth century suggests that the poems had subsisted mainly in the oral tradition. This is not to say that the oral medium was irrelevant for the men: on the contrary, oral performance of Welsh poetry has remained important into modern times. Available evidence from the medieval period onwards for men, and from the eighteenth century in the case of women, reveals that literacy was no obstacle to individuals continuing to give priority to the oral medium when it came to poetry as opposed to the more utilitarian applications of the written word. Hence a woman like Ann Griffiths used writing for letters, but rarely for composition of her hymns. Thus the absence of a substantial body of evidence of women being actively involved in reading and writing should not necessarily be taken to indicate the absence of the involvement of women in literature, whether composing, transmitting or receiving.

It has been argued in the past, notably by scholars such as Morgan Watkin and Saunders Lewis, that Welsh noble households were thoroughly Normanized at a comparatively early date, and it is undeniable that by the fourteenth century French literature had become a major influence on Welsh literature, as the flowering of translation and evidence for French manuscripts circulating in Wales demonstrate. But this does not mean that there existed to any extent amongst Welsh women what one might call a 'boudoir culture' that might have fostered a text-based literary culture such as existed in parts of continental Europe. It is hard to imagine Welshwomen of the later Middle Ages enjoying the kind of life led by noble women in Languedoc, for instance. Outside the Normanized areas the standard of housing was poor; the physical geography and climate of their country were unconducive to the way of life cultivated by their noble counterparts in France. (A quick glance at the best-quality Welsh manuscript of the fourteenth century and at a middling-quality French manuscript of the same period provides an eloquent visual commentary on the difference in material culture.)

The political and military unrest that broke out periodically both before and after the Edwardian conquest deeply affected women's lives. The nunnery at Llanllŷr suffered serious depredations during the late thirteenth century, whilst lay women were left to run and to defend estates and fortified dwellings whilst their husbands were absent on campaign. It is because she died fighting on behalf of her husband that Gwenllian, daughter of Gruffudd ap Cynan, has become a national heroine, honoured by the Welsh women's organization Merched y Wawr. Throughout the Middle Ages, even in the most cultured families, women like Gwenllian became involved in violent struggles or affected by them. A further example is provided by Elen Gethin, wife of Thomas ap Rhosier Fychan or Vaughan of Hergest (c. 1400–69), who came to own the famous late fourteenth-century manuscript compendium, the Red Book of Hergest, now Jesus College MS 111 in the Bodleian Library, which acquired its name from its stay with the Vaughan family at Hergest. The family were also noted patrons of literature, the poet Lewis Glyn Cothi being one of those who regularly benefited from their hospitality and generosity, and Elen also patronized the visual arts by commissioning an elegant tomb for her husband when he was beheaded in 1469 after the battle of Edgecote. However, she is also remembered for killing with her own hands her cousin, Siôn Hir ap Phylip Fychan, because he had killed her brother, Dafydd Fychan of Llinwent, demonstrating unequivocally the normal co-existence of high culture and low violence.[41]

Even in the more privileged classes, then, Welsh women could not be sure of a quiet, domestic existence, any more than could their husbands. In these circumstances literacy and books were a luxury that many women – or their menfolk – could not afford. But we should not forget that the written word was not the only way to preserve literature, especially poetry; and it was not always the best way. Where male poets moved from one court or house to another in search of patronage, of course, they might feel it was in their best interests not to allow written copies to circulate without their control. One poet, of either sex, could share a poem with innumerable listeners, and the poem would live after the poet died, as certainly seems to have happened in the case of Gwerful Mechain. Books were also expensive and vulnerable to loss in times of military conflict or unrest when even the religious houses were not immune to depredations, on top of the usual risk of fire in medieval houses. Bearing these factors in mind, as well as the nature of the native culture where even the most exalted literature, created for the highest social classes, still had its roots in the oral medium, it is not surprising that the relationship between literacy and literary production and transmission should differ from that obtaining in certain other European cultures. We cannot assume that because evidence is available in greater profusion in England, France or Germany, a similar pattern must have obtained in Wales, but all the evidence has simply disappeared. A lack of evidence from within Wales should lead us instead to question the reasons for that paucity. In the case of women and their relationship to literary culture, it would be unwise to assume that there had once existed a substantial body of documentary or visual evidence of medieval Welsh women as readers, scribes, patrons and book-owners, but that somehow it had all mysteriously disappeared. What we know of later centuries, for which more information is available, demonstrates that a written text was not a *sine qua non* for women poets or for their audience. The fact that the women seemed to have more written about them (or ostensibly about them, mediated by male perceptions and assumptions) than they themselves set down in writing did not mean they were excluded from, or even chose to distance themselves from, the production and transmission of literature.

As we gradually and belatedly rediscover our history as Welsh-speaking women, it would be a great mistake to assume that literature and the written word must perforce go hand in hand. A worse mistake would be to assume that no 'great' literature could be produced and transmitted without the intervention of the written word. The fact that the available evidence, scarce as it is, suggests that Welsh women living in the Middle Ages had only restricted access to written texts does not mean that they could not have a highly developed word-culture, a culture of which we can be proud. Literature need not require literacy.

Ceridwen Lloyd-Morgan

NOTES

1 L. Smith and Taylor (eds.), *Women, the Book and the Godly*, pp. x–xi. This volume together with L. Smith and Taylor (eds.), *Women, the Book and the Worldly* and *idem* (eds.), *Women and the Book* contain a wide range of essays on all aspects of women's literacy in England and continental Europe during the medieval period.

2 *Gwaith Sefnyn*, ed. Jones and Rheinallt, pp. 61, 95 (*Moliant Myfanwy wraig Goronwy ap Tudur o Benmynydd*, line 13). I am most grateful to Dr Nerys Ann Jones for this reference.

3 *Cartae*, ed. Clark, vol. 2, pp. 232–3, 244; vol. 6, pp. 2310–11. The last example is also calendared in Birch, *Descriptive Catalogue*, vol. 1, pp. 24–5, where it appears amongst documents of the thirteenth century.

4 The Plymouth Deeds at the National Library of Wales, for example, include a number of such cases, from 1363 onwards, relating to lands in Flintshire.

5 See *Littere Wallie*, ed. Edwards, p. 122, no. 213. In both her case and that of *Thaderech* a conventional formula within the document refers to their sealing. For the late twelfth-century seal of the wife of Gruffudd ap Gwenwynwyn, see D. H. Williams, *Catalogue*, pp. 26, 71, no. D.32.

6 Cf. Smith, below, p. 211 and Carr, below, pp. 225–31.

7 Personal communication; Wendy Armstead is currently preparing a PhD thesis (University of Wales) on misericords.

8 M. Lewis, *Stained Glass*, p. 4; for photographs of the St Apollinaris windows, see ibid., plates 16–17.

9 J. M. Lewis, *Welsh Medieval Tiles*, p. 3.

10 *Vitae Sanctorum Britanniae*, ed. Wade-Evans, pp. 288–9, §3 ('liberalibus artibus . . . tradere').

11 Ibid., pp. 290–7, §7. On Lollard women, see McSheffrey, 'Literacy', esp. p. 165.

12 See e.g. Labarge, *Women*, pp. 230–3, Petersen and Wilson, *Women Artists*, pp. 11–16 (for the Claricia initial see Fig. II.4).

13 Reproduced in Huws, *Peniarth 28*.

14 Williams-Jones, 'Caernarvon', p. 97.

15 See, for example, G. Williams, *Welsh Church*, pp. 19–20.

16 See, for example, Labarge, *Women*, pp. 223–4.

17 For the most comprehensive account to date, see D. H. Williams, 'Cistercian nunneries'.

18 *Giraldi Cambrensis Opera*, ed. Brewer *et al.*, vol. 2, p. 248; vol. 4, pp. 168–9; vol. 6, p. 59.

19 *Littere Wallie*, ed. Edwards, pp. 89, 132, nos. 176, 234.

20 *Gwaith Dafydd ap Gwilym*, ed. Parry, pp. 298–9.

21 *Gwaith Huw Cae Llwyd*, ed. Harries, pp. 69–71: 'Mae merch wen, caenen y côr, / Yma i'th ofyn, math Ifor: / Abades, o dduwies dda, / Llan-llyr wen, llawn lloer yna. / Dâm Annes sy'n damunaw / O bai i'ch llys, âb o'ch llaw' (lines 21–6). Keeping pets was also a common practice in convents outside Wales: see, for example, Labarge, *Women*, pp. 100–1.

22 See, for example, Meale, '". . . alle the bokes"', and Dutton, 'Passing the book'.

23 *Glamorgan Wills*, ed. Riden.

164

24 For a comprehensive survey of surviving wills relating to Wales, see Chandler, 'Will in Medieval Wales', esp. pp. 47–8, 123–70, 136–9, 181–3, 233–63. Chandler notes that barely 3% of wills with Welsh connections proved before 1550 contain bequests of books, and found no such instances in women's wills. From a survey of wills from all sources she lists a total of eleven extant wills made by women before 1500, and thirteen between 1500 and 1540 (pp. 233–63); for our present purposes, however, these figures are slightly inflated, because they include women – like Agnes Rodney – who were domiciled in England but owned land in Wales, and women with overtly non-Welsh personal names, whose Welsh linguistic or cultural identity is at best uncertain.

25 See Smith, below, p. 206.

26 For complete text, see 'Credo Athanasius', ed. Lewis. For discussion, see also J. E. C. Williams, 'Rhyddiaith grefyddol', pp. 331–2.

27 See *Geiriadur Prifysgol Cymru*, s.v. *diddanwch*.

28 For these and similar examples, see Lloyd and Owen, *Drych yr Oesoedd Canol*, pp. 228–31.

29 Peniarth MS 5: see J. G. Evans, *Report*, vol. 1, p. 310. Llyfr Gwyn Rhydderch also contains a copy of the *Credo Athanasius* translated for Efa ferch Maredudd; Rhydderch ab Ieuan Llwyd was the great-great-grandson of her father, Maredudd ab Owain: see ibid., p. 311, and Huws, 'Llyfr Gwyn Rhydderch', 19–20.

30 See, for example, Dutton, 'Passing the book', pp. 47–50.

31 See J. G. Evans, *Report*, vol. 1, p. 311.

32 *Pedeir Keinc*, ed. Williams, p. 38; translation from *Mabinogion*, trans. Jones and Jones, p. 32.

33 *Canu Maswedd*, ed. Johnston, pp. 58–61, lines 6–8.

34 Blamires, 'Limits of bible study', pp. 3–4; Meale, ' ". . . alle the bokes" ', pp. 130–2, 136, 144.

35 McSheffrey, 'Literacy', and Biller, 'Women and texts'. In the context of medieval England, Felicity Riddy has stressed the importance of the oral/aural context of the literary culture of both nuns and pious laywomen, which she describes as 'a textuality of the spoken as well as the written word', which might begin in the book but was 'then transmitted among the women by word of mouth': ' "Women talking" ', esp. pp. 110–12.

36 *Rhagymadroddion*, ed. Hughes, p. viii, quoting Peniarth MS 403D ('ir holl verched or iaith honn, ar ai darlleo neu a glywo i ddarllain').

37 See *Clenennau Letters*, ed. Jones Pierce (and unpublished vol. 2 at NLW) and NLW, *Calendar of Wynn Papers*.

38 *Calendar of Ancient Correspondence*, ed. Edwards, pp. 20, 75, 184.

39 *Giraldi Cambrensis Opera*, ed. Brewer *et al.*, vol. 6, p. 108; *Historia Gruffud*, ed. Evans, p. 7.

40 See Lloyd-Morgan, 'Women and their poetry'.

41 See *Dictionary of Welsh Biography*, pp. 996–7.

9

Celtic literary tradition and the development of a feudal principality in Brittany

NOËL-YVES TONNERRE

Tracing the development of Breton culture between the early Middle Ages and the eleventh and twelfth centuries is no easy task. The problem does not arise from the lack of documentation, as Brittany is relatively rich in documentation, but from the documentary desert of the tenth century.[1] Thus, no study of Breton culture can avoid drawing conclusions about the effects of the Scandinavian invasions of Brittany. Did these invasions bring about violent changes which favoured the rapid spread of the French language, or on the contrary did they only have a limited effect, thereby allowing Celtic cultural traditions to be maintained?

At first sight there is a stark contrast between ninth-century Brittany and Brittany in the eleventh and twelfth centuries. If we confine ourselves to the history of events, we are presented with two very different scenarios. Brittany in the second half of the ninth century was a kingdom. Energetic princes, Nominoë, Erispoë and Salomon, had created a strong principality which was recognized as a kingdom by 851. Military victories ensured not only the conquest of the counties of Rennes and Nantes but also the submission of western Anjou and the Cotentin. Several renowned monks, of whom Conuuoion, abbot of Redon, was the most famous, inspired a remarkable degree of monastic fervour and a wealth of cultural activity, which we can catch a glimpse of in a few rare manuscripts. In contrast, Brittany in the eleventh and twelfth centuries appears a fragile principality. After the death of Alan Barbetorte (952), the count of Rennes Conan I (d. 992) finally won his long struggle to gain recognition of his hegemony over Upper Brittany, that is, the county of Nantes. However, it was a hollow victory: on the one hand Cornouaille and Léon were outside his authority, on the other hand the emergence from 1050 onwards of powerful castellanies weakened the count's power of command. The dynasty of Cornouaille, which ruled the duchy from 1066 onwards through the marriage of Hoël of Cornouaille to the heiress of the dynasty of Rennes, seemed far more likely to succeed, since Hoël already ruled Cornouaille and the Nantais. His reign (1066–84) proved disappointing in so far as he failed to take possession of Rennes. His son Alan IV Fergant (1084–?1115) and his grandson Conan III (1115–48) undeniably extended ducal authority, bringing about the submission of the Rennais and the expansion of the administration and finances of the principality.

However, hardly had these developments begun when a major war of succession broke out. In 1154 Duke Conan IV swore allegiance to Henry II Plantagenet in order to defeat his father-in-law Eudon de Porhoët, who was seeking to rule the duchy. In 1166 Conan IV abdicated in favour of his daughter Constance, who was to marry Geoffrey, the fourth son of Henry II. Because the betrothed couple were so young Henry II decided to govern the duchy himself. Indeed it was not until 1181 that the marriage took place and Geoffrey in fact became duke. His untimely death in 1186 led to Henry II once again taking power, to be followed by his son Richard I. Thus Brittany, which had always lived under the threat of invasion by its neighbours, Normandy and Anjou, the two strongest principalities in northern France, proved incapable of holding out against Henry II Plantagenet, master of Anjou, Normandy and England. For thirty years the Plantagenets held sway over the peninsula: it was not until 1199, with the accession of King John, that Duchess Constance managed to free herself from their tutelage. At that point the peninsula passed into the sphere of influence of the Capetians.[2]

This marked contrast between two Brittanies, a strong ninth-century Brittany and a weak Brittany following the Viking invasions, is largely based on the interpretation of Arthur de La Borderie, the great Breton historian of the late nineteenth century. La Borderie, who was deeply committed to Brittany although he did not speak Breton (he was born in Vitré, in Upper Brittany), idealized the ninth century by glorifying the memory of Nominoë and Salomon, whom he saw as 'the fathers of the Breton nation.'[3] He chose to ignore the extent of Frankish Carolingian influence. However, recent research has shown that this influence was stronger than had been imagined at the beginning of the century.[4] La Borderie also failed to see the importance of a social crisis which already in Salomon's time was weakening the peninsula. On the other hand, he overstated the importance of the Viking invasions. We now know that Brittany was not completely ruined. Even though the monasteries were seriously damaged and abandoned, some members of the secular aristocracy such as Count Berengar of Rennes remained on their lands. The rest of the aristocracy fled for some twenty years at the most. In Nantes episcopal continuity was interrupted for only twenty years or so. Lastly, with regard to the period following the year 1000, La Borderie failed to understand the importance of the twelfth century in the history of Brittany. This century was seen by La Borderie as one long crisis. We now know that on the contrary, in spite of difficulties, the twelfth century was a very productive one. At this point I do not intend to dwell on the rapid development of agriculture, the growth of trade and the increase in the number of market towns; however, I must emphasize the importance of the creation of a feudal principality which united the peninsula and assured the growth in power of the knightly aristocracy. It was in the twelfth century that Brittany finally became united and in this the Plantagenets played a decisive role. Even though they ruled with a very firm hand, the Plantagenets were far from tyrannical. Their rule enabled a strong feudal principality to prevail; it ensured that the Breton people were integrated into a political unit that included England and western France, and the Bretons certainly did not hesitate to serve the Angevin king, especially in Wales where they were not always well received.

These preliminary thoughts lead us to consider the period from 753 (the date of the earliest Carolingian intervention in the province) to the end of the twelfth century as a truly coherent one in the history of Brittany.[5] By this I mean that, even though Frankish – and subsequently French – influence grew ever stronger and Carolingian influence was also strong and persistent (at least until the middle of the eleventh century), there still remained a strong Celtic stamp. This was to become very weak after 1200 when French Capetian influence finally prevailed. There is thus clear continuity between the ninth and eleventh centuries and even part of the twelfth century. Our aim here is to highlight this continuity from the cultural point of view, or more precisely to highlight the way in which the Bretons of the eleventh and twelfth centuries were not only the heirs of the ninth century but also of Breton nationhood from the very early Middle Ages. Indeed there was a tangible sense of Brittonic unity, based on a feeling of linguistic continuity, despite the evolution of diverging forms which were already clearly perceptible.[6] The Welsh scribe of the Book of

Llandaf was able to reconstitute the Welsh version of the Breton name *Withenoc*, namely *Gueithenauc*.[7] Gerald of Wales for his part stated: 'In Cornwall and Brittany they speak almost the same language, a language which, moreover, on account of its common origin, can be understood in many if not all instances by the Welsh.'[8]

It is difficult to make an appraisal of this cultural tradition as evidence is limited.[9] It is worth remembering that we have no text written purely in Breton earlier than the fifteenth century. It was then that the first Breton–Latin–French dictionary was compiled, by Jean de Lagadeuc.[10] Furthermore, the fact that the documentation that we do have comes largely from south-eastern Brittany, the part most Romanized and the most susceptible to external influences, is a further handicap. Most of the Latin works provide us with very scanty direct information, likewise the chronicles such as the *Chronicle of Nantes* and the *Annals of Quimperlé*. The *Chronicle of Saint-Brieuc* is a later work. There is little to be gleaned from the cartularies of Saint-Georges, Saint-Melaine de Rennes or Sainte-Croix de Quimperlé, or the charters of the abbey of Redon relating to the eleventh and twelfth centuries. Admittedly we occasionally find phrases in Breton, but they are much rarer than in the ninth-century Redon charters. Fortunately we have the Lives of saints, which relate to Breton-speaking Brittany. They are written in Latin, but they stem from a long Breton tradition; it may even be that some of the Lives were originally written in Old Breton. Although there is a lack of historical detail concerning these saintly figures, all of whom lived in the early Middle Ages, we find in the Lives the fundamental themes of Celtic culture and the mythical heroes of the Breton world of long ago. Of course there remains the problem of dating, and here we can only consider the Lives written in the tenth and eleventh centuries. In this respect, B. Merdrignac, G. Le Duc and B. Tanguy have significantly enhanced our knowledge.[11] As well as the Lives of saints we have the whole corpus of secondary information contained within that vast collection of writings, the 'Matter of Britain'. There is a wealth of research from the last thirty years which casts new light on the unity of the Brittonic world and the part played by Brittany.[12] Finally, we must draw attention to the contribution of anthroponymy, which shows the remarkable success and continuity of certain names which were typical of the early Middle Ages.

To appreciate the strength of this cultural tradition we must first highlight those factors which allowed it to flourish. Let us begin by

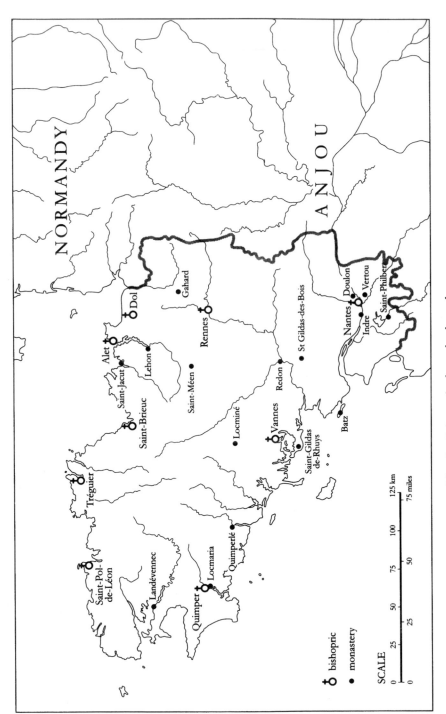

Map 2 Brittany in the early eleventh century

emphasizing that in the eleventh century there existed an educated aristocracy. Even though a large number of knights in eleventh-century Brittany were unable to read, the élite were not all uneducated. Elementary education was certainly available.[13] There were episcopal schools in Nantes, Rennes, Vannes and Quimper. When the abbey of Sainte-Croix de Quimperlé was founded, Alan Canhiart was assisted by a *grammaticus*; similarly we read of *grammatici* in the households of the lords of Porhoët and Dinan. Their presence amongst men of high rank shows that these *grammatici*, most likely members of the clergy, enjoyed real prestige.[14] The dukes held the written culture in high esteem. The cartulary of Quimper contains a very interesting text in which we find Hoël asking for several works belonging to the cathedral to be bound. Moreover, we know that Abelard was taught by his father.[15] It is also worth noting Otto of Freising's comment that Brittany produced gifted clerics dedicated to the liberal arts.[16] However, this was a Latin culture and Latin was certainly predominant in Nantes, Rennes and even in Redon. Nevertheless, there is no doubt that amongst the aristocracy Breton was still in everyday use in the eleventh century. The dukes descended from the house of Cornouaille, Hoël and Alan IV, could speak Breton. Alan was given a Breton appellation, *Fergant*, meaning courageous, perfect. In the north of the peninsula Breton was still spoken as far as the area of Saint-Malo; thus in 1053 we find Breton spoken in Trémeheuc near Combourg. The whole of the area lying between Saint-Brieuc and the Rance remained bilingual until the early thirteenth century. A little further south, in the heart of Upper Brittany, Breton was still spoken in Bréhant-Loudéac in the thirteenth century, and the Forest of Paimpont proved to be a strongly resistant area.[17] There is no doubt that knowledge of the Breton language made it easier for Breton knights to settle in the west of Britain, especially in Cornwall and Wales, following the victory of William the Conqueror. Research based on the great survey in 1166 of the fiefs held by knights shows a figure of 250 fiefs held by Breton knights out of a total of 5,000, that is 5% of all fiefs. However, while the Bretons were to be found in most English counties, they played a particularly important role in the west of the kingdom, as Michael Jones has clearly shown.[18]

It is of course in the field of music and song that the distinctive character of Celtic culture is most clearly seen. Even in ancient times the lyre was depicted on Gaulish coins. The rich musical and choral

171

vocabulary of the Brittonic languages is evidence of the extent to which music and song flourished. In the sixth century Venantius Fortunatus wrote of the richness of Breton poetry, and Hoarvan, the father of St Hervé and one of the most popular saints in Brittany, was a harpist.[19] As with the *chansons de geste*, song ensured that the tales of feats of war would be preserved. Moreover, song was also the guardian of the traditions of the nation, or *senchas* as it is known in Ireland. We are told by Gerald of Wales at the end of the twelfth century that the discovery of Arthur's remains at Glastonbury was due to historical allusions in the songs of Breton singers of history.[20] This tradition survived in Brittany. There are genealogies in the Life of St Guénolé and also in the cartulary of Redon. In the cartulary of Quimperlé, the Breton Juthaël, son of Aidan, appears reciting the genealogy of St Gurthiern, 'not for an earthly reward but for a heavenly one'.[21] Michel Huglo has clearly shown the existence of a notation that is specifically Breton.[22] It seems to have appeared in the ninth century and fell out of use at the end of the twelfth century. Its use contributed significantly to the development of Breton music and song. When in the eleventh century Dudo of Saint-Quentin wished to celebrate the greatness of Richard I he asked for songs by Breton bards to be heard as well as Norman ones. Amongst those whom Conan II called his barons when he paid a ceremonial visit to Thibaud of Blois in 1065 was an individual by the name of Norman, who was described as a *citharedus* (harpist). In the entourage of Duke Hoël near the lords of Clisson and Retz we find a minstrel by the name of Pointel.[23] The *Chanson d'Aquin* has been attributed to Garin Trossebof, a *jongleur* in the service of Roland, archbishop of Dol.[24]

The important corpus of saints' Lives provides the most substantial direct evidence that we possess. It shows the continuity between the early Middle Ages and the ducal period. It also shows the close links between Brittany and the island of Britain. Long before the brilliant success of the 'Matter of Britain' in the twelfth century, saints' Lives tell of the traditional heroes of Breton history: Guénaël is mentioned in the Lives of Gildas, Méen and Ninnoc; Connomor appears in the early Lives of Samson, Gildas and Paul Aurelian and also in the Life of Hervé; to these early heroes we must add Gradlon, Trifin, Judicaël and above all Arthur, mentioned in the Lives of Cadog, Padarn and Gildas.[25] Clearly the key question is what sources were used by the hagiographers. Of course there was the *Historia Brittonum*.[26] Brittany possessed the oldest manuscript of this work, the famous manuscript

172

Celtic literary tradition in feudal Brittany

Z in the archives of Chartres (now destroyed), written *c.* 900.[27] However, there is the question of the existence of a *Historia Britannica*, a legendary tradition prior to the *Historia Brittonum*, used not only by the hagiographers but by Geoffrey of Monmouth in the twelfth century.[28] References can be found in the Legend of St Guethnow written by the priest Guillaume in 1019. The following passage is particularly evocative:

> We have read in the British History (*Ystoria Britanica*) that, when, through their bravery, the Britons under Brutus and Corineus had conquered Albidia, which they called Britain, with the surrounding islands, and having seen their number grow and their kingdom prosper, Conan Meriadec, a catholic and warlike man, accompanied by a vast host of Britons whose number had increased so greatly that no single region could contain them, sailed across to the Armorican Gulf of Gaul.[29]

Similarly, Leon Fleuriot has shown that the *Translatio Mathei* probably contains elements drawn from an old tradition which stretches back beyond the ninth century. The oldest manuscripts are those of Monte Cassino and Rome, which date from the eleventh century.[30] However, considerable difficulties arise in the analysis not only of these manuscripts but also of another very valuable text, the *Livre des faits d'Arthur*, which L. Fleuriot dated to *c.* 1000 because the relics of St Matthew were still to be found in Salerno; they were not brought to Brittany until 1012.[31] As for the manuscript of the cartulary of Quimperlé, it includes a fragment of an ancient Breton tradition within the Life of St Gurthiern. Amongst the saint's mythical ancestors we find *Beli* and *Kenan*, sons of *Outham Senis*.[32]

So it is clear that a historical tradition with a considerable legendary element persisted in Brittany. This tradition was not merely oral but written as well. The monks certainly had at their disposal old manuscripts, written in Latin or in Old Breton. Thus in the later twelfth century Godfrey of Viterbo made use in his *Pantheon* of a very old book at the abbey of Saint-Mathieu which related the voyages of Enoch and Elias and which may have been a source for Irish voyage-legends such as the Voyage of St Brendan.[33] In the prologue to the first *Vita S. Turiavi*, written in the first half of the ninth century, the writer complains about the lack of care which led to the loss of ancient documents.[34]

From this hagiographical literature I wish to draw attention to three significant pieces of evidence.

173

The Life of St Hervé created great interest in Brittany because this saint was held in such high veneration, in Léon of course but also in Trégor and the Nantais, as for a long time the cathedral of Nantes possessed the skull of the saint. We know moreover that the cult of St Hervé was well established before the year 1000, as attested by a liturgical manuscript preserved in Angers which shows on 17 June the *depositio Huiarnvivi confessoris*.[35] However, after the year 1000 veneration of the saint grew rapidly. His name was modified. Huiarnvé became Hervé, no doubt influenced by the Germanic name Hervé. New elements were added, especially toponymic ones, and Hervé was to become one of the two hereditary names of the dynasty of the viscounts of Léon. When it comes to dating the text we are faced with considerable difficulties as it was written at different periods. Undoubtedly the early chapters of the Life of the saint date back to the early Middle Ages. Other chapters must date from the thirteenth century. In the oldest part at the beginning of the work, it is worth noting that the anthroponymic forms remain archaic and are to be found in the personal names of the cartulary of Redon: Wiuhuran rather than Guiuharan, Wicon rather than Guigon. It is also worth noting Hoarvan, the father of Hervé: he was a highly cultured bard and musician who spoke several languages. There are few elements linking with purely Brittonic tradition, but there are many passages in common with Irish folklore, such as the tale of the luminous tooth, which we find in the stories of St Patrick; there are also episodes relating to a solar theme: the miraculous harvest, the blindness of the saint, the orientation of the route taken by Hervé, but these take us out of the Celtic context and into Indo-European themes.[36]

The Life of St Gurthiern, a text of which appears in the cartulary of Quimperlé, was written down in southern Cornouaille in the eleventh century. It contains very ancient elements which relate to Breton traditions about Vortigern.[37] As Fleuriot has shown, the text appears to make considerable use of an original in Old Breton which was very closely related to British traditions. Several expressions seem to derive from the Old Breton text. The mother is carrying the head of her son killed in battle as she has not been able to bury his body, but she has shielded the head from the outrages of the enemy. This is exactly the same theme as in the early Welsh poem *Canu Llywarch Hen*.[38] We must add that the abbey of Quimperlé had links with Wales with regard to another saint, namely Cadog whose Life was written by the

Welsh cleric Lifris; the abbey of Quimperlé owned the little island of Saint-Cado in the River Etel and tried to obtain information about the life of the saint.[39]

The Life of St Judicaël is the masterpiece of this hagiographical literature. Its presumed author, Ingomar, was a monk at Saint-Méen early in the eleventh century. At that time the abbey was rapidly developing again under the leadership of Abbot Hinweten (1008–24) who had come from the abbey of Saint-Jacut and been entrusted with the restoration of the monastery of Gaël by Alan III. The latter monastery moved to Saint-Méen in about 1025. Ingomar wrote a *Vita Mevenni* and a *Vita Judicaelis*. The *Vita Mevenni* offers little historical information. The text is built around three important names: Samson for the account of the immigration, Gueroc for the foundation in the Forest of Brocéliande and lastly Judicaël. The cult of the king of Dumnonia was developing rapidly, for he was mentioned in early tenth-century Breton litanies which reached Anglo-Saxon England as well as in a Welsh martyrology written probably in 1079.[40] The great merit of the *Vita Judicaelis* is that it has preserved for us evidence of the existence of traditions in western Brittany relating to the famous Taliesin. The latter, a bard at the court of King Urien, is said to have stayed in Brittany with St Gildas on the Rhuys Peninsula. In a famous passage, after hunting, Judicaël stayed with Ausoch, 'his client'. He had a dream. The following morning he remembered the premonition in his dream and was astonished by it. He immediately sent one of his faithful servants into Broerec to the monastery of St Gildas, where there was a pilgrim who had been banished overseas from his native land: the bard Taliesin, son of Don, a soothsayer with a great gift for prophecy and interpreting omens, who through divinatory words foretold in wondrous manner the fortunes of both happy and unhappy men.[41] To Ingomar we owe this veritable *gorchan* (panegyric), which is not unlike the *planctus* of the Carolingian era:

> For, surrounded by numerous enemy soldiers, like a brave bull amongst common cattle, he slew them all around with his agile, brawny hands, powerfully brandishing his weapons and fighting ardently. Or, like peasants broadcasting their seed in the countryside, Judicaël threw; wherever he wished, there he brought down his spear. And again, just like a sturdy warrior going into battle, he set off to war against his enemies. Amongst his squires who joyfully marched behind him, he shared many horses bedecked with

phalerae. And many a spearman, who set off behind him on foot, returned home on horseback, laden with booty.[42]

We cannot pick out every reference to this Celtic tradition visible in the Lives of saints. However, we must indicate the success of the Voyage of St Brendan. His name is found in the Life of St Malo, which is one of the oldest Lives of Brittany (ninth century).[43]

It is in the 'Matter of Britain' that we find our richest source of information.[44] Like all their contemporaries, Breton knights certainly took great delight in listening to the epic stories of the *chansons de geste*. A brief study of anthroponymy is sufficient to show the great success of the *Chanson de Roland*. Roland and Olivier feature amongst the commonest first names of the twelfth century, especially in the great castellan families.[45] Moreover, Charlemagne was held in great veneration, as is shown in the *Roman d'Aquin*, the only *chanson de geste* surviving from that period of Breton history. The text tells of Charlemagne's conflict with the Vikings in Brittany.[46]

Alongside this Carolingian tradition, Breton heroes remained very popular. The existence of oral literature is undoubted. Thus Alan of Lille (1128–1203), a great traveller and a man of encyclopaedic culture, wrote:

> Go to the kingdom of Armorica, that is Brittany, and proclaim in the market places and in the villages that Arthur of Britain is as dead as anyone else who has passed away; what follows will show you how true was Merlin's prophecy that Arthur's end would be veiled in uncertainty. You will not escape unharmed from there, for you will either be subjected to the insults of your listeners or will certainly succumb to their stones.[47]

Amongst the earliest writers of the 'Matter of Britain', Marie de France gives invaluable information about the essential role of Brittany in Arthurian literature. Very little is known about Marie's life. Born into the ranks of the high aristocracy (possibly the Plantagenets), she had a good knowledge of Latin and visited important centres of culture, possibly the court of Champagne as according to one tradition she married Count Henry the Liberal.[48] Then she came to England where she stayed at the court of Henry II. She may have died about 1216, while abbess of Shaftesbury.[49] Her fame comes from a dozen tales in octosyllables, inspired, she claims, by the ancient *lais* (poems) of the Breton harpists. While the rendering is her own and whereas we can detect elements foreign to Brittany,

Celtic literary tradition in feudal Brittany

we also find many details drawn from Brittany. In *Guigemar* the hero's father is a character by the name of Oridial, son of the lord of Liun, whose name appears to derive from the old Breton Horetuual. Hoilas, his suzerain, is none other than Duke Hoël. While *Laüstic* takes place in Saint-Malo 'in the country', Dol is the setting for *Le Fresne* and the town's archbishop is mentioned several times. The action of *Chaitivel* takes place entirely in Nantes. The story of *Bisclavret* is about a baron who lived in Brittany. Lastly, even though the plot of *Milun* unfolds on the other side of the Channel, the protagonist crosses the sea, lands in Normandy and then 'went straight to Brittany'. In short, eleven of the twelve *lais* have connections with Brittany which are either obvious or clearly stated by Marie. Several of these *lais* have Breton titles, for instance *Guigemar*, *Bisclavret*, *Yonec* and *Laüstic*. We cannot say for sure that Marie de France came to Brittany, but she certainly had some knowledge of the language. In the prologue to *Laüstic* she explains the meaning of the title: '*Laüstic* is its name, I believe, and that is what the Bretons call it in their land. In French the title is *Rossignol*, and Nightingale is the correct English word.'[50]

Gottfried von Strassburg is another important witness.[51] We know nothing at all about Gottfried's origins, education or status. We may assume that he received a sound clerical education. Moreover, he was referred to as *meister* by the two continuators of his unfinished work, Ulrich von Turheim and Heinrich von Freiberg. What is interesting is that Gottfried referred to Breton vernacular culture. Thus we find in *Tristan und Isolde*: '"Tristan, I heard you singing in Breton just now, and in Welsh, good Latin, and French. Do you know all these languages?" "Yes, tolerably well, Sire."'[52]

This rapid survey of the state of Breton culture in the early Middle Ages reveals the often underestimated vitality of the Celtic cultural tradition in Brittany. The Scandinavian invasions did not cause a real break. They undeniably brought about a weakening, but through the Lives of saints there remained a living, native tradition which linked the saints with a number of heroes from the early Middle Ages. Thus it is possible to speak of a whole clerical Arthurian tradition.[53] In this tradition, Lower Brittany occupies a dominant place. The Lives of saints originated in this region. This native tradition also fostered an oral literature which has been handed down to us for the most part through the complex corpus represented by the 'Matter of Britain'. There is no doubt that the aristocracy remained faithful to the

177

memory of heroes who were common to all the Brittonic lands. The preservation of the Breton language in certain areas of Upper Brittany facilitated this continuity.

At the end of the twelfth century we can detect a break in this cultural tradition. Admittedly during that century the Plantagenets encouraged the development of Arthurian literature; however, the success of Geoffrey of Monmouth and later of Chrétien de Troyes had the effect of diluting the importance of the 'Matter of Britain', as it became part of a far larger body of literature in which French was soon to become the dominant language. Even more significantly, the development of ducal administration,[54] the increase in trade and the growth in the number of market towns favoured the dominance of the French language. A study of anthroponymy is extremely re-vealing.[55] In the eleventh century, family names remain very close to those of the ninth century: single names largely preponderate, con-sisting of elements found in the names of warriors of the early Middle Ages, and there are still some similarities with Welsh names. Even in the Nantais over 35% of names are Breton. The figure is even higher if we confine ourselves to those of castellan lineage and their entourage. It is particularly noticeable that the counts of Nantes have Breton names: Hoël, Guérec, Budic. Out of a total of 230 different Breton names for the whole of Brittany the most frequent names in the eleventh century are Hervé, Guégon, Judicaël, Harscoët and Morvan. The frequency of the name Hervé shows the amazing popularity of the saint of that name from Léon, who was the most famous of the Breton saints; Guégon comes from the Old Breton UUincon, a name found in the Llandaf charters; as for Morvan, he was the hero of the struggle against Louis the Pious; Judicaël reminds us of the king of Dumnonia in the days of Dagobert; Harscoët corresponds to Hoiarnscoët, made up of *Hoiarn* ('iron') and *Scoet* ('shield'). There are names containing Hoiarn in the Book of Llandaf and in the Redon cartulary. Compared with these Breton names, French ones are rare except in the Nantais.

However, in the twelfth century in Upper Brittany there was a swift decline in Breton anthroponymy; in the Nantais the percentage fell to less than 10%. Even in Breton-speaking Brittany there was a marked increase in French names, for they represented a third of all names by the end of the twelfth century. Eudes and Guillaume enjoyed popularity along with Raoul and Robert. At the same time the use of the single name alone disappeared, to be replaced by a name composed of two elements: a single name together with 'son of', or name plus surname.

It was in the field of law that this decisive growth in French influence was to be most marked. In 1185 the Assize of Count Geoffrey brought the legal system of the Breton nobility into line with the one in use in all the lands ruled by the Plantagenets.[56] There followed moves to impose an extremely strict interpretation of the law of primogeniture. From the beginning of the thirteenth century the Capetian dynasty was establishing itself and its influence became stronger and stronger. A century later, around 1312–41, the *Très Ancienne Coutume de Bretagne* was proclaimed. This is a particularly interesting document, for it shows the resurgence of Roman law with some passages very close to the Code of Justinian; however, it is far removed from Celtic practices. Of course we still find traces of strong solidarity within the family unit. Thus the practice of *finport* allowed all those who shared a common ancestry to be summoned when there was a case against any one of them. The existence of the right of relatives to repurchase (*retrait lignager*) ensured the preservation of properties which families jointly owned. However, these Celtic features were few and far between. The wife who enjoyed considerable rights in the Celtic world was now closely dependent on her husband, as also were her children. The settlement of a dower was subject to very strict rules.[57]

Must we conclude that all Celtic influence disappeared? Certainly not. The legal system which was established over the whole of the duchy came from Upper Brittany as Upper Brittany finally gained political supremacy. However, in Lower Brittany, alongside official customary law, local practices were to persist, practices which Jobbé-Duval more than sixty years ago,[58] and more recently Fleuriot, tried to bring to light. Thus the survival into modern times of practices relating to land tenure, such as *domaine congéable* and *quevaise*, has kept alive the distinctiveness of Lower Brittany. This contrast between a dominant Upper Brittany and a subordinate Lower Brittany brings to mind the situation in lowland Scotland, where there was an early decline in the use of the native language and where marked Anglo-French influences were felt from the early twelfth century.[59]

Noël-Yves Tonnerre

NOTES

1 The relative richness of Brittany with regard to source material is particularly true of the ninth century. The cartulary of Redon is an exceptional document. Containing more than 320 charters, it provides us with valuable information about society and the economy but it is only concerned with south-eastern Brittany: *CR*, and see W. Davies, above, pp. 99, 102, 105–7. We also have several Lives of saints. The oldest text, the Life of St Samson, probably dates from the eighth century. The Lives of St Guénolé and St Paul Aurelian and the *Gesta Sanctorum Rotonensium* were written in the ninth century. On this hagiographical corpus, see Duine, *Catalogue*; Fleuriot, *Origines*, pp. 223–86; Merdrignac, *Recherches*; *Monks of Redon*, ed. Brett.

2 Chédeville and Tonnerre, *La Bretagne féodale*, pp. 21–112.

3 A. de La Borderie did a great deal of research on Brittany in the Middle Ages. Although his writings have become dated, it is still necessary to consult his work, especially his monumental *Histoire de Bretagne*.

4 Here we must draw particular attention to the work of Karl-Ferdinand Werner ('Untersuchungen') and also to the researches of Hubert Guillotel: Chédeville and Guillotel, *La Bretagne*. See also J. M. H. Smith, *Province and Empire*.

5 From the point of view of purely political history, this continuity is undeniable. On the one hand the families who built the castles of the second half of the eleventh century were all descended from the high aristocracy which had become established in the ninth century, whether descended from Frankish or Breton aristocracy. On the other hand the dukes of Brittany were conscious of their illustrious past. In the preface to one of the charters of Mont-Saint-Michel Conan I is given the title of *Britannorum princeps*, and according to Raoul Glaber he had himself crowned in the manner of a king: Rodulphus Glaber, *Histories*, ed. France, p. 58; Morice, *Mémoires*, vol. 1, cols. 350–1. Two generations later Alan III and his brother Eudes took the title of king and described their principality as *regnum nostrum*: *CR*, no. 299.

6 Fleuriot, *Origines*, p. 8.

7 *LL*, p. 278.

8 *Giraldi Cambrensis Opera*, ed. Brewer *et al.*, vol. 6, p. 177 (*Descriptio Kambriae* I. 6), and cf. *LL*, p. 181.

9 For a recent discussion, see Brett, 'Breton Latin literature'.

10 Guyonvarc'h, 'Du breton moyen', pp. 193–203.

11 Merdrignac, *Recherches*; Sterckx and Le Duc, 'Les fragments inédits'; Le Duc, 'L'Historia britannica'; Tanguy, 'Les paroisses primitives'.

12 See, for example, Dumville, 'Sub-Roman Britain'; Piriou, 'Contribution à une histoire'; Loomis, 'Le folklore breton', 203–7.

13 On the education of the aristocracy, see my *Naissance de la Bretagne*, pp. 397–400.

14 Fleuriot, 'Le latin', p. 61.

15 Tonnerre, *Naissance de la Bretagne*, p. 397.

16 *Ottonis et Rahewinis Gesta Friderici*, ed. Waitz, p. 68 (I. 49).

17 Chédeville and Tonnerre, *La Bretagne féodale*, p. 305; Tonnerre, *Naissance de la Bretagne*, pp. 152–3.

18 M. Jones, *Creation of Brittany*, pp. 69–93. As P. Flatrès has shown, these Bretons were sometimes held in very low esteem: 'Les Bretons en Galles'.

19 Tanguy, *Saint Hervé*.

20 Chambers, *Arthur of Britain*, pp. 270, 273.

21 Fleuriot, 'Old Breton genealogies' (quotation on p. 2); Piriou, 'Contribution à une histoire'.

22 Huglo, 'Le domaine musical'; on this important point see also Fleuriot, 'Périodiques, VI', 590.

23 *Recueil*, ed. La Borderie, p. 36.

24 On this text in Old French, see ibid., p. 16, and Chédeville and Tonnerre, *Bretagne féodale*, pp. 135–8.

25 The Lives of these saints clearly show the common cultural identity of the Brittonic countries. The Life of Gildas by the Breton monk Vitalis was written between 1010 and 1030. The Life of Cadog was written by Lifris of Llancarfan c. 1100. The story of Padarn is far more complicated but the tradition connecting him with Samson goes back to the ninth century at least.

26 Lot, *Nennius*; Dumville, 'Historical value'.

27 Fleuriot, *Origines*, pp. 247–8.

28 Sterckx and Le Duc, 'Fragments inédits'.

29 Chambers, *Arthur of Britain*, pp. 241–2.

30 Fleuriot, *Origines*, pp. 260–3. The Monte Cassino manuscript is the Codex Casinensis 101 HH, fos. 187v–193v. The Vatican manuscript is MS 7810, fos. 144–5.

31 Fleuriot, *Origines*, pp. 245–6. See also Le Duc, 'L'Historia britannica', pp. 823–31.

32 Fleuriot, 'Old Breton genealogies', 2–4.

33 Esposito, 'Apocryphal "Book"', 196–204.

34 Kerlouégan, 'Littérature hagiographique', p. 85.

35 Fleuriot, *Dictionnaire*, p. 9. In the tenth century we also find this saint (with the spelling *Hoieianvive*) in a psalter of continental origin preserved in Salisbury, and in a liturgical calendar for the abbey of Landévennec preserved in Copenhagen.

36 Tanguy, *Saint Hervé*, p. 53.

37 Chadwick, 'Note on the name', pp. 39–44.

38 Fleuriot, *Origines*, pp. 278–9.

39 'Vie de saint Cadoc', ed. Grosjean.

40 *Anglo-Saxon Litanies*, ed. Lapidge, pp. 81, 84, 261 (XXXVIII. 113), 292 (XLIV. 191); *Psalter and Martyrology of Ricemarch*, ed. Lawlor, vol. 1, pp. xxi–xxii, 28.

41 Fleuriot, 'Sur quatre textes', 207–13.

42 Fleuriot *et al.*, *Récits et poèmes celtiques*, pp. 44–5.

43 Bili, *Vita Machutis*, ed. Le Duc, pp. 50–5.

44 For a recent survey, see J. E. C. Williams, 'Brittany and the Arthurian legend'.

45 For example, Roland at Fougères and Machecoul, Olivier at Dinan and Pontchâteau: Chédeville and Tonnerre, *La Bretagne féodale*, pp. 140–76.

46 See n. 24 above.

47 Chambers, *Arthur of Britain*, p. 265.

48 Foulon, 'Marie de France et la Bretagne'; Marx, 'Monde brittonique et Matière de Bretagne'. In the development of the 'Matter of Britain', we must also draw

attention to the *Prophetia Merlini* of John of Cornwall, although we do not know whether he was Cornish or Breton: Fleuriot, 'La prophetia Merlini'; John of Cornwall, 'New edition of John of Cornwall's *Prophetia Merlini*', ed. Curley.

49 On the problems of identifying Marie, see *The Lais of Marie de France*, trans. Burgess and Busby, pp. 17–19.
50 Ibid., p. 94.
51 *Gottfried von Strassburg: Tristan*, trans. Hatto.
52 Ibid., p. 91.
53 Cf. Brett, 'Breton Latin literature', 9.
54 A ducal chancery originated in the early twelfth century; the first seal appeared in 1108. See Chédeville and Tonnerre, *La Bretagne féodale*, pp. 74–5.
55 On the development of anthroponymy, see Loth, *Chrestomathie bretonne*, and Tonnerre, *Naissance de la Bretagne*, pp. 381–2, 401–2.
56 Ibid., pp. 404–6.
57 Brejon de Lavergnée, 'La Très Ancienne Coutume'.
58 Jobbé-Duval, *Les idées primitives*.
59 See Broun, below, pp. 183–4.

IO

Gaelic literacy in eastern Scotland between 1124 and 1249

DAUVIT BROUN

Scottish experience of the Anglo-French domination of Britain and Ireland in the twelfth and thirteenth centuries appears, on the face of it at least, to be diametrically opposed to that of Ireland and Wales. Politically, Scotland was something of a success story. The kings of Scots, unlike Irish and Welsh rulers, survived relatively unmolested until Edward I's famous onslaught, which was ultimately weathered. The situation was rather different culturally, however. Gaelic and Welsh retained their status in court and cloister under the most powerful Irish and Welsh rulers; the kings of Scots, in contrast, presided over the decisive retreat of Gaelic from the lowlands.[1] Scotland's ruling dynasty enthusiastically embraced the Anglo-French world, initiating what has been described as 'anti-Celtic tendencies' in church and household.[2] By the time of Alexander I's death (1124), important steps in this direction had already been taken. The tempo quickened decisively, however, with the accession of David I (1124–53), who, as earl of Huntingdon and brother-in-law and close friend of Henry I, was already established as a prominent figure in Anglo-Norman circles.[3]

It might be expected that this would have had a serious impact on Gaelic literacy. Although very little material written in Scotland survives from the Gaelic heyday of the tenth or eleventh centuries,[4] there can be little doubt that (as in Ireland) it took place predominantly in monastic scriptoria and, in its secular output, often reflected particular royal interests. If court and cloister turned their back on Gaelic culture, there can be little doubt that this would have been a mortal blow for Gaelic literacy. The other side of the coin was the adoption of new contexts for writing. The bulk of the writing which survives from twelfth-century Scotland is in Latin charters, introduced chiefly by new monastic foundations to record their property rights and, in the case of royal charters, increasingly produced by

183

royal clerks.[5] This overwhelming preponderance of documents owing nothing to earlier models of literacy in Scotland has led an eminent scholar to remark that 'it is hard to avoid the impression that the slate was wiped clean *c.* 1100 and a fresh start made', an impression reinforced by the 'notable lack of churches of ancient foundation which had succeeded in preserving their clerical establishments, or even their buildings, libraries and records, intact'.[6] It might be wondered whether this was because Gaelic manuscripts could no longer be read.

The fate of Gaelic literacy is, however, bound to be difficult to assess. Patrick Sims-Williams has discussed elsewhere in this volume the dangers of reading too much into the absence of evidence of a literate culture.[7] Where a language of literacy has died out, it is easy to appreciate that anything written in the old language would have become unintelligible and devalued. It should not be a surprise, therefore, that the only extant example of written Gaelic prose from eastern Scotland in its original manuscript should be found inserted into a precious item such as an illuminated Gospel Book. This example – the property records in the Book of Deer – has been dated by its most recent editor to between *c.* 1130 and *c.* 1150.[8] This serves to emphasize that what has been lost could be from the twelfth century as much as the eleventh or earlier.

There are, indeed, isolated examples of Gaelic retaining some of its importance at the highest levels of society. It is striking, for instance, that when the matrix of Mael Coluim IV's seal was made on his accession in 1153, it was the Gaelic form of his name, rather than the Latin, which was preferred. *Malcolum Deo Rectore Rex Scottorum* it announced, rather than *Malcolmus . . . .*[9] It does not appear that, even in this vital symbol of the king's authority, David I's largely Anglo-French household was keen to shun Gaelic.

A more arresting example occurs in 1249, almost a century later. There is a famous passage towards the end of the account of Alexander III's inauguration given in the chronicle left unfinished by John of Fordun *c.* 1385:

> Behold! When all was over a certain highland Scot suddenly fell on his knees before the throne and, bowing his head, hailed the king in his mother tongue, saying these words in Gaelic: *Bennachd Dhé, Rí Alban<ach>, Alexanndar mac Alexanndair m<ei>c Uilleim m<ei>c Énri m<ei>c Dáibhidh*, and reciting in this way he read up to the end

of the genealogy of the kings of Scots. That is, in Latin, *Salue Rex Albanorum Alexander filius Alexandri filii Willelmi*...[10]

We are told that the genealogy was *read* in Gaelic.[11] Fordun's account is generally corroborated by a depiction of what seems to be the same inauguration on the seal of Scone Abbey.[12] A figure is dimly discernible on it reading a scroll. John Bannerman has identified another figure close by as possibly a harpist, and suggested that the seal might portray the reading out of the inaugural ode rather than the genealogy itself.[13] He argues persuasively, moreover, that the 'certain highland Scot' is no less a person than the *ollamh ríghe*, the 'King's Poet', who in Fordun's account has taken a leading role in the royal inauguration. It might be objected that this example only shows Gaelic being used at a rare and particularly formal occasion in which links with the past were especially worthy of emphasis – most obviously in the recitation of the royal genealogy itself. It seems unlikely, however, that the King's Poet retained his skills simply for a one-off event.[14]

The question of Gaelic's fate as a language of literacy under David I and his successors promises no clear-cut answers. In this chapter, however, an attempt will be made to identify more evidence for Gaelic literacy in the period between David I's accession and Alexander III's inauguration. This is, of course, a difficult task which, I fear, will sometimes become unavoidably technical. In this way, enough evidence can be assembled to argue that Gaelic literacy was a going concern when the matrix of Mael Coluim IV's seal was struck; and it will also be possible to add something to the indication in Alexander III's inauguration that Gaelic literacy survived into the thirteenth century.

For as long as Gaelic continued as a language of literacy in the context of Anglo-French acculturation, it would, presumably, have retained status in some important households and churches, and have been practised in the course of their duties by Gaelic *literati* – such as poets, clerics and judges – if not by some of the incomers themselves. This raises an intriguing question. Professor Rees Davies has perceptively argued that within the framework of submission and non-interventionist hegemony which evolved in the twelfth and into the thirteenth centuries, the history of Anglo-French political dominance in Ireland and Wales could have been one of 'accommodation rather than conquest, of a *modus vivendi* rather than an *expugnatio*'.[15] Can the process of acculturation in the Scottish royal court and the church also be seen as operating, initially at least, on the level of a *modus vivendi* between Gaelic and Anglo-French? If there was such an accommodation, for how long did it prevail? If it continued up to the end of the reign of Alexander II (1214–49), the demise of Gaelic literacy within the kingdom's heartlands might best be understood as a product of circumstances and forces which came to the fore in the mid- or late thirteenth century, rather than simply as the inevitable result of the enthusiastic embrace of Anglo-French culture in the twelfth century.

Before turning to consider in detail the evidence for Gaelic literacy, it is necessary to explain the parameters of this discussion. The rarity of Gaelic writing surviving from Scotland in this period certainly bodes ill for an attempt to establish workable samples of Gaelic which may yield evidence for Gaelic literacy. There are, however, a few texts which, though written in Latin, involve the handling of large numbers of Gaelic proper nouns, namely texts of the royal genealogy and Scottish king list current in this period. These will form the raw material for the bulk of the discussion which follows. Although the precise provenance of many of these texts cannot be established with confidence, they almost all show specific links, at some early stage in their transmission, with important Gaelic churches in eastern Scotland. This was the region, more than anywhere else in the kingdom, where well-entrenched Gaelic *literati* would have encountered powerful agents of Anglo-French influence in this period. Moreover, it was historically the core area of the kingdom.[16] It is important to bear in mind that there was considerable regional variation throughout Scotland in the degree of cultural and social change, the experience of Gaelic 'high culture', and the relationship with the king of Scots. If these texts are likely to originate in eastern Scotland not only because of what is known about their transmission but also because eastern Scotland provides the most plausible cultural and political context, it follows that whatever evidence may be gleaned from them about Gaelic literacy should probably be applied to eastern Scotland alone. It would be misguided to expect, or attempt on the basis of this evidence, any general comments on the state of Gaelic literacy in lowland Scotland, or in historically strong Gaelic areas like Galloway or the north which had a much less intimate relationship with the kingship, never mind Scotland as a whole. This study, therefore, should be seen as perforce limited to the area between the Forth, the central highlands and Moray.

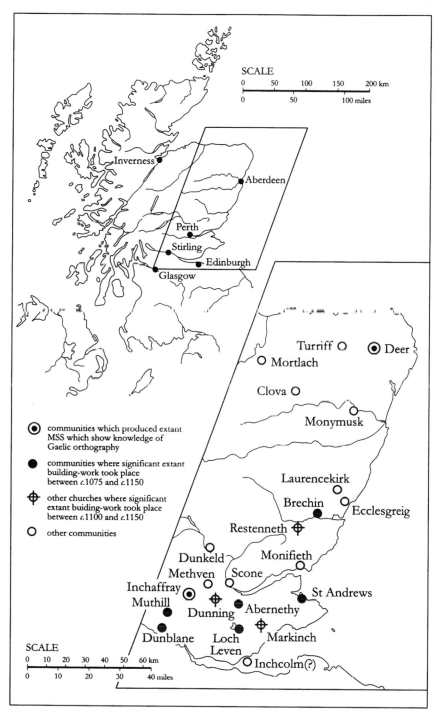

Map 3 Gaelic churches in eastern Scotland in the twelfth century: communities, wealth and literacy

187

The focus of this discussion will be on evidence for the ability to write Gaelic, not simply to read it (as demonstrated by translations from Gaelic into Latin, such as the property records of Loch Leven).[17] This, of course, is a difficult undertaking in the absence of actual survivals of texts written in Gaelic. Gaelic/Irish had an established system of spelling (such as 'p' 't' 'c' for internal or final b, d, g, and 'b' 'd' 'g' for bh, dh, gh). Although there are no survivals of extended Gaelic prose (apart from the property records in the Book of Deer from north of the Mounth), there are many Latin texts which employ Gaelic personal names, place-names and technical terms, which on the face of it offered an opportunity for Gaelic orthographic practice to be employed. A cursory glance at original charters from this period relating to eastern Scotland shows, however, that scribes did not render these according to Gaelic spelling conventions. For example, a charter of *c.* 1200, probably written by a canon of the newly refounded Augustinian priory at Inchaffray, renders the following place and personal names without much regard for Gaelic orthography: *Inse Affren* (Inchaffray) is spelt 'Inche Affren'; *Achad Longseg* is rendered 'Achadlongsih'; *Mael Isu* as 'Malis' and 'Malhis'; *Gille na Naem* as 'Gillenanof'; and *Gille Brec* as 'Gillebrech'.[18] The approach is not necessarily ignorant or chaotic. There is, moreover, a willingness to reflect actual pronunciation – not always admissible in conventional Gaelic orthography (for instance the quality of *ae* in *Naem*, which it renders with 'o').[19] It may be argued, therefore, that where the text is Latin it was not felt necessary, or maybe even appropriate, to use Gaelic orthography for such names, and an alternative approach to spelling was employed. Scribes who wrote Latin but not Gaelic need never, then, have acquired a knowledge of Gaelic spelling conventions. The corollary of this is that Latin texts which do exhibit a number of clear-cut examples of the use of Gaelic conventions may be interpreted either as deriving from a text which was originally Gaelic, or as being written by a scribe who knew how to write Gaelic, and presumably had occasion to do so outside the Latin text(s) which survive from his quill.

Charters rarely have more than a handful of Gaelic names; the royal genealogy, on the other hand, has over a hundred. A number of copies of the genealogy survive whose originals can be traced to the twelfth century. The one which most obviously exhibits characteristically Gaelic orthography in abundance is found in the 'Poppleton manuscript', written *c.* 1360 at York.[20] Molly Miller argued convincingly that the manuscript's collection of Scottish pieces (of which the genealogy is a part) was probably put together in eastern Scotland, possibly at the Augustinian abbey of Scone, between 1202 and 1214.[21] The text of the genealogy, which extends as far back as 'Adam son of the Living God', is duly headed by William I (1165–1214), and has the superficial appearance of being in Latin because of its general use of *filius* (rather than *mac*). The only names which are given in Latin, however, are William I and his father Henry; Gaelic spelling conventions are otherwise generally apparent. The beginning of the text reads: 'Willelmus rex rufus filius Henrici filii Dauid fili Maelcolaim filii Donnchada, que [*sic*] fuit nepos Malcolaim filii Cinada filii Maelcolaim filii Domnaill filii Constantin . . .' A Latin form for all these names was readily available (or at least devisable) in the twelfth century. From David onwards, however, they are rendered much as might be expected in a Gaelic text.[22] It would appear, therefore, that the text probably represents a genealogy of David I updated in Latin in William's reign (perhaps by whoever compiled the Scottish pieces found in the 'Poppleton manuscript'). As far as the remaining hundred and more names are concerned, if run-of-the-mill scribal accidents are taken account of – such as the misreading of minims and confusion between 't' and 'c', 'c' and 'e', and 'i' and 'r' (all of which are attested throughout the collection of Scottish pieces), as well as mistakes in the division of name and epithet – then something which must be close to the 'original' can be reconstructed. From Conaire Mór to Úgaine Mór, for instance, we can read:

> . . . filii Conaire Moir filii Etersceuil filii Eogain filii Elela filii Iair filii Dedaid filii Sin filii Rosin filii Their filii Rothir filii Roin filii Arandil filii Maine filii Forgo filii Feradaig filii Elela Arann filii Fiachra Firmara filii Oengusa Turmig filii Fir Cethairroid filii Fir Roid filii Fir Anroid filii Fir Aibrig filii Labchore filii Echach Altlethin filii Elela Casiaclaig filii Conlaith filii Erero filii Moalgi filii Cobthaig Coel Breg filii Ugaine Moir . . .[23]

Although the spelling is not of such a high standard as in, for instance, the twelfth-century Book of Glendalough's genealogies, it is recognizably written according to Gaelic orthographic conventions. It may reasonably be assumed, therefore, that this was originally a Gaelic text which once had *mac* rather than *filius*, but was given the thinnest of Latin disguises when it was updated in William's reign.

Before David's reign was finished, however, another version of the royal genealogy (extending as far back as Noah) was apparently produced which originally used *filius* and a few more Latin forms. It is found (headed again by William I) in Ralph of Diss's *Imagines Historiarum*.[24] From Conaire Mór to Úgaine Mór it reads:

> filii Conere Mor filii Eders Keol filii Ewein filii Ellela filii Iair filii Dethath filii Sin filii Rosin filii Ther filii Rether filii Rowein filii Arindil filii Mane filii Forgso filii Feredach filii Ellela Earin filii Fiachac Fimmora filii Enegussa Turbinig filii Firketharocht filii Fir Rocht filii An Roth filii Firalmai filii Lamcure filii Liethan filii Ecchach Aldethan filii Elela Cassieclai filii Conletha filii Iretro filii Melge filii Cobthai Cailbrech filii Hugune Mor . . .

Incomplete copies of the genealogy in this form derived from a common ancestor are also found twice in Fordun's Chronicle: one in his account of Alexander III's inauguration, and the other at the end of his account of David I.[25] The latter is described as a text of David I's genealogy supplied by Cardinal Walter Wardlaw, bishop of Glasgow (d. 1387), which suggests that its common source with Diss (and the other Fordun text) was originally headed by David I. Diss is obviously closer to this original than Fordun, whose texts are independent of Diss. Fordun is a valuable witness, however, in that his texts provide corroboration for Diss's readings. How the genealogy reached Diss at all is a matter of speculation. Perhaps it was brought to the archive at St Paul's in London by Gilbert Foliot, bishop of London, a follower of Henry fitz Empress. Henry was supported by David I who knighted him at Carlisle in 1149. Perhaps the genealogy was presented by David to Henry on this occasion and so came into Gilbert Foliot's possession?

The text frequently departs from conventional Gaelic orthography – for instance in its use of 'k' and 'w'; in its marked preference for rendering *dh* as 'th'; and in its sensitivity to pronunciation over convention, as in its admission of the epenthetic vowel in 'Enegussa' (*Oengusa*),[26] its frequent dropping of 'g' for final palatal *gh* and its precocious vocalized internal *gh* (as in *Eogain* as 'Ewein' and 'Owan', and *Rogein* as 'Rowein'). Characteristically Gaelic spellings, however, are also in evidence. This is particularly striking in its treatment of *bh* and *mh*, which in charters are generally rendered 'u'/'v'. It has 'b' for *bh* (in accordance with Gaelic spelling), once uses 'f', but never 'u'/'v'; while for *mh* it frequently employs the conventional Gaelic 'm' (for example, 'Munremor' for *Muinremuir*, 'Almai' for *Almaig*, or 'Lamin' for *Lamfind*), occasionally has 'u'/'v', but never 'f'. It appears, therefore, that the original scribe may have been sensitive to the distinction

190

between *bh* and *mh* (although there is one apparent instance of confusion between the two, where 'Lamcure' appears for *Laebchuire*). The overall impression given by the text is that it was written by someone who knew Gaelic orthography, but who decided to depart from its conventions in a number of instances and adopt an approach which is, at least superficially, similar to that of charter-scribes (often, it seems, with the intention of representing actual pronunciation). A final verdict on this text's orthography will have to await a specialist study by someone better qualified than I for such an undertaking. What can be said, however, is that it is not the work of an ignorant scribe struggling with unfamiliar sounds: there is no sign here, for instance, of the 'general confusion between *ch, gh, th* and *dh*' which Caoimhín Breatnach has noted in Anglo-Norman hands of the Annals of Innisfallen.[27]

The most straightforward answer to why the scribe decided not to employ generally the Gaelic orthography he presumably knew is that the text was conceived as a Latin document. There are, in fact, only a few Latin forms in Diss's copy: *Malcolmi, Dunecani, Constantini* and *Elpini* (for *Ailpín*). They also appear in Fordun's copies, plus a number of other Latin forms which have doubtless been introduced during the text's transmission. It is likely – although incapable of proof – that the Latin forms in Diss reflect the usage of the original scribe himself.

There is one more text of the royal genealogy which arguably descends (ultimately) from a copy made in David I's reign. It is found in the *Original Chronicle* of Andrew of Wyntoun, written in Scots verse in the early fifteenth century,[28] and also (independently) in the commonplace book of John Gray, secretary to two archbishops of St Andrews in the late fifteenth century.[29] Andrew of Wyntoun was himself a canon of St Andrews Priory before becoming prior of Loch Leven (a dependency of St Andrews) in or soon after 1393, so it is likely that the exemplar used by both him and Gray was in St Andrews in the late Middle Ages, and possibly earlier. The text runs from father to son as far as Fergus Mór, proceeding no further towards the present. Compared to the texts discussed already, this one appears seriously corrupt and of little or no value for this enquiry. The names obviously baffled the fifteenth-century scribes who copied Wyntoun's work: some even gave up the effort of writing them all down. This unfortunately includes the scribe of the unique manuscript of Wyntoun's first edition, who protested that 'quhat thare names were callit than . . . were rycht strange for to reherss'.[30] We can readily see why if we look again at the section from Úgaine Mór to Conaire Mór in Wyntoun's second edition (represented best by the earliest extant manuscript of his work):

> . . . And Vsuemoere his sone gat/ Costek Baelbrek eftyre that;/ and his sone callid wes Melge,/ Jero syne thare eft gat he,/ that fadyr wes off Comata;/ and his sone wes callid Elela/ Casiaclek, that eftyre then/ gat Eacak Aldecen;/ his sone Catan gat Cure,/ Fyere Elmael gat he,/ And hys sone Fyere Anroet/ fadyr wes off Fyre Roet;/ Fyre Cetaraot efftyre that/ Angus Turuec to sone gat;/ Fyarak gat Nereon,/ Ellala gat Earen,/ Feraret to sone gat he/ that Fergo gat, and he Mawe;/ Arynden wes syne fardyre/ tyll Regyne, that gat Rotreyre;/ hys sone Trere gat Rosyne,/ and he syne fadyr wes to Syne;/ he had a sone calde Dedaa,/ Jaere his sone gat Elela;/ Elela gat Eogen,/ Edarsce Uyl his sone wes then,/ and he Conare Moere gat . . .[31]

The significance of this mangled text, however, is that it shares a number of errors with Diss (and Fordun), such as merging *Fiachra Tolgach* with his father *Muiredach Bolgrach* to produce 'Fyakak Bolgeg' (Diss has 'Fiechachch Bolgai'); mis-spelling *Nema* as 'Neande' (as does Diss); or misreading the 's' of *Sem* as an 'r' (hence 'Reyne', or in Diss, 'Rein').[32] A comparison of the two, moreover, shows that it often preserves characteristically Gaelic spellings where Diss's (and Fordun's) text does not. For instance, on a number of occasions a 'd' remains visible for what was once *dh*, where Diss's text reads 'th': e.g. 'Dedaa' (for *Dedaid*; Diss reads 'Dethath'); 'Vadek' (*Buadaig*: Diss 'Rothai'); 'Edoym' (*Aedain*: Diss 'Etheon'); 'Moyodade' (*Nuadat*: Diss 'Noethath'); 'Elkada' (*Giallchada*: Diss 'Elchatha'); 'Erkada' (*Erchada*: Diss 'Erchatha'); and 'Gedyll' (*Gaedil*: Diss 'Geithel'). Moreover, it also shows 'g' for original intervocalic *gh* where Diss's text has 'w' or nil: 'Regyne' (for *Rogein*), 'Eogen' and 'Cogyne' (for *Eogain*), and 'Tygerneke' (for *Tigernaig*, as opposed to 'Thiernai' in Diss). All this suggests that Diss's and Fordun's archetype was derived from a distant ancestor of Wyntoun's text which conformed more to Gaelic orthographic conventions. The relationship between Diss's and Fordun's archetype and this distant ancestor of Wyntoun's would, moreover, suggest that the latter may be dated no later than *c.* 1150.

Given the state of Wyntoun's text it is very difficult to say much more about its twelfth-century antecedents. There is one small clue, however, that it has been through the hands of a Gaelic scribe versed in Gaelic pseudo-history. Eochaid Riata, eponym of Dál Riata, appears in Wyntoun's text as 'Eadak Rydesedek Corbre Rygada'.[33] Eochaid Riata is elsewhere called Corpre Rígfata; and in Wyntoun's text *Echdach* (genitive of *Eochaid*) is normally rendered 'Eadak'. This may be unscrambled, therefore, as 'Ec[h]dach Ri[a]d[a] e sede Corbre Rigada' (or, more conventionally, *Echdach Riata é side Corpre Rígfata*), indicating in a shorthand manner that Eochaid Riata was also known as Corpre Rígfata.[34] Whoever wrote this – the scribe of the genealogy or a glossator – evidently had an interest in Gaelic synthetic history and was no doubt, therefore, a fully fledged Gaelic *literatus*.

It is possible, therefore, that the text of the genealogy itself was wholly in Gaelic. There is, moreover, another clue which points in this direction. The phrase *m. Echdach Riata is é side Corpre Rigfota* is also found in the pedigree of David I in the Book of Leinster, and in none of the other Irish manuscripts of the Scottish royal genealogy[35] (although a similar comment in Latin is made elsewhere in the Book of Leinster in its account of the pedigree of St Berchán).[36] It is possible, therefore, that Wyntoun and the Book of Leinster share a source which may have been a glossed copy of David I's pedigree – which would, presumably, have been in Gaelic. This thin thread of evidence may also lend some support to the notion that the ancestral text of the genealogy shared ultimately by Wyntoun and Diss was, indeed, headed by David I.

There are three texts of the royal genealogy, then, which may be traced with varying degrees of plausibility to the reign of David I. One, preserved uniquely in Poppleton's copy of an early thirteenth-century collection of Scottish historical pieces, is likely to have been a Gaelic text; a second, dimly discernible in Wyntoun and Gray, and which may also be behind the copy of David I's pedigree in the Book of Leinster, could also have been written in Gaelic. The third, copied perhaps directly from the second, and preserved by Diss and Fordun, shows knowledge of Gaelic orthography, but was probably conceived chiefly as a Latin text, which might explain why it adopted a less conventional approach to rendering the names. These texts, taken together, suggest therefore that Gaelic literacy was probably still a going concern throughout the region by the end of David's reign.

Evidence of Gaelic literacy after David's reign is more difficult to come by. Something may be gained, however, by turning to another

193

important statement of the kingship's past: the king list. Like the genealogy, it was replete with Gaelic names – especially the longer version which includes kings of Dál Riata. Unfortunately the complex text-history of what survives does not allow the same scope as the genealogical texts for identifying orthographic practices with particular stages in their development. Despite this, there is some indication of Gaelic orthographic practice in the group which Marjorie Anderson has argued derives from an archetype datable to the reign of Alexander II (1214–49).[37] A number of witnesses, for instance, show 'gh' and 'dh' for *gh* and *dh* (e.g. 'Dovenghart' for *Domangart*, 'Heoghan' for *Eogan*, and 'Dunghal' for *Dúngal*; and 'Edhan' for *Aedán*, 'Edh' for *Aed*, and one example of 'Miredhach' for *Muiredach*).[38] One witness, moreover, is not only fairly consistent in giving 'dh' and 'gh', as noted above, but also has Gaelic *Custantin* rather than *Constantinus* four times out of five.[39] This witness is a fourteenth-century English copy of a text datable to between 1286 and 1292, and may only be two copies removed from the archetype of the group.[40] It is possible to envisage, therefore, that all these features were originally found in the group's archetype. If this is so, it would suggest that Gaelic orthographic conventions were still practised during the reign of Alexander II. Indeed, if this line of argument is followed, this text may be seen as an early example of the later convention of using 'h' to denote a lenited consonant (as in 'gh' rather than 'g' for *gh*), which would imply that scribes of Gaelic in eastern Scotland still had contact with the wider world of Gaelic literacy. There can be little doubt, however, that the text itself was written in Latin, and exhibited a number of 'unconventional' orthographic features.

What no copy of the king list or royal genealogy has been able to supply so far, of course, is an example of an original manuscript from this region and period written by a scribe who frequently employed Gaelic spelling conventions. It is a relief, therefore, to find three original Latin charters, written by the same scribe in the first decade of the thirteenth century, which display a knowledge of Gaelic orthography.[41] The scribe was probably a canon of Inchaffray.[42] By a remarkable chance, one of his charters belongs to a pair of almost identical originals produced more or less at the same time.[43] The only significant difference between the two, moreover, is that the other charter in this pair has rendered Gaelic proper nouns without reference to Gaelic orthographic conventions. The difference between the orthographic approach of these two scribes can readily be appreciated if their treatment of Gaelic names is compared. The following are particularly noteworthy:

A	B	Gaelic Forms
Inse affrenn	Inche Affren	*Inse* (or *Inis*) *Affrenn*
Arddeugani	Ardeeweni	?
Achadlongseg	Achadlongsih	*Achad Longseg*
Dubinder	Dufinder	*Dub* ?
Malisio fratre comitis	Malisio fratre comitis	*Mael Ísu*
Gillenanemh	Gillenanof	*Gille na Naem*
Malisio filio suo	Malis filio suo	*Mael Ísu*
Gillebrec	Gillebrech	*Gille Brec*
Duncano filio Maliso	Dunecano filio Malihs	*Donnchad mac Mael Ísu*

Scribe A's knowledge of Gaelic orthography is suggested by his accurate rendering of *Inse Affrenn* (Middle Gaelic for Inchaffray); his use of 'g' in 'Arddeugani', where scribe B has 'w' (apparently for a vocalized intervocalic *gh*); his proficient rendering of *Achad Longseg*, 'Loingsech's field' (including another 'g' for vocalized *gh*); his 'b' for *bh* in 'Dubinder', which scribe B has rendered 'f'; his acceptably Gaelic rendering of *Gille na Naem* (noting especially his use of 'mh' for *m*); and his rendering of *Gille Brec*. All this leaves little doubt that Scribe A knew Gaelic orthographic conventions. It should also be noted that he shows a preference for Latin forms (where these were readily available), which is hardly surprising given that the document is in Latin. He was also willing occasionally to depart from conventional Gaelic orthography (the final 'i' in 'Arddeugani' looks like a case in point:[44] other examples may be found in his other charters, where, for instance, *Craeb* is rendered 'Cref' and *Gaisg* as 'Gaisk').[45] Scribe B, by comparison, shows what can become of the listed names when rendered without regard for conventional Gaelic spelling.[46] It should be noted, however, that he is not antipathetic to Gaelic as such. It is striking, for instance, that he twice renders *Mael Ísu* without resorting to the Latin form *Malisius* (although he does use it in one instance), and that he gives 'Inche Affren' for Inchaffray rather than the Latin *Insula Missarum*, a translation of the Gaelic name which frequently appears elsewhere in the priory's charters.

Scribe A's use of Gaelic orthography for Gaelic proper nouns in Latin charters is highly unusual in a Scottish context. It would not be remarkable in Ireland, however, where the few Latin charters which

195

survive recording grants by Gaelic kings show a much greater adherence to Gaelic spelling conventions, with only a few concessions to the documents' Latin environment.[47] This is not to say that the Inchaffray Scribe A was Irish. His use of Gaelic orthography seems less sustained than that of comparable Irish scribes, and there is nothing in what is known about Inchaffray, or Strathearn generally in this period, which suggests a close link with Ireland. One factor which he had in common with his Gaelic counterparts in Ireland, however, was that he belonged to a milieu where Latin charters were only newly established. It appears that Inchaffray had only very recently started to produce charters when Earl Gille Brígte of Strathearn began to take a close interest in the 'brethren of St John' there, a couple of years before refounding the community in 1200 as an Augustinian priory. Comparison may also be made with Deer, whose earliest Latin charter – written, like the Gaelic property records, into the house's Gospel Book – renders Gaelic names according to Gaelic orthographic conventions.[48] The novelty of charters is not, however, a full explanation of Scribe A's use of Gaelic spellings in this type of document. His approach to orthography stands out from the other early Inchaffray charters – even the three originals which predate 1200.[49] It may be wondered, therefore, if what made him different from his colleagues was a greater experience in writing Gaelic.

There can be little doubt that Scribe A, with his confident book-hand, was a practised scribe in documents other than charters, and that, given his knowledge of Gaelic orthography, he presumably had occasion to write as well as read Gaelic. His charters may be the only surviving example of the script of a Gaelic *literatus* from eastern Scotland in this period. He is not the only Gaelic *literatus*, however, who may be detected in the thirteenth century. As well as the King's Poet at Alexander III's inauguration, there is also the tentative evidence for Gaelic orthographic practice in the archetype of the longest version of the Scottish king list, composed sometime during the reign of Alexander II (1214–49). This is not a lot to go on, but it is perhaps enough to warrant the supposition that Gaelic-named clerics who are found in the early thirteenth century in religious communities with a continuous history from pre-Anglo-French days may have been literate in Gaelic too.[50] There is also specific evidence that such clerics retained an active involvement in education into the thirteenth century – for instance, Mael Domnaig *rex scolarum* with *scolastici* at Muthill (between 1213 and 1223) and Mac Bethad *rex scolarum* with *scolastici* at Dunblane (between 1214 and 1223).[51] It might also be wondered whether Gaelic literacy may also have been found among holders of the Gaelic office of *judex* (in Gaelic *brithem*, 'judge'), such as Cairell mac Mael Coluim, *judex* of Angus *c.* 1220.[52] By the second half of the thirteenth century, however, Gaelic clerics had all but disappeared, the *judices* had decisively lost status, and the King's Poet had performed his last inauguration. If these, as might be suspected, had been the main practitioners of Gaelic literacy, their demise in the middle of the thirteenth century would readily explain the demise of Gaelic literacy in this region.

If Gaelic *literati* such as these continued to copy and write predominantly Gaelic texts, it can only be guessed what these may have been. It is worth asking, however, why the writings from this region which do survive from this period are so predominantly new genres (most notably Latin charters). The lack, for instance, of historical and literary texts, or any Gaelic law tracts and legal commentaries that there might have been, is greatly to be lamented – especially in comparison with the riches from Ireland and Wales. With the exception of a few pieces (especially the collection in the 'Poppleton manuscript'), they are lost.[53]

It can, of course, be argued that this gaping hole represents to some extent the range of Gaelic texts which, once Gaelic literacy was lost, no one could read. Presumably, however, an important factor contributing to their loss was that no one important needed them any more. Most of what little survives did so because it was translated; the rest was presumably abandoned. Gaelic *literati* would not only have helped to perpetuate an interest in (predominantly) Gaelic texts, but would also have been a channel through which the empowered in society would have had access to what they contained – say, in the recitation of poetry or genealogy, or in the courts of *judices*. Perhaps, therefore, it may be assumed that the demise of Gaelic clerics and poets and the decline of *judices* in the middle of the thirteenth century reflects a more general change in society which rendered redundant the need for the learning and expertise which they had to offer.

Even if a balance may have been preserved between Gaelic and Anglo-French for most of this period, in which Gaelic maintained its status as a language of literacy, it is unlikely, of course, that the situation was static and that the literacy of Gaelic *literati* was unaffected. If we wish to understand how Gaelic literacy may have functioned in these conditions we cannot do much better than look ahead to the fifteenth and sixteenth centuries, when literacy in Gaelic and Scots co-existed in areas of the Highlands. Professor Meek's seminal study of this phenomenon has suggested that scribes moved from one orthographic system to the other, depending on the nature of the document.[54] It may be envisaged, therefore, that Gaelic *literati* in eastern Scotland between 1124 and 1249 may have been capable of writing Latin charters without betraying their knowledge of Gaelic orthography. It may also be wondered whether they, too, developed a new, or at least distinctly less conventional, orthography for Gaelic, of which the Diss text of the royal genealogy may be an early example. Another point of comparison is the work of the late-twelfth-century scribes at Núachongbáil in Anglo-French-dominated Leinster, where scribal interest in Gaelic literature continued despite increasing isolation from other Gaelic scholars and peripheralization in the secular and monastic world which now surrounded them.[55] 'In such circumstances', it has been argued, 'orthographic and literary norms would be increasingly prone to give way to unconventional usage and innovations.'[56] Perhaps the Gaelic *literati* in eastern Scotland between 1124 and 1249 should be seen in a similar light. They do, however, appear to have retained a significant role in a society which was, after all, Anglo-French voluntarily rather than by conquest. They, and Gaelic literacy with them, may not have held the predominant position they once did. It would be rash, however, to assume that they were therefore peripheralized. On balance, it seems safer to envisage that, from the early twelfth to the mid-thirteenth centuries, the reality in eastern Scotland was closer to *modus vivendi* than *expugnatio*.[57]

NOTES

1 See Murison, 'Linguistic relationships'.
2 Barrow, *Robert Bruce*, pp. 6–8.
3 Barrow, *Kingship and Unity*, pp. 35ff.; R. R. Davies, *Domination*, pp. 50–1.
4 Part of the problem is that material current in Scotland in this period will in many instances be indistinguishable from Irish, given that the same Gaelic literate culture would have been shared from Munster to Moray. See Hudson, 'Historical literature', for a survey of texts which may have a Scottish provenance.
5 Barrow, *Scotland and its Neighbours*, ch. 5; Broun, *Charters*.
6 Barrow, *Scotland and its Neighbours*, pp. 109, 118–19.

7 Above, pp. 15–38.

8 Jackson, *Gaelic Notes*, esp. pp. 89, 96–7.

9 *Regesta Regum Scottorum*, vol. 1, ed. Barrow, p. 72.

10 *Johannis de Fordun*, ed. Skene, p. 294. For discussion, see Bannerman, 'King's Poet'; Duncan, *Scotland*, pp. 554–6. Most MSS give the Gaelic royal title as 're Albane', which suggests an ungrammatical *rí Albanaigh*. The usual title is *rí Alban* ('king of Scotland'). The Latin translation (*rex Albanorum*), however, suggests that *rí Albanach* ('king of Scots') was intended.

11 Picked up in Bannerman, 'King's Poet', 122; Duncan, *Scotland*, p. 555, n. 5.

12 Bannerman, 'King's Poet', 124, 133–5; Duncan, *Scotland*, pp. 555–6.

13 Bannerman, 'King's Poet', 133–5.

14 Bannerman, ibid., 143–4, has drawn attention to Gille Brígde Albanach, a poet active in Munster *c.* 1220, as a fully fledged representative of Gaelic literary culture who may have originated in eastern Scotland. Some uncertainty remains about his region of origin, which may have been somewhere like Atholl or the Lennox where the leading families remained predominantly Gaelic throughout this period (and beyond). Also, he is not an example of a poet finding patronage in eastern Scotland in the thirteenth century.

15 R. R. Davies, *Domination*, ch. 3, at p. 62.

16 And was, indeed, what was often meant by 'Scotland' up to the early thirteenth century: see Broun, 'Defining Scotland'.

17 *Liber Cartarum Sancti Andree*, pp. 113–17. Dr Simon Taylor is currently preparing a new edition.

18 *Charters of Inchaffray*, ed. Lindsay *et al.*, no. XI. Also edited in Neville, 'Earls of Strathearn', vol. 2, no. 7.

19 For a discussion of this vowel, see Jackson, *Gaelic Notes*, pp. 133–5.

20 Cowan, 'Scottish chronicle'; edited in Anderson, *Kings and Kingship*, 2nd edn, pp. 240–60.

21 Miller, 'Matriliny', pp. 138–42.

22 David spelt 'Dauid' is found in Gaelic texts. See, for example, *Dictionary of the Irish Language*, s.n. *Dauíth* (D, pp. 126–7).

23 If nine simple scribal accidents (as described above, but ignoring word division) are corrected, plus, in one case, ignoring a suspension stroke.

24 Lambeth Palace, MS 8, fo. 107v, a32–b28, Diss's own manuscript, begun in 1188. A copy, begun two years later, is BL Cotton MS Claudius E.3 (the genealogy is at fo. 116r, b26–116v, a29). It is published in *Radulfi de Diceto*, ed. Stubbs, vol. 2, p. 35. See ibid., vol. 1, pp. xciii ff. for the relationship of these two manuscripts.

25 *Johannis de Fordun*, ed. Skene, pp. 251–2, 294–5. I hope to discuss these texts and their relationship to each other at greater length elsewhere. Professor D. E. R. Watt points out to me that Fordun may have already died before David I's genealogy was added to his chronicle.

26 On the epenthetic vowel here, see Jackson, *Gaelic Notes*, p. 108.

27 C. Breatnach, 'Guttural spirants', 186.

28 Published in *Chronicle of Andrew of Wyntoun*, ed. Amours, vol. 2, pp. 114–17, 210–13, 349, 351; and *Androw of Wyntoun*, ed. Laing, vol. 1, pp. 55–6, 102–3, 169–70.

29 National Library of Scotland, Edinburgh, Advocates' MS 34.7.3, fos. 17v–19r.

30 *Chronicle of Andrew of Wyntoun*, ed. Amours, vol. 2, p. 348.

31 BL Royal MS 17 D. 20, fo. 46r vi edited (not entirely accurately) in *Androw of Wyntoun*, ed. Laing, vol. 1, pp. 169–70. See *Chronicle of Andrew of Wyntoun*, ed. Amours, pp. i, xliii-lx, lxxxvii-lxxxix for the relationship between the manuscripts of Wyntoun's work and its three editions.

32 A rare indication that Insular script may have been used. For another possible example, see Anderson, *Kings and Kingship*, 2nd edn, p. 247, n. 83. Presumably scribes used Insular script (certainly in the first half of the twelfth century). There is little indication in what survives that scribes experienced difficulty in reading it. The Cistercian abbey of Coupar Angus possessed (and seems to have used) a psalter from north-east Ireland written in Insular script. See McRoberts, 'A "Continuatio Bedae"?' and Barrow, *Kingship and Unity*, p. 82, for discussion and references.

33 BL Royal MS 17 D. 20, fo. 46v. 'Eadak' is misread as 'Cadak' in *Androw of Wyntoun*, ed. Laing, vol. 1, p. 170. Wyntoun's third edition, in *Chronicle of Andrew of Wyntoun*, ed. Amours, vol. 2, p. 351, has 'Cadak Resedek Corbre Rigada'.

34 A similar statement probably lies behind Éremon's appearance in Wyntoun as 'Ermeon Malanseyde' (*Androw of Wyntoun*, ed. Laing, vol. 1, p. 103). 'Malan' may originally have been presented as an alternative name for Éremon's father Míl Éspáine, in which case 'Malan' may be a garbling of Galam, which is given as Míl's alternative name in some versions of *Lebor Gabála Érenn*.

35 *Book of Leinster*, ed. Best *et al.*, vol. 6, p. 1471 (336b38–c26).

36 Ibid., p. 1558 (350e35–7): 'm. Echach Riata qui 7 Carpre Rigfota a quo Dal Riata'.

37 Anderson, *Kings and Kingship*, 2nd edn, pp. 52–67.

38 Most witnesses are edited ibid., pp. 264–89.

39 List I: ibid., pp. 279–85. It also has 'Finled' (two times out of two) for *Finnlaíg*, which is the first occasion in texts discussed in this paper where *gh* is spelt 'd'. If 'd' for *gh* appeared elsewhere in List I it could suggest that this was an attempt to spell 'by ear'. It is more likely, therefore, to be a slip by a scribe who had some experience of writing Gaelic in the period after *dh* had developed into *gh*, which could lead to one being written for the other by mistake, as in this case. For *dh* changing to *gh*, see O'Rahilly, 'Middle Irish pronunciation', 164–7, 187ff., and Jackson, '"Common Gaelic"', 83, who dates this phenomenon to between the early twelfth and thirteenth centuries.

40 See ibid., 61–3 (though List I's 'Radharc' for *Rhydderch* is preferable to 'Amdarch' in other lists, which Anderson regards as superior).

41 *Charters of Inchaffray*, ed. Lindsay *et al.*, nos. XII (facsimile no. 6), XXVI and XXVII (facsimile no. 8); Neville, 'Earls of Strathearn', vol. 2, nos. 8, 16 and Additional Charters, no. 17.

42 See ibid., vol. 1, p. 339.

43 The pair are *Charters of Inchaffray*, ed. Lindsay *et al.*, nos. XI and XII; Neville, 'Earls of Strathearn', vol. 2, nos. 7 and 8.

44 The facsimile shows that Scribe A gives a stroke above every minim intended as an *i*. The name is now Ardunie. Donald Mackinnon (*Inchaffray Charters*, ed. Lindsay *et al.*, p. 328) suggested *Ard Eógain*, 'Eógan's height', though confessed that 'the final *i* is puzzling, but may represent a diminutive'.

200

45 *Charters of Inchaffray*, ed. Lindsay *et al.*, no. XXVII; Neville, 'Earls of Strathearn', vol. 2, Additional Charters, no. 17.
46 See above, p. 188, for discussion.
47 See Flanagan, above, p. 115.
48 Jackson, *Gaelic Notes*, p. 32. See Barrow, 'Charters of David I', 29.
49 *Charters of Inchaffray*, ed. Lindsay *et al.*, nos. III-V.
50 For example Mael Giric, prior of the *Céli Dé* of Muthill, and his successor Muiredach (who is found in 1235); Gille Anndrais, prior of the *Céli Dé* of Abernethy (mentioned between 1235 and 1239); and Mael Brígte, prior of the *Céli Dé* of Brechin (found by 1189 and between 1204 and 1214). See Cowan and Easson, *Religious Houses*, pp. 46–51.
51 Ibid. For further discussion of Gaelic learned orders in eastern Scotland in this period, see Bannerman, 'King's Poet', 138–49. Cf. also Barrow, 'Some East Fife documents', 24.
52 Bannerman, 'King's Poet', 138–9 (and on *judices* in general, Barrow, *Kingdom of the Scots*, pp. 69–82). Only one document from a *judex* survives (dated 1221) – though only in a sixteenth-century copy (edited in Barrow, *Kingdom of the Scots*, pp. 81–2). It is an official Latin document, and shows no significant signs of Gaelic orthography. The earliest extant manuscript of a collection of Scottish law dates to between 1267 and 1272, and includes a text of miscellaneous items under the heading *leges Scotie* which may (in part) date to the latter half of William I's reign. (See esp. MacQueen, 'Scots law', pp. 85–95, 99–102.) Could any of this (especially the superficially archaic section known since the seventeenth century as the 'laws of the Scots and the Bretts') have been inherited from Gaelic legal texts written or transcribed in the twelfth or thirteenth centuries? Very few charters survive in the name of any *Céli Dé* but those that do, again, show no significant indication of Gaelic spelling (see, for example, Barrow, 'Kinninmonth', 119–120.)
53 Insofar as it may be assumed that they existed: see Sims-Williams, above, pp. 19–20.
54 Meek, 'Gàidhlig is Gaylick'.
55 Mac Gearailt, 'Middle Irish texts'.
56 Ibid., 201.
57 I am very grateful for feedback I received at the conference from Prof. David Dumville and Dr Dáibhí Ó Cróinín, and especially Dr Richard Sharpe whose comments, along with the helpful suggestions made by Dr Huw Pryce, inspired me to rewrite substantially my conference paper for publication. I am also very grateful to Dr Nerys Ann Jones for her constant help and encouragement. Whatever errors remain are entirely my own.

Inkhorn and spectacles: the impact of literacy in late medieval Wales

LLINOS BEVERLEY SMITH

At Llanbeblig church in Caernarfon, some time after 1500, a memorial brass was commissioned to commemorate the life of one Richard Foxwist, 'in whom the glory of writing outshone many' ('in quo pre multis scribendi gloria fulsit'), and, as befitted one who had plied the craft of scrivener in the town, the brass was adorned with the signs of his occupation, an inkhorn and penner. Towards the end of the fifteenth century, the poet Owain ap Llywelyn ab y Moel, in a *cywydd gofyn* or asking poem, had solicited from his patron, Sir Siôn Mechain, the distinguished and well-heeled incumbent of the church of Llandrinio in Powys, a pair of spectacles with handles, to be worn 'between eyebrows and cheeks' ('rhwng dwyael a gên') to dispel the fog and the mists which impeded his vision.[1] Although the scrivener, armed with his inkhorn and pen, and the bespectacled poet provide two vivid and arresting images with which to approach the issues of literacy and the burgeoning literate mentality of late medieval Wales, a consciousness of literate skills and the culture of parchment and ink was, by then, quite widely disseminated. It was with pen and ink, according to the poet Dafydd Nanmor (fl. *c.* 1420–85), that Pilate had inscribed the forehead of Jesus. Parchment and ink, even, perhaps, the new technology of print, likewise became apt metaphors in the poetic armoury to convey the height of perfection achieved by the beloved's skin and brows. Indeed in the fourteenth century the north wind was for Dafydd ap Gwilym the poet's emissary as it blew through the heavens, likened to a notary writing on a page of parchment ('noter wybr natur ebrwydd'). For Iolo Goch (fl. *c.* 1320–1400) a professional scribe or notary public (*notar pyblig*), even if he were to spend an entire year and three days writing with pen and ink (*du*) the life of St David, could scarce recount the saint's numerous miracles. But most revealing of the impact of writing is another of Dafydd Nanmor's poems where the poet, confessing his numerous amorous sins, proposes to send to his loved one 'an eagle's load of letters' ('llwyth eryr o lythyrau') and to write in 'a fair hand in ink' a loving word on the edge of her glove. It would be difficult to find a clearer witness to the mental adjustments and shifts which these words suggest. For whereas the conventional conveyer of the poet's missives was normally a denizen of the natural world, here the skills of paper and pen are to be used.[2]

The fourteenth and fifteenth centuries are, in some ways, the least interesting, and certainly one of the most frustrating, periods in which to study the impact and implications of literacy in medieval Wales. By the time of the Edwardian conquest of 1282–3 Wales had already been exposed to the written word and its culture – in both Latin and vernacular forms – for several centuries, and the period lacks the interest and forensic challenge of an earlier age when language was first committed to writing. Nor can the preoccupations of those who study the burgeoning of literate modes in later centuries be matched in the evidence of the fourteenth and fifteenth centuries, and issues such as the acquisition and diffusion of skills of reading and writing or the consequences, if any, for the development of cognitive processes and abstract thought, for the drawing of boundaries between the inner self and the wider community, for social and cultural differentiation or for individual emancipation are elusive.[3] The society of late medieval Wales was not one of prodigious and feverish letter-writers like the Pastons or Plumptons, still less the lettered, cultured world of the *marchand écrivain* whose *livres de raison* and *ricordanze* betoken, so it is argued, 'a major breakthrough . . . in the use of literacy' and constitute an important 'vehicle of self-expression of the citizen class'.[4] Even if an agreed definition of what is meant by literate skills could be established, no objective and reliable means of measuring such skills in medieval societies has yet been discovered. Even so, this chapter will argue that the two and a half centuries which spanned the period between the Edwardian conquest and the Union with England in 1536 did constitute a crucial and distinctive period in the development of a literate mentality in Wales: a process which may, in some ways, be compared with the twelfth and thirteenth centuries in England, when, as Michael Clanchy has convincingly argued, literate modes spread both territorially and socially, and when a pronounced shift 'from memory to written record, from sacred script to practical literacy' was witnessed.[5] An attempt will be made to identify some of the signs which suggest that the fourteenth and fifteenth centuries in Wales experienced not perhaps the beginning, but a marked intensification, of the process of creating a literate mentality; to try and explain why it was so; and, finally, to account for the enduring force of non-literate modes throughout the late medieval centuries.

Some indication of the impact made by written texts, of the social milieux in which manuscripts were known and respected and the ways in which literate skills were acquired can be gained from a number of sources: from the colophons of surviving texts, from the wills of the period, as well as from anecdotal references in record sources.[6] No attempt will be made here at a comprehensive coverage of the evidence; nor, indeed, can the surviving information be regarded as in any way complete. For instance, written texts as recorded in wills may not be a reliable or a complete index of a testator's literary possessions. It is well known that books in the form of a volume or codex were almost certainly fewer in number than smaller quires or single pages or rolls, which may not always be noted or itemized. Michael Clanchy has written how 'on the threshold of literacy, among knights and minstrels . . . writings were perhaps at first more familiar and inviting in the form of rolls containing short, vernacular texts than in the form of weighty Latin books'.[7] In Wales and its borders there can be little doubt that rolls and quires were important parts of the written culture of our period, as some illustrative examples will show. A Lollard heretic on the Herefordshire borders made in his abjuration a promise not to retain quires or rolls containing heresies or errors written by himself or by others; the Welsh poet Hywel ap Dafydd ab Ieuan ap Rhys refers to the 'books and rolls' ('llyfrau a rholiau') owned by Rhys ap Siancyn at Aberpergwm; a fifteenth-century law-book refers to the information obtained from the 'roll of Dafydd Llwyd'; while Thomas Wiliems, writing in 1600, referred to 'an old roll of parchment written in Welsh after the conquest, which contains the Statute of Rhuddlan and the laws given to the Welsh at the time' ('hen rol ar vemrwn wedy'i scrivenu yn Gymraec er concwest Cymru . . .').[8]

A number of volumes may, however, be linked quite precisely with their owners, of whom, not surprisingly, clerics formed an important and distinctive group. Although few clerical libraries (with the exception of monastic establishments) could match that of Anian, bishop of St Asaph (1268–93), his will, while it does not mention specific titles, refers to his books of canon law, his books of theology and his Bible.[9]

204

The impact of literacy in late medieval Wales

By the end of our period priests like Hugh Robartes or Henry Morgan could bequeath in their wills books of 'grammer and vmanitie', and, more specifically, 'a boke callid Polidorus de Historia Britannorum'. Equally unsurprising were the liturgical books which were in clerical ownership, like the breviary bequeathed by William Rodon or the printed missal, which, as Daniel Huws has suggested, may have belonged to Master Richerd Peicke, vicar of Conwy, in the early sixteenth century, or the gradual or antiphon which Ieuan Du'r Bilwg solicited from Syr Lewis ap Dafydd, a priest of Glyn Nedd.[10] Jurists and experts in native Welsh law were also availing themselves of pocket-sized volumes of specialist texts.[11] By the middle of the fifteenth century, major poets were committing to writing both their own works and those of earlier practitioners, while the names of two – Gwilym Tew and Dafydd Nanmor – were inscribed on the volume which came to be known as *Llyfr Aneirin*.[12] Several of the surviving colophons, likewise, link a manuscript with an owner or attribute its writing or its translating to a patron's instigation. It was at the behest of Gruffudd ap Maredudd of Ceredigion that Madog ap Selyf translated the legendary *Chronicle of Turpin*, while Efa ferch Maredudd instigated the vernacular translation of the Creed of Athanasius, evidence which suggests not only a taste for devotional texts among lay men and women but also the cardinal role of such texts in the mother tongue as an inducement to acquiring literate skills.[13] The White Book of Rhydderch itself was associated with the distinguished *jurisperitus* of Ceredigion, Rhydderch ab Ieuan Llwyd, and in its subsequent peregrinations it may well have reposed in the home of Elise ap Gruffudd ab Einion at Plas-yn-Iâl, near Llandegla.[14] In Glamorgan, likewise, the interest of Hopcyn ap Tomas ab Einion of Ynysdawe, one of the most distinguished of medieval manuscript aficionados, is testified not only by the many poetic salutations to his manuscript collection but also by the explicit reference to the commissioning by him of at least one vernacular manuscript and his presumed association with the celebrated Red Book of Hergest.[15] The rise of the secular book owner may also be illustrated by the will of William Gefferey, who in 1504–5 bequeathed his books, namely 'Pollycronycon Boras, the Fall of Prynces, Dives et Pauper and a book in Latin named Liber Sancte Terre', to the parish of Our Lady in Swansea 'there to be chained in church in such places as the warden thinks best'.[16] Chance references in the record sources of the period also confirm the impression of a book-owning laity. In the court of

205

the borough of Ruthin in 1346 one Bleddyn ap Hochkin brought a case against Adam le Taillour alleging that a book, purchased from Alice Tasket of Denbigh and valued at 10$s.$, had been withheld from him. By the end of the fourteenth century, we may safely assume that primers and missals, sometimes of considerable monetary value, were in lay ownership. Far and away the most intriguing reference, however is that to a 'book of Welsh history', valued at 6$s.$ 8$d.$, and the subject of an extended law-suit in the commote court of Llannerch in Dyffryn Clwyd in 1331 between Ithel ab Einion and Ednyfed ap Carwed when the loan of the book was alleged.[17] The 'explosion in Welsh book production and in the writing down of literature', which Daniel Huws has rightly identified as a significant and enduring achievement of the period between 1250 and 1400, clearly had ramifications not only for the copying and conserving of texts but for their dissemination across a broad swathe of late medieval society.[18]

In what sense were these lay owners of books and manuscripts literate people? Although explicit references to literate skills are exiguous, contemporary poetry and record sources alike suggest that some lay men and women had a measure of competence in reading and writing. 'Llythr a ddysgodd' ('she has learned her letters'), exclaimed the poet Rhisierdyn (fl. *c.* 1360–1400) of Myfanwy, the wife of Goronwy Fychan ap Tudur of Penmynydd, while by the fifteenth century wills and administrative records suggest that some of the gentry and merchants were able to write documents in their own hand. Likewise, to judge from the words of the poets, the reading of works of literature, history and law was a regular feature of their patrons' habits and life-style. Just as Llywelyn Goch ap Meurig Hen recorded how it was his enjoyable duty during his sojourn at Nannau to read with his patrons and nephews the law-texts and ancient history of the Britons, so too was it the custom of Lewys Glyn Cothi, almost a century later, to peruse the chronicles, pedigrees and *ystoria* with his mentor, Gwilym Siôn of Llanegwad.[19] Such inviting and seductive images of cosy, domestic and private study, which seem to speak to us in recognizable tones across the centuries, are, however, delusive. True, the Welsh house was to witness improved standards of comfort in the late fourteenth and fifteenth centuries. It was then that chimneys and dais canopies were introduced in the sturdy, craftsman-built houses of the gentle orders, while the development of the single-celled hall-house into a multi-cellular structure with inner or secondary rooms has also been charted.[20] The letter-loving Welshman,

The impact of literacy in late medieval Wales

however, had not yet withdrawn completely to those secret, intro-
spective parlours or chambers so repellent to Langland. Likewise,
although the habit of private reading was elsewhere reflected in the
graphic language of texts perused by laymen, reading, as we are often
reminded, was also a shared convivial activity and books were
possessed of acoustic properties.[21] The scenes described by the Welsh
poets of the fourteenth and fifteenth centuries seem to belong more to
the world of the 'textual communities' brilliantly revealed by Brian
Stock than to the private, intimate world of the silent reader. But in
that ambience, through the mediation of literate men, the unlettered
were themselves enabled to share in the assumptions and culture of
the literate world.[22]

If reading retained a measure of professional skill, writing was even
more markedly, as we are also often reminded, a craft best left to the
trained practitioners whose identities are now slowly emerging from
the detailed investigations of modern textual scholars. Although
manuscripts such as the Book of Taliesin (NLW, Peniarth MS 2) or
Llawysgrif Hendregadredd (NLW MS 6680B) suggest the continued
importance of the monastic *scriptorium* (in the latter case, indeed, the
variety of hands identified at work on the text suggests a collective
enterprise), Daniel Huws has recently emphasized the importance of
scribes who may well have been working beyond the monastic
penumbra – men like Gwilym Wasta or, notably, Hywel Fychan of
Builth, one of the scribes of the Red Book of Hergest who worked at
the behest of Hopcyn ap Tomas.[23] But besides the copiers and
compilers of some of the greatest treasures of the medieval heritage,
and the notaries public such as John son of William de Bergevenny or
Robert ap Rhys, to whom laymen had access, we must also take note
of the labours of modest scriveners, engrossing the written instruments of the fourteenth and fifteenth centuries.[24] A great deal of work
remains to be done on the identities of these humble but indispensable
men, although careful inspection of surviving deeds, their hands and
their witness-lists helps to establish their careers and connections.
Several of the known examples, such as Henry and Dennis (Diony-
sius), scriveners of Ruthin, or Richard Pygot, scriptor of Denbigh,
may be set in the urban communities of the period.[25] Much the most
distinctive family of scriveners, whose skills were passed down from
father to son in the same way as the skills of the learned professions
reflect a dynastic mentality, was that of the Foxwists of Caernarfon,
to one of whom reference has already been made. A substantial

207

number of written instruments penned by Richard Foxwist, as well as by two of his sons, Rowland and John, survives in a number of important collections of estate records, documents which show not only the extensive scribal practice enjoyed by these men but also the very considerable geographical range of their interests.[26] It was Richard Foxwist also who compiled, in a fair and competent hand, the version of the *Record of Caernarvon* now to be found in BL Harleian MS 696, a copy embellished not with his signature, but with a drawing of a fox to which the words 'Ricardus' and 'Wisti' are added.[27] If he is indeed the beneficiary named in the will of one John Padyngton of London in 1452, a valuable indication of his training may be obtained, for the will directed that the boy Richard Foxwist should be educated for a term of three years, the third of which was to be spent at a writing school where he should be provided with food, linen and wool garments and other necessities.[28] Another Welsh scrivener, albeit one whose working life was spent in the city of London, was Morgan Williams, who, along with bequests to his kinsmen in Llandybïe, left to his apprentice and servant William Goldyng twenty marks in money 'so that he contynue at his lernyng . . . and all my bokes of law and also of presidents [precedents] belongyng to myn occupacyon of scryvener'.[29]

Although the indications are that the skills of reading and writing remained largely specialist ones in late medieval Wales, the literate layman, possessed of technical skills, is also in evidence. We cannot now chart the location of formal educational establishments, nor speak of the men or the women who profited from them. Suffice it to say that formal teaching in school was not the only determinant of elementary literate skills, for these might also be gained by informal instruction.[30] Be that as it may, by the end of the fifteenth century, if not earlier, convincing testimony of pragmatic, practical literacy among laymen can be adduced. One such was Gruffudd ap Aron, builder of the Peniarth estate, who kept, in his own hand, a roll of his *prid* lands, just as the owners of Edwinsford found it prudent to preserve a written memorandum of their own land transactions.[31] A manuscript volume, hitherto little noticed, but one which in the present context is an interesting and revealing survival, is that known as Cardiff MS 51. Written almost entirely in Welsh in a crude and graceless late-fifteenth-century hand, it details a large number of land transactions accomplished in the lordship of Denbigh during the last decades of the century. Over a total of some 166 pages, many of the entries record the purchases of one Rhys ab Einion Fychan, whom John Wynn of Gwydir described as a 'gentleman of the house of Penwyn of Nanconwy and Denbighland', and whose daughter, Gwenhwyfar, was married to Robert Salesbury of Lleweni, taking with her in marriage the greater part of her father's estate, estimated at a thousand marks *per annum*. It seems reasonable to assume that the volume was written by Rhys himself, or by his son-in-law, as an *aide-mémoire* of his landed possessions and especially of those lands taken at mortgage by means of the *prid* transaction.[32] By the same period, also, among men of substance who were also charged with administrative responsibilities in their localities, the practice of keeping books of precedence or commonplace books had developed. We hear of the 'book of Dafydd ap Hywel ap Madog written in a fair hand on paper during the time of Edward IV' ('lyfr Dafydd ap Howel ap Madog wedy ei ysgrifennu yn deg ar bapir yn amser Edward IIII'), the 'book of Edward ap Dafydd ab Edward', the 'book of William ap Gruffydd of Penmynydd' and the 'book of Lawrence Rixton of Conway', although none of these has survived.[33] Of the surviving examples, however, two may be directly connected with their owners and compilers. The first, a volume of miscellaneous materials written throughout in a late-fifteenth-century hand and including materials of mainly administrative importance in French, Latin, English and Welsh, is that of John Edwards of Chirk, a man of property and office in the north-east march, and one of learning and intellectual attainment who was addressed by most of the major poets who plied their craft in the period. Moreover, by happy coincidence, a second volume which may be confidently connected with John Edwards survives in the form of a book of Latin grammar which reveals the pedagogical aids used to inculcate basic linguistic accomplishments in the period.[34] Of similar purpose to John Edwards's commonplace book was a formulary or precedent book compiled somewhat later by Edward ap Rhys of Eglwyseg, in the county of Denbigh, who, like John Edwards of Chirk, was also saluted as a man of learning. The poet Gruffudd Hiraethog described him as 'chief of recorders' ('pen ysgrifenwyr') while another referred to his academic labours and book learning.[35] While these volumes may not be ranked among the most spectacular or prestigious treasures of Wales's literary heritage – they are rather the practical, unstudied gleanings of busy men of affairs, lettered, cultured and entrusted with responsibilities for the business of their neighbourhood – they demonstrate nevertheless the importance of office, no less than landed proprietorship, in fostering literate skills within a significant segment of Welsh society by the end of the fifteenth century.

While the practical, pragmatic skills of these men seems evident, men such as Edward ap Dafydd, John Edwards and Edward ap Rhys formed an important bridge linking the manuscript culture of late medieval Wales with the burgeoning record-making and record-keeping mentality which characterized the post-conquest period. Indeed, the two features were interrelated, for the royal or seignorial functionary and the cultivated connoisseur of books and manuscripts were often one and the same. Two illustrative examples must suffice. Take the case of Ithel ab Einion, whose ownership of a 'book of Welsh history' was noted earlier. Not only was Ithel a man of considerable landed estate but he was also invested with office – *rhaglaw* (bailiff) and farmer of *amobr* (virginity dues) among others – in the lordship of Dyffryn Clwyd.[36] Or again, the case of Dafydd Glais, the perpetrator of a notorious and vicious murder at Aberystwyth in 1440, who in his more sober and reflective moments penned a fifteenth-century manuscript of Geoffrey of Monmouth's *Brut*.[37] Although the space of a century separates Dafydd and Ithel, both may be set in the same social and intellectual milieu, for Dafydd himself (as, indeed, his father before him) served in the royal administration of Aberystwyth town during the first half of the fifteenth century. The administrations in which these men served were themselves cumulatively dominated by the written word.[38] Just as in post-conquest England, first in the king's bureaucracy and then in seignorial administrations, a steady rise in the output of documents was witnessed, so too, in Wales after 1282 a spectacular proliferation of written records is evidenced. Several of the great cadastral surveys belong to the period of the conquest itself or to the ensuing decades. While the castles of Caernarfon and Conwy were building, the king set in train the enquiries which were to result in the extent of Anglesey; Denbigh (1334) and Bromfield and Yale (1391), among secular lordships, and the landed endowments of St David's (1326) among ecclesiastical possessions, were surveyed, while at the end of the fourteenth century the lordship of Chirk, along with the other Arundel lordships, was extented on 'quires of paper afterwards compiled in one book' ('in uno libro').[39] Documents such as these were conserved, examined and scrutinized and became authoritative statements of services, customs and status. Thus a bondman claiming free status had his claim overturned because the name of his grand-father was to be found written among the names of the bondmen of the lordship of Bromfield and Yale; the economic depression at the end of the fourteenth century in Chirk prompted the scrutiny of 'old financial records'. Titles and privileges, individual and collective alike, were inscribed in seignorial charters, and disputes and their resolution were likewise committed to writing in formal and authoritative records of curial proceedings. Everywhere, reliance on and dominance of the written word were growing apace.[40]

The proliferation of written records was not, of course, confined to the higher echelons but was, rather, disseminated throughout the social spectrum. Those who could not themselves read or write were becoming increasingly familiar with the use of, and the need to produce, the written instrument when this was demanded. Bondmen might have in their possession charters of manumission and vaga-bonds might be required to carry a licence to beg.[41] Even an outlaw might address his lord in a letter which, for all its defiant and insolent tone, conformed punctiliously to contemporary epistolary style. Seignorial directives might be conveyed in writing. Marriage contracts and arbitration decrees were committed to writing, while the use of a document under seal in the form of a conditional bond or obligation became widely available to effect a credit transaction or to register an agreement.[42] Habits of personal chronology likewise reflected the increasing importance of writing. Although the keeping of parish registers was made obligatory only in 1538 and the requirement for some time thereafter was 'honoured as much in the breach as in the observance', the more prominent members of Welsh society were already recording the birth of their sons and heirs in writing. The missal of the church of Llandyfeisant near Llandeilo, for instance, was inscribed with the day and year of the birth of Edmund Fitzherbert, just as the birth of John Walwayn at Hay in 1329 was entered in the great psalter of the church, and the date of the birth of Roger Puleston 'in a certain missal in the church of Worthenbury'.[43] Even if the date of birth or baptism had not been deliberately recorded, reliance might be placed on written instruments when verification was needed. Charters of feoffment made on or near the reputed date of birth might be produced when proof of age was required, as were dated financial accounts, arbitration awards or records of entry into Holy Orders.[44] Dates of death and burial were also inscribed on a breviary, while graves were sometimes inscribed with the name of the deceased and

211

the date of his or her death. 'Mae sgrifen uwch ben y bedd / Mae dau o enwau unwedd' ('The grave is inscribed with two names'), noted Lewys Glyn Cothi in his elegy on the death of Thomas ap Rhosier of Hergest as he proceeded to describe the fine family tomb erected to his memory and that of his wife. The scrivener, Morgan Williams, characteristically perhaps, left detailed instructions in his last will that a marble stone should be laid on his grave with his name and the date of his death 'to be gravyd in Latyn fixed on the same stone'.[45] Written remembrances such as these could be, and indeed were, consulted when it was necessary to do so. The altar of the church of Clifford, whose dedication on the last day of April 1329 was commemorated in gold letters, was inspected on the occasion of a proof of age, just as in 1464 the missal recording the date of birth of John Lestrange was scrutinized.[46] Above all, men and women began increasingly to convey their landed properties by means of charters or deeds. Such instruments, in the form both of deeds poll and chirographs, survive in their thousands.[47] They survive as originally issued and given by the donor, on slips of parchment or paper, many with their authenticating features, such as seals, still intact. Moreover, they were now being written and conserved not only in monastic *scriptoria* and ecclesiastical cartularies but by secular scriveners and in private secular archives.

What importance did people attach to the charter or deed and what status was accorded the written instrument? In form and construction the late medieval deed retained the features which marked it out as an evidentiary not a dispositive instrument. Land might be conveyed without the use of a deed, provided livery of seisin was given, although such a course of action would be deemed unwise. Nor was a deed of itself sufficient proof of ownership at law.[48] My concern, however, is not with the legal effects of deeds but with people's perceptions of their value and worth. On occasion, it has to be said, a deed might be very lightly regarded, as was the case when one was sold for 4*d.* and a gallon of ale.[49] Such a cavalier attitude to the written word was, however, exceptional. Charters were themselves valuable objects and substantial monetary compensation as well as damages were claimed when they were eloigned.[50] Small private archives of charters are sometimes revealed in our sources. The writings of substantial landowners, like the house of Avene in Glamorgan, might be housed in a box sealed with the owner's seal and formal safeguards demanded when it left its owner's possession;

but the muniments of smaller landowners might also be kept in a special deed box or pyx, as were those of Dafydd ap Iorwerth and Ithel his brother or Isabella, wife of John ap Dafydd Fychan of Wepre, whose family archive stretched back for a century or more.[51] Moreover, regardless of the status of the deed at law, it is clear that in people's perceptions, the charter embodied the title to land, and was in itself a potent symbol of ownership. Thus, a man made a feoffment of land to take effect after his death, to one of his sons, with successive remainders to two other sons and to his two daughters in turn. On the death of the third of his sons, with a daughter set to inherit, his widow burned the charter of feoffment, fearing, so it was claimed, that if the inheriting daughter were to obtain the deed she would dispose of the estate.[52] Likewise, the annulment of charters, even where livery of seisin had been effected, would be a serious and solemn act requiring a corporal oath on the Gospel and formal registration of the act by a notary public.[53] People were reposing their trust in the written word and responding to the need to produce formal documentation when such was required. Indeed, in the absence of authentic and valid instruments, fabrication was an obvious alternative and a wide range of forged documents – letters of divorce, matrimonial certificates as well as charters and bonds – is revealed in our evidence.[54] As Michael Clanchy observes, forgers are best understood 'not as occasional deviants on the peripheries of legal practice, but as experts entrenched at the centre of literary and intellectual culture'.[55] In that sense, they, too, betoken the strength of the literate mentality in late medieval Wales.

So far, a case has been made for a surge in literate habits in post-conquest Wales and the growing respect for, and trust in, the written word. Such a development was intensified, even if it was not wholly created, by the practices and demands of bureaucratic seignorial regimes, many of whose functionaries were themselves literate men drawn from the selfsame communities which they served. It was enhanced also by the demands of landed proprietorship at all social levels, by men and by women whose land transactions and archives were formed and conserved. By these means, also, illiterate people were increasingly drawn into the ambit of written culture, through contact with instruments which they could not themselves read or fashion. Even so, several important caveats need to be entered before the triumph of literate modes can be taken for granted. Not only was there an oral residue in the literate culture but the spoken word, image, gesture and ritual were important elements in their own right. For all the proliferation of writing, the culture of the late medieval world remained, as we have been reminded, a profoundly memorial one uniting written and oral transmission, eye and ear.[56] Just as Richard de Fournival in his *Bestiaires d'Amours* revealed the equal importance of sight and hearing in his emphasis on *painture* and *parole* as the portals of memory, so also did his Welsh translator describe how *parabl* and *lliw* both represented and recalled the past to memory.[57] Others must make their assessment of the interrelationship of oral and literate, and the relevance of aural and visual to the modes of literary and artistic expression in late medieval Wales.[58] Our purpose is the more modest one of charting the evidence to be found in the processes of administration and law, and the material is copious. Charters, for instance, continued to be addressed to those who had seen and heard, and what was conserved in writing might be communicated also by word. A gift, committed to writing, was read out in the church of Llanasa and a charter likewise publicly proclaimed in the court of Dyffryn Clwyd.[59] Nor had written, documentary proof supplanted the force of common remembrance or the importance of gesture and symbol in the theatre of memory. The 'infourmacions of old men' or the appraising eye of the judge and the court in proving the age of a child, remained firmly entrenched, as did the bestowal of silk purses or arrows, or the holding of banquets, help to fix notable events in men's minds.[60] Nor did the prevalence of the written arbitration award undermine completely the gestures of conciliation, such as the kiss or the public, visible act of contrition.[61] Despite the increasing use of conditional bonds, the oral agreement remained central to the formation of covenants. Even at the turn of the sixteenth century, so we are told, Sir John Wynn of Gwydir could attribute the friendly relations he enjoyed with his tenantry to his use of verbal rather than written agreements when terms were arranged. In late medieval Wales, likewise, the oral agreement, which, it was said, 'counted as much as a deed in England', remained engrained in popular practice. Although the king's courts in England would not entertain actions of covenant except in the form of a written document under seal, local jurisdictions, by contrast, had no hesitation in respecting the oral agreement.[62] Contracts, indeed, were often sanctioned with symbols and rituals, like the ritual drink (*beveragium*) or the token payment of godsilver, and witnesses who had seen and had heard (*audientes et videntes*) were admitted as proof if the deal were not honoured.[63] 'Even if laymen,' writes one legal historian, 'were conscious of the magic of parchment and wax, they often trusted the words of others without further security.' A man's word, was, truly, 'as good as his bond'.[64]

A second caveat concerns the regional contrasts in the impact of writing in late medieval Wales. For although, as we have seen, increasing resort was made to the written instrument when land was conveyed (as evidenced by the many thousands of surviving examples), it is a puzzling fact, and indeed one that demands explanation, that remarkably few charters and deeds of late medieval date have survived from the counties of Carmarthen and Cardigan, and this despite the survival in contiguous areas, and indeed from urban settlements within these two counties, of written modes of conveyance. Such diverse experience cannot be explained by the bias of preserved records alone, and comments made by early modern observers go some way to providing an answer. A survey of the lordship of Cydweli, dating from 1609, for instance, records that 'before the tyme of King Henry the viiith, they held theyre lands in gavelkynd whereof some were bond and the resydue ffreemen, and passed theyre lands allwayes in the Lords courte by the Rodde wherof there was a record kepte', adding that 'now they only paste theyre lands by deede and release from one to another whereof no record is kept'.[65] The importance attached to the record of court was likewise evinced by a deponent aged 'eighty and upwards', who also recalled the procedure used on such an occasion. 'She did take by the rodde herselfe', she declared, for 'her father did delyver her seazon and possession of the tenement she now hath by the rodde att the hands of the stuarde in court, when she was very yonge of ye age of 7 yeares or thereabouts'.[66] The Elizabethan antiquary George Owen likewise made note of how 'all lands' in the area 'passed by surrender in the lord's court according to the laws of Hywel dda, so that in these countries you shall find no deeds, releases, fines or recoveries of any lands before 1536', a practice which is also confirmed by a late-thirteenth-century comment that 'pleas of feoffment and pleas of quitclaim' were held in Wales 'without charter or writing'.[67] The truth of such claims cannot be tested, for no full record of curial proceedings survives from the lands which are the subject of comment. Far more can be said of an area where a similar practice undoubtedly prevailed, namely the lordship of Dyffryn Clwyd.

There, in the fourteenth and fifteenth centuries, transfer of land was likewise accomplished by surrender and regrant in court, a practice observed not only in the courts of the commotes but also in those of the town.[68] True, in this particular area, the use of deeds and charters was by no means unknown. Seignorial grants, for instance, were conveyed by charter, while private transactions might also be effected by deed poll or indenture.[69] The march of the written word in the area is revealed by the increasing resort to the engrossing of deeds and indentures when land was transferred, and is also reflected in an important statement made by five of the lordship's Welsh tenants that an estate in land was not good 'without a charter sealed with the lord's seal'.[70] Enrolment in the records of curial proceedings was, however, the normal and sufficient means of registering title. Indeed, in one instance a prior record enrolled in the court prevailed over a charter, and in the event of dispute it was the court rolls that would be consulted.

Recourse to such methods has, I would argue, profound implications far beyond their importance to investigators of judicial procedure or to students of diplomatic practice. For although we have insisted so far on the growing familiarity with the written modes of doing business, writing was also a symbol of power and control wielded by seignorial regimes. The power of writing resides not simply in the content of texts and the authority to encourage or inhibit their currency, but also in the fact of recording itself and the difficulty or ease with which access to the written word is permitted. Here the Dyffryn Clwyd records provide us with several insights. Although the court records constituted a written authority which litigants, both in inter-party disputes and in cases where the lord's interests were at stake, were required to provide, access was closely controlled. The process of consulting the records was, for the litigant, taxing in time and in money: in time, by the need to approach the lord's treasury, where his records were kept and whose keys were carefully guarded;[71] in money, by the very substantial fines which the lord might require for permission to scrutinize his muniments: 2s., 5s., 13s. 4d., sometimes as much as £1 were regularly demanded.[72] In this way, writing remained at some distance from the common experience, a remote, unfamiliar technology which carried the power to intimidate and to coerce.

From a remote, unfamiliar technology, it is but a short step to the magical-religious aspects of writing and the persistence of letter or literary magic. Indeed Jack Goody has frequently stressed how it was these aspects of writing which most impressed the populations of pre-colonial Africa, who were mainly concerned with writing as 'a means of communicating with God and other supernatural agencies rather than as a means of social and personal advancement'.[73] Such notions clung tenaciously in the mind-set of Welsh men and women, as our records make clear. The survival of charms, embellished with writings which may be dated with confidence to the late medieval period, suggests the persisting regard for the magic of letters in popular practice. Professor Glanmor Williams, for instance, has shown that the custom of hanging 'scrowes' round the necks of men and beasts, albeit condemned by strict moralists, was none the less common. 'Whoever should say these words or should look upon them' ('pwy bynnac a dywetto yr enweu hynn neu ae hedrycho') recites the preamble to one such charm found in a late-fourteenth-century manuscript, while in the reign of Henry VIII a Radnorshire parson was taken to task for making writings to set over the doors for charming sick cattle and for young children 'that cry in their sleep'.[74] Such examples remind us that for all the advancement of parchment and ink, writing retained for centuries its arcane and magical aura, and graphic expression continued to be invested with supernatural powers.

Even so, by the time of the Union with England many of the elements which helped to create a literate society were already firmly in place. Subsequent decades would offer still further prospects for the cultivation of literate habits. The technique of print and the enduring strength of the culture of parchment encouraged the acquisition of literate skills by lay men and women. Building on solid medieval foundations, religious and devotional vernacular texts proclaimed to the laity the authority of the word and the book.[75] But in this slow transformation the fourteenth and fifteenth centuries had played a distinctive and crucial part. It was then that a literate mentality was established and nourished.

NOTES

1 J. M. Lewis, *Welsh Monumental Brasses*, pp. 40–1; *Gwaith Owain ap Llywelyn*, ed. Rolant, pp. 52–3. For the interest shown by Owain and other Welsh poets in the development of optical instruments see Rolant, 'Owain ap Llywelyn', 106–7.

Llinos Beverley Smith

The earliest known spectacle-maker in England is believed to have been a Dutchman working in Southwark in 1458. Rhodes, 'Spectacle frames', and see Rosser, 'London and Westminster', p. 54. For the development of eye-glasses, see Rosen, 'Invention of eyeglasses', and Ilardi, 'Eyeglasses'.

2 *Poetical Works of Dafydd Nanmor*, ed. Roberts and Williams, p. 96; *Gwaith Dafydd ap Gwilym*, ed. Parry, p. 230; *Oxford Book of Welsh Verse*, ed. Parry, p. 104. For references to notaries, see, for example, *Gwaith Dafydd ap Gwilym*, p. 309 and Bowen, 'Nodiadau ar gywydd'; *Gwaith Iolo Goch*, ed. Johnston, pp. 133, 344, n.; *Gwaith Lewys Môn*, ed. Rolant, p. 456, n. Dafydd Nanmor's reference to an 'eagle's load of letters' is to be found in *Poetical Works*, pp. 78–9. A parallel development is the consciousness of administrative documents, such as writs, which is also expressed in the period's poetry: for example, Llywelyn Goch ap Meurig Hen's assertion that writs (*brifiau*) have summoned him from his patrons at Nannau (*Gwaith Dafydd ap Gwilym a'i Gyfoeswyr*, ed. Williams and Roberts, p. 158). For the suggestion that images of print had entered the poetic repertoire, see I. Jones, *History of Printing*, p. 1 (quoting a *cywydd* by Bedo Brwynllys).

3 See in general the studies in McKitterick (ed.), *Uses of Literacy*, and K. Thomas, 'Meaning of literacy'.

4 Klapisch-Zuber, *Women, Family and Ritual*; Bec, *Les marchands écrivains*.

5 Clanchy, *From Memory*, p. 333. For suggestive remarks on quantifying literacy, see Schofield, 'Measurement of literacy', and Poos, *Rural Society*, pp. 280–9.

6 All references to record sources are to documents in the Public Record Office unless otherwise indicated. References to the Dyffryn Clwyd Court Rolls are to the relevant roll and membrane, except for those included in the data base compiled by the Dyffryn Clwyd Court Roll Projects funded by the Economic and Social Research Council (R000232548 and R000234070) where reference is made to the roll and membrane followed by the calendar number. The support of the ESRC is gratefully acknowledged.

7 Clanchy, *From Memory*, p. 143.

8 J. A. F. Thomson, *Later Lollards*, p. 42; C. W. Lewis, 'Literary tradition', p. 668, n. 255; Huws, *Medieval Codex*, p. 16.

9 Anian's will is transcribed in full from Canterbury Cathedral Archives, Dean and Chapter Sede Vacante Scrap Book, II, p. 187 in Chandler, 'Will in medieval Wales', pp. 212–14. For Welsh monastic libraries, see in general Ker (ed.), *Medieval Libraries*, and for that of Margam, Cowley and Lloyd, 'Old Welsh englyn'.

10 J. C. Smith, 'Wills', 199 (will of Hugh Robartes); Palmer, 'Isycoed', 239 (will of William Rodon); PCC F 22 Spert (will of Henry Morgan). See Chandler, 'Will in medieval Wales', pp. 181–2; Huws, 'Earliest Bangor missal', esp. 117–18.

11 Jenkins, *Law of Hywel Dda*, pp. xxi–xxii; Huws, *Medieval Codex*, p. 5.

12 C. W. Lewis, 'Literary tradition', p. 508; Huws, 'Canu Aneirin', p. 45. It is suggested by Huws that the *englynion* to the rood at Carmarthen in NLW MS 6680B, fos. 120r–121r may be in the hand of the young Dafydd ap Gwilym: 'Llawysgrif Hendregadredd', 18 and Plate 4; for the *englynion*, see *Gwaith Llywelyn Brydydd Hoddnant*, ed. Parry Owen, pp. 55–66.

13 *Ystorya de Carolo Magno*, ed. Williams, pp. xxix, xxxi; NLW Llanstephan MS 2;

218

The impact of literacy in late medieval Wales

Jenkins, *Law of Hywel Dda*, pp. xxii–xxiii. See also Lloyd-Morgan, above, pp. 157–8.

14 Huws, 'Llyfr Gwyn Rhydderch'.

15 Roberts, 'Un o lawysgrifau', 223–4; James, ' "Llwyr wybodau" '.

16 PCC 27 Holgrave; *Glamorgan Wills*, ed. Riden, p. 2.

17 SC 2/217/12, m. 22/Roll7/144; SC 2/216/12, m. 24/Llan1/2003. From numerous other references, the following are given as illustrations: SC 2/215/72, m. 1/GC1/ 423 (theft of books); SC 2/220/4, m. 26/GC5/1001 (detinue of a book valued at 4*d.*); SC 2/221/1, m. 28v/H /1590 (detinue of a book called a porthois value 10*s.*); SC 2/220/9, m. 62/D 5219 (detinue of a primer value 100*s.*). More familiar is the reference to the books owned by Llywelyn Bren of Glamorgan which included three in the Welsh language and a copy of the *Roman de la Rose*: J. B. Smith, 'Rebellion of Llywelyn Bren', p. 85.

18 Huws, 'Llyfrau Cymraeg'.

19 *Gwaith Sefnyn*, ed. Jones and Rheinallt, p. 61; Chandler, 'Will in medieval Wales', pp. 182–3; *Gwaith Dafydd ap Gwilym a'i Gyfoeswyr*, ed. Williams and Roberts, p. 159; *Gwaith Lewys Glyn Cothi*, ed. Johnston, p. 135. See also *Gwaith Guto'r Glyn*, ed. Williams and Williams, pp. 240–1, and C. W. Lewis, 'Literary tradition', p. 496. But for the possibility that these descriptions may be poetic *topoi*, see Bowen, 'Beirdd a noddwyr', 251–2 and the sources cited.

20 P. Smith, *Houses*, pp. 37–71; Pantin, 'Instructions', esp. p. 406.

21 Saenger, 'Silent reading'. For suggestive studies of the Welsh texts and manuscripts, see McCann, 'Adeiledd Y Tair Rhamant', esp. 127, n. 18; S. Davies, 'Llafar v. ysgrifenedig'; and also *eadem*, above, pp. 135–46.

22 For the idea of 'textual communities', see Stock, *Implications of Literacy* and *Listening for the Text*. I am using the phrase in the sense of the transmission of a text without necessarily the implications for group behaviour or shared assumptions suggested by Stock.

23 Haycock, 'Llyfr Taliesin', esp. 366–7, although the author is justifiably cautious in attributing provenance; Huws, 'Llawysgrif Hendregadredd'; G. Charles-Edwards, 'Scribes of the Red Book'. For a suggestion that the scribe of BL Add. 22356 may have been a clerk of a secular court, see James, 'Llyfr cyfraith', 390–1.

24 Charles and Emanuel, 'Welsh records', 62; NLW Kinmel Deeds, 58. The poet Lewys Môn also referred to Robert ap Rhys's expertise as a notary: *Gwaith Lewys Môn*, ed. Rolant, p. 456. Walter Blount is recorded as *scriptor* in NLW Kinmel Deeds, 61.

25 SC 2/216/2, m. 23 /GC 1/1460; SC 2/223/17, m. 4. For Richard Pygot, see NLW Kinmel Deeds, 40, 47 where he is described as a *scriptor*, and 37, in the same hand, where he appears as last witness. See also Carr, below, pp. 228–30.

26 The following are examples of the work of John Foxwist, many inscribed with his mark on the bottom right-hand corner of the deed: NLW Brogyntyn Deeds, 3376 (a well-executed and elaborate entail), 3410, 3401, 4575; NLW Llanfair and Brynodol, D. 922, 926–8.

27 *Registrum nuncupatum 'Record of Caernarvon'*, ed. Ellis, p. 116. The drawing of the fox is omitted from the printed text of BL Harleian MS 696.

28 His identification with Richard Foxwist of Caernarfon is suggested by J. M. Lewis, *Welsh Monumental Brasses*, p. 40.

Llinos Beverley Smith

29 PCC 17 Holder.
30 Useful information may be found in D. Thomson, 'Cistercians and schools', and a more general survey by G. Williams, 'Addysg yng Nghymru'. For an intriguing reference to *Lleucu uxor le scolemaster* in Rhuddlan, see Chester 30/8, m. 41v.
31 NLW Peniarth Deeds, 496; NLW Edwinsford, 3227, 3228.
32 The volume is briefly described in J. G. Evans, *Report*, vol. 2, pp. 253–4. For the connection between Rhys ab Einion Fychan and Robert Salesbury, see *History of the Gwydir Family*, ed. Jones, pp. 18, 30–2, 34.
33 Ll. B. Smith, 'Grammar and commonplace books', 174. For the 'book of Lawrence Rixton', a burgess of Conwy in the first half of the fourteenth century, see J. B. Smith, 'Land endowments', 152.
34 Ll. B. Smith, 'Grammar and commonplace books'. The Edwards family is also discussed by Bowen, 'I Wiliam ap Siôn Edwart'.
35 Ll. B. Smith, 'Grammar and commonplace books', 183, and Huws, 'Manuscripts', pp. 129–30.
36 SC 2/216/14, m. 17/Llan1/2384; SC 2/217/7, m. 18/Llan2/342; SC 2/217/6, m. 19/Roll1/771.
37 For Dafydd Glais, see Griffiths, 'Aberystwyth', pp. 40–2 and the sources cited.
38 For a valuable study of fifteenth-century bureaucrats, see Griffiths, 'Public and private bureaucracies', esp. pp. 144–7. There is no reason to believe that the position was markedly different in the fourteenth century.
39 E/101/351/9, mm. 4, 47; *Survey of Denbigh*, ed. Vinogradoff and Morgan. For a description of the compiling of the extent of Chirk, see NLW Chirk Castle, D. 40, D. 41.
40 SC2/226/19; SC 2/216/9, m. 8/Llan1/1759 (privileges granted *per specialem factum* which is to be produced in court); SC 2/216/5, m. 22v/Llan/1470 (charter shown and read in court); NLW Chirk Castle, D. 38.
41 SC 2/217/8, m. 8v/Roll3/421; NLW Peniarth MS 354C, m. 2v.
42 J. B. Smith, 'Last phase', 257 (for the letter of Gruffudd ap Dafydd ap Gruffudd to Reginald Grey); for a seignorial order requiring the production of names of delinquents in writing see SC 2/216/1, m. 15/Llan1/876 (1318). For a relatively early reference to the use of a written bond of obligation (dated 3 July 1338), see *Caernarvon Court Rolls*, ed. Jones and Owen, p. 37, although there are numerous references to later bonds. From among numerous examples of written arbitrations see UWB Penrhyn Additional Personalia (16 August 1449), which specifies that the arbitrators are to deliver their arbitration *in scriptis*. For a written contract SC 2/216/13, m. 16/Llan 1/2230 (1332).
43 Ll. B. Smith, 'Proofs of age'. For the birth of John Walwayn, see *Calendar of Inquisitions Post Mortem*, vol. 10, p. 434, and for that of Roger Puleston, Chester 3/46.
44 See the references cited in Ll. B. Smith, 'Proofs of age', 141–2.
45 *Gwaith Lewys Glyn Cothi*, ed. Johnston, p. 281; PCC 17 Holder.
46 *Calendar of Inquisitions Post Mortem*, vol. 10, pp. 423, 547.
47 See Carr, below, pp. 223–37.
48 For the bestowal of land 'by the glove' in fourteenth-century Rhuddlan, see Chester 30/8, m. 46. Cf. the statement in *Ystorya de Carolo Magno* that seisin was given 'y gan y uanec honn yman' (by this glove): *Ystorya de Carolo Magno*, ed. Williams, p. 97.

220

The impact of literacy in late medieval Wales

49 SC 2/217/11, m. 20/Roll 6/1451.
50 For example, SC 2/226/18, m. 1 (a charter of *prid* in the lordship of Bromfield and Yale valued at £10); SC 2/220/9, m. 28v/D 2303 (damages of 100s. for detinue of a charter).
51 *Cartae*, ed. Clark, vol. 4, p. 1245 (1340); Chester 30/21, mm. 1, 6; Chester 30/18a, m. 3. For the theft of a will kept in a chest in a house at Rhuddlan, see Chester 30/12, m. 33. For the conservation of records in a family cartulary, see Griffiths, 'Cartulary and muniments'.
52 NLW Trovarth and Coed Coch, 812.
53 NLW Plas Iolyn, 280.
54 BL Add. MS 10,013, fo. 171r-v; Herefordshire Record Office O/4, p. 18; O/18, p. 386; O/22, p. 124 (the records of the ecclesiastical courts of the diocese of Hereford).
55 Clanchy, *From Memory*, p. 319. Cf. McKitterick (ed.), *Uses of Literacy*, p. 326.
56 Carruthers, *Book of Memory*, p. 122; Aston, *Lollards and Reformers*, pp. 101–35.
57 The passage in the *Bestiaires* is discussed by Carruthers, *Book of Memory*, pp. 223–4. For the Welsh text, see *Welsh Bestiary of Love*, ed. Thomas. The preface to the Welsh text (which is not illustrated in any of the surviving manuscripts) is a much-condensed version of the French text and it is unknown whether a complete translation of the French original had ever been undertaken. I am grateful to Mr Graham Thomas for his guidance on the problems relating to the Welsh versions.
58 Cf. Lloyd-Morgan, above, pp. 149–65.
59 Chester 30/18, m. 16; SC 2/216/10, m. 19/Llan1/1978.
60 *Marcher Lordships*, ed. Pugh, p. 283; *Cartae*, ed. Clark, vol. 5, pp. 1672–4 (1466) (an inquisition and oath made by the 'twelve men of the eldest and best of credite in the parish of Llangeinor'); ibid., p. 1700 (an oath that the defendant's title was 'better and more rightful by his evidence and auncestors by fore hym' than the plaintiff's 'by his dedes of purcheise'); Chester 30/10, m. 19v (proof of age *per aspectu corporis*).
61 See, in general, Bremner and Roodenburg (eds.), *Cultural History of Gesture*, esp. the contributions by K. Thomas and J.-C. Schmitt. For examples of the importance of the kiss and the handshake in late medieval Wales, see Ll. B. Smith, 'Disputes and settlements'.
62 J. G. Jones, 'Governance, order and stability', 36, quoting NLW 9059E, 1188; SC 2/215/74, m. 13. It should be noted that the assertion was made in response to the defendant's offer of compurgation which would normally be barred when specialty was proffered.
63 Ibbetson, 'Words and deeds'. A good illustration of the rituals used when contracts were agreed may be found in SC 2/218/4, m. 9.
64 Baker, *Introduction*, p. 371.
65 *Survey of Lancaster Lordships*, ed. Rees, p. 177.
66 Ibid., p. 25.
67 *Description of Penbrokshire*, ed. Owen, pp. 169–70; *Welsh Assize Roll*, ed. Davies, p. 245.
68 Numerous examples may be found in the data base noted above, n. 6.
69 For example, SC 2/215/74, m. 11/Llan1/583(1314); SC 2/219/1, m. 20/Llan3/

221

2583 (copy of charter annexed to the court roll); SC 2/ 217/7, m. 16v/Roll1/641 (*prid* land transferred 'by a piece of indentured writing').

70 SC 2/216/6, m. 11v/Llan1/1717 (1326).

71 See, for example, SC 2/217/8, m. 2/Roll3/100 (1342).

72 See, for example, SC 2/217/8, m. 6v/Roll3/344; SC 2/219/7, m. 18b/Llan4/1528; SC 2/217/8, m. 8v/Roll3/422 (1343) for examples of the sums paid.

73 Goody, *Interface*, pp. 139, 161.

74 G. Williams, *Welsh Church*, pp. 332–3; NLW Llanstephan MS 27, fos. 152–3; *Inventory of Chancery Proceedings*, ed. Lewis, p. 181. A late-fifteenth-century charm for the protection of the oxen, cows and beasts of one David ap Rhys ap Jankyn survives in NLW Trovarth and Coed Coch, 30.

75 For a survey and comment on the extent to which these promising developments were fulfilled, see G. Williams, 'Language, literacy and nationality', and *idem*, *Renewal and Reformation*, pp. 143–65, 429–51.

12

'This my act and deed': the writing of private deeds in late medieval north Wales

A. D. CARR

By 1300 the ability to write had long since ceased to be a kind of clerical mystique; the business of government and trade and the buying and selling of rights in land depended more and more on the written word, and the medieval world was often one of multi-lingual literacy where an individual might be able to write Latin and one or more vernaculars.[1] This chapter is a preliminary attempt to examine one aspect of lay literacy in late medieval Wales, the writing of deeds of title. Thousands of such deeds survive; the present exercise is therefore limited to the holdings of the Department of Manuscripts in the library of the University of Wales, Bangor. Many more north Wales deeds may be found in the National Library of Wales and the local record offices at Hawarden, Ruthin, Caernarfon and Dolgellau. The discussion is based on a sample of about 700 documents, drawn from all over north Wales and from both urban and rural communities.[2]

These documents are concerned with the everyday business of buying and selling rights in land. Deeds of title are the records of this activity, and there are more of them than of any other medieval source. As Professor Wendy Davies and others have shown, the charter or written act recording the grant of land was far from unknown in the early medieval Celtic world and a distinct form evolved; examples include the Welsh charters in the Book of Llandaf and the Breton ones in the Landévennec and Redon cartularies.[3] Dr Huw Pryce has drawn attention to the latest surviving Welsh example from Arwystli, dated between 1132 and 1151.[4] But, like the Anglo-Saxon diploma or landbook, this tradition seems, in diplomatic terms, to have been a blind alley. The late medieval private deed in Wales followed the pattern of its English counterpart and, like it, derived originally from the late Anglo-Saxon writ. Even the indigenous Welsh private act, the conveyance in *tir prid* (a gage of land for a term of years), is Anglo-Norman rather than Celtic in its style.

223

Land was the basis of society, and the land market was expanding rapidly in Wales in the fourteenth and fifteenth centuries, as it had already done in England. In English law the conveyance of freehold title to land involved a public ceremony of transfer or livery of seisin; a symbolic object like a twig or a clod of earth was handed by the vendor to the purchaser in the presence of witnesses. This ceremony was geared to the needs of an illiterate society; the root of title lay in the memory of witnesses to the transaction, and the written document or deed was the subsequent record and confirmation of what had already taken place.[5] This is why the operative words, 'dedi, concessi et hac presenti carta mea confirmavi' ('I have given, granted and by this my present charter confirmed'), were in the past tense; the document was evidential rather than dispositive. But as the frontiers of literacy were extended and more and more documents were drawn up, it was the written instrument which came to be regarded as evidence of title.

Surviving acts or charters from pre-1282 Gwynedd and Powys tend to be public ones, that is, acts emanating from native rulers and recording grants of land to churches and religious communities; the church, being a literate organization which operated through the written word, insisted on such acts being recorded in writing, and this task was usually the responsibility of the recipient.[6] The handwriting of many such acts makes this abundantly clear, and when Madog ap Gruffudd Maelor of northern Powys confirmed grants by earlier rulers to the Cistercian abbey of Strata Marcella in 1207 it was actually stated in the document that it had been executed in the hand of Dafydd, abbot of Valle Crucis.[7] For the same reason, most surviving grants of land in Wales before 1300 by private individuals are to religious houses; examples are to be found in the massive Margam Abbey archive and in the twelfth- and thirteenth-century charters contained in the cartulary of Haughmond Abbey in Shropshire.[8] The earliest private act involving two individuals so far located from north Wales is one of 1258 relating to the right of inheritance to lands in the townships of Esclusham, Bersham and Broughton in Maelor Gymraeg in northern Powys;[9] no pre-1282 private acts from Gwynedd Uwch Conwy, that part of Gwynedd which lay to the west of the river, are known. For most of north Wales it could be argued, on the basis of existing evidence, that the written private act did not really become relevant until after the Edwardian conquest of 1282–3 and the introduction of English conveyancing practice. For most people, therefore, charters and written documents had yet to become part of everyday life; in the past they had been so rare as to enjoy a quasi-magical status, as Dr Michael Clanchy has pointed out, and there is an echo of this in Llywelyn ab Iorwerth's letter of 1212 to Philip Augustus of France in which he acknowledges Philip's letter, sealed with his golden seal, 'which I shall cause to be kept in the aumbreys of the church as if it were a sacred relic'.[10] This is a long way from the workaday world of fourteenth- and fifteenth-century private deeds; the situation was very different from that in England, where by the second half of the thirteenth century even the conveyance of small plots of land by villeins had come to be recorded in writing. Dr Clanchy has suggested that some eight million such documents were written during that century at this level of society alone.[11]

When considering private deeds in north Wales in the later Middle Ages, two kinds of act are involved. The first, and the more common, of these is the standard English form, the gift or conveyance in fee simple. But there was also a native Welsh form, the conveyance in *tir prid*, which had its origins in Welsh law before 1282.[12] The *tir prid* conveyance had evolved as a way around the prohibition imposed by native Welsh law on the alienation of free hereditary land, a prohibition which was confirmed by Edward I's son Edward of Caernarfon in his response to a petition from the Welsh of north Wales in 1305.[13] Land could only be alienated for a term of (normally four) years and the *tir prid* conveyance was based on this. It was, in effect, a kind of gage or pledge; the land was conveyed by the gageor to the gagee for a term of years in return for a sum of money. At the end of the term the gageor could repay the money and recover the land; if he failed to do so, the transaction would be renewed for a further period of years and this could continue indefinitely. Some deeds are accompanied by quitclaims in which the gageor relinquishes his right to recover the land. The great advantage of the *tir prid* conveyance was its flexibility; as it was not a conveyance in fee simple, no livery of seisin was involved and lands held in this way could be bequeathed by will.[14] Several hundred such deeds survive; the *tir prid* conveyance came to be used all over north Wales, even by burgesses of English descent in the castle boroughs of the principality.

The value of these medieval deeds to the historian is obvious: they shed light on such topics as the development of the land market, the growth of estates and urban and rural topography. But they can also

225

tell us much about contemporary literacy, and this leads on to the question of who actually wrote them. Early grants to religious foundations would have been written out by the recipients, but this was certainly not the case in the later Middle Ages. Sir Hilary Jenkinson divided the writers of late medieval business hands into four categories: clerks, public scriveners, notaries public and *laici literati*.[15] A clerk was technically a person who had received the tonsure and taken minor orders before or after his education; by the later Middle Ages, however, this was no longer necessarily the case and clerks were often administrative officials or servants who had never seen the schools. Scriveners were professional writers who were trained by apprenticeship and who provided a public service; their main functions were conveyancing and the preparation of written instruments, and most towns of any importance had scriveners' companies or guilds. Notaries public were authorized by the pope or the emperor to draw up and authenticate written instruments; the main reason why the notary did not occupy the position in England and Wales which he enjoyed elsewhere in Europe was that English law had little need of his services. Under English law it was the seal which authenticated any act, as the sealing clause in a deed, 'in cuius rei testimonium sigillum meum huic scripto apposui', indicates.[16] As a result it did not matter who actually wrote the document; it was the person or persons whose seals authenticated it who mattered, whether or not they themselves were able to write, and there was no need to identify the scribe. *Laici literati* or literate laymen were those others whose work or business required the ability to write, particularly Latin; their ranks included merchants, local officials such as sheriffs, bailiffs, escheators and manorial and municipal officers, and landed proprietors.

The writers of deeds were drawn from these four categories. Deeds are local documents and they reflect literacy in the local community about its everyday business. Most of them in north Wales must have been the work of clerks or literate laymen. There is no evidence in the sample studied here of the presence of scriveners in any north Wales towns, although some are attested in documents from other archives, and there were certainly no guilds.[17] The towns of north Wales were small and even Chester, the regional metropolis, had no company of scriveners; those who practised in the city would probably have been members of the Painters', Glaziers' and Stationers' Company.[18] There were some notaries; their professional services would have been needed by the church and one might expect to find them in the two episcopal centres of Bangor and St Asaph, but few others would have found it necessary to employ them to authenticate their acts. It is probable that they often did no more than draw up the deeds which would be authenticated by the parties concerned, and the division between notaries and scriveners was probably a very fluid one.

At the beginning of the period under review deeds often appear to have been written by clerics; there are both diplomatic and palaeographical indications of this. On 1 May 1289 Iorwerth Goch ap Rhirid ap Llywelyn conveyed to his daughter and son-in-law lands and a share of a mill in the Flintshire townships of Trefednywain and Maesbledrys.[19] This was a conveyance in fee simple; the following Michaelmas the same lands were conveyed to the same parties in *tir prid*.[20] The two deeds are written in the same hand, which has more of the characteristics of a bookhand than of a business hand; this suggests the work of a cleric, and the possibility is strengthened both by the fact that the documents are dated by the year of the Incarnation and by the presence in the first one of a clause in which the donor promises not to take advantage of 'omni auxilio canonico et civili omnibus exceptionibus cavillationibus deceptionibus cautelis legibus Howel Da et consuetudinibus per que mihi vel meis in aliquo puncto vel modo poterint in posterum prodesse'.[21] This clause may reflect canonical influence.[22] The witness lists of the two documents do not offer the names of any possible clerical scribes; although the hands are identical, the two lists are entirely different, and the fact that each contains a cleric is therefore immaterial. There is a similar clause in a gift of August 1305 in which Ieuan ap Dafydd ab Adda of Pengwern, Llangollen, conveyed all his lands and tenements there to Cynwrig Feddyg ap Goronwy Goch; here the donor bound himself and his heirs to eschew 'omni auxilio iure canonica et civilis statutis regiis legibus Howel Da et patrie consuetudinibus et omnibus aliis que in aliquo poterunt prodesse'.[23]

There are other formulae which may suggest clerical provenance, in particular the greeting. In the Pengwern deed discussed above this is 'salutem in domino sempiternam' ('eternal greeting in the Lord') and the same greeting appears in a 1306 gift by Dafydd Foel to Ithel Fychan of lands in Bagillt in Flintshire.[24] This document is dated by the year of the Incarnation and is written in a very distinctive and almost certainly clerical hand. A scribal error has been removed by the simple expedient of cutting a hole in the parchment, and a repeated linguistic slip in the witness list suggests that Welsh was the writer's first language; four of the witnesses are described as 'Madoc seys. heylyn yurawt' and 'Gruffyt rwth. Iorwerth yurawt' ('Madog Sais, Heilin his brother' and 'Gruffydd Rwth, Iorwerth his brother') rather than as *fratre suo* in each case. An identical error occurs in a deed of 1305 in the same hand relating to land in Halkyn in the same county.[25] There are at least five deeds in this hand, written between 1305 and 1308; Madog ap Bleddyn ap Cynwrig, described in one of them as Sir Madog ap Bleddyn, is a witness to four of them, but this is not, of course, conclusive proof that they are his handiwork.[26] There are many other examples of deeds which were almost certainly written by clerics and these occur throughout the period, although most of them come from the early fourteenth century; in communities where few laymen were literate in Latin a local cleric would be the natural person to undertake the task.

Other professional writers were the clerks or administrative officials in boroughs, marcher lordships and the headquarters of the administration of the principality of north Wales at Caernarfon. These were the writers of such official documents as accounts and court rolls, and there is considerable scope here for further investigation; the comparison of deeds with surviving official records would be a useful exercise. There is one very obvious example. Among the Baron Hill muniments in the University Library at Bangor is the original text of the great extent of the counties of Anglesey and Caernarfon made in 1352 by the deputy justiciar of north Wales, John de Delves, and published by Sir Henry Ellis in 1838 from an early sixteenth-century transcript in the British Library.[27] At least five private deeds, most of them relating to property in Caernarfon, are written in the same hand as the extent; this indicates that the writer was either a clerk to the justiciar of north Wales or to the chamberlain of the principality at the Caernarfon Exchequer.[28] One of the parties to one of these deeds is William de Cranwell; he was clerk to the chamberlain of north Wales and a burgess of the town of Beaumaris. His daughter and heiress Katherine married Richard Golding, who was also a burgess of Beaumaris and clerk to the justiciar.[29] There is no firm evidence to prove that Cranwell actually wrote the extent and the deeds, but he could be a strong candidate. The fact that he had accumulated a substantial landed estate which was inherited by his daughter suggests that he was a layman and that the literate lay administrator was present in north Wales. But whether or not

Cranwell was responsible for the extent and for this group of deeds, their existence shows that public servants did undertake private work; indeed, this had always been done, for example by royal clerks in the twelfth century. The principality clerks in fourteenth-century Caernarfon may well have performed the functions of professional scriveners in that town.

Many deeds are written in what are obviously professional administrative hands. This would not be surprising in Caernarfon, since experienced clerks were always available there, but the same pattern can be seen elsewhere. At Hope in Flintshire the hand of an administrator can be seen in four fourteenth-century deeds, and there are further examples from the next century which suggest the work of local clerks.[30] One settlement of 1428 looks like the work of a lawyer, being written in an engrossing hand.[31] Fourteenth- and fifteenth-century deeds from Conwy also include more than one professional-looking hand; one group of fourteen deeds, written between 1422 and 1448 in the same hand, includes a 1446 conveyance by the corporation, which could suggest that these were written by the town clerk.[32] One burgess, Lawrence Rixton, appears frequently as a witness in the middle of the century; in several deeds from 1449 onwards he is the last witness and these documents, again, are all the product of a single hand.[33] One certainly cannot assume that by the fifteenth century the last witness was the writer of the deed, as had sometimes been the case in earlier centuries; but Rixton was undoubtedly literate. An early sixteenth-century collection of copies of documents from the Conwy area mentions items 'in the book of Lawrence Rixton of Conwy' and this could suggest that he had been town clerk.[34]

A similar pattern can be seen in Beaumaris, a town from which a large quantity of fifteenth-century deeds has survived. One group of thirty-eight documents, written between 1446 and 1474, emanates from the same hand, along with a number of deeds recording acquisitions of land in the township of Llanddyfnan by William Bulkeley the elder of Beaumaris, the founder of that family's fortunes.[35] The witnesses to several of these deeds include one John Forrest, clerk; on a number of occasions Forrest is described as a notary public. Not one of these documents is a notarial act; in this context there was no use for such documents, and the hand does not have the neatness which one would expect of a notary. It is also unlikely that a notary could make a living solely by the exercise of his profession in fifteenth-century Beaumaris, but scriveners could also be notaries. Forrest was also among the witnesses to a quitclaim by William Bulkeley the younger and his wife in Castell in the Conwy valley in 1446; here, again, he is described as a clerk and the hand is similar to that in the Beaumaris and Llanddyfnan documents.[36] There is, of course, no proof that these deeds are the work of John Forrest, but the fact that he appears as a witness to many of them written in the same hand, and is described as both clerk and notary public, justifies the suggestion. He seems to have had some connection with William Bulkeley the elder, and the group of documents with which he is associated includes a 1467 conveyance by the borough community; although he was not a witness on this occasion, the fact that this document is in the same hand could possibly indicate that, like Lawrence Rixton in Conwy, he acted as town clerk.[37]

Notarial instruments are almost non-existent among the documents which have been examined in the preparation of this chapter. The will of John Audlem, rector of Beaumaris and Llandegfan, who died in 1500, was written by a notary, but this was done at Oxford.[38] From the same year there is an exemplification at the Caernarfonshire Great Sessions of a release of land in Castell which bears a notarial mark, as does a gift from the episcopal township of Gweredros in the commote of Creuddyn in the same county.[39] The latter document has a signum at the end with the motto *Veritas*, but it is not accompanied by an authenticating clause. A letter of attorney issued in 1463 by John Person, archdeacon of Bangor, to William Griffith is particularly well written and bears the name of the writer, Plummer, presumably a professional scrivener; such practitioners were obliged to put their names to the documents which they wrote, and the lack of this feature in the rest of the sample suggests that most of those who produced deeds in north Wales were not members of any guild or company.[40]

There are plenty of other examples of groups of deeds from the same area being the work of the same hand. One interesting feature is the way in which the quality of the writing and the layout can vary, even in the products of a single writer. As Dr Clanchy has pointed out, bad layout is the clearest mark of an amateur, and this is as true of the fifteenth century as it is of the twelfth.[41] *Tir prid* conveyances in particular are often far more slapdash and home-made in their appearance, being cramped and hastily and untidily written on small ill-cut pieces of poor-quality parchment in equally poor-quality ink.[42] This is not always the case; those from Castell, for example, which record acquisitions by the Conwy burgess Bartholomew de Bolde, who was particularly active in the land market in the first half of the fifteenth century, are invariably neatly written on good-quality parchment, which suggests that Bolde was able to call on the services of an experienced clerk. Good examples can also be found elsewhere; a conveyance in *tir prid* of 1488 from Aber-erch near Pwllheli has an initial which is so ornate as to resemble a notarial signum, although the next document in that particular sequence, a conveyance in fee of 1489, looks like the ultimate example of a home-made deed.[43] Deeds from Caernarfon are usually well written on good-quality parchment, possibly an indication that principality clerks were using the prince's parchment in private practice.

Why are so many conveyances in *tir prid* of such poor quality? This is often true even when they have been produced by writers who were perfectly capable of turning out documents of a professional standard. Some bear signs of having been written in a hurry by experienced scribes, while others have a far more amateur look; this may, of course, reflect less practice in the art of writing. On the whole the standard of calligraphy is higher in the fourteenth century than in the fifteenth; it may be that a lower standard reflects a wider ability to write, with writing becoming less of a professional skill. But it is difficult to suggest an explanation for the frequent untidiness of *tir prid* conveyances; although the form was a native Welsh one, it would certainly have been familiar to most practitioners in north Wales. The poor-quality parchment may be explained by the cost of the material and the consequent use of offcuts; one of the deeds examined is actually a palimpsest.[44] Deeds written in English also tend on the whole to be less neat than those in Latin.

In any examination of literacy the question of language is a key factor. The sample includes the occasional Norman French document; one of these is a conveyance in *tir prid* of 1315 relating to land in Golftyn in Flintshire.[45] This is a particularly neat hand, beginning with the words *à tous*; under the fold at its foot the scribe has written *a to*, probably as a trial run. The condition of a bond of 1424 relating to the Penrhyn family and estate in Anglesey and Caernarfonshire is also in French.[46] Deeds in Welsh are very rare indeed; in fact, no conveyances in fee or in *tir prid* in Welsh are known to exist. By the fifteenth century literacy in Welsh was widespread, as Dr Llinos Beverley Smith has shown in her contribution to this volume, but the only Welsh document in the present sample is the record of a division of land between brothers from Aber-erch.[47] This looks a less than professional product and has been dated between 1441 and 1450; the hand, however, seems more likely to be a sixteenth-century one, which could suggest that it is a later copy, the original now being lost.

Vernacular documents, therefore, are almost invariably English, and these do not appear in north Wales before the fifteenth century. The earliest English document in the Bangor repository is probably the condition of a bond from Hope dated 1430; the bond itself and the condition are in different hands and it is the bond which looks the more home-made of the two parts.[48] One of the most interesting English deeds is a conveyance in *tir prid* of 1470 from Beaumaris, one of a number of examples of the use of this Welsh device by English burgesses.[49] This is probably the original conveyance to William Bulkeley the elder of Henblas, the Bulkeley residence in the town, and it includes details of the contents of the house. Some spellings, for example *abofe* for 'above' and *cofur* for 'cover', may reflect Welsh influence. It is in the hand of the usual writer of Beaumaris deeds at this time and John Forrest, described here as 'clerk', is a witness. Other documents provide evidence of literacy in English, not in their content but in notes and endorsements added by the parties themselves.[50] Most of these are from Beaumaris, but there is a long endorsement in English in an appalling hand, dated 1500, on a *tir prid* deed of 1470 from Llaneilian in Anglesey.[51] An exemplification of the inquisition *post mortem* of the Anglesey lands of Gwilym ap Gruffydd of Penrhyn, who died in 1431, bears a note on the dorse in the hand of Gwilym's son Gwilym Fychan or William Griffith I:

> Have in mynde that Ieuan ap Gruff' ap Mortyn tolde to me William Gruffith that the manor of the Penryn that my Fader has bylde stondes uppon the lande of Mad' ap Gron' Vichan fader to my graunt dame Generes verch Mad' ap Gron' Vichan and the saide londe hight y gwaslloyneher' and the lloynehere and the longe hey betwix the waye that gose to Conway and the said lloyneher' and the newe gardyn norchard and the lytyll hey under the newe berne and tythyn hoell ap del' and kelly y managh and halfe Coide Parke was the forsaide Mad' ap Gron' Vich' lande for so Gruff' ap Mortyn his fader tolde him.[52]

This indicates that one of the leading Welshmen in north Wales at this time was both literate and bilingual (although both Gwilym Fychan's mother and his wife were English), and it is therefore a very clear example of lay literacy.

This topic poses many further questions. One of these is the matter of writing: who taught this skill and to whom, and what facilities were available in north Wales in the fourteenth and fifteenth centuries? Did the teaching of writing go alongside the teaching of Latin? How many were literate in English or Welsh but not in Latin? How rapidly did vernacular literacy develop? Sir John Wynn's account of his great-grandfather Maredudd ab Ieuan being sent to school at Caernarfon to learn English and 'to reade, to write and to understand lattin' is well known, and Dr Smith has discussed the ways in which literacy might be imparted in late medieval Wales.[53] One document in the present sample is of particular interest in this respect: it is a conveyance in *tir prid* of 1352 from Pengwern, Llangollen.[54] It is not the content of the deed itself which is interesting but the other things written on it. At the foot of the face is an attempt, in a kind of bookhand, to write the opening of the Pater Noster, along with some genealogical notes; in the same hand is written the phrase 'Ego sum bonus puer' ('I am a good boy'); this suggests a pupil, perhaps a child, learning Latin and possibly also learning to write. The Latin is perfectly correct, but the word-order suggests that English was the medium of instruction, and Dr Smith has shown that surviving Latin grammars from the fifteenth century from north-east Wales indicate that Latin was being taught through the medium of English.[55] This in turn would suggest that the pupil had already mastered the latter language. The dorse of the document contains some further calligraphic attempts, which follow a memorandum of a *tir prid* transaction in 1374–5; this may suggest a *terminus post quem* for these exercises.

This chapter offers questions rather than answers, and in doing so has scratched the surface of a large and potentially rich body of source material from north Wales; Dr Smith has pointed out that there are very few surviving medieval deeds from Cardiganshire and Carmarthenshire.[56] These documents deal with business, perhaps the most important business in local communities, the transfer of rights in land. As a rule they were not written out by the actual parties, despite the steady increase in literacy; they would be drafted and engrossed semi-professionally. It was not an unduly difficult task; the diplomatic forms of conveyances in fee and quitclaims, for example, were familiar and common to England and Wales. The conveyance in *tir prid*, being an indigenous Welsh form, showed some range of variation, but there were plenty of exemplars from which to work and the same men often drew up both kinds of conveyance. In the early fourteenth century deeds tended to be drawn up by clerics and were in a hand more akin to a bookhand than to any kind of courthand, since this was how they had learned to write; the clergy were the most literate element in the community at the beginning of the period, and in rural communities it was probably natural to turn to the parson for help. But the task was also undertaken by professional clerks who used business hands and who were increasingly laymen or, at most, in minor orders. In the fifteenth century an increasing number of deeds, and not only conveyances in *tir prid*, look more and more untidy, as if written in haste, and this may reflect the growth of literacy.

There are numerous examples of substantial numbers of deeds being the work of the same writer, and this was not only the case in the towns; it can also be seen in rural areas. A group of documents from the commote of Menai in the south-east of Anglesey, for example, written between 1465 and 1483, appears to be from the same hand, although the quality varies considerably.[57] One has the impression of a difference between town and country, especially in the case of those who, unlike Bartholomew de Bolde in the Conwy valley who seems usually to have used the same clerk, were not building up estates. The quality of many such deeds is definitely poorer, suggesting that they were often being written by less experienced hands; there is far more variation in deeds from Aber-erch, for example, than there is in those from Beaumaris. It would be interesting to know who wrote them out in the remoter rural areas, where the necessary professional skills might not always have been available; it would be equally interesting to know where many of them were written. It would probably be safer not to draw too many conclusions from place-dates, especially before about 1350, since the transaction might be recorded some time after it had taken place.[58] By the fifteenth century those clerks who wrote out deeds in Beaumaris, Conwy or Hope were really the ancestors of the country attorneys of a later age; the solicitors' profession can trace its ancestry to such men.

This was a multi-lingual world. Latin and Welsh were written languages, and Latin gradually became as much of a lay accomplishment as a clerical one for clerks and officials; it is worth remembering, too, that Latin was the written language of native Welsh administration before 1282. Dr Clanchy, following the distinction drawn by Malcolm Parkes between 'pragmatic' literacy, applied to the business of everyday life, and 'cultivated' literacy, which had to do with a more cultural dimension, makes the point that for the laity literacy was 'a practical convenience long before it became an education.'[59] In the towns of north Wales literacy in English was growing, as it was in England, and this is reflected by the fifteenth century in deeds and in informal writing. What we do not know about late medieval Wales is how many outside the towns could speak and write English; deeds in English seem to be far less common in rural areas. This discussion of deeds does not, of course, consider the widespread use of the written word in Welsh, which Dr Smith has examined in detail, since no deeds in Welsh have yet come to light.[60]

The written deed was not a new phenomenon in the Celtic world in the later Middle Ages. Professor Davies has shown how charters were being used extensively in rural Brittany as early as the ninth century, and they became increasingly familiar as more use was made of the written word and as it came to be perceived as part of everyday life throughout Europe.[61] North Wales was a small part of this world, but the study of private deeds as evidence of lay literacy there, on which this chapter offers a few comments and suggestions, would repay further detailed investigation.[62]

NOTES

1 The best discussion of this question is by Clanchy, *From Memory*, esp. chs. 6 and 7.

2 The documents examined are: Baron Hill MSS: Beaumaris, Llanddyfnan, Llaneilian, Llanfechell (Anglesey); Conwy, Castell, Gweredros, Caernarfon (Caerns.). Penrhyn and Penrhyn Further Additional MSS: Cororion, Bodfaeo, Bangor, Caernarfon (Caerns.). Mostyn MSS: Aber-erch (Caerns.); Whitford Garn, Bagillt, Brynford (Flints.); Pengwern (Denbs.). Bodrhyddan MSS: Hope (Flints.). Plas Coch MSS: commote of Menai (Anglesey). Various individual documents have also been examined.

3 W. Davies, 'Latin charter-tradition'; *eadem, Llandaff Charters*.

4 Pryce, 'Church of Trefeglwys'.

5 Livery of seisin is discussed in detail in Pollock and Maitland, *History of English Law*, vol. 2, pp. 83–90.

6 Cf. Maund, *Handlist*, and also Flanagan, above, pp. 113–24, 129–30.

7 Gwynedd Archives Service, Caernarfon XD2/1113.

8 Birch, *Descriptive Catalogue; idem, History of Margam*, p. 280; *Cartulary of Haughmond*, ed. Rees.

9 Denbighshire Record Office (Ruthin) D/DWY 1737.

10 Clanchy, *From Memory*, p. 161; Treharne, 'Franco-Welsh treaty', 74.

11 Clanchy, *From Memory*, p. 50; *Carte Nativorum*, ed. Brooke and Postan, esp. pp. xxviii–lx; Harvey (ed.), *Peasant Land Market*, esp. pp. 19–23.

12 For the *tir prid* conveyance, see Ll. B. Smith, 'Gage and the land market', and *eadem*, '*Tir prid*'.
13 *Registrum nuncupatum 'Record of Caernarvon'*, ed. Ellis, p. 214.
14 Ll. B. Smith, 'Gage and the land market', 549.
15 Jenkinson, *Later Court Hands*, p. 30.
16 'In witness whereof I have attached my seal to this writing.' See Clanchy, *From Memory*, p. 316.
17 Cf. Smith, above, pp. 207–8.
18 I am grateful to Mrs Marilyn Lewis, the City Archivist of Chester, for this information.
19 UWB, Department of Manuscripts, Mostyn 2940.
20 UWB Mostyn 2941.
21 'all assistance by canon and civil [law], all exceptions, quibbles, deceptions, tricks, laws of Hywel Dda and customs by which they may be able to benefit me or mine in any point or manner in the future'.
22 I owe this point to Mr Dafydd Walters. Cf. Walters, 'Renunciation of exceptions'.
23 UWB Mostyn 1627 (i): 'all assistance by canon and civil law, royal statutes, laws of Hywel Dda and customs of the country and all other things which may be able to benefit [me] in any [way]'.
24 UWB Mostyn 2463. A deed from Llanfechell in Anglesey of 1393 (UWB Baron Hill 1445) has the greeting 'salutem et misericordiam in domino' ('greeting and mercy in the Lord') and the witnesses include the rector, Iorwerth Offeiriad.
25 UWB Mostyn 2441.
26 UWB Mostyn 2463–6, 2441.
27 UWB Baron Hill 6714; *Registrum nuncupatum 'Record of Caernarvon'*, ed. Ellis, pp. 1–89.
28 UWB Baron Hill 3156–7; Penrhyn 285–6; Penrhyn Further Additional, 6.xii.1352. Cranwell was himself a party to the last of these transactions.
29 Carr, *Medieval Anglesey*, p. 254.
30 UWB Bodrhyddan 558–61.
31 UWB Bodrhyddan 568.
32 UWB Baron Hill 2127, 2129, 2131–2, 2134, 2136–41, 2148–9, 2151.
33 UWB Baron Hill 2152–5.
34 J. B. Smith, 'Land endowments', 152 and n. 3.
35 UWB Baron Hill 463, 466–9, 472–5, 477–92, 494–6, 499–504, 506–9 (Beaumaris); 1096–1103, 1105–6, 1107–11, 1114–16 (Llanddyfnan).
36 UWB Baron Hill 2310.
37 UWB Baron Hill 500. For a discussion of the writing and attestation of medieval deeds in English towns, see Bond, 'Medieval private deeds'.
38 UWB Baron Hill 534.
39 UWB Baron Hill 2362, 2803.
40 UWB Penrhyn 316; as Jenkinson pointed out (*Later Court Hands*, p. 84), professional scriveners had to put their names on their deeds. This is the only example of this in the sample, but most documents have a paraph or flourish at the beginning and some of these may be personal marks, although this is certainly not always the case.
41 Clanchy, *From Memory*, p. 132.

The writing of private deeds in late medieval north Wales

42 I am grateful to Tomos Roberts for initially drawing this to my attention.
43 UWB Mostyn 789, 790.
44 UWB Penrhyn 220 (1416).
45 UWB Mostyn 3320.
46 UWB Penrhyn Further Additional, 20.v.1424.
47 UWB Mostyn 786. See above, pp. 206–7, 208–10.
48 UWB Bodrhyddan 575.
49 UWB Baron Hill 502.
50 Examples are UWB Baron Hill 463, 480 (endorsements by Alan Kyghley of Beaumaris, 1446–7, 1457), 489, 509 (Thomas Godfrey, 1462, 1464).
51 UWB Baron Hill 1330.
52 UWB Penrhyn Further Additional, 20.vi.1431.
53 *History of the Gwydir Family*, ed. Ballinger, p. 50; Smith, above, pp. 206–12.
54 UWB Mostyn 1634.
55 Ll. B. Smith, 'Grammar and commonplace books', 181–2. Barnie, *War in Medieval Society*, p. 99, quotes Nicholas of Trevisa's comment in 1385 that in England English had replaced French as the language of instruction for teaching Latin in grammar schools, but there is no evidence from Wales of the use of French. Dr Michael Clanchy pointed out in the discussion following the delivery of this paper that the phrase quoted here is not uncommon in contemporary Latin grammars from Italy.
56 Smith, above, p. 215.
57 UWB Plas Coch 7–10, 13, 16–17.
58 UWB Mostyn 2958 (Whitford Garn, Flints., 1311) is given at the donor's own house and several early fourteenth-century Flintshire deeds are given at the hundred court.
59 Clanchy, *From Memory*, pp. 247, 332.
60 Smith, above, pp. 208–10.
61 W. Davies, above, pp. 99–100.
62 I am grateful to my colleagues Tomos Roberts and Huw Pryce for their assistance and advice in the preparation of this chapter.

237

13

Literacy and the Irish bards

KATHARINE SIMMS

Conventionally students of Irish literature apply the description 'bardic poetry' specifically to Irish syllabic verse composed by hereditary poets in the Classical or Early Modern period of the language, that is, between *c.* AD 1200 and 1650, and this chapter deals with the emergence of that particular kind of verse, and the class who composed it. The English term 'bard', as it appears in the title, is used in a general sense of all who earned their living by the composition of verse eulogies and satires.

The Irish words *bard* and *fili* had technical meanings that varied over the Old Irish (sixth to ninth century), Middle Irish (tenth to twelfth century) and Early Modern Irish (thirteenth to seventeenth century) periods. Liam Breatnach's work on the poetico-legal tract *Uraicecht na Ríar*, discussed elsewhere in this volume,[1] has led him to the conclusion that in early Christian Ireland there was originally a single order of the poetic art (*dán*, *cerd*), categorized according to the learning of the practitioners into six grades, with the *fili* in the highest class, and the *bard* fourth from the top. However, he points out that the evidence of the *Bretha Nemed*, and other related Old and Middle Irish legal and poetic texts, indicates that around the eighth century the poets split into two separate orders, and the *filid*, divided into seven grades according to the degree of learning each possessed, were thenceforth distinguished by their literacy and scholarship from the illiterate order of the *baird*, who were graded only by social class and function.[2]

Subsequently, about the eleventh and twelfth centuries, there was a further change. Gerard Murphy has shown that the oral and literate orders of *bard* and *fili* respectively merged once more to produce the praise-poet of the later Middle Ages. This person described himself as a *file*, performed the functions of the earlier *bard* and was most frequently referred to by the annalists as a *fear dána*, a man of the

238

poetic art, having in his train a lowly assistant or reciter known as his *bard*.[3]

There is no controversy over whether the later medieval poets were literate. Pádraig Ó Macháin, in a wide-ranging article somewhat deceptively entitled 'The Early Modern Irish Prosodic Tracts and the editing of bardic verse',[4] which in fact has important points to make about the whole question of orality and literacy in this context, has listed a number of probable examples of autograph manuscripts of bardic verse dating from the fifteenth to the seventeenth centuries.

Not only did the concept of a bardic poet thus vary considerably, but literacy impinged on bardic poetry in different ways at different times. It would be a mistake, even in the case of poets composing in Classical or Early Modern Irish, to see their relationship to learning and letters remaining as constant and unchanging as the rigid rules of metrics and language which governed *dán díreach*, their strict form of professional verse, from 1200 onwards. Overall the skill of writing and the study of books could be said to have reached the professional orders of poets and affected their art in three main ways at three different periods: through church schools until the twelfth-century reform; through their own secular schools when ecclesiastical estab lishments became closed to them; and through the printing press and the literacy of their lay patrons during the Renaissance period.

The influence of the church on the early Irish *filid* has of course been discussed many times.[5] The Old Irish tract *Coire Goiriath* ('The Cauldron of Poesy'), taught that although the highest secular inspira- tion could be achieved by the master-poet's consumption of the legendary 'nine hazels of wisdom',[6] better still was the combination of divine grace and poetic (or prophetic) learning: 'and as a result there are people who are both divine and secular prophets and commentators both on matters of grace and of (secular) learning and they then utter godly utterances and perform miracles, and their words are maxims and judgements, and they are an example for all speech'.[7]

Just as the highest grade of judge was said to be proficient in three speeches, poetic speech, legal speech and Latin,[8] so this passage implies that the most esteemed of the learned poets were clerics, literate in Latin as well as in the vernacular. Annalistic obits from the tenth to the twelfth century explicitly praise a number of churchmen for their literary skills in both languages.[9] The influence of Latin studies on their art is seen not only in the debt of *Auraicept na nÉces*

('The Poet's Primer'), to the Latin grammarians,[10] and in the spread of rhyming syllabic metres from Latin to Irish verse,[11] but more subtly when early poets such as Flann mac Lonáin are called 'the Irish Virgil'.[12]

By definition we know very little about the oral poets of early Ireland because their work went unrecorded. Paradoxically one of the few things we do know about them is that they too were influenced by the Latin learning of the church, since the rhymed syllabic metres which the *filid* described as 'new forms' invented by 'recent writers' became the hallmark of bardic composition, the prescribed rhyme patterns being recognized 'by ear and mind' without 'knowledge of letters and syllables'.[13] If we follow Gerard Murphy in seeing the poems *Aed oll fri andud náne* ('Áed great at kindling of brilliance'), and *Uasal epscop Éirinn Aodh* ('Aodh is leading bishop of Ireland') as stray examples of the bardic art surviving from the Old and Middle Irish periods respectively, either recorded from an oral source or written in imitation of the oral style,[14] then we can go further and say that the praise poems of the early bards were strikingly similar to the compositions of the 'men of art' in the later Middle Ages, and very unlike the better documented work of the learned *filid*.

Murphy attributed the blurring of the distinction between *fili* and *bard* in the post-Norman period to a decline in the learning of the *fili* brought about by the social disruption of the Norman conquest of the late twelfth century,[15] but there are chronological objections to this interpretation of the evidence: for example, in the two later tracts in Thurneysen's *Mittelirische Verslehren* (nos. iii and iv), both of which date to the middle of the eleventh century and neither of which maintains the earlier distinction between *fili* and *bard* metres.[16]

Two developments can be seen leading up to this convergence of the poetic orders. On the one hand was the rise of the literate bard. Donnchadh Ó hAodha hints that the origins of this new class, and the *filid*'s defensive attitude towards it, can be traced as far back as the tenth or even ninth century, reflected in the comments of the Metrical Tracts.[17] Within the monastic schools during the tenth and eleventh centuries clerical and lay learning were becoming less sharply distinguished. A greater emphasis on Irish history, poetry and law is reflected in the death notices of scholars in the annals at this later time.[18] The increased quantity of prose and verse vernacular literature surviving from the Middle Irish period may be part of this trend, while the same era saw a flood of Irish translations of Latin scriptures, apocrypha and homiletic material,[19] such as would enable a student to acquire a respectable amount of clerical learning without any knowledge of Latin. It seems reasonable to link these developments with the growing number of laymen holding church office in the tenth and eleventh centuries,[20] since there was a legal maxim decreeing that authority in the church should go only to the learned, the word here for 'learning' being *ecnae*, which applied specifically to clerical learning.[21]

Thus the eleventh and early twelfth centuries saw the curriculum of the schools become more accessible to the merely literate, rather than the truly learned, while the high prestige accorded to Irish literary studies at this time, and the wealth of written texts becoming available in this field, would have increased the pressure on the upper ranks of the hitherto oral bards to add the skills of reading and writing to their range of accomplishments. It was the doctrine of the poets that the ranks of the *baird* included the *tigernbard* and the *rígbard*, the lord or king who composed verse without formal study.[22] It would appear that the famous Ó Dálaigh family of poets originated in this category, since one of its members is described in 1185 as high chieftain of Corca Raoidhe and Corca Adhain in the present county of Westmeath.[23] Another transitional figure between the aristocratic amateur and the professional poet was Cú Chollchoille Ó Baoigheallái of the ruling dynasty of Dartraighe in the present Co. Monaghan, who is referred to in most annals by surname only (an indication that he was the reigning chief) but is also styled 'the poet' (*in fer dána*), 'masterpoet of Ireland' (*ollam Érenn* or *ardollamh Éirand ar dán*). He met a spectacular death in 1119 when his house was captured and burned over his head by the neighbouring chief, Ó Flannagáin of Tuath Rátha (in the modern Co. Fermanagh), killing at least thirty-five of his family, guests and servants. In one entry his followers (*muinter*) are referred to as his *cliar*, his bardic retinue.[24]

The late eleventh and early twelfth century was also the period when Guilhem de Poitiers, ninth duke of Aquitaine, and other aristocratic and not-so-aristocratic early troubadours began to commit their compositions to writing, and achieve immense popularity in the process. In Ireland, where the honour-price of an *ollamh* or master-poet was equated with that of a petty king, there existed a greater inducement for an aristocratic versifier who perfected his art to seek recognition as a fully professional poet. The fact that the

241

province of Meath was conquered by Hugh de Lacy at the end of the twelfth century may have helped to complete this transition for the Ó Dálaigh family, but long before that date, in 1139, Cúchonnacht Ó Dálaigh of Leacan Midhe (in Corca Raoidhe) was described on his death as *ardollamh le dán* ('cheefe and arch-poet of Ireland'), while two further members of his family successively filled the office of *ollamh* in south Munster in the middle of the twelfth century, presumably in the employ of the Mac Carthaigh kings.[25]

Rather than joining Gerard Murphy in blaming the Norman invasion for disrupting the studies of the learned *filid* and reducing them to mere praise-poets, it seems more logical to focus, with Alan Harrison,[26] on the 'Cistercian invasion', the twelfth-century reform of the church which brought an end to the study of secular Irish literature and history in church schools. Barry O'Dwyer has traced the progressive abandonment of the practice of compiling Irish annals in Cistercian and other reformed religious houses during the early thirteenth century.[27] Françoise Henry tells us that during the thirteenth century scribal art of the Irish type 'seems to reel under the impact' of political and ecclesiastical change, and virtually the only manuscripts now surviving from thirteenth-century Ireland are of English origin or style.[28] It is not until the fourteenth century that we can document the existence of flourishing secular schools of vernacular law, history, poetry and medicine run by hereditary practitioners under the patronage of lay chieftains.[29]

Explicit statements by medieval scribes and linguistic and textual analysis by modern editors show that didactic compositions by the literate *filid* of the Middle Irish period (900–1200) were transmitted to these later schools as transcriptions derived directly and indirectly from twelfth-century manuscripts of ecclesiastical provenance.[30] Similarly prose annals, genealogies, sagas and laws were copied and continued in the later Middle Ages from the work of twelfth-century churchmen, and there are signs that this transition from one environment to another caused breaks in the continuity of the learned tradition.[31]

Interestingly enough, however, syllabic praise poetry showed no signs of partaking in the general malaise affecting Irish studies in the thirteenth century. On the contrary, Donnchadh Mór Ó Dálaigh was described at his death in 1244 as 'a master of poetry who never has been excelled and never will be', and both he and his celebrated contemporaries Muireadhach Albanach Ó Dálaigh and Giolla

Brighde Mac Con Midhe were quoted as exemplary authors in the bardic grammatical and syntactical tracts of the later medieval schools.[32] The slow perfecting of a consistent pattern of bardic rhyme which Brian Ó Cuív has traced in verse compositions from the Old Irish period onwards culminated about the end of the twelfth century in the set forms of the highly ornamented *dán díreach* metres which were to dominate bardic poetry for the rest of the Middle Ages, while at the same time the poets achieved a new standard in grammar and vocabulary which laid 'the linguistic foundations of classical Modern Irish'.[33] This sudden emergence of the modern language was also the culmination of centuries of hidden development in spoken Irish.[34] The seeming abruptness thus relates to the appearance of these oral developments in the written record, beginning with the texts of poems addressed *c.* 1200 to Cathal Croibhdhearg Ó Conchobhair, king of Connacht and Raghnall mac Gofraidh, king of the Isle of Man,[35] and continuing to be found with remarkable consistency in all *dán díreach* poems thereafter. Rather than attributing the forging of the new literary standard to an unrecorded 'synod of poets' in the late twelfth century, as has been suggested,[36] I would prefer to look to the domination of the bardic art throughout Ireland and Scotland by the Ó Dálaigh family in the twelfth and early thirteenth centuries[37] as a unifying and standardizing influence.

What does seem clearly indicated by the known facts is that the training of praise-poets in the later twelfth century was by no means as heavily dependent on the activities of church schools as was the compilation of Irish annals or prose genealogies. The Middle Irish glosses to the tract *Coire Goiriath* show us glimpses of a system of education and examination administered by the poets themselves. They state that he who has the 'Cauldron of Inspiration' (*Coire Érmae*) 'propagates knowledge to students [*do felmacaib*]'. Its possessor has 'knowledge of the synchronism of kings . . . tales and genealogies . . . He confirms tales and genealogies for all, and they are confirmed for him by another poet [*o file aile*], i.e. he magnifies one who undertakes appointment into a grade [*oirdned i ngradh*], and he is then magnified by his teacher [*o oidi*] for his appointment.'[38] The use of the term *oide* or 'foster-father' for the teacher recalls the pronouncement of the king-bishop Cormac mac Cuilennáin (d. 908) that 'the pupil is always in fosterage with his teacher',[39] and this continued to be the normal expression in the later medieval and early modern bardic schools; but where the student in later centuries was correspondingly termed *dalta* or foster-son, here he is styled *felmac*, a word glossed by Cormac mac Cuilennáin as *mac uad* ('son of poetry') but also used of the beginner's grade in the Latin schools, and of the apprentices of a blacksmith.[40]

In fact in a number of ways the organization of poets in pre-Norman Ireland displays features in common with the craft guilds of ancient and early medieval Europe.[41] According to Cormac's Glossary they originally had a shared religious observance in honour of Brigit, daughter of the Dagda;[42] the practice of their profession was regulated by an abundance of laws peculiar to themselves, including fixed prices for the traditional, presyllabic metres;[43] and as we have seen above they had internal arrangements for education and quality control. We do not have evidence of a common purse to which prosperous members subscribed for the relief of those more needy or of widows and orphans, but there is some circumstantial support for the practice of 'fraternal feasting' such as underpinned the fellowship of corporations elsewhere, from the guilds of ancient Rome to the lord mayors' banquets of modern times. The maintenance of guest-houses by poets in the later Middle Ages[44] is foreshadowed by the gloss on *Coire Goiriath* which says of the fully inspired poet: 'he feeds a person together with [his] retinue, and he is fed together with [his] retinue, i.e. he provides entertainment [*fecht féile*] and entertainment is provided for him',[45] but more intriguing perhaps is the remark of Gofraidh Fionn Ó Dálaigh about the great feast given for all the poets of Ireland by Uilliam Ó Ceallaigh, chief of Uí Mhaine in 1351: 'William . . . a man who never made a stanza, issues a summons of the bardic college – astonishing tidings – as though he were a judge of the schools [*mar do bheith 'na bhreitheamh sgol, tuc gairm sgoile*].'[46] The implication must be that it was customary before that date for invitations to be issued to the general body of poets by a man accustomed to composing verse, whether this 'judge of the schools' who hosted such gatherings is understood as a professional jurist who had qualified as a 'judge of poetic speech',[47] or whether we should be thinking of an eminent *ollamh* of poetry who was held competent to judge the relative merits of compositions recited at a feast of this kind.[48] A parallel for the notion of a periodic banquet, held by the poets themselves under the presidency of one of their number, at which there was a competitive recital of poems may be found in the northern French poetic *confréries* or *puys* of the early thirteenth century, including the celebrated *Puy d'Arras*.[49]

Literacy and the Irish bards

Though the datable poems with named authors which survive from the thirteenth century onwards may seem preferable to vague inferences and Middle Irish glosses, they contain only incidental references to such matters as the education and function of a poet, the recitation or writing of poetry and so on. Still, the meagre harvest of such allusions gleaned from a survey of 900 syllabic compositions of hereditary professional poets between 1200 and 1690[50] showed perceptible changes in treatment from one century to another. The first hundred years of *dán díreach* are particularly interesting. Surnames of later medieval poets demonstrate that some families those of Ó Cuill, Mac Craith and Ó Clúmháin, for example – were descended from men styled *éces*, *file* or *ollamh i bhfilidheacht* in the pre-Norman annal entries,[51] while others such as Mac an Bhaird, Ó hAdhmaill and Ó'n Cháinte were descended from the bardic classes.[52] The disparate influences of both church schools and the oral bards find echoes in poems of the thirteenth century.

Paul Zumthor reminds us of the importance of physical performance as the vehicle by which oral poetry is communicated to its audience, and hence the significance of the poet's appearance, gestures, clothes and musical accompaniment.[53] In the late thirteenth century we are given one of the very few word-pictures of a poet in action when we are told of the *bard*, clad in satin and wearing a sparkling jewelled headdress on his blond hair, stationed in the doorway of the banqueting-hall of the chief Brian Mag Shamhradháin (d. 1298).[54] However optimistic the description of the bard's attire, this figure is surely not to be equated with the insignificant poet's assistant named as a 'bard' by Thomas Smyth in the middle of the sixteenth century.[55] The same patron is assured by Giolla Pádraig Mac Naimhin in another poem 'I am thy bard, thy Bricne', though this author describes himself as the chief's *file* five verses earlier, and insists he is more deserving of payment than the timpanists, who receive lavish rewards from Brian for stories of the Fianna.[56]

Reciting poetry to the music of the sweet-stringed harp or *tiompán* is also mentioned by Giolla Brighde Mac Con Midhe, who elsewhere describes poets as dressed in brown and green clothing, colours appropriate for the nobly born,[57] and holding poets' wands (*fleasga fileadh*), in a vision where all the poets in Ireland inaugurate Roalbh Mac Mathghamhna as king.[58] Both authors cited use fine clothes as a practical sign of the poets' high status, rather than recalling the *filí*'s legendary feathered cloak or *tuigen*, described in Cormac's Glossary

245

and the *Colloquy of the Two Sages*, and referred to allegorically in the erudite seventeenth-century elegy for Eochaidh Ó hEoghusa.[59]

Approving references to pre-Christian practices of the poets may not have been considered tactful during the thirteenth century, when secular Irish learning was coming under increasing criticism from the church.[60] While Giolla Brighde calls his visionary poets 'men of the Tuatha Dé Danann',[61] he is careful to assure us that the vision was revealed to him by an angel of God. In a religious poem the same author criticizes payments not only to the *cáinte*, the professional satirist who had long lain under the church's curse, but to the buffoon, the *crosán* who was also being painted as a villain in church sources of the twelfth and thirteenth centuries.[62] Similarly his younger contemporary Tadhg Ó hUiginn, in a poem to Brian Mag Shamhradháin, describes Crom Cruaich, the pagan idol of Magh Sléacht, as Ceann Cruaiche, chief of the druids, a figure of horror and bloodshed, whose mere memory made women faint.[63]

This Tadhg Ó hUiginn was presumably Tadhg Mór Ó hUiginn, credited with an elegy for Brian Mag Shamhradháin in the same poem-book, and with two magnificent eulogies addressed to Maghnus Ó Conchobhair, king of Connacht (d. 1293) and his daughter Fionnghuala (d. 1310).[64] Both he and Giolla Brighde Mac Con Midhe were 'learned' poets, in the sense that Ó hUiginn illustrated his poem to Mag Shamhradháin with a version of the *dindshenchas* of Magh Sléacht,[65] and littered his ode to Maghnus Ó Conchobhair with apposite references to mythical legendary and historical figures, while Giolla Brighde showed himself familiar with the *dindshenchas* of Inis Saimhéar,[66] poems on the battle of Clontarf,[67] poems on the relative rights of the kings of Tír Eoghain and Tír Conaill,[68] and a wide range of historical, hagiographical and scriptural material.[69] His definition of the poetic art (*dán*) as *Donum Dei*, which he correctly translates as the gift of God,[70] need not necessarily imply that he had any deeper knowledge of Latin, but it certainly recalls the teaching of the *Coire Goiriath* on the grace of God as a source of poetic inspiration. The best-attested poems of Donnchadh Mór Ó Dálaigh are breathtaking in the complexity of their metrical ornamentation, and contain a number of biblical and apocryphal references.[71]

One might well enquire why Gerard Murphy was so emphatically convinced that the era of the learned *fili* came to an end with the Norman invasion. The contrast seems to lie in the fact that syllabic poems of the twelfth century and earlier are principally concerned

246

with recording and communicating knowledge about royal genealogies, origin legends and claims to territory and tribute sometimes, but not always, finishing with verses in praise of a particular patron.[72] In a tail-piece to the late eleventh-century Book of Rights, the legendary fifth-century poet Dubthach Maccu Lugair is made to assert that no poet is entitled to visitation or reward who is not also a learned historian.[73] In the post-Norman period praise of a patron is the central theme of professional poetry, and the labours of the specialist historians are merely drawn on to fuel such praise. As Ádhamh Ó Fialáin pointed out to the chief Tomás Mag Shamhradháin: 'Sweet-voiced Mac Fir Bisigh has told the genealogy – a splendid one! – of thy father; is it not enough for me to repeat it, thou Prince of Cé whom I have ever exalted?'[74]

Giolla Brighde's famous defence of the poetic art, *A theachtaire thig ó'n Rúimh* ('O messenger who comes from Rome'), is more about communication than scholarship: 'Were it not for poetry, sweet-tongued harp or *tiompán* would not know of a goodly hero after his death, nor of his reputation nor his prowess. Noble men would have no knowledge of their traditions and nobility; allow these to be composed in poetry or else bid farewell to their ancient histories.'[75] In discussing the spread of vernacular literatures in medieval Europe, Brian Stock has developed the concept of the 'textual community', where a group of people are bound together by their knowledge of or belief in a particular text. The bond was not merely between those who wrote and those who were able to read it. A wider audience was reached through 'interpreters' who absorbed the message of the text by reading, or word of mouth, and then passed it on orally to the illiterate. These 'interpreters' might be preaching friars, heretic missioners or troubadours.[76] Clearly the bardic poet of the high Middle Ages fits this model very neatly. Whether by reading or otherwise, he absorbs the contents of texts such as the *Lebor Gabála* (Book of Invasions) and the *Táin Bó Cuailnge* and then rather than simply recounting them to his illiterate patrons, he interprets the material and draws a message to suit the society he is addressing, exciting their interest by the beauty of his verse and by a musical accompaniment.

It is hard, if not impossible, to separate the academic knowledge displayed by Ó hUiginn, Mac Con Midhe or Ó Dálaigh from a poetic training that involved book-learning, but there is almost total silence in both annals and poems as to how poetic schooling was organized

247

in the thirteenth century. In an ode to Richard de Burgh doubtfully attributed to Muireadhach Albanach Ó Dálaigh (fl. 1213), the author styles himself *maighistir múinte*, a 'master of teaching' rather than an *ollamh* or *oide* to his poet-band.[77] This might be interpreted as an ironic touch in the late twelfth and early thirteenth century, when church schools were replacing the old-style *fer légind* with the new *magister* as their head teacher of Latin learning,[78] and the use of this fashionable term heralded the end of Irish literary studies in church settlements. On the other hand the expression *maighistir múinte* seems to have the sense of a schoolmaster wielding a cane over a juvenile pupil in the fourteenth to fifteenth century,[79] the period to which this composition must belong if it is judged to be a later pastiche. The only other educational reference I have noted in a thirteenth-century poem comes in the anonymous ode to Cailleach Dé, daughter of Ó Mannacháin, where the author mentions his school as following him in serried ranks to assault the hospitality of his patroness, and uses the word *adhbhar* apparently to mean a student-poet, while he refers to himself as a *saoi* or sage.[80] Again the technical vocabulary of the bardic schools is avoided, perhaps deliberately, if the more learned of the thirteenth-century *fir dhána* were anxious to minimize the contrast between their own schools and those of the church. Standards of education seem to have differed. The surviving poems of the obscure Giolla Pádraig Mac Naimhin, who described himself as *bard* to Mag Shamhradháin, are quite free of learned allusions, and he implies that he is giving his son a practical apprenticeship in his own home. 'I said to him: "Silence, son, thou art young and foolish . . . put on thy (poet's) dress and go thy round with thy poets; if thou takest a poem with thee thou shalt get a horse in return . . . I like not to see poets quiet and dumb; a dog lives by his legs (and so a poet by his mouth)." '[81]

As far as the textual transmission of thirteenth-century poems is concerned, we have only circumstantial evidence. Standish Hayes O'Grady detected a reference to the *duanaire* or poem-book of Muireadhach Albanach in a faint heading on fo. 8 of the fifteenth-century manuscript BL Add. 19,995,[82] but this, of course, is no proof that the hypothetical *duanaire* was compiled in or near the poet's own lifetime. Lambert McKenna has suggested that the group of seven poems to the late-thirteenth-century Brian Mag Shamhradháin which are entered at the beginning of the mid-fourteenth-century Mag Shamhradháin *duanaire* derive from an earlier written collection, though it is hard to isolate examples of corruption in the text which are unambiguously due to mistranscription.[83] In favour of the possibility of oral transmission is the fact that Donnchadh Mór Ó Dálaigh ends his long poem on the necessity of paying tithes to the church with a blessing for every one who memorizes and recites it.[84] However the accuracy of the quotations from these early poems found in the bardic grammatical and syntactical tracts of the later period, and the very elaborateness of the rules for the composition of *dán díreach* metre, support Pádraig Ó Macháin's suggestion that 'if, as the poets themselves affirmed, the spoken form was of primary importance, the written form, and therefore the written text, also had some function in what may be termed the bardic process, that is, the composition of a poem and the presentation of it to the person for whom it was intended'.[85]

It is hardly too much to say that all such doubts and ambiguities are removed by the middle of the fourteenth century. From this period we have the Book of Magauran, a written anthology of contemporary poems transcribed for the patron to whom many of them were addressed.[86] We also have the prose tract on common metrical faults in the Ó Cianáin manuscript (c. 1344–5),[87] the first extant textbook from the post-Norman bardic schools, later followed by others from the fifteenth, sixteenth and seventeenth centuries. Verses by the Munster poet Maolmhuire bacach Mac Craith, complaining of Gofraidh Fionn Ó Dálaigh's ingratitude towards the Mac Craith school where he was educated, make explicit reference to the literate nature of that education: 'We read the same book with the great teacher who taught us.'[88]

There are even signs of literacy, or at least of poetic skill, among some aristocratic patrons during the fourteenth century. Best-known is Gearóid Iarla, or Gerald FitzGerald, third earl of Desmond (d. 1398), thirty of whose poems in *óglachas*, the simplified amateur version of Irish syllabic metres, are found in the Book of Fermoy.[89] However there are also good grounds for identifying Diarmaid Ó Briain, author of the little *óglachas* poem on the river Shannon, *A Shionainn Bhriain Bhóroimhe*, with the king of Thomond who died in 1364.[90] A eulogy describes him going on a visit to the poets of Ireland which enabled him to meet all their demands at once and which honoured the author.[91] This may imply that Ó Briain had attended a general gathering of the men of art (*gairm scoile*) held in some poet's house. Since his one short poem gave rise to a 'poetic contention', it is tempting to see it as his contribution to the festivities on that occasion.

Together with the study of vernacular law and history, bardic poetry enjoyed a revival of interest in the second half of the fourteenth century, overcoming a phase of opposition by Irish churchmen and the cut-price competition offered by genuinely oral balladeers.[92] The Gaelic chieftains, riding high on the crest of a recovery of territory and power, and anxious to legitimize their gains in the eyes of the public, began to issue invitations for poetic gatherings to be held in their own houses.[93] The poets seem filled with a new confidence in their own traditional education. Maolmhuire Mac Craith's poem about Gofraidh Fionn Ó Dálaigh speaks not only of books but of the poet's bed; he calls the testing or selecting process *sgagadh* ('sifting'), a word that occurs in the same context in the contemporary Book of Magauran.[94] The teacher is *oide* or fosterfather, and the pupil *dalta* or fosterling. The same terminology is found in Gofraidh Fionn's lament for his dead son, with the addition of *adhbhar ollaimh*, one eligible for the position of master-poet or court poet.[95] It is no accident that in this elegy Gofraidh compares himself sympathetically with the druid Cathbhadh, mourning for his son Geanann Gruadhsholas, in strong contrast to the horrific depiction of the 'druid' Ceann Cruaiche by the thirteenth-century Tadhg Ó hUiginn. In the course of the controversy with the church some ecclesiastical sources had described druids as poets and poets as druids,[96] and the poets seem to have reacted by taking pride in the term, as enhancing their long tradition, high prestige and reputation for magical powers. In his laudatory poem on the Christmas feast held in 1351 by the chief Uilliam Ó Ceallaigh for all the poets of Ireland and the men of art generally, Gofraidh Fionn mentions that among the guests would be judges, 'druids' and noble poets, authors and those who compose battle-rolls.[97] In the early fifteenth century we find an anonymous elegy using the word *file* to describe the druid who prophesies Art's death in *Cath Muighe Mucraimhe* (The Battle of Mag Mucrama)[98] and by the sixteenth and seventeenth centuries it was commonplace for poets to use *draoi* and *cáinte* unselfconsciously as synonyms for *file* and *bard*.[99] The word *bard* itself, in the sense of an insignificant poet's assistant, a reciter of poems, comes in early seventeenth-century compositions by Fearghal Óg Mac an Bhaird and Tadhg mac Dáire.[100] This tendency to use the terminology of bygone days to cast a veil of immemorial antiquity over institutions that had in point of fact undergone considerable changes reflects a general trend in the culture of the Gaelic Resurgence during the later Middle Ages, found also in political rhetoric and ceremonial and in the visual arts,[101] and is comparable to the movements associated with W. B. Yeats and Pádraig Pearse in more recent times.[102]

Such changes as took place, however, were of necessity gradual. While the education of poets and the transmission of their work to subsequent generations clearly involved the written word from the fourteenth century onwards, the continuing illiteracy of many patrons meant that the oral aspects of the poets' work were still important. It was not until the sixteenth and seventeenth centuries that the familiar pattern of poems addressed to absent patrons, apostrophizing envoys who were to tell the poet's message by word of mouth,[103] was joined by verses addressed to a book or letter being posted to the patron, or indeed released to the general reading public.[104]

The early fifteenth-century address to a messenger by Dubhthach Mac Eochadha in the Leabhar Cloinne Aodha Buidhe, *A theachtaire théid bhu thuaidh* ('O messenger who goes northwards'), is of particular interest, because his insistence that the messenger pass on exactly what he told him, not missing a word, although a literary device, presupposes a situation where the composer repeats his poems to the reciter until the man has the words by heart rather than handing him the text on a piece of paper so that he may go off and learn it for himself.[105]

The spread of literacy among the Irish aristocracy during the fifteenth and sixteenth centuries ultimately played a major part in transforming the nature and function of bardic poetry. The traditional bardic eulogy was semi-public. On the one hand it was commissioned and paid for by an individual patron, whose Christian name and surname, perhaps also that of his wife and his direct ancestors, were woven into the rhyme scheme from verse to verse, making it only of value as a possession to that individual and his (or her) descendants.[106] Since, however, it was declaimed at a banquet, in front of a large assembly, it was not the appropriate vehicle for confidential advice, or genuine declarations of love. Increased lay literacy and the advent of the printing press produced change in two directions. The letter-poem, which could be intended for one pair of eyes only, became more personal and emotional, sometimes containing the name of the author or his reader in a riddle or acrostic.[107] On the other hand, the

251

invention of printing and a wider reading public led to the fully public poem, an exhortation to patriotism, or to piety, or a lament for the changing times addressed to the population in general rather than a particular patron. Eochaidh Ó hEoghusa, who has a number of courtly love-poems in *óglachas* metres ascribed to him, expressed a half-humorous, half-apologetic fear of the displeasure his aristocratic patron, the earl of Tír Conaill, might feel at his descent into popular and profitable 'soft' poetry.[108]

The danger for professional poets of composing in the amateur metres was that they might then find themselves in competition with their own patrons. In the sixteenth century we hear of patrons studying with their poets,[109] composing verse turn about with them,[110] lending them books and reading glasses.[111] In the high Middle Ages when Ireland had no university, the bardic schools of law, poetry and history were the only available centres of secular learning.[112] With the founding of Trinity College Dublin in 1592, where attendance was compulsory for the underage heirs of deceased Irish chieftains,[113] the chances were that the bardic poet's patron would have more Latin learning than his 'man of art'. The seventeenth-century Fear Flatha Ó Gnímh sounds distinctly defensive in his ode to Art Óg Ó Néill of Clandeboy (d. 1677), *Cia as mó comaoin ar chloinn Néill* ('To whom are the O'Neills most indebted?'): 'Information about the descendants of Gaoidheal Glas is not in English or Welsh, and it is not available in Latin books to be researched as we research it.'[114] It is precisely in this age of the printing press and the university that bardic poets are most nostalgic about their traditional schools and tell us about the training of young beginners by setting them to memorize the poems of others,[115] about the poets' practice of composing on beds in darkened huts,[116] about the terrifying criticism which their compositions underwent from their fellow-poets,[117] and about the drinking and feasting that was so much a part of their profession.[118]

However, some poets found the traditional schools inadequate and were tempted by the opportunity to widen their intellectual horizons. It is interesting that the pious Giolla Brighde Ó hEoghusa, the sixteenth-century court poet to Aodh Mag Uidhir who left his post to become a Franciscan friar at the Irish college in Louvain, does not ascribe this change to religious motives in a poem he addressed to a close friend:

I have decided on another profession, to abandon Gaelic poetry . . .
It is not hatred of my forefather's art that has unsettled my mind;
nor the fact that the honour which was once bestowed on it by the
Irish race has disappeared. Though our knowledge of them is small,
it is the study of learned books – the most noble profession known
to me – that has enticed me away from you.[119]

The grammar of Classical Irish that Ó hEoghusa subsequently wrote
in Louvain, and his catechetical work *Teagasg Criosdaidhe* ('Christian
Doctrine'), show that the wheel had come full circle. As in early
Christian Ireland Latin ecclesiastical learning and traditional bardic
training had blended successfully to produce a rich hybrid culture,
shown also in the work of Aodh Mac Aingil, Flaithrí Ó Maolchonaire
and Mícheál Ó Cléirigh.[120] The Franciscans' imaginative move in
setting up their own printing press at Louvain showed how readily
this mixed culture could adapt to contemporary European civilization. It was the political collapse of the Gaelic and Anglo-Irish
autonomous lordships in Ireland that deprived the praise-poets of
their basic function of legitimizing sovereign authority, while the
failure of the Catholic Confederation of Kilkenny left the ecclesiastical patriots without a political goal to reward their efforts. As a
result the bottom fell out of the bardic market, and many a trained
professional poet must have thought like Mathghamhain Ó hIfear-
náin: 'Such an art as this is no profit to me, though it is a misfortune it
should fall to the ground: it were more honourable to become a
maker of combs – what use is it to anyone to profess poetry?'[121]

NOTES

1 See Charles-Edwards, above, pp. 70–2.
2 *UR*, pp. 99–100; see also Ó hAodha, 'Middle Irish metrical tract', pp. 211–22.
3 Murphy, 'Bards and filidh'. On the term *fear dána*, see Simms, 'An eaglais', pp. 22–5.
4 Ó Macháin, 'Irish prosodic tracts'.
5 See, for example, McCone, 'Tale of two ditties', and the works there cited.
6 The author may have thought of this as an actual practice of pagan times, or as an
  allegorical description of the attainment of perfection in their art by contemporary
  secular poets. Either way it was a description of the acquisition of *imbas forosna*
  ('the knowledge which illuminates') more acceptable to Christian ears than the
  banned pagan ritual described in Cormac's Glossary. See Thurneysen, 'Imbas for
  osndai', and editor's notes to this passage (next note).
7 Breatnach, 'Caldron', 68–9.

8 *CIH* vol. 5, p. 1614 (MacNeill, 'Ancient Irish law', 282); see L. Breatnach, 'Lawyers', p. 7.

9 *Chron. Scot.* s.a. 907; *AFM* s.a. 903, 915, 941, 971, 1168; 'A. Tig.' s.a. 1056, 1160(?); *AU* s.a 1086.

10 *Auraicept*, ed. Ahlqvist, pp. 14–16, and cf. Charles-Edwards, above, pp. 76–8.

11 Murphy, *Early Irish Metrics*, pp. 8–12; see also McCone, *Pagan Past*, pp. 38–41.

12 *Chron. Scot.* s.a. 896. Ruman mac Colmain (d. 747) is also compared to Homer and Virgil in *Corpus Genealogiarum Sanctorum*, ed. Ó Riain, p. 126.

13 Ó hAodha, 'Middle Irish metrical tract', pp. 218–21.

14 Murphy, 'Bards and filidh', 205–6; 'Poem to Aodh', ed. Murphy, pp. 140–1.

15 Murphy, 'Bards and filidh', 206–7.

16 Thurneysen, 'Mittelirische Verslehren'. See Ó hAodha, 'Middle Irish metrical tract', pp. 209–10.

17 Ó hAodha, 'An bhairdne', pp. 18–19; *idem*, 'Middle Irish metrical tract', pp. 221–2.

18 By combing through the main annal collections (*AU, AI, AFM,* 'A. Tig.', *A. Clonm., Chron. Scot.*) and collating their entries, I came up with 176 references to Latin learning in the obits during the 300-odd years from 587 to 899 AD (including 80 occurrences of *scriba /scribhnidh /scribhneoir*, 76 *sapiens /suí / eagnaidh*, 7 *doctor /religionis doctor*, 5 *fer léigind*), while there were only nine references to Irish learning (3 *poeta / fili*, 3 *iudex /breithem* and 3 *peritissimus historiarum /seanchaidh*, one of whom was also described as *ollamh aurlabhraidh*). By contrast, in the three centuries from 900 to 1200 AD I found 244 references in the obits to Latin scholars (including 117 *fer léigind*, 93 *sapiens /suí / eagnaidh*, 26 *scriba /scribhnidh*, 4 *magister*, 2 *doctor*). In the same period there were 99 references to Irish learning (including 29 *ollam*, 24 *file /éicces /fer dána*, 20 *sencha*, 9 *breithem*, 5 *egnaidh isin mberla Scoitecedha* or equivalent, 3 *druth*). Thus the proportion of Irish to Latin scholarship recorded has jumped from under 1:15 to over 1:3.

19 Kenney, *Sources*, pp. 11, 681–3, 688, 732–3.

20 Hughes, *Church*, pp. 245–6, 265.

21 *Genealogical Tracts I*, ed. Ó Raithbheartaigh, p. 30; see Byrne, *Irish Kings*, p. 35; McCone, *Pagan Past*, pp. 22, 24; and Charles-Edwards, above, pp. 68–76.

22 *UR*, pp. 51, 87–8.

23 *ALC, AFM.*

24 *Miscellaneous Irish Annals*, ed. Ó hInnse, 'A. Tig.', *AFM* s.a. 1118; *AI, AFM, AU* s.a. 1119. For the use of the terms *fer dána* and *ollamh re dán* rather than *file* and *ollamh i bhfilidheacht* for this new generation of poets, see above, n. 2.

25 *A. Clonm.* s.a. 1131, 1136; 'A. Tig.' s.a. 1139; *AFM* s.a. 1139, 1161; *AI* s.a. 1165 (and see also *ALC* s.a. 1181 for another *ollamh* from this family).

26 Harrison, *Irish Trickster*, p. 50.

27 O'Dwyer, 'Annals of Connacht', 83–101.

28 She notes however, that her collaborator, Geneviève Marsh-Micheli, considers that some undated Irish manuscripts assigned approximately to the twelfth century could in fact have originated in the thirteenth (Henry and Marsh-Micheli, 'Manuscripts', pp. 781, 792, n.).

29 Ibid., pp. 792–801; Simms, 'Brehons', pp. 56–9.

30 See, for example, *Book of Leinster*, ed. Best *et al.*, vol. 1, pp. xii-xiii; *Metrical Dindshenchas*, ed. Gwynn, vol. 5, pp. 3–114, and most recently, P. Smith, 'Aimirgein Glúngel', pp. 120–4.

31 Simms, *From Kings*, pp. 6–7 and 'Brehons', p. 66; MacNiocaill, 'Aspects of Irish law', pp. 30–1; Walsh, *Irish Men*, p. 16; *AC*, pp. xiv-xx.

32 *AC*, *ALC* s.a. 1244; *Dán Dé*, ed. McKenna, pp. viii, 147–8; *Poems of Giolla Brighde*, ed. Williams, p. 5; Bergin, *Irish Bardic Poetry*, p. 93.

33 Ó Cuív, 'Some developments', 290.

34 McCone, 'Würzburg and Milan glosses', 101; *idem*, 'Zur Frage der Register', pp. 93–5.

35 'Poem in praise of Raghnall', ed. Ó Cuív, 283–301; 'Poem by Gilbride', ed. Quiggin, pp. 241–5. See Murphy, 'Bards and filidh', 206, n.

36 MacCana, 'Rise', 139 and n.

37 Simms, 'An eaglais', p. 24.

38 Breatnach, 'Caldron', 71, 73. The reciprocal magnifying mentioned here could refer to a praise-poem addressed by the candidate for promotion as a form of test-piece to the king who should officially receive him into the next grade (*UR*, pp. 104–5), followed by a congratulatory poem from the examining *ollam* to the successful candidate. It is clearly stated in the same group of glosses that the essence of *érma* is making praise (poetry) and being paid for it.

39 'is i n-ace bís an deiscipal acind aiti': *Sanas Cormaic*, ed. Meyer, p. 10, no. 88.

40 Ibid., p. 49, no. 599; *Dictionary of the Irish Language*, s.v. 'felmac'.

41 See Epstein, 'Guilds', pp. 13–15.

42 *Sanas Cormaic*, ed. Meyer, p. 15, no. 150.

43 *CIH* vol. 2, pp. 648–52 (*Ancient Laws*, vol. 5, ed. Atkinson, pp. 56–71); see Ó hAodha, 'Middle Irish metrical tract', pp. 218–19.

44 Mac Cana, 'Rise', 132–3.

45 Breatnach, 'Caldron', 73.

46 Knott, 'Filidh Éireann', 52–3.

47 Compare n. 8, above, and n. 90, below.

48 See *Dioghluim*, ed. MacCionaith, no. 73, verse 32.

49 Strayer (ed.), *Dictionary*, vol. 5, p. 117a, vol. 10, p. 218, vol. 12, p. 218b.

50 This figure represents the stage so far reached in my slow attempt to compile a descriptive catalogue of extant published and unpublished bardic poems. My first-line index contains over 2,000 entries in all, but this would include an error margin of up to ten per cent of duplicate or inappropriate entries, while doubtless omitting further suitable items that I have failed to locate.

51 *AI* s.a. 1048, 1097; *AFM* s.a. 1098, 1143, 1170. Presumably in the same category are those families whose early members are styled *ollam* without further indication of profession (Ó Sléibhín *AFM* s.a. 1022, 1031, 1168; and Ó Ruanadha *AFM* s.a. 1079).

52 Ó hAodha, 'An bhairdne', p. 19. Of course the law from the earliest period allowed progression from the lower to the higher class of poets in three generations: *UR*, pp. 94–8, 106–7, 114–15.

53 Zumthor, *Introduction*, ch. 11. Cf. also S. Davies, above, pp. 135–6.

54 *Book of Magauran*, ed. McKenna, pp. 4–5, 291.

55 Hore, 'Irish bardism', 166.

56 *Book of Magauran*, ed. McKenna, pp. 54–7, 310.
57 *CIH* vol. 5, p. 1759, line 14.
58 *Poems of Giolla Brighde*, ed. Williams, pp. 175, 212.
59 *Sanas Cormaic*, ed. Meyer, pp. 91, 107; Bergin, *Irish Bardic Poetry*, pp. 183–4, 299.
60 Simms, 'An eaglais', pp. 25–32 and 'Brehons', p. 67.
61 It is possible Giolla Brighde alludes here to the doctrine repeated by Dubhaltach Óg Mac Firbhisigh that every Irishman who is blond and practises arts such as poetry, music or metalworking descends from the Tuatha Dé Danann. See *Genealogical Tracts I*, ed. Ó Raithbheartaigh, p. 21.
62 *Poems of Giolla Brighde*, ed. Williams, p. 242, where I emend line 28 against the editor's interpretation to read *a bhfuighle ag conaibh na* (g)*cáinte* on grounds of both context and morphology. See Simms, 'An eaglais', pp. 25–6, esp. n. 22; Harrison, *Irish Trickster*, pp. 31–3, 41–53.
63 *Book of Magauran*, ed. McKenna, pp. 14–15, 294–5.
64 Ibid., p. 30; *Dioghluim*, ed. MacCionaith, nos. 98, 114.
65 Ó Caithnia, *Apalóga*, pp. 101–2.
66 Ibid., p. 106.
67 *Poems of Giolla Brighde*, ed. Williams, no. xiii; compare 'Cath Cluana Tairbh', ed. MacNeill, 10; 'Leabhar Oiris', ed. Best, 90–5; *Cogadh Gaedhel*, ed. Todd, p. 138.
68 *Poems of Giolla Brighde*, ed. Williams, nos. i and iii; compare *Book of Fenagh*, ed. Hennessy and Kelly, pp. 312–31, 355–9.
69 Ó Caithnia, *Apalóga*, pp. 63, 74, 80, 92, 98, 103, 107, 109, 121, 136, 143, 145, 152, 162, 169, 178, 180, 184.
70 *Poems of Giolla Brighde*, ed. Williams, pp. 204–5.
71 Ó Caithnia, *Apalóga*, pp. 144, 148–52, 158–9.
72 For example, *Metrical Dindshenchas*, ed. Gwynn, vol. 1, pp. 50–3; Byrne, 'Clann Ollaman Uaisle Emna', 79–80.
73 *Lebor na Cert*, ed. Dillon, pp. 120–3.
74 *Book of Magauran*, ed. McKenna, p. 370.
75 *Poems of Giolla Brighde*, ed. Williams, p. 213.
76 Stock, *Listening to the Text*, pp. 23, 36, 140–58.
77 Bergin, *Irish Bardic Poetry*, p. 89.
78 Simms, 'Brehons', pp. 55–6, 66–7.
79 See *Dictionary of the Irish Language*, s.v. 'múnad'.
80 *Aithdioghluim*, ed. McKenna, vol. 1, pp. 2, 4; vol. 2, pp. 2, 3.
81 *Book of Magauran*, ed. McKenna, pp. 52–9, 309–11.
82 See Murphy, 'Two Irish poems', 74–5.
83 A possible example occurs on line 186 (see *Book of Magauran*, ed. McKenna, pp. viii, 14–15, 401–2).
84 *Dán Dé*, ed. McKenna, pp. 51, 117.
85 Ó Macháin, 'Irish prosodic tracts', p. 277.
86 *Book of Magauran*, ed. McKenna, p. viii.
87 Bergin, 'Irish Grammatical Tracts V'. See Ní Shéaghdha, *Catalogue*, vol. 1, pp. 13, 17.
88 *Dioghluim Dána*, ed. MacCionaith, no. 104, verse 7.

Literacy and the Irish bards

89 'Duanaire', ed. MacNiocaill. See Carney, 'Literature', pp. 697–8.

90 Bergin, *Irish Bardic Poetry*, pp. 46–7, 238. See Simms, 'Brehons', p. 64, n. 75, and *Measgra Dánta*, ed. O'Rahilly, vol. 1, p. 71. One of the manuscripts (Royal Irish Academy 467) containing the poem by Tadhg an Gharadh MacAodhagáin which delivered 'judgement' as between Ó Briain and a certain 'Tadhg Mór (*al.* Óg) Ó hUiginn' appears to be early sixteenth-century in date. This would rule out Eleanor Knott's identification of the 'Tadhg Óg' in question as an early seventeenth-century son of Tadhg Dall Ó hUiginn. See Ó Cuív, 'Poetic contention', 90 and Wulff and Mulchrone, *Catalogue*, p. 1222.

91 'Cuairt ele uaisleochus sionn . ruccais d'fhios fhileadh nÉireann . dá bfhuile gan oilbhéim uaidh . dá gcoimhréir uile a néanuair': 'An Appeal', ed. Ó Cuív, 101. In a paper read to the Seventh Irish Conference of Medievalists at Maynooth 25/6/93, Professor Ann Dooley of Toronto University suggested on grounds of style, content and verbal correspondences that the author of this anonymous address to Ó Briain was Gofraidh Fionn Ó Dálaigh.

92 Carney, 'Literature', pp. 689–93; Simms, 'An eaglais', pp. 29–32; *Book of Magauran*, ed. McKenna, pp. 236–47, 379–83; Murphy, *Early Irish Metrics*, p. 24, n. 1.

93 Simms, 'Guesting', 91–2.

94 *Book of Magauran*, ed. McKenna, p. 234, line 3634.

95 *Dioghluim*, ed. MacCionaith, no. 65.

96 *Bethada*, ed. Plummer, vol. 1, pp. 33–7, vol. 2, pp. 32–6; *Book of Fenagh*, ed. Hennessy and Kelly, pp. 126–9, 188 9. See Simms, 'An eaglais', pp. 30–2.

97 'Beidh breitheamhain bhreath ndligidh . beid draoithe & deighfhilidh beid 'na phurt ughdair Éirionn . lucht cumhdaigh na ccaithréimionn': Knott, 'Filidh Éireann', 56.

98 *Dioghluim*, ed. McKenna, no. 86, verses 2, 5; Ó Caithnia, *Apalóga*, pp. 83–4.

99 *Leabhar Branach*, ed. Mac Airt, lines 840, 1328, 2731, 3715, 4042, 4177, 4187, 4215, 6385; *Leabhar Cloinne Aodha Buidhe*, ed. Ó Donnchadha, pp. 77, 190; *Poems on the O'Reillys*, ed. Carney, p. 11, line 259; *Dioghluim Dána*, ed. McKenna, no. 115, verses 1, 4. See *Dictionary of the Irish Language* s.v. 'druí' (c).

100 *Dioghluim*, ed. McKenna, pp. 141, 384; see *Dán na mBráthar*, ed. MhágCraith, vol. 1, p. 190.

101 Simms, *From Kings*, pp. 17, 29, 48–9; Henry and Marsh-Micheli, 'Manuscripts', pp. 784, 794–5, 802.

102 Kiberd, 'Irish literature', pp. 284–8.

103 For example, *Dioghluim*, ed. McKenna, no. 66; *Leabhar Cloinne Aodha Buidhe*, ed. Ó Donnchadha, pp. 65, 124; *Bardic Poems of Tadhg Dall*, ed. Knott, vol. 1, p. 156; Bergin, *Irish Bardic Poetry*, no. 55.

104 Bergin, *Irish Bardic Poetry*, pp. 25, 40, 139, 151. For some Welsh parallels, see Smith, above, pp. 202–3.

105 Compare Ó Macháin, 'Irish prosodic tracts', p. 279.

106 As witness the well-known anecdote about the Dublin merchant who attempted to sell an old, irrelevant ode to Ó Conchobhair Sligigh (*Leabhar Branach*, ed. Mac Airt, pp. 215–16).

107 For example, *Dánta Grádha*, ed. O'Rahilly, nos. 23, 32, 36, 43,47, 101.

257

108 Bergin, *Irish Bardic Poetry*, no. 30; *Dánta Grádha*, ed. O'Rahilly, nos. 47(?), 88, 96.
109 *Bardic Poems of Tadhg Dall*, ed. Knott, no. 23; *Duanaire Mhéig Uidhir*, ed. Greene, pp. 78, 82, 200.
110 Ibid., p. 82.
111 Bergin, *Irish Bardic Poetry*, no. 14; O'Sullivan and Herbert, 'Provenance of Laud Misc. 615', 183–8.
112 See Simms, 'Bards and barons', pp. 195–6.
113 A. S. Green, *Making of Ireland*, p. 423.
114 'Eolus sleachta Gaoidhil Glais . ní bhí i mBérla nó i mBrethnais . 's ní fhuil i leabhraibh Laidne . a leanmhoin mur leanmaidne': *Leabhar Cloinne Aodha Buidhe*, ed. Ó Donnchadha, p. 227.
115 Bergin, *Irish Bardic Poetry*, no. 42.
116 Ibid., no. 27.
117 *Dioghluim*, ed. MacCionaith, no. 73.
118 Bergin, *Irish Bardic Poetry*, no. 7; *Dioghluim*, ed. MacCionaith, p. 384.
119 *Dán na mBráthar*, ed. MagCraith, vol. 2, p. 11.
120 Walsh, *Irish Men*, pp. 246–51.
121 Bergin, *Irish Bardic Poetry*, p. 279.

Works Cited

I PRINTED PRIMARY SOURCES

Aithdioghluim Dána, ed. L. McKenna, 2 vols., Dublin, 1939–40.

Amra Choluim Chille, ed. W. Stokes, 'The Bodleian Amra Choluim Chille', *Revue Celtique* 20 (1899), 30–55, 132–83, 248–89, 400–37.

Ancient Laws of Ireland, vol. 5, ed. R. Atkinson, Dublin, 1901.

Androw of Wyntoun, The Orygynale Cronykil of Scotland, ed. D. Laing, 3 vols., Historians of Scotland, Edinburgh, 1872–9.

Anglo-Saxon Litanies, ed. M. Lapidge, Henry Bradshaw Society, vol. 106, London, 1991.

Annála Connacht: The Annals of Connacht (A.D. 1224–1544), ed. A. M. Freeman, Dublin, 1944.

Annála Ríoghachta Éireann: Annals of the Kingdom of Ireland by the Four Masters, ed. J. O'Donovan, 7 vols., Dublin, 1851.

Annála Uladh: Annals of Ulster, ed. W. M. Hennessy and B. MacCarthy, 4 vols., Dublin, 1887–1901.

The Annals of Clonmacnoise, ed. D. Murphy, Dublin, 1896.

The Annals of Inisfallen, ed. S. Mac Airt, Dublin, 1951.

The Annals of Loch Cé, ed. W. M. Hennessy, 2 vols., London, 1871; repr. Dublin, 1939.

'The Annals of Tigernach', ed. W. Stokes, *Revue Celtique* 16 (1895), 374–419; 17 (1896), 6–33, 119–263, 338–420; 18 (1897), 9–59, 150–97, 374–91.

'An appeal on behalf of the profession of poetry', ed. B. Ó Cuív, *Éigse* 14 (1972), 87–106.

Augustine, *Confessiones*, ed. L. Verheijen, CCSL 27, Turnhout, 1981.

Augustine, *De Ciuitate Dei*, ed. B. Dombart and A. Kalb, CCSL 47, Turnhout, 1955.

Auraicept na nÉces, ed. A. Ahlqvist, *The Early Irish Linguist: An Edition of the Canonical Part of the* Auraicept na nÉces, Societas Scientiarum Fennica: Commentationes Humanarum Litterarum 73, Helsinki, 1983.

The Bardic Poems of Tadhg Dall Ó hUiginn, ed. E. Knott, 2 vols., London, 1922–6.

Bede, *Historia Ecclesiastica Gentis Anglorum*, ed. B. Colgrave and R. A. B. Mynors, Oxford, 1969.

Bergin, O., 'Irish Grammatical Tracts V: Metrical Faults', *Ériu* 17 (1955), Supplement, 259–93.

Berrad Airechta, ed. R. Thurneysen, *Die Bürgschaft im irischen Recht, Abhandlungen*

Works Cited

der Preussischen Akademie der Wissenschaften, phil.-hist. Klasse (1928), no. 2; trans. R. Stacey, 'Translation of the Old Irish tract *Berrad Airechta*', in T. M. Charles-Edwards, M. E. Owen and D. B. Walters (eds.), *Lawyers and Laymen*, Cardiff, 1986, pp. 210–33.

Bethada Náem nÉrenn: Lives of Irish Saints, ed. C. Plummer, 2 vols., Oxford, 1922.

Bili, *Vita Machutis, Vie de Saint-Malo, Evêque d'Alet*, ed. G. Le Duc, Dossiers du Centre Régional Archéologique d'Alet B, Saint-Malo, 1979.

Black Book of Limerick, ed. J. MacCaffrey, Dublin, 1907.

Blake, M. J., 'King Dermot Mac Carthy's charter, A.D. 1174, to the church at Cork afterwards called Gill-Abbey', *Journal of the Cork Historical and Archaeological Society* 10 (1904), 145–6.

The Book of Ballymote, ed. R. A. Atkinson, Dublin, 1887.

The Book of Fenagh, ed. W. M. Hennessy and D. H. Kelly, Dublin, 1875.

The Book of Lecan: Leabhar Mór Mhic Fhir Bhisigh Lecain, ed. K. Mulchrone, Dublin, 1937.

The Book of Leinster, formerly Lebor na Núachongbála, 6 vols., ed. R. I. Best, O. Bergin, M. A. O'Brien and A. O'Sullivan, Dublin, 1954–83.

The Book of Magauran, ed. L. McKenna, Dublin, 1947.

The Book of Settlements: Landnámabók, trans. H. Pálsson and P. Edwards, Winnipeg, 1972.

Breatnach, L., 'The Caldron of Poesy', *Ériu* 32 (1981), 45–93.

Butler, C. M. and Bernard, J. H., 'The charters of the abbey of Duiske', *PRIA* 35 C (1919–20), 1–188.

Byrne, F. J., 'Clann Ollaman Uaisle Emna', *Studia Hibernica* 4 (1964), 54–94.

Caernarvon Court Rolls 1361–1402, ed. G. P. Jones and H. Owen, Caernarfon, 1951.

Caesarius of Arles, *Sermones*, ed. G. Morin, part 1, CCSL 103, Turnhout, 1953.

Calendar of Ancient Correspondence Concerning Wales, ed. J. G. Edwards, Cardiff, 1935.

Calendar of Archbishop Alen's Register, ed. C. MacNeill, Dublin, 1950.

Calendar of Inquisitions Post Mortem, vol. 10, London, 1921.

Calendar of Ormond Deeds, ed. E. Curtis, 6 vols., Dublin, 1932–43.

Canu Maswedd yr Oesoedd Canol: Medieval Welsh Erotic Poetry, ed. D. Johnston, Cardiff, 1991.

Cartae et Alia Munimenta quae ad Dominium de Glamorgancia Pertinent, ed. G. T. Clark, 2nd edn, 6 vols., Cardiff, 1910.

Carte Nativorum: A Peterborough Abbey Cartulary of the Fourteenth Century, ed. C. N. L. Brooke and M. M. Postan, Northampton, 1960.

Le Cartulaire de l'Abbaye de Landévennec, ed. A. de la Borderie, Rennes, 1888.

Le Cartulaire de Redon, ed. A. de Courson, Paris, 1863.

The Cartulary of Haughmond Abbey, ed. U. Rees, Cardiff, 1985.

'Cath Cluana Tairbh', ed. J. MacNeill, *The Gaelic Journal* 7 (1896), 8–11, 41–4, 55–6.

Charles, B. G. and Emanuel, H. D., 'Welsh records in the Hereford capitular archives', *NLWJ* 8 (1953–4), 59–73.

Chartae, Privilegia et Immunitates, Dublin, 1829–30.

Charters, Bulls and Other Documents Relating to the Abbey of Inchaffray, ed. W. A. Lindsay, J. Dowden and J. M. Thomson, Scottish History Society, Edinburgh, 1908.

Works Cited

Chartularies of St Mary's Abbey, Dublin, ed. J. T. Gilbert, 2 vols., Rolls Series, London, 1884–6.

Chronicle of Andrew of Wyntoun, ed. F. J. Amours, 6 vols., Scottish Texts Society, Edinburgh, 1903–14.

Chronicles of the Picts, Chronicles of the Scots, and Other Early Memorials of Scottish History, ed. W. F. Skene, Edinburgh, 1867.

Chronicum Scotorum, ed. W. M. Hennessy, Rolls Series, London, 1866.

Clenennau Letters and Papers, ed. T. Jones Pierce, *NLWJ* Supplement 4, part 1, Aberystwyth, 1947.

Codex Diplomaticus Langobardiae, ed. G. Porro-Lambertenghi, Turin, 1873.

Cogadh Gaedhel re Gallaibh, ed. J. H. Todd, Rolls Series, London, 1867.

Collectio Canonum Hibernensis: Die irische Kanonensammlung, ed. H. Wasserschleben, 2nd edn, Leipzig, 1885.

Corpus Genealogiarum Hiberniae, vol. 1, ed. M. A. O'Brien, Dublin, 1962; revd. imp. J. V. Kelleher, 1976.

Corpus Genealogiarum Sanctorum Hiberniae, ed. P. Ó Riain, Dublin, 1985.

Corpus Iuris Hibernici, ed. D. A. Binchy, 6 vols., Dublin, 1978.

Crede Mihi, ed. J. T. Gilbert, Dublin, 1897.

'Credo Athanasius Sant', ed. H. Lewis, *BBCS* 5 (1929–31), 193–203.

Críth Gablach, ed. D. A. Binchy, Dublin, 1941.

Cummian's Letter De Controuersia Paschali and the De Ratione Conputandi, ed. M. Walsh and D. Ó Cróinín, Toronto, 1988.

Cyfreithiau Hywel Dda yn ôl Llyfr Blegywryd, ed. S. J. Williams and J. E. Powell, 2nd edn, Cardiff, 1961.

Dán Dé, ed. L. McKenna, Dublin [1922].

Dán na mBráthar Mionúr, ed. C. Mhágcraith, 2 vols., Dublin, 1967–80.

Dánta Grádha, ed. T. F. O'Rahilly, Dublin and Cork, 1926.

The Description of Penbrokshire by George Owen of Henllys, vol. 1, ed. H. Owen, London, 1892.

Dioghluim Dána, ed. L. Mac Cionaith, Dublin, 1938.

'Duanaire Ghearóid Iarla', ed. G. Mac Niocaill, *Studia Hibernica* 3 (1963), 7–59.

Duanaire Mhéig Uidhir, ed. D. Greene, Dublin, 1972.

Dugdale, W., *Monasticon Anglicanum*, ed. J. Caley *et al.*, 6 vols. in 8, London, 1817–30.

Early Welsh Genealogical Tracts, ed. P. C. Bartrum, Cardiff, 1966.

Facsimiles of the National Manuscripts of Ireland, ed. J. T. Gilbert, 4 vols., Dublin, 1874–84.

Falkenstein, L., 'Ein vergessener Brief Alexanders III. an einen "Rex Hibernorum"', *Archivum Historiae Pontificiae* 10 (1972), 107–60.

Förster, M., 'Die Freilassungsurkunden des Bodmin-Evangeliars', in N. Bøgholm, A. Brusendorff and C. A. Bodelsen (eds.), *A Grammatical Miscellany offered to Otto Jespersen on his Seventieth Birthday*, London and Copenhagen, 1930, pp. 77–99.

Genealogical Tracts I, ed. T. Ó Raithbheartaigh, Dublin, 1932.

Gerald of Wales, *The Journey through Wales and the Description of Wales*, trans. L. Thorpe, Harmondsworth, 1978.

Gildas, *De Excidio Britanniae*, ed. M. Winterbottom, London and Chichester, 1978.

261

Works Cited

Giraldi Cambrensis Opera, ed. J. S. Brewer, J. F. Dimock and G. F. Warner, 8 vols., Rolls Series, London, 1861–91.

Glamorgan Wills Proved in the Prerogative Court of Canterbury 1392–1571, ed. P. Riden, Cardiff, 1985.

Gottfried von Strassburg: Tristan, trans. A. T. Hatto, 2nd edn, Harmondsworth, 1967.

Gregory the Great, *Dialogues*, ed. A. de Vogüé, *Grégoire le Grand: Dialogues*, Sources Chrétiennes, no. 260, Paris, 1979.

Gregory of Tours, *Libri de Virtutibus Sancti Martini Episcopi*, ed. B. Krusch, MGH Scriptores Rerum Merovingicarum, vol. 1, part 2, Hanover, 1885, pp. 584–661.

Griffiths, R. A., 'The cartulary and muniments of the Fort family of Llanstephan', *BBCS* 24 (1970–2), 311–84.

Gwaith Cynddelw Brydydd Mawr, I, ed. N. A. Jones and A. Parry Owen, Cardiff, 1991.

Gwaith Dafydd ap Gwilym, ed. T. Parry, 3rd edn, Cardiff, 1979.

Gwaith Dafydd ap Gwilym a'i Gyfoeswyr, ed. I. Williams and T. Roberts, Cardiff, 1935.

Gwaith Guto'r Glyn, ed. J. Ll. Williams and I. Williams, Cardiff, 1939.

Gwaith Huw Cae Llwyd ac Eraill, ed. L. Harries, Cardiff, 1953.

Gwaith Iolo Goch, ed. D. R. Johnston, Cardiff, 1988.

Gwaith Lewys Glyn Cothi, ed. D. R. Johnston, Cardiff, 1995.

Gwaith Lewys Môn, ed. E. Rolant, Cardiff, 1975.

Gwaith Llywelyn Brydydd Hoddnant, Dafydd ap Gwilym, Hillyn ac Eraill, ed. A. Parry Owen, Aberystwyth, 1996.

Gwaith Owain ap Llywelyn ab y Moel, ed. E. Rolant, Cardiff, 1984.

Gwaith Sefnyn, Rhisierdyn, Gruffudd Fychan ap Gruffudd ab Ednyfed a Llywarch Bentwrch, ed. N. A. Jones and E. H. Rheinallt, Aberystwyth, 1995.

Haycock, M., *Blodeugerdd Barddas o Ganu Crefyddol Cynnar*, Swansea, 1994.

The Hisperica Famina: 1. The A-text, ed. M. W. Herren, Pontifical Institute of Mediaeval Studies, Toronto, 1974.

Historia Gruffud vab Kenan, ed. D. S. Evans, Cardiff, 1977.

History of the Gwydir Family and Memoirs, ed. J. G. Jones, Llandysul, 1990.

The History of the Gwydir Family Written by Sir John Wynn of Gwydir, ed. J. Ballinger, Cardiff, 1927.

An Inventory of the Early Chancery Proceedings Concerning Wales, ed. E. A. Lewis, Cardiff, 1937.

Irische Texte mit Wörterbuch, ed. W. Stokes and E. Windisch, 4 vols., Leipzig, 1880–1909.

The Irish Penitentials, ed. L. Bieler, Scriptores Latini Hiberniae, vol. 5, Dublin, 1963.

Jenkins, D., *The Law of Hywel Dda: Law Texts from Medieval Wales*, Llandysul, 1986.

Johannis de Fordun Chronica Gentis Scotorum, ed. W. F. Skene, Historians of Scotland, Edinburgh, 1871.

John of Cornwall, 'A new edition of John of Cornwall's *Prophetia Merlini*', ed. M. J. Curley, *Speculum* 57 (1982), 217–49.

Jonas, *Vita S. Columbani*, ed. B. Krusch, *Ionae Vitae Sanctorum Columbani, Vedastis, Iohannis*, MGH Scriptores Rerum Germanicarum, Hanover, 1905.

262

Works Cited

Knott, E., 'Filidh Éireann go haointeach', *Ériu* 5 (1911), 50–69.

La Borderie, A. de, 'Chartes inédites de Locmaria de Quimper 1022–1336', *Bulletin de la Société Archéologique du Finistère* 24 (1897), 96–113.

The Lais of Marie de France, trans. G. S. Burgess and K. Busby, Harmondsworth, 1986.

Lawrie, A. C., *Early Scottish Charters prior to AD 1153*, Glasgow, 1905.

Leabhar Branach, ed. S. Mac Airt, Dublin, 1944.

Leabhar Cloinne Aodha Buidhe, ed. T. Ó Donnchadha, Dublin, 1931.

'The Leabhar Oiris or Book of Chronicles [A.D. 979–1027]', ed. R. I. Best, *Ériu* 1 (1904), 74–112.

Lebor na Cert, ed. M. Dillon, London, 1962.

The Letters of Lanfranc, Archbishop of Canterbury, ed. H. Clover and M. Gibson, Oxford, 1979.

Liber Cartarum Prioratus Sancti Andree in Scotia, Bannatyne Club, Edinburgh, 1841.

Littere Wallie, ed. J. G. Edwards, Cardiff, 1940.

The Mabinogion, trans. G. Jones and T. Jones, revd. edn, London, 1974.

The Mabinogion from the Llyfr Coch o Hergest and Other Welsh MSS, trans. C. Guest, 3 vols., London, 1849.

MacNeill, E., 'Ancient Irish law: the law of status or franchise', *PRIA* 36 (1923) C, 265–316.

MacNiocaill, G., 'The Irish "charters"', in P. Fox (ed.), *The Book of Kells, MS 58, Trinity College Library, Dublin: Commentary*, Lucerne, 1990, pp. 153–65.

The Marcher Lordships of South Wales 1415–1536: Select Documents, ed. T. B. Pugh, Cardiff, 1963.

The Martyrology of Tallaght, ed. R. I. Best and H. J. Lawlor, Henry Bradshaw Society, vol. 68, London, 1931.

Measgra Dánta, vol. 1, ed. T. F. O'Rahilly, Cork, 1927.

The Metrical Dindshenchas, ed. E. Gwynn, 5 vols., Dublin, 1935.

Meyer, K., 'The expulsion of the Déssi', *Ériu* 3 (1907), 135–42.

'The expulsion of the Dessi', *Y Cymmrodor* 14 (1901), 101–35.

Miscellaneous Irish Annals (A.D. 1114–1437), ed. S. Ó hInnse, Dublin, 1947.

The Monks of Redon: Gesta Sanctorum Rotonensium and Vita Conuuoionis, ed. C. Brett, Studies in Celtic History 10, Woodbridge, 1989.

Morice, H., *Mémoires pour servir de preuves à l'histoire ecclésiastique et civile de Bretagne*, 3 vols., Paris, 1742–6.

Murphy, G., 'Two Irish poems written from the Mediterranean in the thirteenth century', *Éigse* 7 (1953), 71–8.

Nennius: British History and the Welsh Annals, ed. J. Morris, London and Chichester, 1980.

Nicholls, K. W., 'The charter of John, lord of Ireland, in favour of the Cistercian abbey of Baltinglass', *Peritia* 4 (1985), 187–206.

NLW, *Calendar of Wynn (of Gwydir) Papers*, Aberystwyth, Cardiff and London, 1926.

Notitiae as Leabhar Cheannanais, 1033–1161, ed. G. MacNiocaill, Dublin, 1961.

O'Donovan, J., 'The charter of Newry', *Dublin Penny Journal* 1 (1832–3), 102–4.

Ottonis et Rahewinis Gesta Friderici I. Imperatoris, ed. G. Waitz, MGH Scriptores Rerum Germanicarum, 3rd edn, Hanover, 1912.

Works Cited

The Oxford Book of Welsh Verse, ed. T. Parry, Oxford, 1962.

The Patrician Texts in the Book of Armagh, ed. L. Bieler, Scriptores Latini Hiberniae, vol. 10, Dublin, 1979.

Pedeir Keinc y Mabinogi, ed. I. Williams, Cardiff, 1930.

Pender, S., 'Two unpublished versions of the Expulsion of the Déssi', in *idem* (ed.), *Féilscríbhinn Torna*, Cork, 1947, pp. 209–17.

Phillimore, E., 'The *Annales Cambriæ* and Old-Welsh genealogies from *Harleian MS.* 3859', *Y Cymmrodor* 9 (1888), 141–83.

Picard, J. M. and Pontfarcy, Y. de, *The Vision of Tnugdal*, Dublin, 1989.

'A poem by Gilbride MacNamee in praise of Cathal O'Conor', in O. Bergin and C. Marstrander (eds.), *A Miscellany presented to Kuno Meyer*, Halle, 1912, pp. 241–5.

'A poem in praise of Raghnall, king of Man', ed. B. Ó Cuív, *Éigse* 8 (1957), 283–301.

'A poem to Aodh Ua Forreidh, bishop of Armagh', ed. G. Murphy, in S. Ó Briain (ed.), *Measgra i gCuimhne Mhichíl Uí Chléirigh*, Dublin, 1944, pp. 140–64.

The Poems of Giolla Brighde Mac Con Midhe, ed. N. J. A. Williams, Dublin, 1980.

Poems on the O'Reillys, ed. J. Carney, Dublin, 1950.

The Poetical Works of Dafydd Nanmor, ed. T. Roberts and I. Williams, Cardiff, 1923.

The Poetical Works of Gray and Collins, ed. A. L. Poole, London, 1926.

The Psalter and Martyrology of Ricemarch, ed. H. J. Lawlor, Henry Bradshaw Society, vols. 47–8, London, 1914.

Radulfi de Diceto Opera Historica, ed. W. Stubbs, 2 vols., Rolls Series, London, 1876.

Recueil d'actes inédits des ducs de Bretagne, ed. A. de la Borderie, Rennes, 1888.

Die Regensburger Schottenlegende: Libellus de Fundacione Ecclesie consecrati Petri: Untersuchung und Textausgabe, ed. P. A. Breatnach, Munich, 1977.

Regesta Regum Scottorum, vol. 1, *The Acts of Malcolm IV King of Scots 1153–1165*, ed. G. W. S. Barrow, Edinburgh, 1960.

Register of the Abbey of St Thomas, Dublin, ed. J. T. Gilbert, Rolls Series, London, 1889.

Registrum Prioratus Omnium Sanctorum iuxta Dublin, ed. R. Butler, Dublin, 1845.

Registrum vulgariter nuncupatum 'The Record of Caernarvon' e codice MS. Harleiano 696 descriptum, ed. H. Ellis, London, 1838.

Rhagymadroddion 1547–1659, ed. G. H. Hughes, Cardiff, 1951.

Rodulfus Glaber, *The Five Books of Histories*, ed. J. France, Oxford, 1989.

'The saga of Fergus mac Léti', ed. D. A. Binchy, *Ériu* 16 (1952), 33–48.

Sanas Cormaic, ed. K. Meyer, *Anecdota from Irish Manuscripts*, vol. 5, ed. O. Bergin *et al.*, Dublin, 1913.

Sancti Columbani Opera, ed. G. S. M. Walker, Scriptores Latini Hiberniae, vol. 2, Dublin, 1957.

Sheehy, M. P., 'Diplomatica: unpublished medieval charters and letters relating to Ireland', *Archivium Hibernicum* 25 (1962), 123–35.

Pontificia Hibernica, 2 vols., Dublin, 1962–5.

Smith, J. C., 'Wills of Welsh ecclesiastics holding appointments in England', *Archaeologia Cambrensis* 7th series 7 (1927), 197–9.

Works Cited

Smith, P., 'Aimirgein Glúngel Tuir Tend: a Middle-Irish poem on the authors and laws of Ireland', *Peritia* 8 (1994), 120–4.

A Survey of the Duchy of Lancaster Lordships in Wales 1609–1613, ed. W. Rees, Cardiff, 1953.

Survey of the Honour of Denbigh 1334, ed. P. Vinogradoff and F. Morgan, London, 1914.

The Text of the Book of Llan Dâv, ed. J. G. Evans with J. Rhys, Oxford, 1893.

Thurneysen, R., 'Imbas for osndai', *ZCP* 19 (1933), 163–4.

'Mittelirische Verslehren', in *Irische Texte*, ed. Stokes and Windisch, vol. 3 (1), pp. 67–106.

Trioedd Ynys Prydein: The Welsh Triads, ed. R. Bromwich, 2nd edn, Cardiff, 1978.

Two Lives of Saint Cuthbert, ed. B. Colgrave, Cambridge, 1940.

Uraicecht na Ríar, ed. L. Breatnach, Dublin, 1987.

Die Urkunden Friedrichs I., ed. H. Appelt, MGH Diplomata Regum et Imperatorum Romanorum Germaniae X, 4 vols., Hanover, 1975–90.

Die Urkunden Konrads III. und seines Sohnes Heinrichs, ed. F. Hausmann, MGH Diplomata Regum et Imperatorum Germaniae IX, Vienna, 1969.

Urkunden und erzählende Quellen zur deutschen Ostsiedlung im Mittelalter, ed. H. Helbig and L. Weinrich, vol. 1, 2nd edn, Darmstadt, 1975.

'Vie de saint Cadoc par Caradoc de Llancarfan', ed. P. Grosjean, *Analecta Bollandiana* 60 (1942), 35–67.

Visio Tnugdali: Lateinisch und Altdeutsch, ed. A. Wagner, Erlangen, 1882.

Vitae Sanctorum Britanniae et Genealogiae, ed. A. W. Wade-Evans, Cardiff, 1944.

Vitae Sanctorum Hiberniae, ed. C. Plummer, 2 vols., Oxford, 1910.

The Welsh Assize Roll 1277–1284, ed. J. C. Davies, Cardiff, 1940.

A Welsh Bestiary of Love, ed. G. C. G. Thomas, Dublin, 1988.

The White Book Mabinogion, ed. J. G. Evans, Pwllheli, 1907; 2nd edn, *Llyfr Gwyn Rhydderch: Y Chwedlau a'r Rhamantau*, Cardiff, 1973.

Ystorya de Carolo Magno, ed. S. J. Williams, Cardiff, 1930.

2 SECONDARY WORKS

Allen, J. R. and Anderson, J., *The Early Christian Monuments of Scotland*, Edinburgh, 1903, repr. Forfar, 1994.

Anderson, M. O., *Kings and Kingship in Early Scotland*, Edinburgh and London, 1973; 2nd edn, Edinburgh, 1980.

Armstrong, E. R. C. and Macalister, R. A. S., 'Wooden book with leaves indented and waxed found near Springmount Bog, Co. Antrim', *Journal of the Royal Society of Antiquaries of Ireland* 50 (1920), 160–6.

Aston, M., *Lollards and Reformers: Images and Literacy in Late Medieval Religion*, London, 1984.

Baker, J. H., *An Introduction to English Legal History*, London, 1990.

Balcou, J. and Le Gallo, Y. (eds.), *Histoire littéraire et culturelle de la Bretagne*, 3 vols., Paris and Geneva, 1987.

Bannerman, J., 'The King's Poet and the inauguration of Alexander III', *Scottish Historical Review* 68 (1989), 120–49.

Studies in the History of Dalriada, Edinburgh, 1974.

265

Works Cited

Barnie, J., *War in Medieval Society: Social Values and the Hundred Years War*, London, 1974.

Barrow, G. W. S., 'The charters of David I', *Anglo-Norman Studies* 14 (1991), 25–37.

'The early charters of the family of Kinninmonth of that Ilk', in D. A. Bullough and R. L. Storey (eds.), *The Study of Medieval Records*, Oxford, 1971, pp. 107–31.

The Kingdom of the Scots, London, 1973.

Kingship and Unity: Scotland 1000–1306, London, 1981.

Robert Bruce and the Community of the Realm of Scotland, 3rd edn, Edinburgh, 1988.

Scotland and its Neighbours in the Middle Ages, London, 1992.

'Some East Fife documents', in G. W. S. Barrow (ed.), *The Scottish Tradition*, Edinburgh, 1974, pp. 23–43.

Bartlett, F. C., *Remembering: A Study in Experimental and Social Psychology*, Cambridge, 1932.

Bartlett, R., *The Making of Europe: Conquest, Colonization and Cultural Change 950–1350*, Harmondsworth, 1993.

Basgöz, I., 'Formula in prose narrative *hikaye*', *Folklore Preprint Series* 6 (1978), 1–25.

Bauman, R., *Verbal Art as Performance*, Prospect Heights, Ill., 1977.

Bäuml, F. H., 'Medieval texts and the two theories of oral-formulaic composition: a proposal for a third theory', *New Literary History* 16 (1984), 31–49.

Bec, C., *Les marchands écrivains à Florence, 1375–1434*, Paris, 1967.

Benedict, W. C. and Voigtlander, E. von, 'Darius' Bisitun inscription, Babylonian version, lines 1–29', *Journal of Cuneiform Studies* 10 (1956), 1–10.

Bergin, O., *Irish Bardic Poetry*, ed. D. Greene and F. Kelly, Dublin, 1970.

Berschin, W., *Greek Letters and the Latin Middle Ages*, Washington, 1988.

Biebuyck, D., 'The epic as a genre in Congo oral literature', in R. M. Dorson (ed.), *African Folklore*, New York, 1972, vol. 1, pp. 257–73.

Biller, P., 'Women and texts in Languedocian Catharism', in Smith and Taylor (eds.), *Women, the Book and the Godly*, pp. 171–82.

Birch, W. de G., *A Descriptive Catalogue of the Penrice and Margam Abbey Manuscripts*, 6 vols., London, 1893–1905.

A History of Margam Abbey, London, 1897.

Bischoff, B., 'Die alten Namen der lateinischen Schriftarten', in *idem, Mittelalterliche Studien*, 3 vols., Stuttgart, 1966–81, vol. 1, pp. 1–5.

'Wendepunkte in der Geschichte der lateinischen Exegese im Frühmittelalter', *Sacris Erudiri* 6 (1954), 189–279, repr. in *idem, Mittelalterliche Studien*, Stuttgart, 1966–81, vol. 1, pp. 205–73.

Bischoff, B. and Bieler, L., 'Fragmente zweier Schulbücher aus Glendalough', *Celtica* 3 (1956), 211–20.

Bishop, T. A. M., 'The Corpus Martianus Capella', *Transactions of the Cambridge Bibliographical Society* 4 (1964–8), 257–75.

Black, R. I. M., 'The Gaelic manuscripts of Scotland', in W. Gillies (ed.), *Gaelic and Scotland: Alba agus a' Ghàidhlig*, Edinburgh, 1989, pp. 146–74.

Blamires, A., 'The limits of bible study for medieval women', in Smith and Taylor (eds.), *Women, the Book and the Godly*, pp. 1–12.

Bohannen, L., 'A genealogical charter', *Africa: Journal of the International African Institute* 22 (1952), 301–15.

266

Works Cited

Bond, S., 'The attestation of medieval private deeds relating to New Windsor', *Journal of the Society of Archivists* 4 (1971), 276–84.

Bowden, C. T., *Tour through Ireland*, Dublin, 1791.

Bowen, D. J., 'Beirdd a noddwyr y bymthegfed ganrif (rhan II)', *Llên Cymru* 18 (1994–5), 221–57.

'I Wiliam ap Siôn Edwart, cwnstabl y Waun', *Ysgrifau Beirniadol* 18 (1992), 137–60.

'Nodiadau ar gywydd Y Gwynt', *Ysgrifau Beirniadol* 9 (1976), 57–60.

Bowman, A. and Woolf, G. (eds.), *Literacy and Power in the Ancient World*, Cambridge, 1994.

Breatnach, C., 'The treatment of guttural spirants by Anglo-Norman hands', *Ériu* 40 (1989), 185–6.

Breatnach, L., 'Lawyers in early Ireland', in D. Hogan and W. N. Osborough (eds.), *Brehons, Serjeants and Attorneys*, Blackrock, Co. Dublin, 1990, pp. 1–13.

Review of Tranter and Tristram (eds.), *Early Irish Literature*, in *CMCS* 23 (Summer 1992), 120–2.

Breatnach, P. A., 'The origins of the Irish monastic tradition at Ratisbon (Regensburg)', *Celtica* 13 (1980), 58–77.

Brejon de Lavergnée, J., 'La Très Ancienne Coutume de Bretagne', in Balcou and Le Gallo (eds.), *Histoire littéraire*, vol. 1, pp. 44–60.

Bremner, J. and Roodenburg, H. (eds.), *A Cultural History of Gesture from Antiquity to the Present Day*, Oxford, 1991.

Brett, C., 'Breton Latin literature as evidence for literature in the vernacular, A.D. 800–1300', *CMCS* 18 (Winter 1989), 1–25.

'John Leland, Wales and early British history', *WHR* 15 (1990), 169–82.

Bromwich, R., 'The Celtic literatures', in J. E. C. Williams (ed.), *Literature in Celtic Countries*, Cardiff, 1971, pp. 25–57.

Broun, D., *The Charters of Gaelic Scotland and Ireland in the Early and Central Middle Ages*, Quiggin Pamphlet no. 2, Cambridge, 1995.

'Defining Scotland and the Scots before the Wars of Independence', in D. Broun, R. Finlay and M. Lynch (eds.), *Image and Identity*, Edinburgh, forthcoming.

'The origin of Scottish identity in its European context', in B. E. Crawford (ed.), *Scotland in Dark Age Europe*, St John's House Papers 5, St Andrews, 1994, pp. 21–31.

Brown, T. J., 'The oldest Irish manuscripts and their late antique background', in P. Ní Chatháin and M. Richter (eds.), *Irland und Europa*, Stuttgart, 1984, pp. 311–27.

'St Ninian's Isle silver hoard: the inscriptions', in *A Palaeographer's View: The Selected Writings of Julian Brown*, ed. J. Bately, M. Brown and J. Roberts, London, 1993, pp. 245–51.

Bruford, A., *Gaelic Folk-Tales and Mediaeval Romances*, Dublin, 1969.

'Recitation or re-creation? Examples from South Uist storytelling', *Scottish Studies* 22 (1978), 27–44.

Butler, L. A. S., 'A fire at Clynnog church', *Transactions of the Caernarvonshire Historical Society* 27 (1966), 98–106.

Byrne, F. J., *Irish Kings and High-Kings*, London, 1973.

'A note on Trim and Sletty', *Peritia* 3 (1984), 316–19.

Works Cited

One Thousand Years of Irish Script: An Exhibition of Irish Manuscripts in Oxford Libraries, Oxford, 1979.

'*Senchas*: the nature of Gaelic historical tradition', *Historical Studies* 9 (1971), 137–59.

Campbell, J., *Essays in Anglo-Saxon History*, London, 1986.

Carey, J., 'The ancestry of Fénius Farsaid', *Celtica* 21 (1990), 104–12.

Review of Sharpe, *Medieval Irish Saints' Lives*, in *Speculum* 68 (1993), 260–2.

Carney, J., 'The dating of archaic Irish verse', in Tranter and Tristram (eds.), *Early Irish Literature*, pp. 39–56.

'Literature in Irish, 1169–1534', in Cosgrove (ed.), *New History of Ireland*, pp. 688–707.

'Three Old Irish accentual poems', *Ériu* 22 (1971), 23–80.

Carr, A. D., *Medieval Anglesey*, Llangefni, 1982.

Carruthers, M., *The Book of Memory: A Study of Memory in Medieval Culture*, Cambridge, 1990.

Chadwick, N. K., 'Early culture and learning in North Wales', in N. K. Chadwick *et al.*, *Studies in the Early British Church*, Cambridge, 1958, pp. 29–120.

'A note on the name of Vortigern', in H. M. Chadwick *et al.*, *Studies in Early British History*, Cambridge, 1954, pp. 34–46.

Chafe, W. L., 'Integration and involvement in speaking, writing and oral literature', in D. Tannen (ed.), *Spoken and Written Language: Exploring Orality and Literacy*, New Jersey, 1982, pp. 35–53.

Chambers, E. K., *Arthur of Britain*, London, 1927.

Chandler, H., 'The will in medieval Wales to 1540', MPhil thesis, University of Wales, Aberystwyth, 1991.

Chaplais, P., 'The letter from Bishop Wealdhere of London to Archbishop Brihtwold of Canterbury: the earliest original "letter close" extant in the west', in M. B. Parkes and A. G. Watson (eds.), *Medieval Scribes, Manuscripts and Libraries: Essays presented to N. R. Ker*, London, 1978, pp. 3–23.

Chapman, M., *The Celts: The Construction of a Myth*, Basingstoke, 1992.

Charles-Edwards, G., 'The scribes of the Red Book of Hergest', *NLWJ* 21 (1979–80), 246–56.

Charles-Edwards, T. M., 'Boundaries in Irish law', in P. H. Sawyer (ed.), *Medieval Settlement*, London, 1976, pp. 83–7.

Early Christian Ireland, Cambridge, forthcoming.

'Early medieval kingships in the British Isles', in S. Bassett (eds.), *The Origins of Anglo-Saxon Kingdoms*, Leicester, 1989, pp. 28–39.

'Language and society among the Insular Celts AD 400–1000', in M. Green (ed.), *The Celtic World*, London, 1995, pp. 703–36.

'Review article: the *Corpus Iuris Hibernici*', *Studia Hibernica* 20 (1980), 141–62.

The Welsh Laws, Cardiff, 1989.

Chaytor, H. J., *From Script to Print: An Introduction to Medieval Vernacular Literature*, Cambridge, 1945.

Chédeville, A. and Guillotel, H., *La Bretagne des saints et des rois Ve-Xe siècle*, Rennes, 1984.

Chédeville, A. and Tonnerre, N.-Y., *La Bretagne féodale XIe-XIIIe siècle*, Rennes, 1987.

Works Cited

Clanchy, M., *From Memory to Written Record: England 1066–1307*, 2nd edn, Oxford, 1993.

'Remembering the past and the Good Old Law', *History* 55 (1970), 165–76.

Clancy, T. O. and Markús, G., *Iona: The Earliest Poetry of a Celtic Monastery*, Edinburgh, 1995.

Clover, C. J., 'The long prose form', *Arkiv för Nordisk Filologi* 101 (1986), 10–39.

Coleman, J., 'Interactive parchment: the theory and practice of medieval English aurality', *The Yearbook of English Studies* 25 (1995), 63–79.

Public Reading and the Reading Public in Late Medieval England and France, Cambridge, 1996.

'The solace of hearing: late medieval views on the reading aloud of literature', *ARV: Scandinavian Yearbook of Folklore* 46 (1990), 125–35.

Conran, T., 'The ballad and Taliesin', *CMCS* 28 (Winter 1994), 1–24.

Constantine, M.-A., *Breton Ballads*, Aberystwyth, 1996.

Contreni, J. J., 'The Irish contribution to the European classroom', in D. E. Evans *et al.* (eds.), *Proceedings of the Seventh International Congress of Celtic Studies*, pp. 79–90.

Corthals, J., 'Irland im frühen Mittelalter: die Entstehung einer Schriftkultur', in R. Ansorge (ed.), *Schlaglichter der Forschung: Zum 75. Jahrestag der Universität Hamburg 1994*, Hamburg, 1994, pp. 237–56.

Cosgrove, A. (ed.), *A New History of Ireland*, vol. 2, *Medieval Ireland 1169–1534*, Oxford, 1987; 2nd imp. 1993.

Cowan, E. J., 'The Scottish chronicle in the Poppleton manuscript', *Innes Review* 32 (1981), 3–21.

Cowan, I. B. and Easson, D. E., *Medieval Religious Houses: Scotland*, 2nd edn, London, 1976.

Cowley, F. G. and Lloyd, N., 'An Old Welsh *englyn* in Harley Charter 75 C 38', *BBCS* 25 (1972–4), 407–17.

Crosby, R., 'Oral delivery in the middle ages', *Speculum* 11 (1936), 88–110.

Dabbs, J. H., *Dei Gratia in Royal Titles*, The Hague, 1971.

Dark, K., 'Epigraphic, art-historical, and historical approaches to the chronology of Class I inscribed stones', in N. Edwards and A. Lane (eds.), *The Early Church in Wales and the West*, Oxford, 1992, pp. 51–61.

Davies, R. M. M., 'The moral structure of *Pedeir Keinc y Mabinogi*', PhD thesis, University of Wales, Cardiff, 1993.

Davies, R. R., *Conquest, Coexistence and Change: Wales 1063–1415*, Oxford, 1987.

Domination and Conquest: The Experience of Ireland, Scotland and Wales 1100–1300, Cambridge, 1990.

Davies, S., *Crefft y Cyfarwydd: Astudiaeth o Dechnegau Naratif yn Y Mabinogion*, Cardiff, 1995.

The Four Branches of the Mabinogi, Llandysul, 1993.

'Llafar v. ysgrifenedig yn *Culhwch ac Olwen*', *Ysgrifau Beirniadol* 19 (1993), 46–53.

Davies, W., 'Celtic kingships in the early middle ages', in A. Duggan (ed.), *Kings and Kingship in Medieval Europe*, London, 1993, pp. 101–24.

'Les chartes du cartulaire de Landévennec', in M. Simon (ed.), *Landévennec et le monachisme breton dans le haut moyen âge*, Actes du Colloque du 15^e

Works Cited

Centenaire de l'Abbaye de Landévennec 25–26–27 Avril 1985, Landévennec, 1986, pp. 85–95.

'The composition of the Redon cartulary', *Francia* 17 (1990), 69–90.

'Forgery in the *Cartulaire de Redon*', in *Fälschungen im Mittelalter: Internationaler Kongress der MGH München 16–19 September 1986* (MGH Schriften 33), 6 vols., Hanover, 1988, vol. 4, pp. 265–74.

'The Latin charter-tradition in western Britain, Brittany and Ireland in the early mediaeval period', in Whitelock *et al.* (eds.), *Ireland in Early Mediaeval Europe*, pp. 258–80.

The Llandaff Charters, Aberystwyth, 1979.

'The myth of the Celtic church', in N. Edwards and A. Lane (eds.), *The Early Church in Wales and the West*, Oxford, 1992, pp. 12–21.

'People and places in dispute in ninth-century Brittany', in W. Davies and P. Fouracre (eds.), *The Settlement of Disputes in Early Medieval Europe*, Cambridge, 1986, pp. 65–84.

'Property rights and property claims in Welsh *Vitae* of the eleventh century', in E. Patlagean and P. Riché (eds.), *Hagiographie, cultures et sociétés, IVe-XIIe siècles*, Paris, 1981, pp. 515–33.

'Protected space in Britain and Ireland in the middle ages', in B. Crawford (ed.), *Scotland in Dark Age Britain*, St Andrews, 1996, pp. 1–19.

Small Worlds: The Village Community in Early Medieval Brittany, London, 1988.

Wales in the Early Middle Ages, Leicester, 1982.

Delargy, J. H., 'The Gaelic story-teller', *Proceedings of the British Academy* 31 (1945), 172–221.

Dictionary of the Irish Language Based Mainly on Old and Middle Irish Materials, ed. E. G. Quin *et al.*, Dublin, 1983.

The Dictionary of Welsh Biography down to 1940, London, 1959.

Doane, A. N., 'The ethnography of scribal writing and Anglo-Saxon poetry: scribe as performer', *Oral Tradition* 9 (1994), 420–39.

Doherty, C., 'The Irish hagiographer: resources, aims, results', in T. Dunne (ed.), *The Writer as Witness: Literature as Historical Evidence = Historical Studies* 16, Cork, 1987, pp. 10–21.

Doyle, A. I. and Parkes, M. B., 'The production of copies of the *Canterbury Tales* and the *Confessio Amantis* in the early fifteenth century', in M. B. Parkes and A. G. Watson (eds.), *Medieval Scribes, Manuscripts and Libraries: Essays presented to N. R. Ker*, London, 1978, pp. 163–210.

Driscoll, S. T., 'Power and authority in early historic Scotland: Pictish symbol stones and other documents', in Gledhill *et al.* (eds.), *State and Society*, pp. 215–35.

Duine, F., *Catalogue des sources hagiographiques pour l'histoire de la Bretagne jusqu'à la fin du XIIe siècle*, Paris, 1922.

Dumville, D. N., 'Early Welsh poetry: problems of historicity', in Roberts (ed.), *Early Welsh Poetry*, pp. 1–16.

'The historical value of the *Historia Brittonum*', *Arthurian Literature* 6 (1986), 1–26.

'The importation of Mediterranean manuscripts into Theodore's England', in M. Lapidge (ed.), *Archbishop Theodore: Commemorative Studies on his Life and Influence*, Cambridge, 1995, pp. 96–119.

270

Works Cited

'Kingship, genealogies and regnal lists', in P. H. Sawyer and I. N. Wood (eds.), *Early Medieval Kingship*, Leeds, 1977, pp. 72–104.

'Late-seventh- or eighth-century evidence for the British transmission of Pelagius', *CMCS* 10 (Winter 1985), 39–52.

'Sub-Roman Britain: history and legend', *History* 62 (1977), 173–92.

Duncan, A. A. M., 'Bede, Iona, and the Picts', in R. H. C. Davis and J. M. Wallace-Hadrill (eds.), *The Writing of History in the Middle Ages: Essays presented to R. W. Southern*, Oxford, 1981, vol. 1, pp. 1–42.

Scotland: The Making of the Kingdom, Edinburgh, 1975.

Dutton, A. M., 'Passing the book: testamentary disposition of religious literature to and by women in England 1350–1500', in Smith and Taylor (eds.), *Women, the Book and the Godly*, pp. 41–54.

Eben Fardd, *Cyff Beuno*, Tremadog, 1863.

Edel, D. (ed.), *Cultural Identity and Cultural Integration: Ireland and Europe in the Early Middle Ages*, Blackrock, Co. Dublin, 1995.

Edwards, N., *The Archaeology of Early Medieval Ireland*, London, 1990.

Eggers, H., *Symmetrie und Proportion epischen Erzählens*, Stuttgart, 1956.

Epstein, S., 'Guilds and métiers', in J. R. Strayer (ed.), *Dictionary of the Middle Ages*, vol. 6 (New York, 1985), pp. 13–15.

Esposito, M., 'An apocryphal "Book of Enoch and Elias" as a possible source of the *Navigatio Sancti Brendani*', *Celtica* 5 (1960), 192–206.

Evans, D. F., Griffith, J. G. and Jope, E. M. (eds.), *Proceedings of the Seventh International Congress of Celtic Studies*, Oxford, 1986.

Evans, D. S., *Llafar a Llyfr yn yr Hen Gyfnod*, Cardiff, 1982.

Evans, J. G., *Report on Manuscripts in the Welsh Language*, 2 vols., London, 1898–1910.

Fawtier, R., *The Capetian Kings of France*, London, 1960.

Fentress, J. and Wickham, C., *Social Memory*, Oxford, 1992.

Fichtenau, H., *Das Urkundenwesen in Österreich von 8. bis zum frühen 13. Jahrhundert* (Mitteilungen des Instituts für Österreichische Geschichtsforschung, Ergänzungsband 23), Vienna, 1971.

Finnegan, R., *Literacy and Orality: Studies in the Technology of Communication*, Oxford, 1988.

Oral Literature in Africa, Oxford, 1970.

Oral Poetry: Its Nature, Significance and Social Context, Cambridge, 1977.

Oral Traditions and the Verbal Arts: A Guide to Research Practices, London and New York, 1992.

Flanagan, M. T., *Irish Society, Anglo-Norman Settlers, Angevin Kingship*, Oxford, 1989.

'St Mary's Abbey, Louth, and the introduction of the Arrouaisian order into medieval Ireland', *Clogher Record* 10 (1980), 223–34.

Flatrès, P., 'Les Bretons en Galles du XIe au XIIIe siècle', *Mémoires de la Société d'Histoire et d'Archéologie de Bretagne* 36 (1956), 41–6.

Fleuriot, L., *Dictionnaire des gloses en vieux breton*, Paris, 1964.

'Le latin dans l'ancienne société bretonne', in Balco and Le Gallo (eds.), *Histoire littéraire*, vol. 1, pp. 61–70.

'Old Breton genealogies and early British traditions', *BBCS* 26 (1974–6), 1–6.

271

Works Cited

Les origines de la Bretagne, Paris, 1980.

'Périodiques, VI', Etudes Celtiques 11 (1964–7), 589–90.

'La prophetia Merlini', Etudes Celtiques 14 (1974), 31–56.

'Sur quatre textes bretons en latin, le "liber vetustissimus" de Geoffroy de Monmouth et le séjour de Taliesin en Bretagne', Etudes Celtiques 18 (1981), 197–213.

Fleuriot, L., Lozac'hmeur, J.-C. and Prat, L., Récits et poèmes celtiques, Paris, 1981.

Foley, J. M., The Singer of Tales in Performance, Bloomington and Indianapolis, 1995.

Traditional Oral Epic: The Odyssey, Beowulf, and the Serbo-Croatian Return Song, Berkeley, Los Angeles and London, 1990.

'Word-power, performance, and tradition', Journal of American Folklore 105 (1992), 275–301.

Foley, J. M. (ed.), Oral-Formulaic Theory: A Folklore Casebook, New York, 1990.

Forsyth, K., 'The inscriptions on the Dupplin Cross', in C. Bourke (ed.), From the Isles of the North: Medieval Art in Ireland and Britain, Belfast, 1995, pp. 237–44.

'The ogham-inscribed spindle-whorl from Buckquoy: evidence for the Irish language in pre-Viking Orkney?', Proceedings of the Society of Antiquaries of Scotland 125 (1995), 677–96.

'The ogham inscriptions of Scotland: an edited corpus', PhD thesis, Harvard University, 1996 (Ann Arbor, Michigan, 1996).

'Symbols: the third Pictish writing system?', in D. Henry (ed.), Studies in Insular Art, Balgavies, Forfar, forthcoming.

Foulon, C., 'Marie de France et la Bretagne', Annales de Bretagne 60 (1952), 243–58.

Frame, R., Colonial Ireland, 1169–1369, Dublin, 1981.

The Political Development of the British Isles 1100–1400, Oxford, 1990.

Freedman, M., Chinese Lineage and Society: Fukien and Kwangtung, London, 1966.

Geiriadur Prifysgol Cymru: A Dictionary of the Welsh Language, Cardiff, 1950– .

Genicot, L., Les Généalogies, Turnhout, 1975.

Gledhill, J., Bender, B. and Larsen, M. T. (eds.), State and Society: The Emergence and Development of Social Hierarchy and Political Centralization, London, 1988.

Gneuss, H., 'A preliminary list of manuscripts written or owned in England up to 1100', Anglo-Saxon England 9 (1981), 1–60.

Goody, J., The Domestication of the Savage Mind, Cambridge, 1977.

The Logic of Writing and the Organization of Society, Cambridge, 1986.

The Interface between the Written and the Oral, Cambridge, 1987.

Goody, J. (ed.), Literacy in Traditional Societies, Cambridge, 1968.

Goody, J. and Watt, I., 'The consequences of literacy', in Goody (ed.), Literacy in Traditional Societies, pp. 27–68.

Gough, K., 'Literacy in Kerala', in Goody (ed.), Literacy in Traditional Societies, pp. 132–61.

Grant, A., Independence and Nationhood: Scotland 1306–1469, London, 1984.

Gratwick, A. S., 'Latinitas Britannica: was British Latin archaic?', in N. Brooks (ed.), Latin and the Vernacular Languages in Early Medieval Britain, Leicester, 1982, pp. 1–79.

Works Cited

Green, A. S., *The Making of Ireland and its Undoing, 1200–1600*, London, 1908.

Green, D. H., *Medieval Listening and Reading: The Primary Reception of German Literature 800–1300*, Cambridge, 1994.

Greene, D., 'Linguistic considerations in the dating of early Welsh verse', *Studia Celtica* 6 (1971), 1–11.

Griffiths, R. A., 'Aberystwyth', in *idem* (ed.), *Boroughs of Mediaeval Wales*, Cardiff, 1978, pp. 19–45.

'Public and private bureaucracies in England and Wales in the fifteenth century', in *idem, King and Country: England and Wales in the Fifteenth Century*, London, 1991, pp. 137–59.

Gruffydd, R. G., 'Where was *Rhaeadr Derwennydd* (*Canu Aneirin* line 1114)?', in A. T. E. Matonis and D. F. Melia (eds.), *Celtic Language, Celtic Culture: A Festschrift for Eric P. Hamp*, Van Nuys, Calif., 1990, pp. 261–6.

Guyonvarc'h, C.-J., 'Du breton moyen au breton moderne', in Balcou and Le Gallo (eds.), *Histoire littéraire*, vol. 1, pp. 193–230.

Guyonvarc'h, C. J. and Le Roux F., *Les druides*, 4th edn, Rennes, 1986.

Gwynn, A., 'The Irish missal of Corpus Christi College, Oxford', *Studies in Church History* 1 (1964), 46–68.

'Tomaltach Ua Conchobair, coarb of Patrick (1181–1201): his life and times', *Seanchas Ardmhacha* 8 (1975–7), 231–74.

Harbison, P., 'The extent of royal patronage on Irish high crosses', *Studia Celtica Japonica* new series 6 (1994), 77–105.

Harrison, A., *The Irish Trickster*, Sheffield, 1989.

Harvey, A., 'The Cambridge Juvencus Glosses – Evidence of Hiberno Welsh Literary Interaction?', in P. S. Ureland and G. Broderick (eds.), *Language Contact in the British Isles*, Tübingen, 1991, pp. 181–98.

'Early literacy in Ireland: the evidence from ogam', *CMCS* 14 (Winter 1987), 1–15.

'Latin, literacy and the Celtic vernaculars around the year AD 500', in C. J. Byrne, M. Harry and P. Ó Siadhail (eds.), *Celtic Languages and Celtic Peoples: Proceedings of the Second North American Congress of Celtic Studies, Halifax 1989*, Halifax, Nova Scotia, 1992, pp. 11–26.

Harvey, P. D. A. (ed.), *The Peasant Land Market in Medieval England*, Oxford, 1984.

Havelock, E., *The Muse Learns to Write: Reflections on Orality and Literacy from Antiquity to the Present*, New Haven, 1986.

'The oral-literate equation: a formula for the modern mind', in D. R. Olson and N. Torrance (eds.), *Literacy and Orality*, Cambridge, 1991, pp. 11–27.

Preface to Plato, Cambridge, Mass., 1963.

Haycock, M., 'Early Welsh poetry', in P. Ryan (ed.), *Memory and Poetic Structure: Papers of the Conference on Oral Literature and Literary Theory held at Middlesex Polytechnic, 1981*, London, n.d., pp. 91–135.

'Llyfr Taliesin', *NLWJ* 25 (1987–8), 347–86.

'Medd a mêl farddoni', in M. E. Owen and B. F. Roberts (eds.), *Beirdd a Thywysogion: Barddoniaeth Llys yng Nghymru, Iwerddon a'r Alban*, Cardiff, 1996, pp. 39–59.

'The significance of the "Cad Goddau" tree-list in the Book of Taliesin', in M. J. Ball, J. Fife, E. Poppe and J. Rowland (eds.), *Celtic Linguistics/ Ieithyddiaeth*

Works Cited

Geltaidd: Readings in the Brythonic Languages, Festschrift for T. Arwyn Watkins, Amsterdam, 1990, pp. 297–331.

Head, T. and Landes, R. (eds.), *The Peace of God: Social Violence and Religious Response,* Ithaca, 1992.

Henderson, I., 'Early Christian monuments of Scotland displaying crosses but no other ornament', in A. Small (ed.), *The Picts: A New Look at Old Problems,* Dundee, 1987, pp. 45–58.

'Pictish art and the Book of Kells', in Whitelock *et al.* (eds.), *Ireland in Early Mediaeval Europe,* pp. 79–105.

The Picts, London, 1967.

'The shape and decoration of the cross on Pictish cross-slabs carved in relief', in R. M. Spearman and J. Higgitt (eds.), *The Age of Migrating Ideas: Early Medieval Art in Northern Britain and Ireland,* Edinburgh, 1993, pp. 209–18.

Henige, D. P., *The Chronology of Oral Tradition: Quest for a Chimera,* London, 1974.

'The disease of writing', in J. C. Miller (ed.), *The African Past Speaks: Essays on Oral Tradition and History,* Dawson, 1980, pp. 240–61.

Oral Historiography, London, 1982.

'Truths yet unborn? Oral tradition as a casualty of culture contact', *Journal of African History* 23 (1982), 395–412.

Henry, F. and Marsh-Micheli, G., 'Manuscripts and illuminations 1169–1603', in Cosgrove (ed.), *New History of Ireland,* pp. 781–815.

Herbert, M., 'Charter material from Kells', in F. O'Mahony (ed.), *The Book of Kells,* Aldershot, 1994, pp. 60–77.

Iona, Kells, and Derry: The History and Hagiography of the Monastic Familia of Columba, Oxford, 1988.

Herren, M. W., 'Hisperic Latin: luxuriant culture-fungus of decay', *Traditio* 30 (1974), 411–19.

Higgitt, J., 'The display script of the Book of Kells and the tradition of Insular decorative capitals', in F. O'Mahony (ed.), *The Book of Kells,* Aldershot, 1994, pp. 209–33.

'*Legentes quoque uel audientes*: early medieval inscriptions in Britain and Ireland and their audiences', in D. Henry (ed.), *Studies in Insular Art,* Balgavies, Forfar, forthcoming.

'The Pictish Latin inscription at Tarbat in Ross-shire', *Proceedings of the Society of Antiquaries of Scotland* 112 (1982), 300–21.

Review of Okasha, *Corpus,* in *Early Medieval Europe* 4 (1995), 240–1.

'The stone-cutter and the scriptorium: early medieval inscriptions in Britain and Ireland', in W. Koch (ed.), *Epigraphik,* pp. 149–62.

'Words and crosses: the inscribed stone cross in early medieval Britain', in *idem* (ed.), *Early Medieval Sculpture in Britain and Ireland,* British Archaeological Reports, British Series 152, Oxford, 1986, pp. 125–52.

Hore, H. F., 'Irish bardism in 1561', *Ulster Journal of Archaeology* 1st series 6 (1858), 165–7, 202–12.

Houston, S., 'Literacy among the Pre-Colombian Maya: a comparative perspective', in E. Hill Boone and W. D. Mignolo (eds.), *Writing Without Words: Alternative Literacies in Mesoamerica and the Andes,* Durham, NC, 1994, pp. 27–49.

Works Cited

Howlett, D., '*Orationes Moucani*: early Cambro-Latin prayers', *CMCS* 24 (Winter 1992), 55–74.

Hudson, B. T., 'Historical literature of early Scotland', *Studies in Scottish Literature* 26 (1991), 141–55.

Hughes, K., 'The Book of Deer', in *eadem, Celtic Britain*, pp. 22–37.

Celtic Britain in the Early Middle Ages: Studies in Scottish and Welsh Sources, Studies in Celtic History 2, Woodbridge, 1980.

The Church in Early Irish Society, London, 1966.

'Early Christianity in Pictland', in *eadem, Celtic Britain*, pp. 38–52.

'Where are the writings of early Scotland?', in *eadem, Celtic Britain*, pp. 1–21.

Huglo, M., 'Le domaine musical de la notation bretonne', *Analecta Musicologica* 35 (1963), 54–84.

Hunt, T., 'The art of *Iarlles y Ffynnawn* and the European *volksmärchen*', *Studia Celtica* 8–9 (1973–4), 107–20.

Hunter, T. G., 'Onomastic lore in the native Middle Welsh prose tales', MPhil thesis, University of Wales, Aberystwyth, 1988.

Huws, D., '*Canu Aneirin*: the other manuscripts', in Roberts (ed.), *Early Welsh Poetry*, pp. 43–56.

'The earliest Bangor missal', *NLWJ* 27 (1991–2), 113–30.

Five Ancient Books of Wales, H. M. Chadwick Memorial Lectures, 6, Cambridge, 1995.

'Llawysgrif Hendregadredd', *NLWJ* 22 (1981–2), 1 26.

'Llyfr Gwyn Rhydderch', *CMCS* 21 (Summer 1991), 1–37.

Llyfrau Cymraeg 1250–1400, Aberystwyth, 1993; also in *NLWJ* 28 (1993–4), 1–21.

'The making of *Liber Landavensis*', *NLWJ* 25 (1987–8), 133–60.

'The manuscripts', in T. M. Charles-Edwards, M. E. Owen and D. B. Walters (eds.), *Lawyers and Laymen*, Cardiff, 1986, pp. 119–36.

The Medieval Codex, Aberystwyth, 1980.

Peniarth 28: Darluniau o Lyfr Cyfraith Hywel/Illustrations from a Welsh Lawbook [Aberystwyth] 1988.

'The transmission of a Welsh classic: Dafydd ap Gwilym', in C. Richmond and I. Harvey (eds.), *Recognitions: Essays Presented to Edmund Fryde*, Aberystwyth, 1996, pp. 179–202.

'A Welsh manuscript of Bede's *De Natura Rerum*', *BBCS* 27 (1976–8), 491–504.

Ibbetson, D. J., 'Words and deeds: the action of covenant in the reign of Edward I', *Law and History Review* 4 (1986), 71–94.

Ilardi, V., 'Eyeglasses and concave lenses in fifteenth-century Florence and Milan: new documents', *Renaissance Quarterly* 29 (1976), 341–60.

Irvine, M., *The Making of Textual Culture*, Cambridge, 1994.

Isaac, G. R., '*Canu Aneirin* Awdl LI', *Journal of Celtic Linguistics* 2 (1993), 65–91.

Jackson, K. H., '"Common Gaelic": the evolution of the Goidelic languages', *Proceedings of the British Academy* 37 (1951), 71–97.

The Gaelic Notes in the Book of Deer, Cambridge, 1972.

The Gododdin: The Oldest Scottish Poem, Edinburgh, 1969.

Language and History in Early Britain, Edinburgh, 1953.

James, C., 'Llyfr cyfraith o Ddyffryn Teifi: disgrifiad o BL. Add. 22,356', *NLWJ* 27 (1991–2), 383–404.

Works Cited

' "Llwyr wybodau, llên a llyfrau": Hopcyn ap Thomas a'r traddodiad llenyddol Cymraeg', in H. T. Edwards (ed.), *Cwm Tawe*, Llandysul, 1993, pp. 4–44.

Jarman, A. O. H., 'Cerdd Ysgolan', *Ysgrifau Beirniadol* 10 (1977), 51–78.

Jenkins, D., 'From Wales to Weltenburg? Some considerations on the origins of the use of sacred books for the preservation of secular records', in N. Brieskorn, P. Mikat, D. Müller and D. Willoweit (eds.), *Vom mittelalterlichen Recht zur neuzeitlichen Rechtswissenschaft: Bedingungen, Wege und Probleme der europäischen Rechtsgeschichte*, Paderborn, 1994, pp. 75–88.

Jenkins, D. and Owen, M. E., 'The Welsh marginalia in the Lichfield Gospels, Part I', *CMCS* 5 (Summer 1983), 37–66.

'The Welsh marginalia in the Lichfield Gospels, Part II: the "surexit" memorandum', *CMCS* 7 (Summer 1984), 91–120.

Jenkinson, H., *The Later Court Hands in England: From the Fifteenth to the Seventeenth Century*, Cambridge, 1927.

Jobbé-Duval, E., *Les idées primitives dans la Bretagne contemporaine*, 2 vols., Paris, 1920.

Jones, I., *A History of Printing and Printers in Wales*, Cardiff, 1925.

Jones, J. G., 'Governance, order and stability in Caernarfonshire c. 1540–1640', *Transactions of the Caernarvonshire Historical Society* 44 (1983), 7–52.

Jones, M., 'L'aptitude à lire et à écrire des ducs de Bretagne à la fin du moyen âge et un usage précoce de l'imprimerie', *Mémoires de la Société d'Histoire et d'Archéologie de Bretagne* 62 (1985), 37–53.

The Creation of Brittany: A Late Medieval State, London and Ronceverte, 1988.

Jones, R. M., 'Tri mewn llenyddiaeth', *Llên Cymru* 14 (1981), 92–110.

Kelleher, J. V., 'The pre-Norman Irish genealogies', *Irish Historical Studies* 16 (1968–9), 138–53.

Keller, H., 'Die Entwicklung der europäischen Schriftkultur im Spiegel der mittelalterlichen Überlieferung: Beobachtungen und Überlegungen', in P. Leidinger and D. Metzler (eds.), *Geschichte und Geschichtsbewusstsein*, Münster, 1990, pp. 171–204.

Keller, H., Grubmüller, K. and Staubach, N. (eds.), *Pragmatische Schriftlichkeit im Mittelalter*, Münstersche Mittelalter-Schriften, vol. 65, Munich, 1992.

Kellogg, R. L., 'Varieties of tradition in medieval narrative', in H. Bekker-Nielsen *et al.* (eds.), *Medieval Narrative: A Symposium*, Odense, 1979, pp. 120–9.

Kelly, F., *A Guide to Early Irish Law*, Dublin, 1988.

Kelly, S., 'Anglo-Saxon lay society and the written word', in McKitterick (ed.), *Uses of Literacy*, pp. 36–62.

Kendrick, T. D., *The Druids*, 2nd edn, London, 1928.

Kenney, J. F., *The Sources for the Early History of Ireland: Ecclesiastical*, New York, 1929.

Ker, N. R. (ed.), *Medieval Libraries of Great Britain*, London, 1964.

Kerlouégan, F., 'La littérature hagiographique latine', in Balcou and Le Gallo (eds.), *Histoire littéraire*, vol. 1, pp. 77–95.

Keynes, S., 'Royal government and the written word in late Anglo-Saxon England', in McKitterick (ed.), *Uses of Literacy*, pp. 226–57.

Kiberd, D., 'Irish literature and Irish history', in R. F. Foster (ed.), *The Oxford Illustrated History of Ireland*, Oxford, 1989, pp. 275–338.

Works Cited

Klapisch-Zuber, C., 'The genesis of the family tree', *I Tatti Studies* [The Harvard University Center for Italian Renaissance Studies] 4 (1991), 105–29.
Women, Family and Ritual in Renaissance Italy, Chicago, 1985.
Knight, J. K., 'Penmachno revisited: the consular inscription and its context', *CMCS* 29 (Summer 1995), 1–10.
Koch, J. T., 'The conversion and the transition from Primitive to Old Irish *c*. 367–*c*. 637', *Emania* 13 (1995), 39–50.
'The Cynfeirdd poetry and the language of the sixth century', in Roberts (ed.), *Early Welsh Poetry*, pp. 17–41.
'Gleanings from the *Gododdin* and other early Welsh texts', *BBCS* 38 (1991), 111–18.
'The loss of final syllables and loss of declension in Brittonic', *BBCS* 30 (1983), 201–33.
'Thoughts on the Ur-*Godoδin*: rethinking Aneirin and Mynyδawc Mŵynvawr', *Language Sciences* 15 (1993), 81–9.
'When was Welsh literature first written down?', *Studia Celtica* 20/21 (1985–6), 43–66.
Koch, W. (ed.), *Epigraphik 1988: Fachtagung für mittelalterliche und neuzeitliche Epigraphik, Graz 10–14 Mai 1988*, Österreichische Akademie der Wissenschaften, Philosophisch-Historische Klasse, Denkschriften, vol. 213, Vienna, 1990.
Labarge, M. W., *Women in Mediaeval Life*, London, 1986.
La Borderie, A. de, *Histoire de Bretagne*, 6 vols., Rennes, 1896–1904.
Lambert, P.-Y., *La langue gauloise*, Paris, 1994.
' "Thirty" and "sixty" in Brittonic', *CMCS* 8 (Winter 1984), 29–43.
Lapidge, M., 'Gildas's education and the Latin culture of sub-Roman Britain', in Lapidge and Dumville (eds.), *Gildas*, pp. 27–50.
'Latin learning in Dark Age Wales: some prolegomena', in D. E. Evans *et al.* (eds.), *Proceedings of the Seventh International Congress of Celtic Studies*, pp. 91–107.
'Surviving booklists from Anglo-Saxon England', in M. Lapidge and H. Gneuss (eds.), *Learning and Literature in Anglo-Saxon England: Studies presented to Peter Clemoes*, Cambridge, 1985, pp. 33–89.
'The Welsh-Latin poetry of Sulien's family', *Studia Celtica* 8/9 (1973–4), 68–106.
Lapidge, M. and Dumville, D. (eds.), *Gildas: New Approaches*, Studies in Celtic History 5, Woodbridge, 1984.
Lapidge, M. and Sharpe, R., *A Bibliography of Celtic-Latin Literature, 400–1200*, Dublin, 1985.
Law, V., *The Insular Latin Grammarians*, Studies in Celtic History 3, Woodbridge, 1982.
Le Duc, G., 'L'Historia britannica avant Geoffroy de Monmouth', *Annales de Bretagne* 79 (1972), 819–35.
Leerssen, J. Th., *Mere Irish & Fíor-Ghael: Studies in the Idea of Irish Nationality, its Development and Literary Expression prior to the Nineteenth Century*, Amsterdam, 1986.
Lerer, S., *Literacy and Power in Anglo-Saxon England*, Lincoln, Nebraska, 1991.
Levy, E., *West Roman Vulgar Law: The Law of Property*, Philadelphia, 1951.
Lewis, C. W., 'The literary tradition of Morgannwg down to the middle of the

Works Cited

sixteenth century', in Pugh (ed.), *Glamorgan County History*, vol. 3, pp. 449–554, 657–79.

Lewis, I. M., 'Literacy in a nomadic society: the Somali case', in Goody (ed.), *Literacy in Traditional Societies*, pp. 266–76.

Lewis, J. M., *Welsh Medieval Paving Tiles*, Cardiff, 1976.

Welsh Monumental Brasses: A Guide, Cardiff, 1974.

Lewis, M., *Stained Glass in North Wales up to 1850*, Altrincham, 1970.

Lhuyd, E., *Archaeologia Britannica*, Oxford, 1707.

Lindsay, W. M., *Early Welsh Script*, Oxford, 1912.

Lloyd, N. and Owen, M. E., *Drych yr Oesoedd Canol*, Cardiff, 1986.

Lloyd-Morgan, C., 'Narrative structure in *Peredur*', *ZCP* 38 (1978), 187–231.

'Women and their poetry in medieval Wales', in Meale (ed.), *Women and Literature*, pp. 183–201.

Loomis, R. S., 'Le folklore breton et les romans arthuriens', *Annales de Bretagne* 56 (1949), 203–7.

Lord, A. B., *The Singer of Tales*, Cambridge, Mass., 1960.

Lot, F., *Nennius et l'Historia Brittonum*, Paris, 1934.

Loth, J., *Chrestomathie bretonne*, Paris, 1890.

Lowe, E. A., *Codices Latini Antiquiores: A Palaeographical Guide to Latin Manuscripts prior to the Ninth Century*, 11 vols. plus Supplement, Oxford, 1935–71.

Lüthi, M., 'Imitation and anticipation in folktales', in N. Burlakoff and C. Lindahl (eds.), *Folklore on Two Continents*, Bloomington, 1980, pp. 3–13.

Lyle, E., 'Parity of ignorance: Child's judgment on "Sir Colin" and the Scottish verdict "not proven"', in J. Harris (ed.), *The Ballad and Oral Literature*, Cambridge, Mass., 1991, pp. 109–15.

Macalister, R. A. S., *Corpus Inscriptionum Insularum Celticarum*, vol. 2, Dublin, 1949.

Mac Cana, P., 'David Greene (1915–1981)', *Ériu* 34 (1983), 1–10.

The Learned Tales of Medieval Ireland, Dublin, 1980.

The Mabinogi, 2nd edn, Cardiff, 1992.

'Mongán Mac Fiachna and Immram Brain', *Ériu* 23 (1972), 102–42.

'Rhyddiaith Gymraeg', *Ysgrifau Beirniadol* 10 (1977), 79–93.

'The rise of the later schools of *filidheacht*', *Ériu* 25 (1974), 126–46.

McCann, W. J., 'Adeiledd y Tair Rhamant: Gereint, Owein, Peredur', *Ysgrifau Beirniadol* 13 (1985), 123–33.

McCone, K., *Pagan Past and Christian Present in Early Irish Literature*, Maynooth, 1990.

'A tale of two ditties: poet and satirist in *Cath Maige Tuired*', in Ó Corráin *et al.* (eds.), *Sages, Saints and Storytellers*, pp. 122–43.

'The Würzburg and Milan glosses: our earliest sources of "Middle Irish"', *Ériu* 36 (1985), 85–106.

'Zur Frage der Register im frühen Irischen', in Tranter and Tristram (eds.), *Early Irish Literature*, pp. 57–97.

Mac Gearailt, U., 'The language of some late Middle Irish texts in the Book of Leinster', *Studia Hibernica* 26 (1991–2), 167–216.

McKitterick, R., *The Carolingians and the Written Word*, Cambridge, 1989.

McKitterick, R. (ed.), *The Uses of Literacy in Early Mediaeval Europe*, Cambridge, 1990.

Works Cited

McManus, D., *A Guide to Ogam*, Maynooth, 1991.

'*Linguarum diversitas*: Latin and the vernaculars in early medieval Britain', *Peritia* 3 (1984), 151–88.

MacMullen, R., 'The epigraphic habit in the Roman Empire', *American Journal of Philology* 103 (1982), 233–46.

Mac Niocaill, G., 'Aspects of Irish law in the late thirteenth century', in G. A. Hayes-McCoy (ed.), *Historical Studies* 10 [Indreabhán] 1976, pp. 25–42.

MacQueen, H. L., 'Scots law under Alexander III', in N. H. Reid (ed.), *Scotland in the Reign of Alexander III, 1249–1286*, Edinburgh, 1990, pp. 74–102.

McRoberts, D., 'A "Continuatio Bedae" from Whithorn?', *Innes Review* 24 (1973), 69–71.

McSheffrey, S., 'Literacy and the gender gap in the middle ages', in Smith and Taylor (eds.), *Women, the Book and the Godly*, pp. 157–70.

Marrou, H.-I., *A History of Education in Antiquity*, London, 1956.

Marx, J, 'Monde brittonique et Matière de Bretagne', *Etudes Celtiques* 10: 2 (1963), 10–27.

Matchak, S., 'Aspects of structure and folklore in *Culhwch and Olwen*', MA thesis, University of Wales, Aberystwyth, 1975.

Maund, K. L., *Handlist of the Acts of Native Welsh Rulers 1132–1283*, Cardiff, 1996.

Meale, C., '" . . . alle the bokes that I haue of latyn, englisch, and frensch": laywomen and their books in late medieval England', in *eadem* (ed.), *Women and Literature*, pp. 128–58.

Meale, C. (ed.), *Women and Literature in Britain 1150–1500*, 2nd edn, Cambridge, 1996.

Meek, D. E., 'Gàidhlig is Gaylick anns na meadhon aoisean', in W. Gillies (ed.), *Gaelic and Scotland: Alba agus a' Ghàidhlig*, Edinburgh, 1989, pp. 131–45 (English abstract, pp. 233–5).

Meid, W., *Gaulish Inscriptions*, Budapest, 1992.

Merdrignac, B., *Recherches sur l'hagiographie armoricaine du VIIème au XVème siècle*, 2 vols., Dossiers du Centre Régional Archéologique d'Alet, Saint-Malo, 1985–6.

Meyer, E. A., 'Explaining the epigraphic habit in the Roman Empire: the evidence from epitaphs', *Journal of Roman Studies* 80 (1990), 74–96.

Miller, M., 'The disputed historical horizon of the Pictish king-lists', *Scottish Historical Review* 58 (1979), 1–34.

'The foundation-legend of Gwynedd in the Latin texts', *BBCS* 27 (1976–8), 515–32.

'Matriliny by treaty: the Pictish foundation-legend', in Whitelock *et al.* (eds.), *Ireland in Early Mediaeval Europe*, pp. 133–61.

Moisl, H., 'Anglo-Saxon royal genealogies and Germanic oral tradition', *Journal of Medieval History* 7 (1981), 215–48.

Morris, C., *The Papal Monarchy: The Western Church from 1050 to 1250*, Oxford, 1989.

Mortimer, R., 'The charters of Henry II: what are the criteria for authenticity?', *Anglo-Norman Studies* 12 (1989), 119–34.

Mostert, M., 'Celtic, Anglo-Saxon or Insular? Some considerations on "Irish" manuscript production and their implications for Insular Latin culture, c. AD 500–800', in Edel (ed.), *Cultural Identity*, pp. 92–115.

Works Cited

Murison, D., 'Linguistic relationships in medieval Scotland', in G. W. S. Barrow (ed.), *The Scottish Tradition*, Edinburgh, 1974, pp. 71–83.

Murphy, G., 'Bards and filidh', *Éigse* 2 (1940), 200–7.

Early Irish Metrics, Dublin, 1961.

'Saga and myth in ancient Ireland', in E. Knott and G. Murphy, *Early Irish Literature*, London, 1966, pp. 97–142.

Nash-Williams, V. E., *The Early Christian Monuments of Wales*, Cardiff, 1950.

Nelson, J. L., 'Literacy in Carolingian government', in McKitterick (ed.), *Uses of Literacy*, pp. 258–96.

Neville, C. J., 'The earls of Strathearn from the twelfth to the mid-fourteenth century, with an edition of their written acts', 2 vols., PhD thesis, University of Aberdeen, 1983.

Nicholls, K. W., 'The Mac Coghlans', *Irish Genealogist* 6 (1980–5), 445–9.

Nicolaisen, W. F. H., 'Concepts of time and space in Irish folktales', in P. K. Ford (ed.), *Celtic Folklore and Christianity: Studies in Memory of William B. Heist*, Santa Barbara, 1983, pp. 150–8.

'Time in folk-narrative', in V. J. Newall (ed.), *Folklore Studies in the Twentieth Century: Proceedings of the Centenary Conference of the Folklore Society*, Woodbridge, 1980, pp. 314–19.

Ní Dhonnchadha, M., 'The guarantor list of *Cáin Adomnáin*, 697', *Peritia* 1 (1982), 178–215.

Nieke, M., 'Literacy and power: the introduction and use of writing in early historic Scotland', in Gledhill *et al.* (eds.), *State and Society*, pp. 237–252.

Niermeyer, J. F., *Mediae Latinitatis Lexicon Minus*, Leiden, 1976.

Ní Shéaghdha, N., *Catalogue of Irish Manuscripts in the National Library of Ireland*, vol. 1, Dublin, 1961.

Norberg, D., *Manuel pratique de latin médiéval*, Paris, 1968.

Ó hAodha, D., 'An bhairdhne i dtús a ré', in P. Ó Fiannachta (ed.), *An Dán Díreach* = *Léachtaí Cholm Cille* 24, Maynooth, 1994, pp. 9–20.

'The first Middle Irish metrical tract', in H. L. C. Tristram (ed.), *Metrik und Medienwechsel/Metrics and Media*, Tübingen, 1991, pp. 211–22.

Ó Caithnia, L. P., *Apalóga na bhFilí 1200–1650*, Dublin, 1984.

Ó Coileán, S., 'Oral or literary? Some strands of the argument', *Studia Hibernica* 17–18 (1977–8), 7–35.

Ó Conbhuidhe, C., 'The origins of Jerpoint Abbey, Co. Kilkenny', *Cîteaux: Commentarii Cistercienses* 14 (1963), 293–306.

Ó Corráin, D., 'The early Irish churches: some aspects of organisation', in *idem* (ed.), *Irish Antiquity: Essays and Studies presented to Professor M. J. O'Kelly*, Cork, 1981, pp. 327–41.

'Foreign connections and domestic politics: Killaloe and the Uí Briain in twelfth-century hagiography', in Whitelock *et al.* (eds.), *Ireland in Early Mediaeval Europe*, pp. 213–31.

'Historical need and literary narrative', in D. E. Evans *et al.* (eds.), *Proceedings of the Seventh International Congress of Celtic Studies*, pp. 141–58.

'Irish origin legends and genealogy: recurrent aetiology', in T. Nyberg *et al.* (eds.), *History and Heroic Tale*, Odense, 1985, pp. 51–96.

280

Works Cited

'Legend as critic', in T. Dunne (ed.), *The Writer as Witness: Literature as Historical Evidence* = *Historical Studies* 16, Cork, 1987, pp. 23–38.

'Nationality and kingship in pre-Norman Ireland', in T. W. Moody (ed.), *Nationality and the Pursuit of National Independence* = *Historical Studies* 11, Belfast, 1978, pp. 1–35.

Ó Corráin, D., Breatnach, L. and McCone, K. (eds.), *Sages, Saints and Storytellers: Celtic Studies in Honour of Professor James Carney*, Maynooth, 1989.

Ó Cuív, B., 'The poetic contention about the River Shannon', *Ériu* 19 (1962), 89–110.

Review of *CGH*, *Éigse* 10 (1961–3), 328–32.

'Some developments in Irish metrics', *Éigse* 12 (1967–8), 273–90.

O'Dwyer, B. W., 'The Annals of Connacht and Loch Cé and the monasteries of Boyle and Holy Trinity', *PRIA* 72 (1972) C, 83–101.

Okasha, E., *Corpus of Early Christian Inscribed Stones of South-West Britain*, London, 1993.

Hand-list of Anglo-Saxon Non-Runic Inscriptions, Cambridge, 1971.

'Literacy in Anglo-Saxon England: the evidence from inscriptions', in *Medieval Europe 1992*, vol. 7: *Art and Symbolism*, York, 1992, pp. 65–70.

'The non-ogam inscriptions of Pictland', *CMCS* 9 (Summer 1985), 43–70.

'A supplement to *Hand-list of Anglo-Saxon Non-Runic Inscriptions*', *Anglo-Saxon England* 11 (1983), 83–118.

'Vernacular or Latin? The languages of Insular inscriptions, AD 500–1100', in W. Koch (ed.), *Epigraphik*, pp. 139–47.

Okpewho, I., 'Does the epic exist in Africa? Some formal considerations', *Research in African Literatures* 8 (1977), 171–200.

Olrik, A., 'Epic laws of folk narrative', in A. Dundes (ed.), *The Study of Folklore*, Englewood Cliffs, NJ, 1965, pp. 129–41.

Olson, L., *Early Monasteries in Cornwall*, Studies in Celtic History 11, Woodbridge, 1989.

Ó Macháin, P., 'The Early Modern Irish prosodic tracts and the editing of bardic verse', in H. L. C. Tristram (ed.), *Metrik und Medienwechsel/Metrics and Media*, Tübingen, 1991, pp. 273–87.

Ong, W. J., *Orality and Literacy: The Technologizing of the Word*, London and New York, 1982.

'Writing is a technology that restructures thought', in G. Baumann (ed.), *The Written Word: Literacy in Transition*, Oxford, 1986, pp. 23–50.

O'Rahilly, T. F., 'Middle Irish pronunciation', *Hermathena* 44 (1926), 152–95.

Orchard, A., *The Poetic Art of Aldhelm*, Cambridge, 1994.

Ó Riain, P., 'The Psalter of Cashel: a provisional list of contents', *Éigse* 23 (1989), 107–30.

Ó Riain-Raedel, D., 'Aspects of the promotion of Irish saints' cults in medieval Germany', *ZCP* 39 (1982), 220–34.

'Irish kings and bishops in the *memoria* of the German *Schottenklöster*', in P. Ní Chatháin and M. Richter (eds.), *Irland und Europa: Die Kirche im Frühmittelalter*, Stuttgart, 1984, pp. 390–403.

'Twelfth- and thirteenth-century Irish annals in Vienna', *Peritia* 2 (1983), 127–36.

Works Cited

Oskamp, H., 'The Irish material in the St. Paul Irish codex', *Éigse* 17 (1977–9), 385–91.

O'Sullivan, A. and Herbert, M., 'The provenance of Laud Misc. 615', *Celtica* 10 (1973), 174–92.

Owen, M. E., 'Gwŷr dysg yr oesoedd canol a'u dulliau rhyddiaith', *Ysgrifau Beirniadol* 17 (1990), 42–62.

' "Hwn yw e Gododin. Aneirin ae cant" ', in R. Bromwich and R. B. Jones (eds.), *Astudiaethau ar yr Hengerdd*, Cardiff, 1978, pp. 123–50.

Padel, O., 'The inscriptions of Pictland', MLitt thesis, University of Edinburgh, 1972.

Page, R. I., *An Introduction to English Runes*, London, 1973.

Palmer, A. N., 'Isycoed, County Denbigh', *Archaeologia Cambrensis* 6th series 10 (1910), 229–70.

Pantin, W. A., 'Instructions for a devout and literate layman', in J. J. G. Alexander and M. T. Gibson (eds.), *Medieval Learning and Literature: Essays presented to R. W. Hunt*, Oxford, 1976, pp. 398–422.

Parry, M., *The Making of Homeric Verse: The Collected Papers of Milman Parry*, Oxford, 1971.

Pattison, R., *On Literacy: The Politics of the Word from Homer to the Age of Rock*, Oxford, 1982.

Peden, A., 'Science and philosophy in Wales at the time of the Norman conquest: a Macrobius manuscript from Llanbadarn', *CMCS* 2 (Winter 1981), 21–45.

Pelteret, D. A. E., *Slavery in Early Mediaeval England*, Studies in Anglo-Saxon History 7, Woodbridge, 1995.

Petersen, K. and Wilson, J. J., *Women Artists: Recognition and Reappraisal from the Early Middle Ages to the Twentieth Century*, New York and London, 1976.

Piggott, S., *The Druids*, new edn, London, 1975.

Piriou, J. P., 'Contribution à une histoire de littérature bretonne perdue', Thèse d'état, University of Rennes, 1982.

Pollock, F. and Maitland, F. W., *The History of English Law before the Time of Edward I*, 2nd edn with introduction by S. F. C. Milsom, Cambridge, 2 vols., 1968.

Poos, L. R., *A Rural Society after the Black Death: Essex 1350–1525*, Cambridge, 1991.

Poppe, E., 'The list of sureties in *Cáin Éimíne*', *Celtica* 21 (1990), 588–92.

'A new edition of *Cáin Éimíne Báin*', *Celtica* 18 (1986), 35–52.

Pryce, H., 'The church of Trefeglwys and the end of the "Celtic" charter tradition in twelfth-century Wales', *CMCS* 25 (Summer 1993), 15–54.

'Early Irish canons and medieval Welsh law', *Peritia* 5 (1986), 107–27.

'Ecclesiastical wealth in early medieval Wales', in N. Edwards and A. Lane (eds.), *The Early Church in Wales and the West*, Oxford, 1992, pp. 22–32.

Native Law and the Church in Medieval Wales, Oxford, 1993.

'The origins and the medieval period', in P. H. Jones and E. Rees (eds.), *A Nation and its Books: A History of the Book in Wales*, Aberystwyth, forthcoming.

Pugh, T. B. (ed.), *Glamorgan County History*, vol. 3, *The Middle Ages*, Cardiff, 1971.

Radner, J. N., 'Interpreting irony in medieval Celtic narrative: the case of *Culhwch and Olwen*', *CMCS* 16 (Winter 1988), 41–59.

Works Cited

Randsborg, K., *The Viking Age in Denmark*, London, 1980.

RCAHMS, *Inventory of the Ancient and Historic Monuments of Argyll*, vol. 4, *Iona*, Edinburgh, 1984.

Redknap, M., *The Christian Celts: Treasures of Late Celtic Wales*, Cardiff, 1991.

Reuter, T., 'Property transactions and social relations between rulers, bishops and nobles in early eleventh-century Saxony', in W. Davies and P. Fouracre (eds.), *Property and Power in the Early Middle Ages*, Cambridge, 1995, pp. 165–200.

Reynolds, R. E., '"At sixes and sevens" – and eights and nines: the sacred mathematics of sacred orders in the early middle ages', *Speculum* 54 (1979), 669–84.

Rhodes, M., 'A pair of fifteenth-century spectacle frames from the City of London', *Antiquaries Journal* 62 (1982), 57–73.

Rhys, J., *Lectures on the Origin and Growth of Religion as Illustrated by Celtic Heathendom*, London, 1888.

Richards, M., 'The "Lichfield" Gospels (Book of "Saint Chad")', *NLWJ* 18 (1973–4), 135–46.

Richardson, H. G., 'Some Norman monastic foundations in Ireland', in J. A. Watt, J. B. Morrall and F. X. Martin (eds.), *Medieval Studies presented to Aubrey Gwynn, S. J.*, Dublin, 1961, pp. 29–43.

Richter, M., *The Formation of the Medieval West: Studies in the Oral Culture of the Barbarians*, Blackrock, Co. Dublin, 1994.

'Writing the vernacular and the formation of the medieval West', in *idem*, *Studies in Medieval Language and Culture*, Blackrock, Co. Dublin, 1995, pp. 218–27.

Riddy, F., '"Women talking about the things of God": a late medieval sub-culture', in Meale (ed.), *Women and Literature*, pp. 104–27.

Ritchie, J. N. G. and Fraser, I., *Pictish Symbol Stones: A Handlist 1994*, RCAHMS, Edinburgh, 1994.

Roberts, B. F., 'Oral tradition and Welsh literature: a description and survey', *Oral Tradition* 3 (1988), 61–87.

Studies on Middle Welsh Literature, Lewiston, Queenston and Lampeter, 1992.

'Un o lawysgrifau Hopcyn ap Thomas o Ynys Dawy', *BBCS* 22 (1966–8), 223–8.

'Ystoria', *BBCS* 26 (1974–6), 13–20.

Roberts, B. F. (ed.), *Early Welsh Poetry: Studies in the Book of Aneirin*, Aberystwyth, 1988.

Rolant, E., 'Owain ap Llywelyn ab y Moel', *Ysgrifau Beirniadol* 9 (1976), 100–14.

Rosen, E., 'The invention of eyeglasses', *Journal of the History of Medicine and Allied Sciences* 11 (1956), 13–46, 183–218.

Rosenberg, B. A., 'The message of the American folk sermon', in J. M. Foley (ed.), *Oral-Formulaic Theory: A Folklore Casebook*, New York, 1990, pp. 137–68.

Ross, J., 'Formulaic composition in Gaelic oral literature', *Modern Philology* 57 (1959), 1–12.

Rosser, G., 'London and Westminster: the suburb in the urban economy in the later middle ages', in J. A. F. Thomson (ed.), *Towns and Townspeople in the Fifteenth Century*, Gloucester, 1988, pp. 45–61.

Rowland, J., *Early Welsh Saga Poetry*, Cambridge, 1990.

'Genres', in Roberts (ed.), *Early Welsh Poetry*, pp. 179–208.

'Horses in the *Gododdin* and the problem of Catraeth', *CMCS* 30 (Winter 1995), 13–40.

Works Cited

Rowlands, E. I., 'Bardic lore and education', *BBCS* 32 (1985), 143–55.

Rowlands, H., *Mona Antiqua Restaurata*, Dublin, 1723, 2nd edn, London, 1766.

Russell, P., *An Introduction to the Celtic Languages*, London and New York, 1995.
'Recent work in British Latin', *CMCS* 9 (Summer 1985), 19–29.

Ryding, W. W., *Structure in Medieval Narrative*, The Hague, 1971.

Saenger, P., 'Silent reading: its impact on late medieval script and society', *Viator* 13 (1982), 367–414.

Sawyer, B., 'Viking-Age rune-stones as a crisis symptom', *Norwegian Archaeological Review* 24: 2 (1991), 97–112.

Schofield, R. S., 'The measurement of literacy in pre-industrial England', in J. Goody (ed.), *Literacy in Traditional Societies*, pp. 311–25.

Sharpe, R., *Medieval Irish Saints' Lives*, Oxford, 1991.
'Palaeographical considerations in the study of the Patrician documents in the Book of Armagh', *Scriptorium* 36 (1982), 3–28.

Sheehy, M. P., 'Influences of ancient Irish law on the *Collectio Canonum Hibernensis*', in S. Kuttner (ed.), *Proceedings of the Third International Congress of Medieval Canon Law*, Monumenta Iuris Canonici Series C, vol. 4, Vatican City, 1971, pp. 31–42.

Simms, K., 'Bards and barons: the Anglo-Irish aristocracy and the native culture', in R. Bartlett and A. MacKay (eds.), *Medieval Frontier Societies*, Oxford, 1989, pp. 177–97.
'The brehons of later medieval Ireland', in D. Hogan and W. N. Osborough (eds.), *Brehons, Serjeants and Attorneys*, Blackrock, Co. Dublin, 1990, pp. 51–76.
'An eaglais agus filí na scol', in P. Ó Fiannachta (ed.), *An Dán Díreach = Léachtaí Cholm Cille* 24, Maynooth, 1994, pp. 21–36.
From Kings to Warlords: The Changing Political Structure of Gaelic Ireland in the Later Middle Ages, Studies in Celtic History 7, Woodbridge, 1987.
'Guesting and feasting in Gaelic Ireland', *Journal of the Royal Society of Antiquaries of Ireland* 108 (1978), 67–100.

Sims-Williams, P., 'The additional letters of the ogam alphabet', *CMCS* 23 (Summer 1992), 29–75.
'Byrhtferth's ogam signature', in T. Jones and E. B. Fryde (eds.), *Essays and Poems Presented to Daniel Huws*, Aberystwyth, 1994, pp. 283–91.
'Dating the transition to Neo-Brittonic: phonology and history, 400–600', in A. Bammesberger and A. Wollmann (eds.), *Britain 400–600: Language and History*, Heidelberg, 1990, pp. 217–61.
'The early Welsh Arthurian poems', in R. Bromwich, A. O. H. Jarman and B. F. Roberts (eds.), *The Arthur of the Welsh*, Cardiff, 1991, pp. 33–71.
'Edward IV's confirmation charter for Clynnog Fawr', in C. Richmond and I. Harvey (eds.), *Recognitions: Essays presented to Edmund Fryde*, Aberystwyth, 1996, pp. 229–41.
'The emergence of Old Welsh, Cornish and Breton orthography, 600–800: the evidence of Archaic Old Welsh', *BBCS* 38 (1991), 20–86.
'The evidence for vernacular Irish literary influence on early mediaeval Welsh literature', in Whitelock *et al.* (eds.), *Ireland in Early Mediaeval Europe*, pp. 235–57.
'Gildas and vernacular poetry', in Lapidge and Dumville (eds.), *Gildas*, pp. 169–92.

284

Works Cited

'Historical need and literary narrative: a caveat from ninth-century Wales', *WHR* 17 (1994–5), 1–40.

'The invention of Celtic nature poetry', in T. Brown (ed.), *Celticism*, Amsterdam, 1996, pp. 97–124.

'"Is it fog or smoke or warriors fighting?"': Irish and Welsh parallels to the *Finnsburg* Fragment', *BBCS* 27 (1976–8), 505–14.

Religion and Literature in Western England, 600–800, Cambridge, 1990.

Review of W. Davies, *Llandaff Charters* and *An Early Welsh Microcosm* (London, 1978), in *Journal of Ecclesiastical History* 33 (1982), 124–9.

Review of Hughes, *Celtic Britain*, in *Journal of Ecclesiastical History* 36 (1985), 306–9.

Review of McCone, *Pagan Past*, in *Éigse* 29 (1996), 179–96.

Review of *The Welsh Life of Saint David*, ed. D. S. Evans (Cardiff, 1988), in *Journal of Ecclesiastical History* 43 (1992), 468–70.

'Some functions of origin stories in early medieval Wales', in T. Nyberg *et al.* (eds.), *History and Heroic Tale*, Odense 1985, pp. 97–133.

'Some problems in deciphering the early Irish ogam alphabet', *Transactions of the Philological Society* 91 (1993), 133–80.

'William of Malmesbury and *La silloge epigrafica di Cambridge*', *Archivum Historiae Pontificiae* 21 (1983), 10–33.

Slotkin, E. M., 'The fabula, story, and text of *Breuddwyd Rhonabwy*', *CMCS* 18 (Winter 1989), 89–111.

Smith, J. B., 'Land endowments of the period of Llywelyn ap Gruffudd', *BBCS* 34 (1987), 150–64.

'The last phase of the Glyndŵr rebellion', *BBCS* 22 (1966–8), 250–60.

'The rebellion of Llywelyn Bren', in Pugh (ed.), *Glamorgan County History*, vol. 3, pp. 72–86, 593–6.

Smith, J. H. M., 'Oral and written: saints, miracles, and relics in Brittany, c.850–1250', *Speculum* 65 (1990), 309–43.

Province and Empire: Brittany and the Carolingians, Cambridge, 1992.

Smith, L. and Taylor, J. H. M. (eds.), *Women, the Book and the Godly: Selected Proceedings of the St Hilda's Conference, 1993*, Cambridge, 1995.

Women, the Book and the Worldly: Selected Proceedings of the St Hilda's Conference, 1993, vol. 2, Cambridge, 1995.

Women and the Book: Assessing the Visual Evidence, British Library Studies in Medieval Culture, London and Toronto, 1997.

Smith, Ll. B., 'Disputes and settlements in medieval Wales: the role of arbitration', *English Historical Review* 106 (1991), 835–60.

'The gage and the land market in late medieval Wales', *Economic History Review*, 2nd series 29 (1976), 537–50.

'The grammar and commonplace books of John Edwards of Chirk', *BBCS* 34 (1987), 174–84.

'Proofs of age in late-medieval Wales', *BBCS* 38 (1991), 134–44.

'*Tir prid*: deeds of gage of land in late-medieval Wales', *BBCS* 27 (1976–8), 263–77.

Smith, P., *Houses of the Welsh Countryside*, 2nd edn, London, 1988.

Smyth, A. P., *Warlords and Holy Men: Scotland AD 80–1000*, London, 1984.

285

Works Cited

Sterckx, C. and Le Duc, G., 'Les fragments inédits de la vie de Saint-Goëznou', *Annales de Bretagne* 78 (1971), 227–85.

Stevenson, J., 'The beginnings of literacy in Ireland', *PRIA* 89 C 6 (1989), 127–65.
'Literacy and orality in early medieval Ireland', in Edel (ed.), *Cultural Identity*, pp. 11–22.
'Literacy in Ireland: the evidence of the Patrick dossier in the Book of Armagh', in McKitterick (ed.), *Uses of Literacy*, pp. 11–35.

Stevenson, R. B. K., 'Further thoughts on some well known problems', in R. M. Spearman and J. Higgitt (eds.), *The Age of Migrating Ideas: Early Medieval Art in Northern Britain and Ireland*, Edinburgh, 1993, pp. 16–26.

Stock, B., *The Implications of Literacy*, Princeton, 1983.
Listening for the Text: On the Uses of the Past, Baltimore and London, 1990.

Strayer, J. R. (ed.), *Dictionary of the Middle Ages*, 13 vols., New York, 1982–9.

Street, B. V., *Literacy in Theory and Practice*, Cambridge, 1984.

Swift, C., 'Tírechán's motives in compiling the *collectanea*: an alternative interpretation', *Ériu* 45 (1994), 53–82.

Tanguy, B., 'Les paroisses primitives en plou- et leurs saints éponymes', *Bulletin de la Société Archéologique du Finistère* 109 (1981), 121–55.
Saint Hervé: vie et culte, Minihi Levenez, 1990.

Thomas, C., *And Shall These Mute Stones Speak? Post-Roman Inscriptions in Western Britain*, Cardiff, 1994.
'The early Christian inscriptions of southern Scotland', *Glasgow Archaeological Journal* 17 (1994 for 1991–2), 1–10.

T[homas], E. (= Eben Fardd), 'Clynnog Fawr yn Arfon', *Y Gwladgarwr* 6 (1838), 40–5.

Thomas, K., 'The meaning of literacy in early modern England', in G. Baumann (ed.), *The Written Word*, Oxford, 1986, pp. 97–131.

Thomas, R., *Oral Tradition and Written Record in Classical Athens*, Cambridge, 1989.

Thomas, R. J., 'Enwau afonydd â'r ôlddodiad -wy', *BBCS* 8 (1935–7), 27–43.

Thomson, D., 'Cistercians and schools in late medieval Wales', *CMCS* 3 (Summer 1982), 76–80.

Thomson, D. S., 'Gaelic learned orders and literati in medieval Scotland', *Scottish Studies* 12 (1968), 57–78.

Thomson, J. A. F., *The Later Lollards 1414–1520*, Oxford, 1965.

Thornton, D. E., *Kings, Chronologies, and Genealogies: Studies in the Political History of Early Mediaeval Ireland and Wales*, Woodbridge, forthcoming.
'A neglected genealogy of Llywelyn ap Gruffudd', *CMCS* 23 (Summer 1992), 9–23.
'Power, politics, and status: aspects of genealogy in mediaeval Ireland and Wales', PhD thesis, University of Cambridge, 1991.

Thurneysen, R., 'Colmán mac Léníni und Senchán Torpéist', *ZCP* 19 (1933), 193–209.

Tomlin, R. S. O., *Tabellae Sulis: Roman Inscribed Tablets of Tin and Lead from the Sacred Spring at Bath*, part 4 of B. Cunliffe (ed.), *The Temple of Sulis Minerva*, vol. 2, Oxford, 1988.
'Was ancient British Celtic ever a written language? Two texts from Roman Bath', *BBCS* 34 (1987), 18–25.

Works Cited

Tonnerre, N.-Y., *Naissance de la Bretagne: géographie historique et structures sociales de la Bretagne méridionale (Nantais et Vannetais) de la fin du VIIIe à la fin du XIIe siècle*, Angers, 1994.

Tranter, S. N. and Tristram, H. L. C. (eds.), *Early Irish Literature – Media and Communication: Mündlichkeit und Schriftlichkeit in der frühen irischen Literatur*, Tübingen, 1989.

Treharne, R. F., 'The Franco-Welsh treaty of alliance in 1212', *BBCS* 18 (1958–60), 60–75.

Tristram, H. L. C., 'The "Cattle-Raid of Cuailnge" in tension and tradition: between the oral and the written, classical subtexts and narrative heritage', in Edel (ed.), *Cultural Identity*, pp. 61–81.

Early Insular Preaching: Verbal Artistry and Method of Composition, Österreichische Akademie der Wissenschaften, Philos.-hist. Kl., Sitzungsberichte 623, Veröffentlichungen der keltischen Kommission, 11, Vienna, 1995.

'Early modes of Insular expression', in Ó Corráin *et al.* (eds.), *Sages, Saints and Storytellers*, pp. 427–48.

Vansina, J., *Oral Tradition as History*, London, 1985.

Oral Tradition: A Study in Historical Methodology, London, 1961.

Walker, D., *Medieval Wales*, Cambridge, 1990.

Walsh, P., *Irish Men of Learning*, Dublin, 1947.

Walters, D. B., 'The renunciation of exceptions: Romano-canonical devices for limiting possible defences in thirteenth-century Welsh law suits', *BBCS* 38 (1991), 119–28.

Warner, R., *A Walk through Wales in August 1797*, 3rd edn, Bath, 1799.

Watson, W. J., *The History of the Celtic Place-Names of Scotland*, Edinburgh, 1926.

Webster, C. A., *The History of the Diocese of Cork*, Cork, 1920.

Wenzel, S., *Macaronic Sermons: Bilingualism and Preaching in Late-Medieval England*, Ann Arbor, Michigan, 1994.

Werner, K.-F., 'Untersuchungen zur Frühzeit des französischen Fürstentums (9.-10. Jarhundert)', *Die Welt als Geschichte* 18 (1958), 256–89, 19 (1959), 146–93.

Whitelock, D., McKitterick, R. and Dumville, D. (eds.), *Ireland in Early Mediaeval Europe*, Cambridge, 1982.

Williams, D. H., 'Cistercian nunneries in Wales', *Cîteaux* 3 (1975), 155–71.

Catalogue of Seals in the National Museum of Wales, vol. 1, Cardiff, 1993.

Williams, G., 'Addysg yng Nghymru cyn 1536', in *idem, Grym Tafodau Tân*, Llandysul, 1984, pp. 9–23.

'Language, literacy and nationality in Wales', in *idem, Religion, Language and Nationality in Wales*, Cardiff, 1979, pp. 127–48.

Renewal and Reformation: Wales c.1415–1642, Oxford, 1993.

The Welsh Church from Conquest to Reformation, Cardiff, 1962.

Williams, I., 'Notes on Nennius', *BBCS* 7 (1933–5), 380–9.

Williams, J. E. C., 'Brittany and the Arthurian legend', in R. Bromwich, A. O. H. Jarman and B. F. Roberts (eds.), *The Arthur of the Welsh*, Cardiff, 1991, pp. 249–72.

'Celtic literature: origins', in K. H. Schmidt and R. Ködderitzsch (eds.), *Geschichte und Kultur der Kelten*, Heidelberg, 1986, pp. 123–44.

'Rhyddiaith grefyddol Cymraeg Canol', in G. Bowen (ed.), *Y Traddodiad Rhyddiaith yn yr Oesau Canol*, Llandysul, 1974, pp. 312–407.

Works Cited

Williams-Jones, K., 'Caernarvon', in R. A. Griffiths (ed.), *Boroughs of Mediaeval Wales*, Cardiff, 1978, pp. 73–101.

Wilsher, B. and Hunter, D., *Stones: A Guide to Some Remarkable Eighteenth Century Gravestones*, Edinburgh, 1978.

Wilson, R. R., *Genealogy and History in the Biblical World*, New York and London, 1977.

Winterbottom, M., 'Columbanus and Gildas', *Vigiliae Christianae* 30 (1976), 310–17.

'On *Hisperica Famina*', *Celtica* 8 (1968), 126–39.

Woolf, G., 'Power and the spread of writing in the west', in Bowman and Woolf (eds.), *Literacy and Power in the Ancient World*, pp. 84–98.

Wormald, P., 'The emergence of the *regnum Scottorum*: a Carolingian hegemony?', in B. Crawford (ed.), *Scotland in Dark Age Britain*, St Andrews, 1996, pp. 131–60.

'A handlist of Anglo-Saxon lawsuits', *Anglo-Saxon England* 17 (1988), 247–81.

'The uses of literacy in Anglo-Saxon England and its neighbours', *Transactions of the Royal Historical Society* 5th series 27 (1977), 95–114.

Wright, D., 'The tablets from Springmount Bog: a key to early Irish palaeography', *American Journal of Archaeology* 67 (1963), 219.

Wright, N., 'Gildas's prose style and its origins', in Lapidge and Dumville (eds.), *Gildas*, pp. 107–28.

Wulff, W. and Mulchrone, K., *Catalogue of Irish Manuscripts in the Royal Irish Academy*, fasc. 10, Dublin, 1933.

Youngs, S. (ed.), *'The Work of Angels': Masterpieces of Celtic Metalwork, 6th - 9th Centuries AD*, London, 1987.

Zimmer, H., *Nennius Vindicatus: Über Entstehung, Geschichte und Quellen der Historia Brittonum*, Berlin, 1893.

Zumthor, P., *Histoire littéraire de la France médiévale*, Paris, 1954.

Introduction à la poésie orale, Paris, 1983.

Index

289

Index

Index

Index

292

Index

Index

294

Index

Index

Index

CAMBRIDGE STUDIES IN MEDIEVAL LITERATURE

Titles published